Wooden Ships and Iron Men

The U.S. Navy's Ocean Minesweepers 1953–1994

Cdr. David D. Bruhn, USN (Retired)

EAGLE EDITIONS
2007

EAGLE EDITIONS
AN IMPRINT OF HERITAGE BOOKS, INC.

Books, CDs, and more—Worldwide

For our listing of thousands of titles see our website
at
www.HeritageBooks.com

Published 2007 by
HERITAGE BOOKS, INC.
Publishing Division
100 Railroad Ave. #104
Westminster, Maryland 21157

Library of Congress Control Number: 2006929957

International Standard Book Number: 978-0-7884-4325-1

To my sons David and Michael

Contents

Photographs

Maps, Diagrams, and Tables

Foreword

Far more than any ship type in the post–WW II United States Navy, there is uniformity among minesweepers. The similarities go well beyond their unique construction of wood and non-magnetic engines, anchor chains, screws, and nails. Some of the ships are good, some very good, some not so good; and, like all Navy ships, each is to some degree a reflection of the Captain's personality, competence, and style. However, the one thing that makes every minesweeper like all the others is its crew. Walk aboard any wooden ship, spend a few minutes on the quarterdeck, and it becomes obvious that the Sailors speak a common language unique to the mission of the ships in which they serve.

During the Vietnam era the "sweeps" were often deployed for long and repetitive assignments. Those Sailors who did their best under the difficult circumstances were either bachelors or lucky enough to have very understanding and self-sufficient wives. Most had to be young and in good shape just to survive life at sea in small ships never intended by their naval architects to stay in the open ocean long enough to require alongside service from fleet oilers and stores ships. They had to endure constant motion even in calm seaways and stand seemingly never-ending watches, as well as conduct repairs and maintenance under way. Even eating and sleeping were chores that sapped all but the most robust of energy when the patrol lasted for thirty days or more. Board and search during MARKET TIME operations added another degree of risk and discomfort as small boats of questionable seaworthiness were launched from friendly pitching decks to visit sometimes-unfriendly pitching decks. Going to sea in a minesweeper was definitely a young Sailor's game.

Minesweeper Sailors were masters of multitasking before the term was invented. Almost everybody on board except the Captain and the Corpsman stood watches outside his/her rate on a regular basis. Minesweeping quarters and sea details for entering port and for going alongside replenishment ships were in every way "all hands" evolutions. It was not unusual to see lines or cables being manhandled by a First Class Sonarman on a station supervised by a Third Class Boatswainsmate who was ten years his junior in the service. Willing and unselfish sacrifice for the good of the ship was the mark of every minesweeper crew and in my many years of observing ships, including my own, I have never seen tighter esprit than among these tough young Sailors.

Wooden Ships and Iron Men is a complete work of more than forty years of ocean-going minesweeper operations. It describes the amazing versatility and endurance of these small but mighty warships. That they could consistently accomplish so much with such modest resources is a tribute to the crews that sailed them into harm's way.

Rear Admiral Stephen K. Chadwick, USN Retired
Commanding Officer USS *Warbler* (MSC 206) 1966–1968

Foreword

Wooden Ships and Iron Men thoroughly captures the legacy of our Navy's Ocean Minesweepers (MSOs) and their courageous crews! Commander Bruhn has superbly researched the many major tasks and interesting assignments of MSOs from 1953 to 1994 and surveyed their tremendous and wide-ranging contributions to our nation.

As a former Commander Mine Warfare Command 1979–1984, I had the privilege of going on board many Minesweepers throughout the world. I was always singularly impressed by the outstanding esprit de corps of the crews on each and every Minesweeper and their special contributions with their "wooden" ships.

Since 1950 up to the present (2004), including the Korean and Vietnam Wars, Operations EARNEST WILL, DESERT STORM, and IRAQI FREEDOM, the U.S. Navy has had nineteen ships either damaged or sunk by hostile weapons. (USS *Liberty* AGTR 5 suffered damage from both torpedo and aerial attack.) Of these nineteen ships:

- One was damaged by torpedoes
- One was damaged by missiles
- One was damaged by terrorist attack
- Two were damaged or sunk by aerial attacks
- *Fifteen* were damaged or sunk by *mines*

These statistics are powerful and real evidence of why our Minesweepers and current Minehunters have been, are, and always will be so vital to our Navy. For the twenty-first century, our Navy has placed "assured access" as one of its highest priority missions, to be able "to go anywhere—anytime." Our Minesweepers and Minehunters will be crucial to this top-priority mission. As recently as Operation IRAQI FREEDOM, our Navy's Minesweepers and Minehunters performed admirably and contributed greatly to the assured access of our critical troop and supply ships.

"Where the Fleet goes—we have been!" This famous saying of our Minesweepers illustrates how important our Mine Countermeasures ships were and will continue to be in this century! Commander Bruhn's thorough research has produced a book that should be compelling reading not only to former Minesweeper crews, but to a public that needs to know about one of the Navy's most important tasks.

Rear Admiral Charles F. Horne, III, USN Retired
Commander Mine Warfare Command 1979–1984

Acknowledgments

I would like to thank the many people who contributed to or influenced this book.

Richard DeRosset, noted maritime artist, graciously agreed to paint the scene used for the book cover. A former Navy "bluejacket," crewmember of the fishing boat *Petrel*, which caught fire and sank seventy-five miles off the southern California coast, and master of the small merchant tanker MV *Pacific Trojan*, he reflects in the authenticity of his work talent, extensive research, and much time at sea.

YNCM (SW/AW) Robert Meindl, USNR (Ret.), an English professor at California State University, Sacramento, edited the multiple versions of the text and made many suggestions that substantially improved the book. He served as a selected reservist on USS *Excel* (MSO 439) and Mine Division 52 staff from 1983 to 1987 and sailed with the sweeps for several extensive deployments.

Pelham Boyer, the Managing Editor of the Naval War College Press, was kind enough to review an early draft of the book. Jo-Ann Parks, also associated with the Naval War College, designed and typeset the final work.

Retired Navy Captains Richard Farrell, Ronald Moser, and Michael Hacunda, "shipmates" during my last tour on active duty, reviewed early drafts and provided valuable information.

Michael Goss, a former lieutenant who, between 1958 and 1963, served aboard three mine warfare ships and was assigned to the Mine Force Pacific staff, reviewed the material and provided perspective based on his experience in the mine force.

Retired Chief Dennis L. Moore contributed many remembrances, including a very compelling story about the shock of finding a Soviet defector aboard his ship in the Mediterranean.

Retired Navy Captain Charles R. Schlegelmilch and Boatswainmate Second Class Michael Wark recounted the actions of *Endurance* during a nighttime sea battle with a Vietcong armed trawler.

Retired Navy Captain David Grieve, commander of the U.S. mine countermeasures forces deployed to the Persian Gulf to support Operation DESERT SHIELD/STORM, reviewed the material related to this operation and the conclusion to the book. His unique perspective and expertise were particularly valuable. Then Capt. George Smith and

Cdr. Steven Lehr, active-duty naval officers, provided comments regarding their participation in Operation DESERT SHIELD/STORM. Dr. Edward Marolda, John Reilly, Bernard Cavalcante, and Edwin Finney of the Naval Historical Center, Washington, D.C., assisted with research, as did Todd Warger, Project Archivist of the Bellingham Shipyards Documentary Film Project.

Special thanks are due Dick Lewis, W. W. "Mike" Warren, Richard Szpyrka, and others responsible for the formation of the Navy MSO Association and creation of an "MSO challenge coin" to help sort out "good and true sweep sailors" from other patrons of establishments where one goes to "bend an elbow." Mike was also the driving force behind the Save an MSO Association's acquisition of the USS *Lucid* (MSO 458), located at Bradford Island in the California delta near Rio Vista and Antioch, for display as a museum ship. With assistance from Rick Christie, Mike has begun restoration of the ocean minesweeper. Persons interested in supporting or participating in this laudable effort may obtain information about it online at http://usslucid.org or contact Mike at usslucid@usslucid.org.

Many other individuals also made contributions. For the sake of brevity, I have omitted their military rank: Bob Adelwerth, Mark Bradley, Stan Cockran, Jerry Coppage, Michael Cosgrove, Richard Crank, Gary Grewell, Joe Gross, Dale Henry, Harry Keith, J. Daniel Mathis, Reid Morris, Rick Newkirk, Matthew Prager, John Riker, Dennis J. Robinson, Dan Smith, Jamie Smith, Richard Tarbuck, Joe Treat, Bill Vaughn, Steve Walter, and Charles Wymer.

Preface

I first became acquainted with U.S. Navy ocean minesweepers (MSOs) in 1979 when I toured USS *Dash* (MSO 428), the first of her class to be commissioned (14 August 1953), at her berth in Newport, Rhode Island. At the time I was a young sailor assigned to a frigate moored nearby. Being naturally curious about wooden ships, I asked to be shown around—and was immediately impressed by the comradeship of her crewmembers and their obvious pride in their ship. The ship was immaculate, there was plenty of hot coffee on the messdecks, and the men assigned were noticeably cheerful. Most intriguing, however, were the crew's berthing spaces. My escort, noting my admiration for the bunks, crafted of carved and lacquered wood headboards, footboards, and siderails, explained that a reservist had done the fine work. A cabinetmaker by trade and a part-time sailor by choice, he had invested many of his free hours in a labor of love.

My experience in one of these ships is especially noteworthy because I had the good fortune to take part in the first extended deployment of Pacific Fleet MSOs since the return to the United States of the ten ocean minesweepers that had participated in Operation END SWEEP in 1973. In 1984, shortly after I reported aboard as a junior officer, USS *Excel* (MSO 439) and seven of the other eight Pacific Fleet minesweepers rendezvoused in San Francisco Bay before departing in company with USS *Durham* (LKA 114) en route to Hawaii.

The group deployment was motivated in part by the desire of Captain Wright, then Commander, Mine Squadron 5, to demonstrate conclusively that the material condition of his nearly thirty-year-old ships was good enough to justify their continued existence. This belief was not universally held after the many years of service during which MSOs had endured transfer to the Naval Reserve, reduced manning, and insufficient maintenance. However, operations confirmed that the MSOs had life left in them; indeed, three of them would deploy four years later to the Persian Gulf to join three sister ships from the Atlantic Fleet in Operation EARNEST WILL. After a ten-day transit to the island of Maui and participation in exercise RIMPAC 84, five of the eight ships returned home. The remaining three, *Enhance* (MSO 437), *Esteem* (MSO 438), and *Excel* (MSO 439), steamed on to Adak via the Bering Sea, making stops at Dutch Harbor, Kodiak, and Ketchikan between training exercises, finally arriving three months later at their respective homeports.

Life aboard a minesweeper was generally harsh, as a result of which the day-to-day appearance of some "minesweep" sailors would probably not pass muster on a cruiser. However, their sins were forgivable in light of the myriad demands that the MSOs placed on their keepers. For one thing, the constant motion of the ships often kept washers and dryers from operating, limiting changes of clothes to those on hand, as well as keeping crewmembers with weak stomachs from digesting regular meals. Water permeated throughout the ships during storms and a squat funnel designed to improve stability sent stack gases into the open bridge when the wind was astern.

Additionally, the ships could be temperamental. The engineers aboard ships with Packard engines occasionally harbored ill feelings toward conning officers because frequent bell changes were apt to result in blown head gaskets or ruptured jacket-water hoses. Engine vibration periodically loosened the rings that retained the sodium-filled exhaust valves, which then dropped, were struck by pistons, and exploded, causing severe damage to engines whose manufacture had ceased two decades earlier.

I first considered this book when I learned during a tour in the Pentagon that *Excel* had been decommissioned and relegated to the "ghost fleet" at Suisun Bay, near San Francisco. This news gave rise to thoughts of a book about her—on the lines of *Little Ship Big War*, which traces the life of a destroyer escort in World War II. Research, however, revealed that there was not enough riveting material about *Excel* alone to fill a text—but that collectively MSOs had, during nearly four decades of service, participated in many interesting events. Thus was borne the idea of recording their history before it would all be obscured by the passage of time.

I was impressed in my research by the regularity with which many of these ships battled violent storms during nearly annual deployments in the 1950s, 1960s, and early 1970s. The most notable storm incident I found documented was Mine Division 45's encounter with Hurricane Inez at Guantanamo Bay, Cuba, in 1966. The base commander issued storm warnings on 28 September, and the following day Commander Mine Division 45 was assigned as commander task element 134.2.4.3 in command of the nine ships in the harbor. These included *Affray* (MSO 511), *Alacrity* (MSO 520), *Exploit* (MSO 440), and *Observer* (MSO 461), the ships of his division, along with USS *Shakori* (ATF 162), USS *Petrel* (ASR 14), USS *Sennet* (SS 408), USS *Pinnacle* (MSO 462), and USS *Sagacity* (MSO 469). Due to an engine casualty, *Alacrity* remained at the pier, as did *Sennet*. The remaining ships were assigned anchorages to ride out the storm. The eye of the hurricane approached the bay during the morning hours of 30 September, bringing with it winds up to 100 knots and nine-foot seas. The edge of Inez' eye was plotted to have passed directly over *Exploit*. Abatement of the storm revealed no personnel casualties and only minor damage to the ships.

Excel did not during my tour on board encounter storms of that severity, although we did once roll fifty-three degrees in heavy seas off Maui (tossing the Captain out of his bunk), and on another occasion in the Gulf of Alaska lost hull sheathing stripped by wind and wave. My next duty in the mine warfare community, a decade later, began with orders to command one of the new *Avenger*-class mine countermeasures ships—replacements for the MSOs, which by now had all been decommissioned. The actions and events described in the following chapters, and the rigors of day-to-day life at sea, give me an appreciation for the deeds of the estimated fifty thousand sailors who roamed the world's oceans in these small wooden ships. I hope that this book pays adequate tribute to the "iron men" who served proudly from the commissioning of USS *Dash* (MSO 428) in 1953 until the decommissioning of USS *Implicit* (MSO 455) in 1994 and to the sailors, male and female, who continue to serve in follow-on classes of ships in the mine force today.

This work is intended for those who served aboard the ocean minesweepers and their families and friends, students and practitioners of mine warfare, scholars interested in naval history, naval architects, wooden ship enthusiasts, sailors and seamen, and others who enjoy experiencing (vicariously) life at sea.

In some cases I have used representative examples to provide an overview of the involvement of MSOs in particular events or activities. Because of the breadth of the book both in span of years (1953 to 1994) and number of ships (sixty-five), I was unable to develop some events as much as I might have liked. Moreover, some readers may wonder about the omission of events of which they have personal knowledge or the absence of their ship in the description of a particular event. Information may be omitted because it is classified, I found no reference to it in my research, or I chose to omit it to minimize redundant events. Hopefully, however, any errors I have made are due to omissions and not commissions. I have tried not to draw any conclusions about the outcome of events in the absence of corroborating information.

I hope readers who do not find reference to an important event in which their ship participated find solace in and enjoy reading about the exploits of sister ships even though all good and true sailors believe their ship was the best. It is also my hope that the many events and stories depicted herein will bring back fond memories and, perhaps, spur additional works about the mine force.

Overview

Sea mines sank or damaged many merchant and naval vessels in the twentieth century and still pose a potential threat today. During the past fifty years, a total of nineteen U.S. Navy ships were damaged or sunk by missiles, torpedoes, aerial attack, terrorist attack, or mines. More startling than total numbers is that casualties to fifteen of the ships, nearly 80 percent, were due to mines, and not, as one might imagine, by more sophisticated and expensive weapons or, most recently, terrorist-employed explosives (see chart). Moreover, the countermeasures utilized against mines have changed relatively little since large-scale production of ocean minesweepers in the 1950s, and the locating and disposing of them is still time consuming and now even more dangerous. While the physics of the ocean have remained the same, sea mines are now much more sophisticated and difficult to thwart. Although the Navy continues to seek more effective and efficient ways to deal with this threat through the discovery and

U.S. Casualties by Weapon Type, 1950–2000

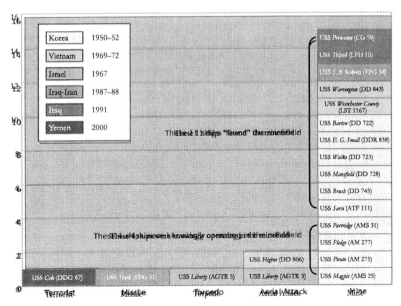

application of new technology, mine countermeasures ships, helicopters, and explosive ordnance disposal divers continue to be the mainstays of U.S. Navy countermeasure capabilities.

To gain an appreciation for the deadliness of weapons that wait and their effect on military operations and the economies of countries, one need only review the summaries of Navy and merchant ship losses from past wars. The United States lost only three ships to mines in World War I. However, the allies lost 586 merchant vessels and 87 warships, not counting 152 small patrol boats and minesweepers, and total ship damage from mines was greater than that from gunfire or torpedoes. Sea mines laid during World War II sank or damaged, during the war or in its aftermath, 213 U.S. ships. The Navy lost 72 ships (including 24 minecraft) to mines, and mines sank or damaged an additional 9 Army and Coast Guard ships and 132 merchant vessels. Fifteen of the ship casualties were due to American mines in U.S.-laid defensive minefields.[1]

Mines can also preclude, delay, or modify planned military operations. During the Korean War, the U.S. Navy was not prepared at Wonsan (see map 2-1) to counter some 3,000 Soviet mines spread over 400 square miles of water that North Korean sampans and junks, assisted by Soviet military personnel, had laid to prevent U.S. troops from landing. Planned military operations were held up a week while the Navy did what it could, in the process losing minesweepers *Pirate* and *Pledge* to mines. Six members of *Pirate*'s crew went down with their ship and more than forty survivors were injured. For *Pledge*, six men were lost and more than fifty injured. Even more devastating, a mine explosion that sank the South Korean minesweeper ROKN *YMS-516* killed half her crew. The greatest sea power in the world in 1945, five years later the United States lost control of the sea for want of an adequate number of minesweepers. At the end of World War II, the U.S. Navy's Pacific mine force alone numbered more than 500 ships, some 3,000 officers, and about 30,000 men. When the Korean War began, the Navy could muster only two divisions of steel-hulled destroyer minesweepers, two divisions of fleet minesweepers, and twenty-one smaller minesweepers.[2]

One might reasonably inquire "What caused this deplorable state of affairs?" What happened was that about 99 percent of the WWII minecraft crews were Reserves, and between 1945 and 1950, due to demobilization, budgetary cuts, and a lack of naval interest and emphasis on mine warfare, the trained crews had vanished and their ships had been mothballed, sold, or scrapped. In an interview, the Chief of Naval Operations said of the mines at Wonsan:

> They caught us with our pants down. Those damn mines cost us eight days delay in getting the troops ashore and more than two hundred casualties. That's bad enough. But I can all-too-easy think of circumstances where eight days' delay offshore could mean losing a war. . . . We've been plenty submarine-conscious and air-conscious. Now we're going to start getting mine-conscious—beginning last week.[3]

The painful lessons learned at Wonsan, Korea, spurred construction of a large number of mine warfare ships, including the ocean minesweepers that are the subject of this book.

However, although few adversaries have had the military strength to face the U.S. Navy in combat upon the sea, enemies in previous and ensuing conflicts have successfully hindered or prevented naval and amphibious operations though the employment of low-cost weapons in lieu of expensive warships. A review of naval history from World War I to the present reveals that, sadly, despite the extraordinary dedication and hard work of many individuals within the mine warfare community and supporting organizations, the U.S. Navy has generally been either ill prepared for or not fully tested in its encounters with mines.

The customary practice within the U.S. Navy has been to maintain a skeleton mine force until faced with the reality of large numbers of enemy mines, then to modify existing ships or, if necessary, construct new ones, and finally to let the capability lapse during peacetime. It was not unique to the period following World War II. During the aftermath of World War I, British and U.S. minesweepers cleared 70,000 U.S. Mk 6 mines, comprising the 230-mile-long North Sea Barrage. The mines had been laid in an attempt to bottle up U-boats in German waters to keep them out of the Atlantic, where they had wreaked havoc among allied shipping. In February 1917 alone, German submarines sank 800,000 tons. Because the "Yankee Mining Squadron" had laid 56,571 of the 70,117 total mines comprising the field, in water depths ranging from 80 to 240 feet, the U.S. Navy had complete knowledge of the characteristics of the American mines and first-hand knowledge of the location of most of them. Even so, the U.S. Navy's eighty-two minesweepers were employed (along with British minesweepers) in clearance operations for six months, from 30 April 1919 to 31 September 1919, to remove the deadly menace from the North Sea. The minesweeping ships arrived in New York City on 24 November 1919 and were reviewed by Secretary of the Navy Josephus Daniels, following which most of them were sold or consigned to "red-lead row" and their crews sent home.[4]

Caught with inadequate capability to deal with enemy mines at the beginning of World War II, possessing only remnants from the last war (*Bird*-class minesweepers and "flush deck" destroyers converted for use as high speed minesweepers), the Navy purchased thirty-five commercial fishing vessels, mostly wooden-hulled tuna boats, and converted them to coastal minesweepers. Ultimately, a massive shipbuilding effort would produce *Raven*-, *Auk*-, *Adroit*-, and *Admirable*-class steel-hulled minesweepers, and wooden-hulled *Accentor*-class coastal minesweepers and "Yard-class" auxiliary motor minesweepers, the latter 136-foot vessels too numerous to be given names. Although the scrappy little ships were nameless, their crews had mettle as demonstrated by an anonymous ditty sung to the tune of "McNamara's Band":

> Oh, the mines go bang and the winches clang,
> And the guns they blaze away,
> We rescue men and pick up stiffs
> To pass the time of day.
> We carry freight and stay out late,
> No matter what the mess.
> The tighter the spot when things are hot
> Is the place for a YMS.

To augment what minecraft it did have while awaiting new construction, the Navy pressed old steel-hulled destroyers, landing craft, and fishing vessels into service (see table 1).[5]

This scenario would be repeated twice more during the next fifty years. The U.S. Navy mine force would be wholly unprepared at the onset of the Korean War and Operation DESERT STORM, better known as the "Persian Gulf War." The inadequate mine force fielded for DESERT STORM resulted from a massive post–Vietnam War reduction in numbers of minesweepers and a decline in the material condition of those that remained in service. Following the Vietnam War and transfer of a majority of the MSOs not mothballed, sold to foreign countries, or struck from service, to the Naval Reserve, the ships' active duty

Table 1

Type of ship	Class	Designation	Hull	Length	Number
High speed Minesweeper	Converted "flush-deck" destroyers	DMS	steel hull	314 feet	18
High speed Minesweeper	*Ellyson*-class	DMS	steel hull	348 feet	24
Minesweeper	*Lapwing* ("bird")-class	AM	steel hull	187 feet	24
Minesweeper	*Raven/Auk*-class	AM	steel hull	220 feet	72
Minesweeper	*Adroit*-class	AM	steel hull	173 feet	18
Minesweeper	*Admirable*-class	AM	steel hull	180 feet	113
Coastal Minesweeper	Converted fishing trawlers	AMc	wood hull	various	35
Coastal Minesweeper	*Accentor/Acme*-class	AMc	wood hull	97–98 feet	67
Coastal Minesweeper	Other converted vessels	AMc	wood hull	various	9
Coastal Minesweeper	Converted Landing Craft Tank and Landing Craft Infantry Large	AMc(U) Underwater Locator	steel hull	119 feet (hulls 1-6) 159 feet (hulls 7-11)	11
Auxiliary Motor Minesweeper	"Yard class" Minesweeper	YMS	wood hull	136 feet	481
Total Number					872

U.S. Navy World War II Mine Countermeasures Vessels and Craft

crews were cut in half and complemented by a reservist contingent that was normally aboard only one weekend a month and two weeks in the summer. The inevitable result was a constant high level of crew fatigue. Funding for fuel and maintenance was reduced, and as the material conditions of the ships deteriorated over time, the outside inspection and assessment necessary to maintain fleet standards was similarly reduced. Consequently, the Navy would deploy only three aged ocean minesweepers and USS *Avenger* (MCM 1), the first vessel in a replacement class of ships, to the Persian Gulf during Operation DESERT SHIELD/STORM to counter (overall unsuccessfully) both Iraqi- and Iranian-laid mines.

Experiences during the Gulf War would demonstrate that, due to both the complexity and the deadliness of modern mines and associated difficulty in countering them, the U.S. Navy could no longer ignore their potential threat during peacetime and, in the final hour, press elderly ships into action or employ other stopgap methods to deal with the threat. Despite this stark reality, the Navy today has only a very modest surface mine force, and it looks as if it is starting to repeat history to its own disadvantage. Fourteen of the twenty-six mine warfare ships in the U.S. Navy (five of fourteen *Avengers* and nine of twelve *Ospreys*) have been transferred to the Naval Reserve Force, and implementation of a current proposal would decommission all twelve *Ospreys* within the next two years. Hopefully, a review of history and recognition of the importance of a ready mine force will spur adequate funding for today's surface mine force and the model from the 1970s–1990s will not be replicated.

None of the above discourse is intended to diminish the accomplishments or commitment of people who served or are serving in the U.S. mine force, but instead to caution policy makers and students of mine warfare to consider how today's mine force would fare against thousands or tens of thousands of modern sophisticated mines employed by a knowledgeable foe. During World War II, thousands of brave men carrying out their duty aboard hundreds of new rapidly constructed scrappy little minesweepers were adequate to thwart the mine threat, although the loss of many ships still resulted. Today, and for the foreseeable future, in view of the expense and length of time required to construct modern mine warfare ships and train the highly skilled crews needed to man them to counter relatively inexpensive, easily obtainable, and very deadly sea mines, such policy and practice is untenable.

Photo 1-1

USS *Endurance* (MSO 435) engages North Vietnamese gunrunner in historic wooden versus steel ship confrontation (painting by Richard DeRosset)

Richard,

Your painting of the USS Endurance's night engagement off the coast of Vietnam is both vivid and accurate in the finest detail. The dramatic portrayal clearly captures the intensity of the engagement and gives a perspective that those who were there will readily recall. I have already set it up as my desktop.

Captain Charles R. Schlegelmilch, USN (Ret.)
Former Commanding Officer USS *Endurance*

Richard DeRosset's depiction is chillingly accurate and brings back a flood of memories. The streams of incoming and outgoing tracers still stand out in my mind. His ability to capture that eerie scene is amazing.

John Cotton
Former USS *Endurance* crewmember

David,

As the ship's signalman, I experienced the battle off the mouth of the Cua Co Chien River first-hand. I was fascinated to read about its full dimensions in your well-researched and -written account. Richard DeRosset's painting is stunning and very accurate in detail, right down to the color of the trawler and the focus of our fire on its deckhouse.

Judge Dan Hyatt
Former USS *Endurance* crewmember

Praise for *Wooden Ships and Iron Men*

Wooden Ships and Iron Men *is a fitting tribute to the ocean minesweepers and Sailors who crewed them during a critical time in the U.S. Navy's modern history. While enduring all the hardships common to life at sea in small vessels, these men contributed significantly to the Navy's successful operations, from 1953 to 1994, in the Atlantic and Pacific oceans, off the coast of Vietnam, and in the volatile Persian Gulf. This work is a must read.*

> Edward J. Marolda
> Senior Historian
> Naval Historical Center

Cdr. Bruhn's history of the Ocean Minesweeper will delight all those who served in and worked with these fine wooden ships. It will also provide much interesting detail on their employment to anyone concerned with the U.S. Navy's mine countermeasures efforts between the Korean War and DESERT STORM. Bruhn reviews many of the ongoing issues and competing priorities that have crippled this important warfare area. Wooden Ships and Iron Men *is a real walk down memory lane for a former MSO Commanding Officer and Mine Group Commander. Worth the read!*

> Captain David J. Grieve, USN (Ret.)
> Commander U.S. Mine Countermeasures Force 1990–1991
> Operation DESERT SHIELD/STORM ("Persian Gulf War")

Thank you, David, for the jacket painting. It is out of this world—very, very accurate, and I can't imagine that anyone else could have done such an excellent job. It is so real it takes me right back to that night in 1970. Please pass a "Bravo Zulu" to Richard DeRosset for his rendition of Endurance *in action. I was on the fo'c'sle throughout the battle and I can testify that he did indeed get it right. Can't wait to get my copy of the book!*

> BM2 Michael Wark, USN (Ret.)
> Former Endurance crewmember

I don't normally read military nonfiction books, but Wooden Ships and Iron Men *reads like an action adventure novel. The first-person accounts and Bruhn's writing style put you right in the middle of the action, almost as if you were really there.*

> Andrew Baran
> High school science teacher

Reading Dave Bruhn's important book on mine warfare, I was delighted to return to sea on an MSO without the usual seasickness caused by its endless corkscrewing and the nausea induced by stack gas blowing into the bridge on a following wind. I could actually walk a deck without leaving heel prints three feet up a bulkhead! Thank you, David, for returning me to the days of my youth and callow innocence.

> Mike Goss, Former Lt., USN

Many adventurous men and women served their country by both "jumping fire" and, during military service, "sailing in harm's way," and while I'm unsure whether any smokejumpers served aboard the small wooden ships, I am certain they would have had an affinity for sweep sailors and well understood one another. You have done a masterful job in describing a tough and sometimes dangerous job of which few people were aware.

> Chuck Sheley, editor, *Smokejumper* magazine

1 Commence Firing

The role USS Endurance (MSO 435) played in the destruction of the enemy infiltration trawler was of a nature reminiscent of an earlier time in the U.S. Navy's history when "iron men and wooden ships" were the rule of the day.

Vice Admiral Jerome H. King Jr.
Commander U.S. Naval Forces Vietnam

Late on the night of 22 November 1970, in the combat zone off South Vietnam, a 172-foot wooden U.S. Navy vessel proceeded at "darken ship" (all except navigation lights extinguished) through coastal waters off the mouth of the Mekong River to challenge a large heavily armed steel-hulled vessel making for the coast of South Vietnam. Devoid of running lights, it was violating the rules of the road, something a ship might do when fearful of being detected. A U.S. Navy P3 patrol aircraft had initially spotted the suspect vessel in international waters well off the coast and classified it as a possible Vietcong type SL-3 infiltration trawler. At the time, Navy maritime patrol aircraft routinely searched at considerable distances offshore for mother ships that might be supplying coastal smugglers. When it appeared that trailing the enemy ship would be a long-term effort, the responsibility for radar surveillance was passed to a U.S. Coast Guard high endurance cutter (WHEC). She, with other Coast Guard vessels and a large number of Navy ships and patrol craft, was assigned to Task Force 115 in support of Operation MARKET TIME, all stationed in a picket line along a thousand-mile coastline from the 17th parallel to the Cambodian border to search for Vietcong seaborne infiltrators trying to move enemy troops, munitions, and miscellaneous war materials into South Vietnam.[1]

USS *Endurance* (MSO 435) had entered Vung Tau, South Vietnam (see map 1-1), earlier in the day in the hopes that technicians aboard a

Map 1-1

During the Vietnam War, ocean minesweepers operated routinely along the coastline of South Vietnam from the DMZ to the Thailand border and, immediately prior to and during Operation End Sweep, off North Vietnam.

repair barge could fabricate a part needed to return one of its main engines to service. Due to a previous commitment to rendezvous at sea with a service ship for an underway replenishment, the ocean minesweeper had then departed port, leaving its chief engineer behind to expedite repair work. Informed that the trawler was apparently making a move toward the coast, Navy planners vectored *Endurance* for the area projected to be the trawler's goal. However, the suspect vessel's intentions were not at all clear, and in previous incidents suspected infiltration trawlers had transited the South China Sea as far as Cambodia only to return to North Vietnam without entering the contiguous waters of South Vietnam. The outer boundary of this area marked entry into international waters twelve miles from shore.[2]

Through use of information provided by the cutter, the minesweeper was able to gain a position ahead of the projected track of the trawler. Because of communications difficulties, little information was exchanged among the U.S. components involved except via secure teletype. *Endurance* provided tracking and contact information to Commander Task Force 115 using a single-sideband circuit, but since it was an "uncovered net," all reports had to be hand encrypted and transmitted to provide some degree of operational security. To avoid alerting the trawler prior to its entering South Vietnamese waters, where it could be engaged in combat, CTF 115 directed *Endurance* to clear the area. She responded that she would clear to the north, which would place her in an ideal position to close the trawler when it entered the contiguous zone.[3]

When it appeared that the trailing ships, the Coast Guard cutters *Rush* (WHEC 723) and *Sherman* (WHEC 720), would be too far seaward and thus unable to close the trawler before it transited an area of shoal water and small concentrations of fishing boats, *Endurance* requested permission from the on-scene commander to proceed and challenge the vessel. Permission was immediately granted, whereupon the minesweeper maneuvered to close and challenge the vessel, using existing rules of engagement (ROE). Drawing about nine feet less than the much larger 378-foot cutters, the minesweeper could follow the trawler through waters they could not and maintain contact should it try to lose itself amongst fishing boats as she held it both visually and on radar. *Endurance*'s commanding officer recalls the ensuing sequence of events:

The initial challenge was by flashing signal light sending the international AA (what ship) and the VNN challenge codes. The trawler made no reply to these challenges but did turn on its navigation lights. When no reply was forthcoming, we illuminated the trawler with the 24-inch searchlight and identified it as a SL-3 type suspected infiltration trawler, with a green hull and white superstructure. The trawler reversed course and headed out to sea. Since we were still within the 12-mile limit and the ROE permitted more aggressive action, we fired across the trawler's bow, then into the bow area, and followed with destructive fire to the bridge and their firing positions when they returned fire.[4]

The above brief summary of the sea battle between *Endurance* and the enemy trawler may not convey to readers the novel and courageous action of the minesweeper in engaging in battle at close range a larger and more heavily armed ship constructed of steel. Ocean minesweepers were but lightly armed, provided only with the capability to destroy floating mines with gunfire and to permit some means of self-defense. Because MSO guns had little penetrating power, while enemy large-caliber gunfire could inflict great damage, loss of life, or total destruction, Navy commanders normally assigned cruisers, destroyers, frigates, or, occasionally, battleships to provide force protection if they thought danger was imminent. Usually, minesweepers were at greatest risk while conducting clearance operations off a hostile shore, within range of enemy aircraft, ships, patrol craft, or shore-based missile or gun batteries. However, like other lightly armed ships, such as the intelligence-gathering vessels USS *Pueblo* (AGER 2) and USS *Liberty* (AGTR 5), they sometimes unexpectedly found themselves in harm's way. Of course, the reason minesweepers were assigned to patrol duties during the Vietnam War was because there were simply not enough "steel-hulls" to meet all existing requirements.

At one time in the U.S. Navy's history, before the advent of steam-propelled vessels, fighting ships were constructed of wood. USS *Constitution*, the famous three-masted frigate, was launched and christened at Edmond Hartt's Shipyard in Boston on 21 October 1797. As a point of interest, let's compare her to *Endurance*. Although only slightly larger, 175 feet long at the waterline with a 45-foot beam, the frigate was more massively built and more heavily armed. Designed to both give and receive damage, she was fitted with thirty-two 24-pounder long guns, twenty 32-pounder carronades, and two 24-pounder bow chasers. Commonly referred to as "Old Ironsides" because cannon-balls bounced off her, *Constitution* was built of resilient live oak planks seven inches thick in places, contributing, with the heavy armament, to her displacement of 2,200 tons. Somewhat smaller with an overall length of 172 feet and a 35-foot beam, *Endurance*, with a 755-ton maximum displacement, was much lighter, and her hull was designed to keep out the sea, not gun rounds. Armed with a single 20mm gun mount on her foc'sle, two .50-caliber machine guns on her port and starboard bridge wings, and a single .30-caliber machine gun on her fantail, *Endurance* was unlikely to cripple or destroy the trawler. However, by exposing herself to enemy fire she might delay the trawler trying to make the Mekong River long enough to allow more formidable U.S. assets to arrive on scene.

Uncloaked from darkness by *Endurance*'s searchlight, the trawler responded by directing 75mm rounds at the minesweeper's signal bridge in an attempt to extinguish the bright light blinding its gunners and bridge watch team, followed by 75mm recoilless rifle and 12.75mm machine gun fire to other locations, visible by their respective red and brilliant green tracer. During the battle, gun flashes from the engaged combatants were visible on the dark clear night to crewmen aboard the cutter *Sherman* a few miles to the east. Taking fire, *Endurance* engaged the enemy vessel with her small gun mount and three machine guns. The action of *Endurance*'s signalman in keeping the searchlight directed at the enemy ship throughout the engagement probably saved the lives of some of his shipmates, as it blinded the enemy gunners. The bravery of all crewmembers manning topside General Quarters stations was highlighted in *Endurance*'s After Action Report:

> SM3 Hyatt stood completely exposed on the 04-level, fully aware that it was an obviously well-defined target above the bridge; SM3 Hyatt remained at his post and effectively carried out his duties despite tracers and 75mm recoilless rifle rounds passing directly overhead. All gunners, loaders, and other mount personnel also displayed a high degree of heroism and disregard for their own personal safely while returning the enemy's fire from their completely unprotected mounts.[5]

Leading seaman Michael Wark, the battle phone talker stationed on the foc'sle to relay orders to the 20mm gun, remembers the intensity of the engagement:

We hit them with all our firepower. Although the night was very dark, it soon lit up when the action started. Gunfire seemed to be coming from everywhere and tracers lit up the night. They seemed to have us outgunned. I am not sure, but don't think they could have seen us very well, since they were blinded by our searchlight. We were really tearing them up. [6]

The trawler, located off *Endurance*'s starboard bow, steering roughly a parallel course and getting the worse of it, then turned to port and tried to ram the minesweeper. *Endurance*'s commanding officer had not wanted to allow the enemy vessel an opportunity to close his ship, because he believed, based on intelligence reports received, that Vietcong arms carriers in danger of being seized might try to blow up not only their cargo and themselves but also their interdictors. (One such report provided pictures and layout for the explosive devices and hypothesized that an enemy vessel would conceivably try to get alongside to self-destruct. Of course, enemy intent to try to take out their U.S. opponents was at best speculation. It is more realistic to conclude that the crew would have destroyed the vessel once it had been offloaded.) However, this may have been the trawler's intention when it suddenly made a sharp turn to port and tried to ram the MSO's starboard side, or it may have been trying to disable and disengage from *Endurance* in an effort to make shallow waters off the Mekong River mouth before the more heavily armed cutters could close her. [7]

Wark remembers his view of the action from the foc'sle:

When they saw they weren't doing any good, they attempted to ram us. I remember I saw tracers coming from the 20mm going in the portholes in their pilothouse and bouncing out their port and starboard side doors. Anyway, they barely missed colliding with us. As they passed close by, they hit us with some type of rocket. It hit the port quarter at deck level. [8]

The commanding officer of *Endurance* had to maneuver quickly to avoid collision while keeping his gun batteries unmasked and firing into the trawler. He also elected to turn to port because *Endurance*'s 20mm gun had jammed and by this maneuver the MSO could continue to engage the enemy vessel with the .30- and port .50-caliber machine guns as she came about. *Endurance*'s timely maneuver prevented the trawler from ramming, but the enemy vessel was able to close to within 300 yards. Additionally, the turn to port exposed the minesweeper's port quarter and a 75mm round fired by the trawler struck her hull on the portside fantail area just below the deck edge, fortunately not penetrating the skin of the ship. The tailfin of the round was embedded in the hull and later recovered to identify the round. A second 75mm round was evaluated as a near miss on the port side, amidships [9]

As *Endurance* was turning hard to port, Wark walked aft to see where the trawler was so that he could inform the 20mm gunner when it was going to clear the pilothouse and he could fire on it. He was knocked off his feet by the detonation of the round, which was fortuitous as shrapnel hit the deckhouse near where he had been standing. Meanwhile, GMG3 Cotton, the port .50-caliber machine gunner, had come to the foc'sle and changed out the 20mm gun barrel, even though there was a chance the round might "cook off" (detonate in the barrel and propel shrapnel in all directions) before he could get it over the side. The gun had jammed from a "misfire," perhaps due to the age of the ammunition it was firing, part of a lot that had been manufactured during World War II. By the time Cotton had replaced the gun barrel, the trawler had broken away, although *Endurance* still got off a few more rounds.[10]

Escaping after the mêlée, the trawler set course north-northwest for shallow water and cover of a cluster of fishing boats in the area. However, the actions of *Endurance* had delayed the trawler, enabling the more heavily armed Coast Guard cutters to close her position. With the Vietcong vessel disengaged from *Endurance*, *Rush* fired 5-inch rounds without scoring any hits. *Rush* then directed *Sherman* to engage the enemy, and she hit it repeatedly with 5-inch 38-caliber rounds from her forward mount. As each point-detonating round struck the trawler, there was an accompanying explosion and bright illumination of the enemy vessel until it stopped, exploded, and sank. *Endurance* meanwhile had been sending contact range and bearing reports to *Sherman* via flashing light (reliable voice radio communications were not available) to ensure that the cutter engaged the correct target since there were a number of VN fishing boats in the area of the trawler. Before *Sherman* commenced firing point-detonating rounds, she fired three star shells to illuminate the target and to ensure identification.[11]

Wark remembers viewing the trawler's final death throes, and recalls with obvious pride *Endurance*'s significant role in both denying the enemy the cargo and in subsequently attempting to recover it:

The trawler had made its pass and fired its rocket [exploding 75mm round] in one last attempt to sink us. We just kept firing our guns. The trawler got clear of us, and a few minutes later as I saw fire consuming its superstructure it exploded into bits. The fire got to some of the ammunition she was carrying. She went to the bottom.

I know we saved a lot of soldiers' lives by denying the enemy the ammunition that was put on the bottom. We stayed on station where we sank the trawler for about ten days, assisting the Navy UDTs [Underwater Demolition Team divers] in the recovery of the ammo from that ship. Because it was in very shallow water, not more than 5 to 7 fathoms deep, Charley would have recovered it if we hadn't. I picked up a piece of wood from the sunken ship that was floating on the surface and brought it back as a souvenir. It was painted the color of the ocean and may have been part of the deckhouse. The trawler appeared to be approximately 190 feet long.[12]

Endurance's commanding officer, Lieutenant Commander Charles R. Schlegelmilch, later received the Silver Star medal and members of his crew a total of seven Bronze Stars, seven Navy Commendation medals and nine Navy Achievement medals. All hands received Combat Action Ribbons and Navy Unit Commendations. In total, the ocean minesweeper had expended during the sea battle one hundred thirty 20mm rounds, eight hundred fifty .50-caliber rounds, and three hundred .30-caliber rounds while suffering no casualties to crewmembers.[13]

The morning after the engagement, Vice Adm. King and the VNN Chief of Naval Operations visited *Endurance*. Following their departure, the MSO was directed to attempt to locate the sunken trawler by use of her sonar so that divers could investigate the site. *Endurance* immediately located the trawler on sonar and, after arriving at the plotted location, visually sighted a mast protruding above the water. Embarked Navy UDT divers from Harbor Clearance Unit 1 dove on the site and confirmed the presence of the trawler, noting that its superstructure had been demolished by explosions. Initial diving efforts were directed toward obtaining codebooks, charts, radio settings, and selections of weapons and ammunition that would provide intelligence concerning trawler infiltration operations. From 22–25 November U.S. and South Vietnamese Navy divers participated in the operation, which required the use of a YHLC (non-self-propelled heavy salvage lift craft) to surface munitions recovered from cargo holds, while *Endurance* remained on-station to provide support services. When a tropical storm moved through the area, the minesweeper left for open seas and the divers returned to base.[14]

Endurance and the salvage ship USS *Conserver* (ARS 39) later completed salvage operations on the sunken infiltration trawler. Following a conference on 30 November aboard the salvage ship at Vung Tau, *Conserver* relieved *Endurance* as on-scene commander. Diving operations began on 2 December when *Endurance* arrived at the site of the wreck at first light and, using her sonar, began vectoring *Conserver*'s workboat over the trawler. She located the trawler immediately and "buoyed off" the area above it. The Republic of South Vietnam craft YLLC1 (a former USN non-self-propelled light salvage lift craft transferred less than a month earlier by the United States to the Vietnamese Navy as part of its "Accelerated Turn Over to Vietnam" Program), with VNN divers aboard, anchored near the wreck, passed a bowline to the stern of the trawler, and began diving operations. These were extremely hazardous due to zero visibility, strong currents, and jagged metal edges protruding from the vessel's hull. When the currents were at maximum ebb or flood, the divers could not descend to the wreck, and slack water occurred for only about fifteen minutes, usually once per day. Although diving efforts were suspended on 2 December due to deteriorating weather, the divers had been able to become familiar with the trawler and associated working conditions and to recover a drum magazine with a carrying case for a type 56 light machine gun as well as a light canvas cover. *Endurance* moved two miles seaward of the site for night anchorage, while the VNN YLLC1 proceeded up river to seek shelter from bad weather. Slightly improved weather conditions the following day allowed a more thorough investigation and recovery of the following armaments:

• Four birdcage underwater pressure actuating devices plus carrying case
• Thirty-one boxes of 82mm mortar rounds (2 per box) with accessories
• One case (968 rounds) TSPE 53, 7.62mm ammunition
• Approximately 20,000 rounds of AK-47 ammunition in 16–20 round packages.[15]

Relieved of her MARKET TIME duties by ocean minesweeper USS *Dynamic* (MSO 432), *Endurance* proceeded to Subic Bay, Republic of the Philippines, for a change of command and upkeep before commencing her return voyage with the other units of Mine Division 73 to Long Beach, California.[16]

2 Design, Construction, and Alteration

"The true poem is the poet's mind; the true ship is the ship-builder."
Emerson, "Of History," *Essays.*

IMPETUS FOR THE POST-KOREAN WAR MINE FORCE

Because of the U.S. Navy's inability to rapidly clear enemy-laid mines in the approaches to Wonsan Harbor (see map 2-1) during the Korean War (1950–1953), a total of 101 ocean minesweepers (MSOs) were built in ship and boat yards in the United States in the 1950s. This massive shipbuilding program occurred in response to extensive North Korean use of Soviet-supplied mines, which at Wonsan had forced some 250 ships with 50,000 men embarked to wait a week to make a landing because of a lack of minesweeping capability. (The problem arose when North Korean sampans and junks laid an estimated 3,000 Soviet mines in combinations of old 1908-vintage moored mines and modern bottom mines that presented a new menace to existing minecraft. Of these, only 225 were subsequently cleared or destroyed in the swept channel, with resulting casualties of two U.S. and one South Korean minesweepers.) Sixty-five of the 101 new ocean minesweepers were commissioned for service in the U.S. Navy, and the remaining thirty-six were transferred immediately to allies as part of the Mutual Defense Assistance Program (MDAP). These vessels were a portion of a larger shipbuilding program that also produced twenty-four coastal and two inshore minesweepers for service in the U.S. Navy, as well as another 171 coastal and six inshore minesweepers for transfer to allies and other friendly countries.

Map 2-1

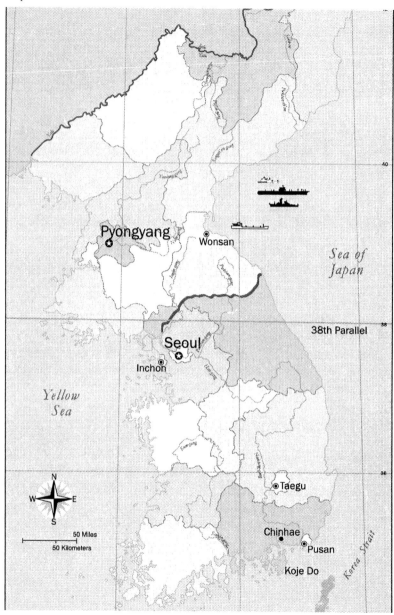

Korea: The Navy's inability to clear mines at Wonsan during the Korean War spurred construction in the 1950s and early 1960s of large numbers of wooden ocean, coastal, and inshore minesweepers.

COMPOSITION OF THE MINE FORCE

Between 1953 and 1994, a total of ninety-one wooden mine warfare ships, constructed during the post–Korean War era, served in the U.S. Navy. In addition to ocean, coastal, and inshore minesweepers, the mine force included smaller craft built of wood or Fiberglas, fifty-seven-foot minesweeping boats and thirty-six-foot launches for operations in shallow waters not accessible to larger vessels. A few "steel hulls" were converted for use as mine countermeasures support ships or as "guinea pigs," Styrofoam-filled vessels that steamed through areas believed to contain pressure mines triggered by ship passage for which no countermeasure existed.

In the late 1950s and early 1960s, the Navy redesignated as mine countermeasures vessels seven ships that had been constructed for other missions. Four of them, *Orleans Parish* (MCS 6), *Epping Forest* (MCS 7), *Catskill* (MCS 1), and *Ozark* (MCS 2), underwent conversion and served in the Atlantic and Pacific Fleets; *Catskill* and *Ozark* were the last to leave service (in the early 1970s). The other three vessels, the former vehicle landing ships *Osage* (MCS 3), *Saugus* (MCS 4), and *Monitor* (MCS 5), were redesignated as mine countermeasures support ships while they were laid up in the reserve fleet in the 1950s, but were never "brought out of mothballs" and were subsequently struck. *Epping Forest*, *Catskill*, and *Ozark* carried minesweeping launches; *Orleans Parish*, a converted World War II tank landing ship, did not have this capability. The "guinea pig ships," formally termed "special devices," were the former World War II Liberty ship *Harry L. Glucksman* (2445) and the former tank landing ship USS *Washtenaw County* (LST 1166). The latter vessel was modified specifically during the Vietnam War to perform "check sweeping" as part of a U.S. effort in 1973 to render safe mines that U.S. Navy carrier aircraft had planted earlier in Haiphong Harbor. Following mine countermeasures performed by ocean minesweepers and minesweeping helicopters, it ran the channel to check effectiveness. The operation itself was aptly codenamed END SWEEP.

The service of the coastal minesweepers, inshore minesweepers, and smaller craft is not covered in this work. When their history is written, most notable will be the seven-man enlisted crews that took in harm's way the fifty-seven-foot minesweeping boats that served in Vietnam. Duty in the boats, even more unheralded than that in minesweepers, presented almost daily the possibility of injury or death by mines or enemy attack as the small craft worked ceaselessly to keep the waterways leading into Saigon open. The crews of other, nontraditional, minecraft deserve equal recognition for the dangers and hardships they faced during their service with the "brown water Navy." These included landing craft (LCM 6) rigged with minesweeping gear and redesignated river mine-sweepers (MSM) and smaller 30-ton patrol minesweepers (MSR).[1]

PHILOSOPHY BEHIND AND DESIGN OF THE OCEAN MINESWEEPERS

During World War II, minesweeping had become, in a sense, hazardous duty. The various warring navies had developed mines that were increasingly difficult to sweep. This was true of our own program as well as the mine warfare programs of our enemies. In an action as large as World War II, men and ships were expendable and it was often the fate of minecraft to fall within the expendable category. Immediately after the war, however, the Navy was diminished considerably in size and its thinkers and planners wrestled with problems that had been glossed over before. One of these problems was minesweepers. Thus, when the Korean conflict broke out, the Navy was ready to promote a new type of minesweeper to counter the enemy's inventiveness in mine warfare. The ineffectiveness of older-type minesweepers with metal hulls was illustrated graphically in Wonsan Harbor, where such ships fell victim to magnetic mines. To combat a deadly menace it became necessary to construct a vessel displaying no magnetic characteristics, or "signature." Designing a completely new type of vessel is at best arduous, but when the design must embody an entirely new engineering concept—in this case exclusive use of nonmagnetic materials—the inherent problems become nearly insurmountable.[2]

The concept of building wooden-hulled ocean minesweepers grew out of the inadequacies of their predecessor steel-hulled *Raven*- and *Auk*- and *Admirable*-class fleet minesweepers (AM) that had occasionally detonated mines during minesweeping operations. Six steel-hulled minesweepers and one high-speed minesweeper were lost to mines in World War II and another was severely damaged. While making a preinvasion sweep in Brunei Bay, Borneo, during World War II, USS *Salute* (AM 294) struck a mine and sank while she led several minesweepers through waters believed to have been swept. USS *Perry* (DMS 17), a converted destroyer, was sunk by a mine off Peleliu

Island. *Osprey* (AM 56) was blown up in the English Channel, *Skylark* (AM 63) off Haguchi Beach, Okinawa, *Portent* (AM 106) and *Swerve* (AM 121) off Anzio, and *Tide* (AM 125) off Normandy. *Skirmish* (AM 303) struck a mine in Manila Bay but survived.[3]

Following the war, many minesweepers spent months clearing mines in Japanese and Korean waters. While operating with Japanese minesweepers, *Minivet* (AM 371) stuck a mine, rolled over, and sank within minutes. During the Korean War, *Pirate* (AM 275) and *Pledge* (AM 277) sank while conducting preinvasion sweeping off the enemy-held island of Sin-Do.

The tremendous task of creating a modern minesweeper was given to the prolific and versatile marine designer Philip L. Rhodes of New York, whose career spanned more than five decades from 1919 until his death in 1974; during that time he designed a wide variety of craft for clients ranging from Rockefellers to Sears and Roebuck. His twelve-meter yacht *Weatherly* would win the America's Cup in 1962. During World War II, he had developmental responsibilities for such naval auxiliaries as patrol craft, minelayers, minesweepers, school ships, salvage vessels, tugs, barges, and sub chasers. He also supervised conversion of large liners into troopships and worked on hospital ship projects. His biographer Richard Henderson emphasizes that Rhodes was not only an excellent engineer but a true artist. "Whatever kind of vessel he produced, it invariably had the look of rightness about it. His sailing yachts in particular, with their beautifully proportioned hulls and graceful sheerlines, are works of true design harmony."[4]

Rhodes and his staff deliberately aimed at producing the finest wooden-hulled oceangoing naval ship ever produced. What emerged from his drawing board and from the forests and foundries of America was the MSO 421-class minesweeper. A wooden-hulled ship with a low magnetic signature, it was specifically designed not to detonate magnetic mines and to safely sweep and destroy any mine likely to be encountered at that time. However, there were, as in any new class of ship, some design flaws. For instance, life aboard an MSO was often difficult because Rhodes had given little consideration to crew comfort. Deck seams opened in any sort of heavy weather and cascading waters left crewmembers wet and miserable, and the lively motion of the ships meant seasickness was always a problem for some. Subsequent improvements helped matters. Some of the most significant were installation of a taller stack to help move engine exhaust away from the bridge and other topside areas, reducing the nausea resulting from breathing "stack gas," air conditioning to cool crew and equipment, and additional freshwater-making capability. (One problem in the original design was the lack of adequate water-making capability, compounded by temperamental evaporators and limited water storage capacity. Accordingly, sailors sometimes had to stream their laundry astern of the ship.) Little could be done, however, about the heavy weather that caused the ships to roll and pitch violently, resulting in crew fatigue and often forcing sailors on watch or performing work to hang tightly onto or wedge themselves against or between immobile objects to prevent being washed overboard or suffering bruises or cuts from hard spills. During such periods, many of those off watch spent their time in their "racks," trying to get what little rest was possible before they had to stand their next watch or take part in ship's evolutions.[5]

Photo 2-1

Model of USS *Conflict* (MSO 426) by Rick Szpyrka depicting the original configuration of the ocean minesweepers designed by Philip L. Rhodes (courtesy of Rick Szpyrka)

MISSIONS AND CAPABILITIES OF OCEAN MINESWEEPERS

In order to understand the mission of a minesweeper, it is useful to know something about the sea mine, which, after all, was the reason for the MSOs' existence. The word "mine" usually conjures up a mental picture of a spherical, spiked object anchored on a cable and riding below the surface of the sea. This is known as a moored, or mechanical, mine. The terms "moored" and "mechanical" refer to the fact that the mine is moored in place and that physical contact is necessary to detonate it. Another class of mines, the "influence" type, is detonated by such forces as disturbances in the earth's magnetic field, sound, and pressure; these do not require physical contact to be set off. Influence mines lie on the sea bottom and are for this reason sometimes known as "bottom" mines. The bottom mine is most effective in relatively shallow waters, for at greater depths the force of its explosion is diminished during propagation through the water column to the ocean's surface. Notwithstanding, bottom mines are relatively easy to lay and fairly difficult to counter. The new state-of-the-art ocean minesweepers were designed to be virtually invulnerable to influence mines and equipped with the gear necessary to deal with both contact and influence types.[6]

Generally, minesweepers must pass over mines to sweep them; therefore, designers gave primary consideration to the safety of ship and personnel. Because 1950s mines were activated by physical contact or by magnetic or acoustic disturbances, the MSO influence signature had to be eliminated or reduced to a minimum. This requirement was met by constructing ships with wooden hulls, by using nonmagnetic aluminum, bronze, brass, or stainless steel fittings, and by employing noise reduction strategies. (This approach, however, would present reliability and maintenance challenges, as nonmagnetic metals aren't the most durable materials with which to build ships.) Magnetic materials, where necessary for strength or durability, were compensated for by a degaussing system designed to eliminate the disturbance they cause in the earth's magnetic field, which triggers magnetic mines. The ships' nimble maneuverability (with controllable-pitch propellers like those of DC-6 aircraft) and a policy of stationing all hands topside during sweeping operations added to safety. The new minesweepers could utilize all known minesweeping techniques with reasonable safety and, although small, were able to sail all the oceans, bays, and waterways of the world.[7]

The MSOs had "moored" gear for cutting the moored or mechanical mines and "influence" gear for sweeping influence mines. The moored gear essentially consisted of two cables (known as wires) streamed off the stern, diverted by "kites" to the port and starboard sides of the ship at a certain depth below the surface and held down by a "depressor." Members of the minesweep detail attached mechanical or explosive cutters to the wires at regular intervals. A float, or "pig," with a jackstaff and flag on top as a visual reference, was attached to the port and starboard wires to keep the gear from "bottoming out." If the wires, streaming astern of, downward, and outward from the ship, caught a mine cable, they guided it to the cutters, which severed it, causing the mine to surface so it could be destroyed by gunfire. (The U.S. Navy mine force no longer practices this method of destruction, having learned through experience that a gunfire-induced explosion can also damage the minesweeper.) This type of sweep is referred to as a "Single-O" if streamed to only one side of the ship or a "Double-O" if streamed to both port and starboard. The "O-sweep," invented by the British and used in World War I, is short for *Oropesa*, the name of the British ship that perfected its use.[8]

In fact, the predecessors of all sweep gear fitted in the MSOs, as well as the degaussing systems used to help protect the ships from magnetic mines, were invented by the British, with variants adopted and manufactured by the United States for use in its minesweepers. It's been said that necessity is the mother of invention and, during World War I, Britain faced daily the possibility of loss of ships and men due to mines laid by German naval vessels the preceding night. The Royal Navy's counter to this threat, sending out minesweepers each day to keep open the English Channel, so vital to the survival of Britain, was described thus by Rudyard Kipling:

DAWN off the Foreland—the young flood making
Jumbled and short and steep—
Black in the hollows and bright where it's breaking—
Awkward water to sweep.
Sent up *Unity, Claribel, Assyrian, Stormcock,* and *Golden Gain.*
Noon off the Foreland—the first ebb making
Lumpy and strong in the bight.
Boom after boom, and the golf-hut shaking
And the jackdaws wild with fright!
Mines located in the fairway,
Boats now working with chain,
Sweepers—*Unity, Claribel, Assyrian, Stormcock,* and *Golden Gain.*

Dusk off the Foreland—the last light going
And the traffic crowding through,
And the five damned trawlers with their syreens blowing

Heading for the whole review!
Sweep completed in the fairway.
No more mines remain.
Sent back *Unity, Claribel, Assyrian, Stormcock,* and *Golden Gain.*

For magnetic minesweeping, the MSOs streamed a long insulated copper cable astern and "pulsed" an electrical current to replicate the magnetic field associated with cable-detonated magnetic mines. To sweep sound-influenced mines, which use microphones to listen for the noises made by machinery and propellers of an approaching ship, the minesweepers deployed an acoustic device, essentially a noise-maker employing either a vibrating diaphragm or a hammer-struck plate to set up a sound level high enough to detonate the mines before ships neared their danger zone. The two acoustic devices employed by MSOs were commonly referred to by the ships' crews as the "4 Victor" and the "6 Bravo" (used to counter mines detonated by the noise produced by a ship's propellers and its machinery, respectively). Magnetic and acoustic minesweeping could be done simultaneously, using one of several different configurations. Probably the most dangerous mine, because neither the MSOs nor any other type of minesweeper had a countermeasure for it, was the pressure mine, triggered by a change in water pressure caused by the passage of a ship. There were two defenses for this type of weapon. The first was for ships to proceed at dead slow speed, at high tide, to minimize water disturbance and maximize the vertical column of water between any pressure-mines and own ship, and hope for the best. The second means was to steam a "guinea pig" minesweeper, a large steel-hulled low-value or derelict vessel, modified to minimize danger to its crew, through dangerous waters in the hopes of purposely setting off mines.[9]

In the 1950s, sweeping was the only sure countermeasure against mines. If time did not permit sweeping, however, the MSOs could use short-range, high-resolution sonar for mine hunting or mine location. Using this sonar, as well as electronic and visual navigation, the ship could clear a temporary safe channel until sweep operations could be conducted. Mine hunting was also used to confirm the presence of suspected minefields and for cleanup after clearance sweeps. In the twilight of their service, fitted with much better navigation and sonar equipment, remotely operated vehicles (ROVs) and, sometimes, embarked explosive ordnance disposal (EOD) divers, MSOs were

Photo 2-2

MSO fantail crew streaming a "magtail" (courtesy of Charles Wymer)

directed by Navy policy to "mine hunt if you can, mine sweep if you must." This caution was driven home during the Persian Gulf War, when an ocean minesweeper streaming "sweep gear" was severely damaged by a detonated mine. With mine neutralization vehicles (successors to the ROVs) or EOD divers available, mine countermeasures ships today are able to locate mine-like objects with sonar, mark their location on a chart, stand off at a safe distance to neutralize them if investigation proves them to be mines, or maneuver around them, continue to mine hunt, and deal with them later. The policy of the mine countermeasures forces of some countries is to immediately dispose of mines as they are found; U.S. Navy policy in some cases is to rapidly search as large an area as possible in hopes of finding an alternate route around the minefield before beginning laborious and time consuming mine neutralization. Depending on geography and operational requirements, of course, such a course may not be possible.[10]

OCEAN MINESWEEPER CHARACTERISTICS AND VARIANTS

Normally a new class of ship is named after the first vessel in the class. However, *Agile* (hull number 421) was so unique she is considered the only ship of her class, largely because her engineering plant was unlike that of subsequent minesweepers. (She had V-16 Packard main propulsion engines that provided a total of 3,200 shaft horsepower and an eight-cylinder 250-kilowatt ship's service generator.) The *Aggressive* class, named after the ship with the next hull number (422), comprised fifty-three of the sixty-five U.S. Navy MSOs: 422–427, 432–449, 455–474, and 488–496. The four ships of the *Dash* class, 428–431, were fitted with two eight-cylinder General Motors main propulsion engines, providing 1,600 total shaft horsepower. With an overall length of 172 feet, 35-foot beam, 755-ton maximum displacement and 10-foot draft, *Agile*, *Aggressive*, and *Dash* ships, which used the same hull design, could make fourteen knots through the water.[11]

Photo 2-3

USS *Agile* (MSO 421) under way (Courtesy of Dick Lewis)

The vessels constituting the *Acme* (508–511) and *Ability* (519–522) classes were improved and slightly larger than the *Agile*, intended to serve as mine squadron or division flagships. The four *Acme*-class ships, a little longer at 173 feet, were also fitted with Packard engines. The largest of the MSOs, however, were four *Ability*-class ships. One, *Assurance* (521), was commissioned on 21 November 1958. The cost of her construction was estimated to be $9,500,000. One hundred ninety-one feet long, she had a draft of eleven feet five inches, a displacement of 957 tons, and was propelled by two General Motors V8-diesel engines rated at 1,400 horsepower each to a maximum speed of 15 knots—one knot faster than the other ocean minesweepers.[12]

In 1955, *Avenge*, *Pivot*, and *Firm* underwent conversion to MSO 421-class flagships, a modification accomplished by enlarging the wardroom and office spaces. As flagships they served as tactical and administrative command posts for a number of similar ships.[13]

Photo 2-4

USS *Assurance* (MSO 521), one of three U.S. Navy 191-foot flagships (Official U.S. Navy Photograph from the National Archives)

BUILDERS' YARDS

In order to construct and take receipt of 101 wooden minesweepers within the 1950s, the U.S. government had to mobilize the combined resources of public and private shipyards and boatyards located across America, on the East, West, and Gulf coasts, as well as the inland waterways of the Great Lakes. *Bold* and *Bulwark* were built by the Norfolk (Virginia) Naval Shipyard, the others by private ship and boat yards as follows:

Builders' Yards

Astoria Marine Construction Company Astoria, Oregon	*Dash* (MSO 428)
	Detector (MSO 429)
	Hulls 480, 481, 482 to the Netherlands
Bellingham Shipyards Company Bellingham, Washington	Hulls 450 (M613), 451 (M614), 452 (M617), 453 (M612), 454 (M616), 475 (M618), 476 (M615), 477 (M619), 500 (M620), 501 (M621), 502 (M622) to France
	Hulls 478 (M415) and 479 (M416) to Portugal (the latter transferred to Belgium)
	Hulls 498 (M950) and 499 (M951) to Norway
Broward Marine, Inc. Fort Lauderdale, Florida	*Stalwart* (MSO 493)
	Sturdy (MSO 494)
	Swerve (MSO 495)
	Venture (MSO 496)
Burger Boat Company Manitowoc, Wisconsin	*Valor* (MSO 472)
	Vigor (MSO 473)
	Vital (MSO 474)
	Hulls 486 (M417) and 487 (M418) to Portugal
Colberg Boat Works Stockton, California	*Dynamic* (MSO 432)
	Engage (MSO 433)
	Embattle (MSO 434)
Frank L. Sample Jr., Inc., Shipyard Boothbay Harbor, Maine	*Acme* (MSO 508)
	Adroit (MSO 509)
	Advance (MSO 510)
	Affray (MSO 511)

Builders' Yards, continued

Fulton Shipyard Company Antioch, California	*Conflict* (MSO 426) *Constant* (MSO 427)
Higgins, Inc. New Orleans, Louisiana	*Excel* (MSO 439) *Exploit* (MSO 440) *Exultant* (MSO 441) *Fearless* (MSO 442) *Fidelity* (MSO 443) *Lucid* (MSO 458) *Nimble* (MSO 459) *Notable* (MSO 460) *Observer* (MSO 461) *Pinnacle* (MSO 462)
C. Hiltebrant Drydock Company Kingston, New York	*Direct* (MSO 430) *Dominant* (MSO 431)
J. M. Martinac Shipbuilding Corporation Tacoma, Washington	*Endurance* (MSO 435) *Energy* (MSO 436) *Firm* (MSO 444) *Force* (MSO 445) *Conquest* (MSO 488) *Gallant* (MSO 489) *Leader* (MSO 490) *Persistent* (MSO 491) *Pledge* (MSO 492)
Luders Marine Construction Company Stamford, Connecticut	*Agile* (MSO 421) *Aggressive* (MSO 422) *Avenge* (MSO 423) *Rival* (MSO 468) *Sagacity* (MSO 469) *Salute* (MSO 470) *Skill* (MSO 471)
Martinolich Shipbuilding Company San Diego, California	*Enhance* (MSO 437) *Illusive* (MSO 448) *Impervious* (MSO 449) *Esteem* (MSO 438)

Builders' Yards, continued

Martinolich Shipbuilding Company San Diego, California, continued	Hulls 506 (M5431) and 507 (M5430) to Italy
Peterson Builders Inc. Sturgeon Bay, Wisconsin	*Ability* (MSO 519) *Alacrity* (MSO 520) *Assurance* (MSO 521) Hull 522 (M902) to Belgium Hulls 483 (M886), 484 (M887), 485 (M889) to the Netherlands Hulls 512 (M609), 513 (M610), and 514 (M624) to France
Seattle Shipbuilding and Drydocking Company Seattle, Washington	*Fortify* (MSO 446) *Guide* (MSO 447)
Tacoma Boatbuilding Company Tacoma, Washington	Hulls 503 (M907) and 504 (M906) to Belgium Hull 505 (M623) to France
Tampa Marine Company Tampa, Florida	Hulls 515 (M908) and 516 (M909) to Belgium Hulls 517 (M5432) and 518 (M5433) to Italy
Wilmington Boat Works, Inc. Wilmington, California	*Implicit* (MSO 455) *Inflict* (MSO 456) *Loyalty* (MSO 457) *Pivot* (MSO 463) *Pluck* (MSO 464) *Prestige* (MSO 465) *Prime* (MSO 466) *Reaper* (MSO 467)

The last MSOs built by the Navy were included in the 1954–55 shipbuilding program and were commissioned in 1958. The U.S. minesweepers originally were designated as Wooden Minesweepers (AM), and later reclassified on 7 February 1955 as Ocean Minesweepers (MSO). The design for the 172-foot length MSO 421 class ships, which included the *Agile*, *Aggressive*, *Dash*, and *Acme* variants, was completed in 1951 and that for the four 190-foot MSO 519 *Ability-*class vessels in 1955. Drawings for a larger 200-foot length MSO 523 class of ship were completed in 1966, but no vessels were constructed due to a lack of funding and associated changes in priorities within the Navy resulting from the prolonged war in Vietnam.[14]

POST-CONSTRUCTION CHANGES AND ALTERATIONS

As the ocean minesweepers were commissioned, they underwent thorough testing and evaluation to determine their fitness for duty and to identify improvements for planned ships and those under construction in builders' yards. These tests and trials began in 1953.

In 1955, the Navy conducted extensive tests on *Valor* at the Engineering Experimental Station at Annapolis, Maryland, the ship having been assigned as the prototype for the evaluation of the main propulsion plant of MSO-class ships. The following year, the main propulsion engines in *Illusive* were replaced with experimental Packard engines for an evaluation by the Bureau of Ships. Changes made later to the engines increased their reliability and improved their performance, and modified diesels were installed in later ships.[15]

Photo 2-5

Packard turbocharged 600 HP Marine Propulsion Engine (courtesy of ENCS Richard Crank, USN [Ret.])

However, the modifications did not correct all existing problems, and experimentation with other engines continued. In January 1962, *Loyalty* received two Curtiss-Wright 3D-1700 nine-hundred-horsepower main propulsion diesel engines. The Navy, however, replaced the engines with Packards in 1965. The Packard engines installed in MSOs continued to be challenging and maintenance intensive and were themselves eventually replaced with Waukeshas. *Agile* became the prototype in 1968 when her Packard diesel main engines and generator prime movers were replaced with Waukeshas. On 28 October she completed sea trials and transmitted a radio message that she was "Underway on Waukesha power-101240Z Oct 68," a variant of the historic message sent by USS *Nautilus* (SSN 571), the world's first nuclear-powered submarine, on 17 January 1955.[16]

To assess the strength and integrity of the ships' hulls and equipment, the Navy employed post-construction shock testing. These tests, which involved exploding depth charges at various depths in the water and distances from the hull, often revealed other design and installation problems as well. During shock testing of *Aggressive* in late 1955, she received little hull damage, but suffered major machinery derangement. The concussion knocked all four diesel-main propulsion engines, and the diesel engine for the 300KW variable frequency generator in the forward engine room, off their mounts, rolled the generator prime mover onto its side, and caused other lesser damage to machinery and equipment. The Navy used the findings from these and other tests to make corrections to initial ships of the class and improvements to the design of ocean minesweepers remaining to be constructed.[17]

After leaving the builders' yards and completing initial shakedown training, the new wooden ships reported to mine divisions homeported in Charleston, South Carolina, or Long Beach, California, and thereafter began deploying to the North Atlantic, Mediterranean, and Western Pacific for duty with the 6th and 7th fleets. A decade of operations identified some equipment limitations and problems of obsolescence, but proved the overall design and structural integrity of the hulls, although some degradation occurred due to leaky weather decks and, in voids beneath freshwater tanks and refrigeration boxes and in chain lockers, some problems resulted from freshwater leakage, condensation, and poor ventilation. There was also some criticism leveled at the ocean minesweepers due to their relatively low hull efficiency compared to other Navy ships. A disproportionate amount of their total displacement was dead hull weight. Accordingly, if the proportion could be lowered, the payload or fuel capacity could be increased. However, reducing the weight and robustness of the hulls would likely induce another problem, by making the vessels more susceptible to damage from exploding mines. During subsequent modernization, the installation of additional equipment (and placement of lead ballast in bilge areas to offset the added topside weight and maintain ship stability) increased gross tonnage of the ocean minesweepers, reducing their top speed and maximum range.[18]

MODERNIZATION AND REHABILITATION

In fiscal year 1968, the Navy began a program to modernize the MSOs, providing improvements in mine detection, engineering, communications, and habitability. However, costs and shipyard delays caused the program to be halted after only thirteen ships had been fully modernized at three yards. These vessels were *Engage, Enhance, Esteem, Exultant, Fearless, Fidelity, Force, Fortify, Illusive, Impervious, Inflict, Conquest*, and *Leader* (Mine Divisions 71, 82, and 93). A fourteenth ship, *Avenge*, was damaged by fire during the conversion and later stricken. Several other MSOs were partially modernized, receiving some upgrades and the SQQ-14 variable-depth sonar.

The original AN/UQS-1 sonar was replaced over time by the AN/SQQ-14 sonar, the predecessor to the AN/SQQ-30 and AN/SQQ-32 sonars later installed in the 1990s in *Avenger* (MCM 1) and *Osprey* (MHC 51) class mine countermeasures ships and coastal mine hunters. The sonar transducer was normally hoisted and stored inside the ship when not in use and lowered through a sea chest in the hull during mine hunting operations. Installation of a winch (from which the transducer was suspended) on the foc's'le required removal of the larger 40mm gun mount, which was replaced with a single- or twin-barrel 20mm machine gun. Although its primary purpose had been destruction of sea mines, the 40mm was used very effectively for shore bombardment during the Vietnam War and its removal decreased the versatility of the class. The new 20mm gun was nearly useless for suppressing shore fire, due to its limited range and the lightness of its projectile. (Two .50-caliber machine guns were also fitted on the bridge wings for close-in work, and a .30-caliber gun was mounted aft when required in Vietnam for ship self-defense.)[19]

Photo 2-6

A gunner firing *Leader*'s 20mm gun at a target off the port beam (courtesy of Rick Newkirk)

The forward deckhouse was enlarged to provide room for a new radar set and Identification of Friend or Foe (IFF) equipment, which necessitated moving the signal bridge immediately aft of the bridge. The ships' superstructures were reconfigured to allow for enlargement of the Combat Information Center and the communications spaces. A secure teletype system was installed in Radio Central, and both short- and long-range transmitters and receivers ("Teds" and "Reds") were replaced with modern, high-power, transistorized equipment. The-up-to-date radio gear enabled the ships to copy dual-channel fleet broadcasts and transmit and receive using on-line encryption.[20]

In part for habitability and in part to cool the new electronics equipment, air conditioning was also installed to serve mess decks, crew berthing, wardroom, commanding officer's cabin, Combat Information Center, Radio Central, and IFF spaces. The crew appreciated the installation because of the dramatic improvement in living conditions and because it markedly reduced the frequency of electronics breakdown due to overheating; both advantages later proved particularly valuable to Pacific Fleet ships operating in the South China Sea.[21]

An Aquafresh evaporator was also installed, doubling best freshwater-making capability from two thousand gallons per day to forty-four hundred. The second evaporator meant that MSOs were now normally able to make enough fresh water to provide crewmembers a daily shower and weekly laundry.[22]

In addition to installation of new sophisticated electronic equipment and replacement of seven Packard diesels with Waukesha engines, the degaussing system was to be improved and the SPS-5C radar overhauled. Moreover, the Aquachem evaporator and AN/SQQ-14 replaced the Badger evaporator and AN/UQS-1 sonar, respectively. Lead ballast in the amount of nearly fifty tons was mounted in the bilge areas of both engine rooms to offset the new topside weight added by expansion of the superstructure and new equipment. It was decided not to install an 81mm mortar, as originally planned, but rather a 20mm turn-around gun (swapped between ships upon return to Long Beach from Vietnam).

CONVERSION OF USS *ALACRITY* (AG 520) AND USS *ASSURANCE* (AG 521)

Of the three *Ability*-class ships remaining, *Ability* (MSO 519) was stricken in 1971 and *Assurance* and *Alacrity* were converted in 1973 to towed array surveillance system (TASS) vessels. On 1 March 1973, the designations of the wooden ships were changed from ocean mine-sweepers (MSOs) 520 and 521 to miscellaneous ships (AGs) 520 and 521. Their new mission would be to locate and track submarines, using the AN/SQR-15 passive sonar. (These two ships were precursors to the small fast frigate sister ships USS *Bronstein* [FF 1037] and USS *McCloy* [FF 1038], in which this equipment was later installed; to succeeding larger and more capable combatants; and, finally, to civilian-operated TAGOS SURTAS [Surveillance Towed Array Sensor System] ships built in the 1980s for employment as gap-fillers in the U.S. Navy's SOSUS [Sound Surveillance System] submarine tracking system.)[23]

The new mission required installation of equipment and modifications to enable the vessels to remain unsupported at sea for longer periods. *Assurance* entered first the Atlantic Drydock Corporation, Fort George Island, Florida, for the removal of all minesweeping gear and installation of new evaporators to increase the ship's production of fresh water, and then Detyens Shipyard at Wando, South Carolina, for remaining conversion work and habitability improvements. The AN/SQQ-14 mine hunting sonar and minesweeping gear were removed, including all moored, magnetic, and acoustic mine countermeasures equipment and devices. The reel well, formerly used to store the magnetic cable ("magtail"), was converted to an electrical and TASS workshop. The AN/SQR-15 passive towed array system itself was installed under the direction of the Supervisor of Shipbuilding, Charleston, and the Naval Undersea Center, San Diego. The ship's fuel storage capacity was also increased by approximately twenty-five percent. *Assurance* returned to the Naval Station, Charleston, for in-port certification of the AN/SQR-15 and then left for Exuma Sound in the Bahamas for tests required for her final certification in January 1974, assisted by *Fearless*.[24]

Alacrity underwent conversion at Detyens Shipyard before entering the Atlantic Drydock yard for removal of her minesweeping

Photo 2-7

Alacrity and *Assurance* in port Naples, Italy, in 1974 (courtesy of Reid Morris)

equipment and installation of TASS. The change in her mission area resulted in reduced manning for the deck and operations departments, but the arrival of nine Ocean Systems Technicians brought her complement to four officers and sixty-one men. *Alacrity* left Charleston on 10 January 1974 for the Exuma Sound Range for final certification. *Fidelity* sailed a day later to assist her in testing and checking out the towed arrays recently installed in the converted MSO.[25]

Alacrity and *Assurance* stood out from Charleston on 16 July 1974 for a Mediterranean deployment to test their towed arrays against Soviet submarines. They operated during the next four months under the operational control of Commander Anti-Submarine Force, 6th Fleet, with Navy P3 patrol aircraft based at Sigonella, Italy, tracking Soviet submarines. Between TASS operations, the sister ships visited Rota, Palma de Mallorca, and Barcelona, Spain, and Naples and Brindisi, Italy.[26]

MSO FORCE REDUCTIONS

Beginning in 1970, a relatively brief time after a substantial post–Korean War build-up of the surface mine force, large numbers of ocean and coastal minesweepers were already being decommissioned, transferred to foreign countries, or turned into Naval Reserve Force training platforms. (The last of the coastal minesweepers left service in May 1976. One of the first ocean minesweepers was *Swerve*, commissioned on 27 July 1957 and struck after a mere fourteen years of service.) Having recognized the importance of a credible mine force after the Korean conflict, the Navy had already begun to dismantle it by the end of the Vietnam War, returning to its age-old practice, between conflicts, of mothballing ships and reducing manning aboard reserve ships remaining in service to skeleton caretaker crews. (The Navy did retain a few active duty MSOs with full crews in service.) Recognizing its resulting inability to field adequate numbers of capable minesweepers to deal with any future large-scale mine threats, the Navy would be forced in coming decades to rely increasingly on NATO allies to carry out most of the taskings in this mission area. The consequences of this policy have already proven to be problematic in the Middle East and have the potential to be disastrous as the United States finds itself increasingly distanced from allies whose warfare capabilities were factored into its plans for the future.

3 Organization, Support, and Manning

MINE FORCE ORGANIZATION

Following the humiliation of the U.S. Navy at Wonsan, Korea, where an ill-prepared and under-equipped minesweeping force was unable to deal with mines, Vice Adm. Struble, Commander 7th Fleet, recommended major changes. He concluded that only an integrated mine countermeasures (MCM) force would provide effective assault clearance in future wars. Accordingly, he urged the development of a sufficient mix of MCM-specific surface vessels, assisted by helicopters visually searching for mines, divers to detonate mines, and advanced theater-level intelligence gathering to facilitate true mine countermeasures operations and readiness throughout the Navy. He added that adequate mine countermeasures forces with trained personnel and equipment should be a ready component of each fleet.[1]

Historically, interest within the Navy in mine warfare and resources devoted to it have peaked following wartime exposure of glaring weaknesses and subsided rapidly thereafter as the memories of bitter lessons fade. The Navy was ill prepared to combat mines at the onset of World War I, World War II, and the Korean War, and immediately inactivated the capable mine forces it had scrambled to put together following the world wars. Twice stung, the Navy resolved not to make the same mistake a third time. The mine force was expanded, not downsized, following the Korean War. A first step by the Navy in correcting existing deficiencies was reestablishment in January 1951 of Mine Force, Pacific Fleet, which had been disestablished in 1947 as part of a post–World War II downsizing. Subsequently, both the Atlantic and Pacific Fleets acquired parallel type commanders, responsible solely for the readiness of mine force ships. The 1950s and early 1960s initially proved to be a renaissance for mine warfare.

In succeeding decades, however, emphasis on mine warfare would slowly wane due to a host of factors, including a service culture that had never embraced the warfare area, the necessary diversion of resources to support the prolonged war in Vietnam, and an honest belief that a small mine force would suffice. For two decades, from the end of the Korean War through Operation END SWEEP, conducted in 1973 during the Vietnam War, the minesweepers were but rarely called upon to clear mines and had instead been employed for a myriad of other tasks and duties, some that could have been performed better by more versatile and durable steel-hulled vessels.

There were during this era periodic reorganizations within the mine force, particularly following a massive reduction in numbers of minesweepers in the early 1970s. The changes primarily sought to husband declining resources by consolidating remaining ships under fewer commanders and to improve oversight and support through assignment to groups or squadrons in specific geographical areas. During the 1950s and 1960s, four MSOs were normally assigned to a division, although this number might vary for short periods. In the 1970s, there were frequently more ships per division, with the MSOs of some parent commands based at different locations. As part of the reorganization in the 1970s, five Pacific Fleet MSOs were transferred to the Atlantic Fleet, where a greater demand for the remaining ships existed. The last Pacific Fleet minesweepers deployed for operations in Vietnam would return to the United States in 1973, transfer to the Naval Reserve, and be homeported at one of three major West Coast ports, San Diego, San Francisco, or the Seattle/Tacoma area. Their mission was primarily defensive in nature: to maintain a high order of proficiency and be prepared to conduct mine clearance operations to open ports should an enemy force mine any. The Atlantic Fleet minesweepers had more approaches and seaports along the Eastern Seaboard to cover, and a few deployed periodically to northern Europe to conduct mine countermeasures exercises with NATO allies.[2]

Atlantic Fleet Organization
Ocean minesweepers reporting to the Atlantic Fleet were homeported at Charleston, South Carolina, to which in December 1958 Commander Mine Force relocated its headquarters from Norfolk, Virginia. The following year the U.S. Navy Mine Warfare School at Yorktown, Virginia also moved to Charleston, further establishing it as the principal home for mine warfare in the Atlantic Fleet. In April 1960, a new Mine Force, U.S. Atlantic Fleet organization went into effect. Mine

Division 43 changed its homeport from Charleston to Little Creek, Virginia, to be colocated with the amphibious force based there and provide pre-assault mine clearance during training exercises and operations, and Mine Division 81 relocated to the Naval Mine Defense Laboratory at Panama City, Florida, to support efforts to develop and perfect new methods of mine warfare.[3]

On 1 July 1971, as part of a downsizing of the mine force, the Navy disestablished the two fleet type commands, Mine Force, U.S. Atlantic Fleet and Mine Force, U.S. Pacific Fleet, replacing them with a single centralized command, Mine Warfare Force, U.S. Navy, at Charleston, South Carolina. Mine Squadrons Four and Eight and their subordinate divisions 43, 44, 45, 81, 82, 83, and 85 were disestablished, and Mine Squadron Four was redesignated Mine Flotilla Two. The new flotilla assumed operational control of all Atlantic Fleet mine warfare ships, including Mine Squadrons Ten and Twelve.

Between June and September 1971, fifteen Atlantic Fleet ocean minesweepers were decommissioned and four more transferred to the Naval Reserve Force. As a result of the reorganization, five MSOs scheduled for decommissioning, but still in service, were assigned to the flotilla commander and the remaining seventeen ships to Mine Divisions 21, 22, 23, and 24 (the former Mine Divisions 81, 82, 43, and 45).

With the eventual decommissioning of these ships came the disestablishment of parent commands and more streamlining. The Navy disestablished Mine Division 23 on 1 July 1971 and a year later Mine Divisions 21 and 22. Additional ocean minesweepers were transferred to the Naval Reserve Force. On 30 June 1973, Mine Flotilla Two and its remaining division (MinDiv 24) were disestablished. All remaining active MSOs were assigned to Mine Squadron Ten and all Naval Reserve Force ships to Mine Squadron Twelve. The former squadron, located at Charleston, was subsequently disestablished on 1 July 1975.

Commander, Mine Warfare Force was disestablished on 1 July 1975, and the Atlantic and Pacific Fleet MSOs became units of Commander, Naval Surface Forces, Atlantic and Pacific, respectively. On 16 July 1981, Mine Squadron Twelve was redesignated Mine Group Two and, on 1 March 1985, Mine Group Two was redesignated Mine Squadron Two and assigned to the administrative command of Cruiser Destroyer Group Two instead of Naval Surface Force, Atlantic. With this change, the three minesweepers homeported at Charleston remained under the command of Mine Squadron Two, which enabled the squadron to devote more time to its role of mine countermeasures commander. The administrative and operational control of nine other ships was transferred to new intermediate unit commanders (Destroyer Squadron Eight, Service Squadron Eight, and Surface Group Four). These changes placed the ships in a group or squadron located in the same geographical area and thereby afforded them constant and direct support from a more senior officer.

In late December 1991, Mine Squadron Two was redesignated Mine Countermeasures Group Two and, on 1 October 1992, the homeport of the group was changed from Charleston to Ingleside, Texas. The last Atlantic Fleet ocean minesweeper, USS *Exploit* (MSO 440), was decommissioned on 15 December 1993. Today, the Navy mine force is based at Ingleside, its surface component comprised of the fourteen *Avenger*-class mine countermeasures ships that replaced the MSOs, twelve smaller *Osprey*-class mine hunters, and a command and control ship, the high-speed vessel HSV 2 *Swift*.

Pacific Fleet Organization

In the early 1950s, the first Pacific Fleet MSOs reported to Mine Squadron Nine, Mine Division 91, located in Long Beach, California. As more minesweepers left the builders' yards in 1954–56, they were assigned to Mine Divisions 92 through 96, also based in Long Beach. On 1 January 1957, Mine Squadron Nine was reorganized to form two smaller squadrons (Seven and Nine). This change redesignated Mine Divisions 91 through 96 as Mine Divisions 71, 72, 73, 91, 92, and 93.

Eleven years later, on 1 January 1968, Mine Division 94 was formed with ships from the existing six divisions, essentially to ease the burden on minesweepers serving in Vietnam by increasing, through the addition of a seventh division, the length of time between deployments of individual divisions to the war zone. Mine Squadron Nine was disestablished on 1 June 1968 and Mine Flotilla Three was established, formed from Mine Squadron Seven and Mine Squadron Nine ships. Thereafter, beginning with massive downsizing of the minesweeper force in the early 1970s through the remaining service of the ocean minesweepers, periodic reorganizations would occur in an effort to better utilize and support with too few resources the remaining ships.

On 1 July 1971, Mine Force, U.S. Atlantic Fleet and Mine Force, U.S. Pacific Fleet were disestablished and replaced with Mine Warfare Force, U.S. Navy, at Charleston, South Carolina. As part of the reorganization, Mine Divisions 71, 72, 73, 91, 92, and 93 were disestablished, and Mine Divisions 31, 32, 33, 34, and 35 established. Mine Flotilla One was established at Guam, Marianas Islands, with USS *Force* (MSO 445), USS *Impervious* (MSO 449), USS *Inflict* (MSO 456), USS *Engage* (MSO 433), and USS *Fortify* (MSO 446) assigned. Now sited much closer to Vietnam, the flotilla units continued to operate there regularly. The other Pacific Fleet MSOs were assigned to Mine Flotilla Three at Long Beach, comprised of Mine Divisions 32, 33, 34, and 35. Reserve Mine Squadron Five was established on 1 July 1971 for Pacific Fleet MSOs newly assigned to the Naval Reserve Force. The operational control of minesweepers in the Naval Reserve Force came under the control of the Commander in Chief, Pacific Fleet.

The following year, the Mine Warfare Force was reorganized yet again. On 1 July 1972, Mine Division 32 was disestablished and two days later, Mine Division 33. On 1 September 1972, Mine Division 34 was disestablished and a new division 54 established at Pearl Harbor, Hawaii, assigned to Mine Flotilla Three. Associated changes included reassignment of some Pacific Fleet MSOs to different administrative commands or homeports.

On 30 June 1973, Mine Flotilla Three was redesignated Mine Squadron Five and Mine Flotilla One was disestablished, the latter replaced the following day by the newly established Mine Squadron One. The former flotilla ships left Guam on 1 May 1974 for the United States and their new homeports on the East Coast. Mine Squadron One was disestablished on 1 June 1974.

Following the disestablishment of Mine Squadron One and transfer of its minesweepers to the Atlantic Fleet, all remaining Pacific Fleet MSOs became part of the Naval Reserve Force, assigned to Commander, Mine Squadron Five, located at Seattle, Washington. In the summer of 1984, MinRon 5 was redesignated Mine Group One.

SUPPORTING AND SUPPORTED COMMANDS

As the post–Korean War mine force expanded, there was increased activity within supporting organizations, principally the Navy Mine Warfare School at Yorktown, Virginia, and the Mine Countermeasures

Station at Panama City, Florida. The existing school had passed out its first graduates, 50 officers and 175 men, in May 1941, as part of the Navy's effort to train the sailors it needed to man eventually hundreds of mine countermeasures ships in World War II. The mission of the second facility (for which the cornerstone was dedicated in 1956) was to search for and perfect new and improved ways to defeat mines. Its name changed during the service of the ships, first to the U.S. Naval Mine Defense Laboratory and then to the Naval Coastal Systems Laboratory, the latter change reflecting a somewhat expanded mission that included swimmers and their vehicles. Minesweepers also regularly provided services to other organizations charged with developing and testing mines and mine countermeasure capabilities. These commands included the U.S. Naval Ordnance Laboratory at White Oaks, Maryland, and the Naval Weapons Center at China Lake, California. Atlantic Fleet ships provided direct fleet support to the Naval Underwater Ordnance Laboratory Test Facility at Fort Monroe, Virginia, the Naval Ordnance Laboratory Test Facility at Fort Lauderdale, and the Naval Mine Warfare Evaluation Detachment at Key West, Florida.[4]

Other test facilities and ranges supported these organizations. The Commander, Operational Test and Evaluation Force U.S. Atlantic Fleet operated a test facility at Port Everglades, the port of Fort Lauderdale. A range near Fort Story, Virginia, in the channel leading to the port and naval base at Norfolk, supported the efforts of Naval Underwater Ordnance Laboratory Test Facility, Fort Monroe. The Gulf Test Range at the Naval Coastal Systems Center in Panama City, as well as the one at the Naval Undersea Center at Exuma Sound, Bahamas, also supported research.

Dedicated Support for Research and Development
In the late 1950s, Mine Division 81—*Assurance, Valor, Venture, Vigor,* and *Vital*—was transferred from Charleston to the U.S. Naval Mine Defense Laboratory at Panama City, where it remained until 1971. The ships were dedicated to the support of the lab's research and development efforts, which included work on advanced mine countermeasures equipment for a 1965–1966 minesweeper design intended to replace the MSOs. (Ultimately, the high costs of operations in Vietnam would preclude construction of the planned ships. However, research supported by the MSOs would lead to the follow-on generation of

equipment eventually installed in the *Avengers* that would begin to replace them after 1989.)[5]

The length of time required to install, test, and evaluate major shipboard equipment and systems demanded specialized test platforms. Accordingly, the Navy assigned *Acme*, *Pluck*, *Fidelity*, *Dominant*, and *Exploit* to priority projects. Other minesweepers played a role in research activities from time to time, but only a handful of MSOs bore the main burden and made the major contributions.

FLEET SERVICE MINE TESTS

The intertwined relationship of sword and shield required within the mine force a continued emphasis on both mining and defensive mine countermeasures. Accordingly, minesweepers were involved in periodic Fleet Service Mine Tests (FSMTs). The primary purpose of the tests was to prove new mines and evaluate routinely the reliability of stockpiled U.S. service mines. An added benefit was the opportunity these exercises afforded minelayers, minesweepers, patrol aircraft, submarines, and divers to perform their primary or collateral missions.

Mine tests were conducted many times each year during the late 1950s, the 1960s, and the early 1970s off the East and West Coasts of the United States and, for deployed U.S. and allied forces, in the Mediterranean and Pacific. Responsibility for the tests was rotated among participating mine division and aircraft squadron commanders. Tests in which Pacific Fleet ships participated were normally conducted either at Santa Rosa Island off southern California or, for deployed ships, at Pearl Harbor or in the Western Pacific, normally in conjunction with allies. Atlantic Fleet FSMTs usually took place near Charleston, South Carolina, and in the Mediterranean off the coast of Italy.

If required for the tests, MSOs conducted bottom surveys to aid in mine planting by identifying with their sonar any obstructions that had to be removed. Attack or patrol aircraft and/or submarines then planted the exercise minefield while the minesweepers charted ("raked") the location of the mines. MSOs coordinated aircraft mine drops and prepared overlays of mine positions to speed the relocation and recovery of drill mines (normally a statistical sample from various mine stockpile points) following completion of exercises. The recovery of the mines was essential for the successful analysis of the test and to generate research data on new-model mines.[6]

When the exercise minefield had been prepared, ships and submarines made repeated runs, on different headings and at various speeds, to test the mine actuators. After the vessels challenged the exercise mines with representative targets, MSOs conducted mine clearance to test their sonars and countermeasures (mechanical and combination influence sweeps) against the ordnance. Throughout the exercise, if required, minesweepers patrolled the field to keep shipping and small craft clear. After the MSOs had attempted to locate and trigger the mines, EOD divers (embarked in the minesweepers, salvage ships, or self-propelled barges) recovered the ordnance for return to mine depots.[7]

Photo 3-1

Coastal minesweeper *Warbler* fantail crew recovering a submarine-laid drill mine (courtesy of Capt. Richard Tarbuck, USN [Ret.])

In a representative test in March 1968, Mine Division 93 left Long Beach for Santa Rosa Island. At Becher's Bay, the ships, with their division commander in tactical command, took part in Fleet Service Mine Test 5-68. Participating units included, besides *Leader*, *Guide*, *Excel*, and *Enhance*, the submarine USS *Raton* (SS 270), the self-propelled harbor utility craft YFU-37, an EOD Unit detachment, and mine-laying aircraft. During the test, *Guide* performed a variety of duties: mine watching, minefield patrol, magnetic and acoustic minesweeping, and mine hunting. *Guide* crewmembers also planned and directed mine-marking parties ashore for the mine-laying segment.[8]

THE SHIPS' CREWS

Before readers proceed into the heart of this work, ship operations, it's both appropriate and important to describe the heart of the ships themselves, the officers and men who served aboard them. Admirals Horne and Chadwick both acknowledge and describe the unique qualities and attributes of minesweep sailors and their environment at sea in the book's forewords. The following overview of the composition of the ocean minesweepers' crews and their duties is intended to complement their heartfelt words.

The shipboard organizations of the ocean minesweepers changed somewhat over the years, particularly following the transfer of many to the Navy Reserve Force and the reduced manning resulting from reserve status. Moreover, it wasn't uncommon aboard individual ships for there to be some variations based on the experience, skill, and unique abilities of the people assigned. However, as aboard any small ship in any Navy, crewmembers had to be self-reliant and they had to be tough.

The ships were generally commanded by lieutenant commanders, and occasionally by a more junior or senior officer, an officer in the rank of lieutenant or commander. Seagoing commands are highly sought after by naval officers, and the Navy vests command responsibility only in those it considers most worthy. The commanding officers of the minesweepers were often of two very different sorts: bright and accomplished young men viewed by the Navy as having much future potential, or seasoned "mustangs," older officers risen from the enlisted ranks for whom command of a small ship would most likely be the pinnacle of their careers. Because remaining in the mine force would likely be the death knell for an officer's career, few individuals with aspirations for their futures did, and during the service of the ocean minesweepers the Navy ascribed different career equivalencies to a commanding officer's tour of duty in one. At one point, command of a sweep was viewed as equivalent to a department head tour in a larger vessel, later as in lieu of the second in command (executive officer) aboard a larger ship. Eventually, late in the service of the ships, an officer could be certified "qualified for command" of a larger ship based on a successful command tour in a minesweeper.

Mustangs in command generally tended to be a colorful lot, with some occasionally bending the rules in order to, in their view, get the job done. Such behavior did not always set well with "regular officers." A graduate of the Naval Academy once remarked about a fellow commanding officer, "If he's ever seen a copy of *Navy Regulations*, it's only by accident." A common denominator among commanding officers is love of one's ship, and mustangs savored theirs, recognizing that it was likely the top of the ladder for them and not a step en route to anything higher.

The complement of an ocean minesweeper was originally eight officers, including the commanding officer, and seventy enlisted men. However, shipboard manning varied over time, based on needs of the Navy, funding, and numbers of personnel available. The composition of departments and divisions also varied based on the numbers of officers and Chief Petty Officers assigned and their respective experience and abilities. Junior officers served as the heads of the engineering, operations, deck/weapons, and supply departments, which, with the commanding officer and executive officer, totaled six officers. If two additional officers were available, they might serve as the damage control assistant/electrical officer under the engineer officer, and the combat information center/communications officer working for the "Ops Boss." However, many other variations were possible, including an officer serving as head of both the deck and supply departments at the same time. Because the minesweepers did not rate a Supply Corps officer, the latter position was filled by a surface warfare officer.

The number of Chief Petty Officers aboard an ocean minesweeper also varied, based on distribution of personnel within the Navy and advancement aboard individual ships. Ideally, however, due to the multitude of equipment crammed aboard, the CPO Mess would include a Chief Engineman, Electrician, Boatswainmate, and Operations Specialist. In addition to leading the enlisted men in their respective department or division, Chief Petty Officers might also serve as division officers in lieu of commissioned officers.

In addition to the four departments previously mentioned, there was a fifth, Executive/Medical/Navigation, overseen by the executive officer. Second in command of the ship, he was also directly responsible for the ship's office (to which a yeoman and one or more personnelmen were assigned), the independent duty corpsman, one or two quarter-masters, and the signalman. The latter two ratings normally carried out navigational duties at sea, for which the XO was responsible. In port, the operations officer was normally responsible for overseeing the daily activities of these men. There were within the operations department radiomen, sonarmen, operations specialists (radar operators) and electronics technicians. The engineering department was comprised of enginemen, electricians, interior communications electricians, hull technicians (damage control men), and a few non-rated firemen. A few rated boatswainmates and many non-rated seamen, and normally one gunnersmate (referred to as "gunner"), made up the deck/weapons department. The supply department was comprised of cooks (mess management specialists) and storekeepers. Dispersing and postal functions, traditional supply department duties in larger vessels, were performed by ship's office personnel and mess cooking and laundry duties by seamen and firemen temporarily assigned a tour of duty in the supply department. Haircuts were provided crewmembers by a qualified shipmate, although some recipients might dispute his qualifications. It was generally best to get a haircut ashore well before one was mandated by the "Chief" before he granted permission to leave the ship for liberty. The ship's store, dispersing, and postal functions were not under the purview of the supply department, as surface warfare officers (functioning as supply corps officers aboard small ships) could not by regulations oversee them. The "ships store," run out of a cabinet or small storage area by a member of the crew, normally offered only candy bars and warm sodas although some ship's emblematic items might also be available for sale.

The above overview of a minesweeper crew does not adequately describe how most minesweep sailors viewed themselves and the "sweeps they rode." Minesweep sailors were convinced they were simply the biggest and baddest in the fleet. This sentiment, and pride in ship and crew, may be gleaned from an excerpt from the mid-watch entry made in the deck log of USS *Bold* (MSO 424) on 1 January 1969:

In Charles Towne, as said in old
South Carolina, rides the *BOLD*.
Moored at the U.S. Naval Base,
A bright NEW YEAR for us to face.
A happy new year and it should be,
For all good men who sail on wood.
To hell with hulls of steel so cold,
Iron men live on the *BOLD*.

4 Atlantic Fleet Operations

This chapter depicts representative deployments and operations of Atlantic Fleet ocean minesweepers that, taken together with their participation in search and salvage activities, provides a broad overview of their employment from the late 1950s through the late 1980s. Information about their remaining service through the early 1990s is contained in succeeding chapters devoted to support provided by Atlantic Fleet minesweepers to the space program, the Naval Reserve Force, and Operations EARNEST WILL and DESERT SHIELD/STORM. For the first three decades of their service, the wooden ships deployed routinely to the Mediterranean and North Atlantic for operations with the 6th Fleet as components in the NATO force structure designed to confront the Soviet Union. Because Soviet influence extended to Cuba, some island nations in the Caribbean, and parts of South America, the MSOs also operated as a component of a standing U.S. Navy Caribbean Readiness Force.

Ocean minesweepers took part in amphibious and other actions of the 6th Fleet in response to the appeal of the Lebanese government in 1958; operations off the Dominican Republic in 1961; Caribbean Contingency Operations, operations off Haiti, and the Cuban Missile Crisis in 1962; and the Dominican Republic operations in 1965 and 1966.

Because of the economic and military importance of the Panama Canal, minesweepers periodically conducted sonar surveys of the ocean approaches to the waterway as well as along its fifty-one-mile length. Such operations, by both Atlantic and Pacific Fleet MSOs, complemented the efforts of smaller coastal minesweepers, two of which were permanently stationed for a period in the late 1950s and early 1960s in the Canal Zone.

Although designed specifically to locate and dispose of mines, ocean minesweepers provided services and assistance to many organizations outside mine warfare within the Navy, other military services, and federal and state agencies. Because of the accurate and high-resolution, albeit short-range, sonar gear they were fitted with, MSOs were frequently called upon to search for objects scattered on the ocean floor, including mislaid munitions, downed aircraft, sunken ships, and other miscellaneous items. The most momentous hunt was that to find and recover a nuclear bomb lost in the sea off Spain because of the mid-air collision of two U.S. Air Force planes.

Faced with more requirements than vessels, fleet commanders also employed MSOs for a myriad of odd jobs, among them delivering mail and supplies, towing targets for surface gunnery practice by combatant ships, and serving as communications relay ships. Due to their innocuous appearance and shallow draft, minesweepers were also, if infrequently, ordered to perform such tasks as shadowing foreign intelligence-gathering ships, collecting information, and performing humanitarian missions. The most common task, certainly the most popular with the crews, was representing the United States by official port calls. One of the most interesting of these was the transit of USS *Valor* (MSO 472), in company with Belgian division 191, up the Congo River in central Africa in 1959.

When the Navy began, as part of a post–Vietnam War drawdown, decommissioning or transferring to the Naval Reserve Force large numbers of MSOs, the resulting reduction in minesweepers meant both less U.S. capability to support allies and also greater U.S. reliance on NATO mine countermeasure capabilities for any future mine clearance requirements. A permanent NATO squadron of mine countermeasures ships was created on 11 May 1973, titled Standing Naval Force Channel, comprising vessels from different NATO navies, including the United States, appointed for six to twelve months in rotation. The U.S. Navy, which did not always assign minesweepers to the Force, was usually represented by active duty ships, although it did deploy reserve ships *Fearless* and *Exultant* in 1983.

INITIAL MSO DEPLOYMENT TO THE MEDITERRANEAN

On 4 January 1956, the four bright and shiny new ocean minesweepers of Mine Division 81 sailed for the Mediterranean from Charleston, South Carolina, on a maiden five-month cruise. Three days later, *Direct* collided while refueling with the fleet oiler USS *Canisteo* (AO 99) due to faulty steering gear. Her bow badly damaged, she was ordered to return to Charleston for repairs. En route, the injured minesweeper encountered a storm of gale strength, said to be the worst of its type in the Atlantic in ten years. After battling the nor'easter for two days, *Direct* finally made port.[1]

The remaining three "D-boats"—*Dash*, *Detector*, and *Dominant*—continued onward and arrived at La Spezia in northwest Italy (see map 4-1) after stopping briefly in Gibraltar. Minesweeping exercises occupied the ships for the next few days before their departure on 2 February. They arrived on 4 February in Palma de Mallorca, Spain, one of the Balearic Islands (see map 4-2), after stopping at Cannes, France the previous day. The division next called at Genoa, Italy. The three Ds left Genoa on the 24th and, after conducting exercises en route, arrived at Naples, Italy, on 1 March.[2]

Leaving Naples on 22 March upon completion of a maintenance period, the ships made Cannes two days later. Having attended to both work and play—minesweeping exercises and liberty in the famous French resort—the division left for the Principauté de Monaco. The three ships arrived on 5 April at the second smallest independent state in the world (after Vatican City). Occupying a tiny corner of southwestern Europe and measuring only a little over one-half square mile in area, Monaco is surrounded on three sides by France (see map 4-3). Its ruler, Prince Rainer, would marry Grace Kelly, the American motion picture actress, two weeks later.

The minesweepers next called at Bizerte, Tunisia, arriving 12 April at the North African city. Formerly one of the Barbary States, Tunisia was then a monarchy that would in 1957 become a republic. The following day the division shifted to Tunis to conduct minesweeping exercises, returning to Bizerte on 17 April for more exercises. Departing on 21 April, the division visited Rhodes, Greece, then sailed to Izmir, Turkey and back to Rhodes (see map 4-4). Leaving Rhodes, the MSOs stopped at Piraeus, the port for Athens. On 21 May, the division sailed for home, stopping briefly at Tangier in north Morocco.[3]

The division next touched Ponta Delgada, San Miguel to receive fuel. One of the Azores Islands, which belong to Portugal, it lies about eight hundred miles west of that country in the Atlantic (see map 4-5).[4]

The three Ds returned to Charleston on 11 June 1956. *Detector* also visited Mendorica and Villa-Franche, France, and *Dominant*, Patras, Greece.[5]

Map 4-1

Italy: Deployed MSOs routinely conducted minesweeping exercises off La Spezia, participated in 6th Fleet operations in the Straits of Sicily, entered Naples for voyage repairs and maintenance, and called at other Italian ports for liberty.

MILITARY AND PEACEKEEPING OPERATIONS

The participation of minesweepers in military actions and shows of force is a reminder of turbulent times in which the Navy performed multiple peacekeeping duties. Divisions of ocean minesweepers were deployed continuously to the Mediterranean and Caribbean to provide fleet commanders an on-scene mine countermeasure capability. In the absence of a requirement to clear mines, the MSOs performed support roles, normally patrolling off the coasts of strife-torn or hostile countries as components of larger "shows of force." The first such military operation in which they participated was the Lebanon Intervention in 1958.

Map 4-2

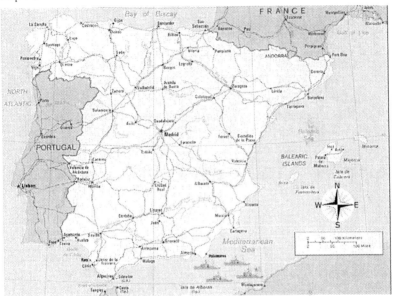

Spain: MSOs normally touched Rota en route and departing "the Med," enjoyed liberty in the Balearic Islands, and in 1966 were dispatched to Palomares to locate a nuclear bomb in the deep ocean waters off the farming hamlet.

On 1 February 1958, Egypt and Syria, recipients of military aid from the Soviet Union, joined to form the United Arab Republic, a single state headed by Egyptian president Gamal Abdel Nasser and dedicated to Arab nationalism and unity. In May, civil unrest broke out in Lebanon between Muslim and Christian factions.[6]

On 12 May, Mine Division 84 ships—*Nimble, Pinnacle, Sagacity,* and *Skill*—stood out of Charleston on a regularly scheduled deployment. After arriving at Gibraltar on 28 May, the division operated in the Eastern Mediterranean, calling occasionally at Italian and Greek ports.[7]

Soon afterwards, President Camille Chamoun of Lebanon charged that the UAR had instigated violent opposition to his regime and

Map 4-3

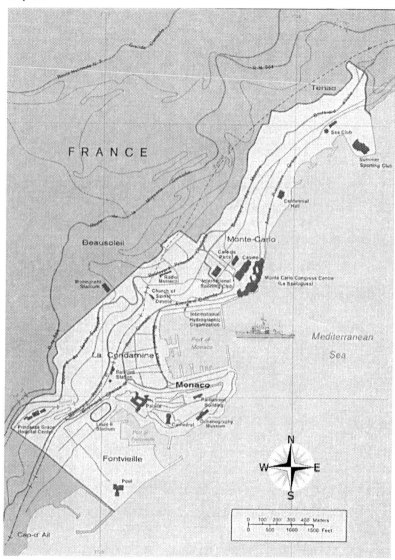

Monaco: An independent state in the heart of Europe, nestled between mountain and sea, the picturesque Principality of Monaco borders France on the Mediterranean coast.

Photo 4-1

Assurance (MSO 521) entering Monte Carlo, Monaco, in 1964 (courtesy of Dan Smith)

appealed for United Nations intervention to halt the unrest. However, UN observers sent to Lebanon in June were unable to substantiate Chamoun's allegations of interference by Nasser in Lebanese internal affairs. Then on 14 July, King Faisal II of Iraq was killed and his pro-Western government overthrown in a UAR-inspired coup. Alarmed by the Iraqi revolt and its implications for the turmoil in his own country, Chamoun appealed to President Eisenhower for help.[8]

Responding immediately, Eisenhower on 15 July ordered five thousand U.S. Marines from the 6th Fleet to land in Lebanon. The resulting operation, code-named BLUE BAT, involved about 14,000 troops, including 8,509 Army personnel and 5,670 officers and men of the Marine Corps. The plan was to occupy the Beirut International Airport and then secure the port of Beirut (see map 4-6) and the approaches to the city. The supporting 6th Fleet naval force, which conducted air operations and Marine assault landings beginning 15 July, comprised over sixty vessels, including eight ocean minesweepers. The first Army forces arrived in Beirut on 19 July. The Marines, four battalion-sized landing teams and a logistical support group, were

Map 4-4

Greece: Ocean minesweepers operated throughout the waters off Greece, enjoyed the time spent in her port cities, and occasionally conducted surveillance on Soviet fleet units at the Kithira Anchorage north of Crete.

deployed on 26 July in and around Beirut. Meanwhile, at the request of King Hussein, cousin of Iraq's murdered Faisal, British troops were flown into neighboring Jordan, which was also under pressure from pro-Nasser elements. Citing the 1957 Eisenhower Doctrine, the president declared Lebanese independence and territorial integrity vital to U.S. interests.[9]

As elements of the 6th Fleet, now ordered to protect Lebanon, the MSOs patrolled off the coast of Beirut with other units. *Sagacity* was among the first to arrive, just before the Marine landings. She patrolled the transport and landing areas and was employed as a communications relay ship. *Nimble* and *Skill* were on station from 17 July to 15 August and

Map 4-5

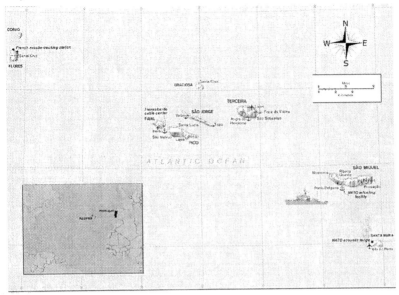

Azores: Minesweepers welcomed stops for fuel, and sometimes brief layovers, at the Azores during their Atlantic crossings.

from 9 September to 2 October, *Sagacity* from 17 July to 2 August, and *Sagacity* and *Pinnacle* from 21 August to 2 October 1958.[10]

A second division of minesweepers covered the periods that MinDiv 84 ships were not on task. On 22 July, Mine Division 44 deployed to support the U.S. military forces in Lebanon. It was composed of *Adroit* and *Stalwart*, with *Fidelity* and *Aggressive* assigned temporarily from Mine Divisions 82 and 83. *Fidelity* sailed from Yorktown, Virginia, to rendezvous with the MSOs and the repair ship USS *Amphion* (AR 13) en route to Beirut. Making a twenty-four-day passage and a brief stop to refuel at Gibraltar, the ships arrived on 15 August to support the Marines who had landed a month earlier. *Stalwart* and *Adroit* were on task between 15 August and 4 September, *Aggressive* and *Fidelity* from 15 to 23 August and 2 to 9 September 1958.[11]

Mine Division 84 was detached from the 6th Fleet on 16 October. At Alicante, Spain, en route home, *Pinnacle* aided in extinguishing a fire in the engineering spaces of the S.S. *Janus*, an abandoned Liberian freighter. The minesweeper fired her 40mm gun at the waterline of the

Map 4-6

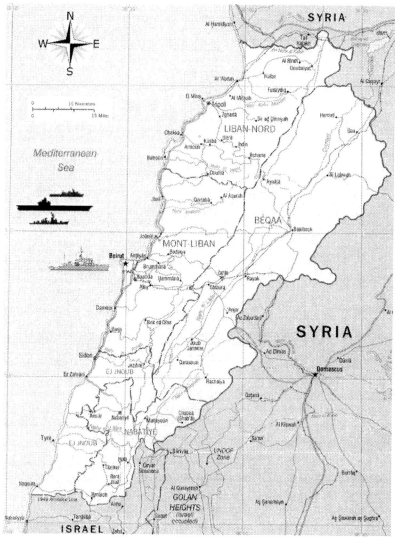

Lebanon: During Operation BLUE BAT in 1958, units of the 6th Fleet including MSOs operated off Lebanon in support of the 14,000 U.S. soldiers and marines deployed to Beirut to halt civil unrest in the country.

Photo 4-2

Assault wave of 3rd Battalion 6th Marines lands ashore from USS *Rockbridge* (APA 228) LCVPs at Red Beach, Beirut, Lebanon, on 16 July 1958 (Official U.S. Navy Photograph from the National Archives)

vessel to pierce the hull, flooding the engineering spaces and quenching the fire without sinking the ship.[12]

SUPPORT OF ALLIES AND SHOWING THE FLAG

Following the U.S. construction and transfer of large numbers of ocean, coastal, and inshore minesweepers to allies in the 1950s and early 1960s, there was, of course, emphasis on training and sharing new technology with other navies. In addition to their role as a ready mine force, the U.S. MSOs worked with allies in the Mediterranean and northern Europe to clear mines remaining from previous wars and called at various seaports, some of which the Navy no longer routinely visits, to "show the flag."

The first deployment to northern Europe began on 12 May 1958, when *Dominant*, with Commander, Mine Division 43 embarked and in company with *Detector*, put to sea from Yorktown, Virginia. After stopping at Portsmouth, England, the ships arrived at Copenhagen, Denmark, the capital city and a major seaport for trade in and out of the Baltic Sea (see map 4-7). The subdivision participated during the next three months in Operations COMPLETE SWEEP I and II, a "special" hydrographic survey in the Baltic Sea. The minesweepers operated from Copenhagen and Kiel, Germany, visiting Svendborg,

Map 4-7

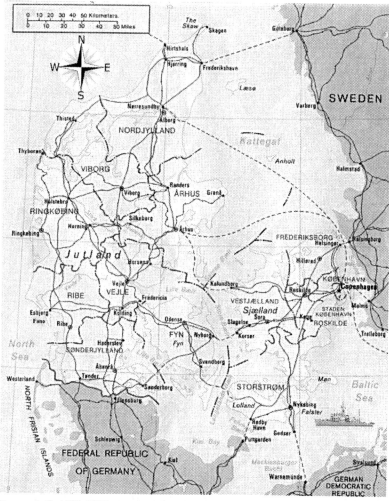

Denmark: In 1958, MSOs conducted operations in the Baltic Sea and thereafter visited Scandinavia infrequently during northern Europe deployments.

Denmark in July. Returning home, the minesweepers stopped at Lisbon, Portugal; Porta Delgada, Azores; and Bermuda (see map 4-8). They arrived in Yorktown on the last day of September.[13]

Map 4-8

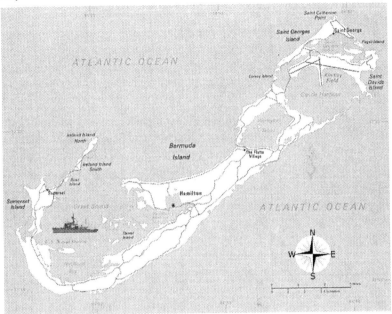

Bermuda: Settled in 1609 by shipwrecked British colonists bound for Virginia aboard the *Sea Venture*, Bermuda was normally the first stop for minesweepers en route the Mediterranean and the last stop before their return home.

TRANSIT UP THE CONGO RIVER

The rise of African nationalism, which began at the end of World War II, spurred an independence movement among colonies in the mid-1950s, one of them the Belgian Congo. Belgium did not seriously consider political changes until the end of 1959, when it agreed to grant independence in less than six months, partially in response to similar movements in nearby French and British colonies. In hastily arranged elections, Patrice Lumumba became the prime minister of the Belgian Congo and Joseph Kasavubu president. Soon afterward, on 30 June 1960, the new nation proclaimed its independence as the Republic of the Congo. (That year, in support of the independence of the Belgian Congo, nearly the entire Belgian fleet would operate in equatorial waters.) The name Zaire was later adopted in 1971. Derived from a local word for "river," the name refers to the great Congo (or Zaire) River, which is the country's chief geographical feature. In 1997, the country was renamed the Democratic Republic of the Congo after Laurent Desire Kabila seized power from Marshal Mobutu's government and exiled the former president (see map 4-9).[14]

Minesweeper *Valor* visited the Belgian Congo immediately preceding the new nation's receipt of independence. On 24 July 1959, she sailed under special orders from Charleston in company with Mine Division 82 and tank landing ship USS *Tallahatchie County* (LST 1159) for northern Europe. *Valor* detached on 7 August near the Azores and proceeded northward along the coast of Portugal and France and through the English Channel to Ostende, Belgium, where she and the Belgium minesweeper *G. Truffaut* (M 908) exchanged divisions. The U.S. MSO sailed thereafter with Belgian division 191 and the *G. Truffaut* with Mine Division 82. *Valor* reported for duty under the operational control of the Belgian Force Navale, and departed with the division for Banana at the mouth of the Congo River in the Belgian Congo.[15]

The division reached Congolese waters on 9 September, arriving at Banana on the Atlantic coast after a transit that included ceremonies appropriate for crossing the equator and a tri-nation exercise involving Portuguese, Belgian, and American ships. Former *Valor* crewmember John Riker recalls the major problem encountered during the exercise:

> The biggest problem *Valor* had was with the incoming radio traffic. It was all in French, and we in the radio shack did not understand the language. We just copied what we heard and hoped for the best. Fortunately the officers managed to translate what we had typed.[16]

In all, *Valor* steamed eighty miles up the Congo River in company with the Belgian ships and visited the two important river ports of Boma and Matadi. The latter, located on the left bank of the river about halfway between the Atlantic Ocean and the Congolese capital of Kinshasa, is today the country's main seaport. Riker describes the journey as uneventful:

> The trip up (river) was a big disappointment. We were expecting to see crocodiles, hippos and all sorts of other different animals, something like the old Tarzan movies, but saw nothing. . . . It was also not kind to

Map 4-9

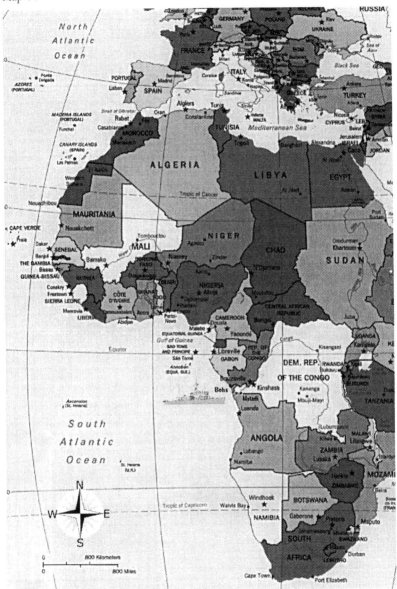

Africa: USS *Valor* (MSO 472) had the distinction of being the only American ocean minesweeper to sail up the Congo River when, in 1959 as part of Belgian Division 191, she visited the river ports Boma and Matadi.

the *Valor*. Our (auxiliary) boilers had to be shut down because they were fouled up with mud from the river and the captain put a water restriction on the whole ship. What water was left in the holding tanks was kept for cooking purposes only. . . . The crew finally got to take a saltwater shower once we got back to sea. . . . While we were up river, the cook submitted a stores requisition for some provisions. The stores came about 8:30 one night and the cook had a real surprise when he saw that the meat he had ordered was freshly killed. I often wondered what kind of meat it was; we ended up giving it to the Belgians.[17]

Returning to Ostende after traveling five thousand miles, the division commenced local minesweeping exercises in the North Sea. Riker describes the period:

We set sail for Ostende on September 21 and arrived on October 17. While we were in the Congo, there was no trouble with the population. It was on our trip back to Belgium that we learned about the rebellion in the Congo. Once we got back to Ostende the crew was given much needed R & R [rest and relaxation]. The nice thing about Belgium was that it was one of only two countries where the crew was allowed to have overnight liberty; England was the other.[18]

Operating from Ostende, the division also participated in a NATO minesweeping exercise off Cherbourg, a seaport at the mouth of the Divette River in northwestern France. Situated along the English Channel, the historical port benefits from a harbor that is well sheltered except to the north. Minesweepers from France, England, Belgium, the Netherlands, and the United States joined in the exercise. *Valor* also made an operational visit to England during this period.[19]

Valor sailed from Ostende for the last time for the U.S. naval base at Rota, Spain. Upon arrival, she reported to Commander, Mine Division 82. The division left for home on 25 January, escorted by *Tallahatchie County*. South of Bermuda, *Valor* was detached to proceed independently to Panama City, Florida, arriving on 14 February. Riker remembers that the crew was very happy to be home:

The *Valor* had visited nine countries and steamed close to 25,000 miles. As interesting as this cruise was, everyone was glad to get back to Panama City.[20]

Valor called at Lisbon, Portugal; Ostende, Belgium; Portland and Portsmouth, England; Banana, Boma, and Matadi, Belgian Congo; Abidjan,

Ivory Coast; Freetown, Sierra Leone; Gibraltar; Cherbourg, France; and
Las Palmas, in the Canary Islands, during the deployment.[21]

OPERATIONS IN THE CARIBBEAN

Many missions require an innocuous ship or simply a presence at a particular location. Minesweepers conducted surveillance of Soviet vessels at anchorages in the Mediterranean and, when deployed with the
Ready Caribbean Force and not otherwise engaged, in the Windward
Passage off Cuba. In the early 1960s, the MSOs conducted many patrols in the passage between Cuba and Haiti (see map 4-10), keeping an
eye on Soviet ships and carrying out other fleet tasks. During one
cruise, *Fearless* towed a water barge, an old converted tanker, back and
forth from San Juan (see map 4-11) to Guantanamo Bay after Fidel
Castro cut off the water supply to the base, providing the service until
the U.S. Navy relocated the desalinization plant in San Diego, California to the base at Cuba. Operations in the Caribbean provided Atlantic
Fleet sailors a change of pace from "Med deployments," and their arrival in the tropics could be almost surreal after leaving only a few days
earlier the snow and wind chill of East Coast ports.

A former *Pinnacle* crewmember fondly recalls that MSO life in this
era included movies on the fantail, great food, and card tournaments.
The cribbage champion of the ship, whom even the old salty boatswain mates couldn't beat, remembers the captain trolling for fish
while on plane guard duty for practice invasions off Vieques Island,
Puerto Rico, and once, when he had a strike, having the ship stopped
until be boated his albacore. He also recollects that when the ship practiced mine-destruction techniques using an empty orange-colored
fifty-five-gallon drum as a target, the gun crew, comprised of cooks,
could rarely, if ever, hit the drum. Accordingly, *Pinnacle* usually had to
steam very close and the Gunner's Mate would finish the job with his
BAR (Browning automatic rifle).[22]

However, duty in the Caribbean was not always carefree. In the
1960s, threats to democracy existed throughout the world, and the Caribbean was no exception as many island nations were experiencing internal strife or external threats to their peace and stability. Accordingly,
MSO divisions routinely sailed south from their East Coast homeports
for duty with the Caribbean Readiness Force. The Force (composed
primarily of amphibious ships) symbolized U.S. presence and resolve.

Map 4-10

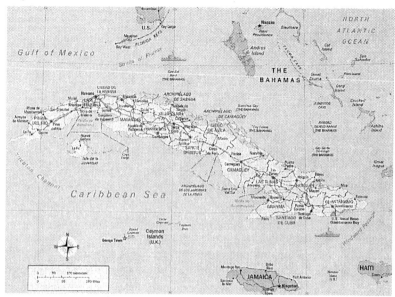

Cuba: MSOs deployed to the Caribbean often patrolled the Windward Passage between Cuba and Haiti conducting surveillance on Soviet ships, and were less frequently assigned harbor patrols at U.S. Naval Base, Guantanamo Bay, Cuba.

Map 4-11

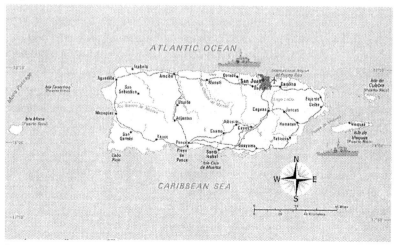

Puerto Rico: Deployed mine divisions participated with amphibious forces in practice landings at Vieques, obtained logistics support at Naval Station Roosevelt Roads, and visited San Juan and other port cities for liberty.

It practiced frequent landings at Vieques, Puerto Rico after the minesweepers had cleared staging areas and boat lanes of practice mines. The U.S. Marines aboard ships in the region ensured the Navy could quickly stage amphibious demonstrations in "shows of force" or, if necessary, land troops ashore to quell trouble—as occurred in 1965 in the Dominican Republic when events culminated that had begun a few years earlier.

On 24 April 1961, in response to a political crisis in the Dominican Republic, Mine Division 82 deployed from Charleston for contingency operations in the Caribbean with Amphibious Squadrons 8 and 10. The division included *Avenge*, *Fearless*, and *Fidelity*, as well as *Valor*, assigned temporarily from Mine Division 81 to replace *Exultant*, which was undergoing a shipyard overhaul.[23]

On 30 May, Rafael Leonidas Trujillo Molina, the president of the Dominican Republic, was assassinated by elements of his army. The following day, Mine Division 82 sailed to rendezvous with other Atlantic Fleet units south of the Dominican Republic for fleet operations. The division participated until 17 June in a demonstration of seapower and then proceeded to Roosevelt Roads for an upkeep period. During the remainder of the deployment, the division took part in two limited amphibious exercises and visited the ports of San Juan and Ponce, Puerto Rico, and St. Thomas in the Virgin Islands.[24]

On 25 October 1961, Mine Division 43, composed of the "D-boats" *Dash*, *Detector*, *Direct*, and *Dominant*, departed Charleston for contingency operations in the Caribbean, arriving five days later at San Juan, Puerto Rico. It was the second deployment of the year for the division, which had returned home on 4 May from the Caribbean. The minesweepers operated that fall in support of Task Group 84.1, deployed off Santo Domingo (see map 4-12) due to the recurrent internal disorders in the Dominican Republic.[25]

During the deployment, the division participated in several fleet maneuvers related to the political tensions in the area and in limited amphibious exercises. *Direct* was assigned to Dominican Republic patrol duties for two weeks and *Dominant* spent two weeks operating in support of TG 84.1. *Detector* visited Antigua, British West Indies (see map 4-13) in November 1961 to represent the United States at the formal reopening of Nelson's Dockyard. In December, she operated between San Juan, Puerto Rico, and the amphibious force off Santo Domingo, delivering mail and supplies.[26]

Map 4-12

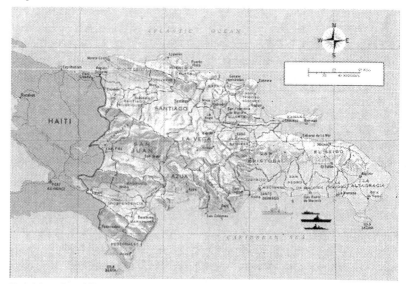

Dominican Republic: Ocean minesweepers operated as a part of larger fleets off the Dominican Republic in the early- to mid-1960s due to internal disorder that ultimately resulted
in civil war

On 20 July 1962, Mine Division 83, with *Agile, Aggressive, Bold,* and
Bulwark, left Charleston for a deployment to the West Indies. That
summer the division joined other naval units off Port au Prince, Haiti
for a "show of force" during another of that country's frequent periods of internal disorder. (When *Alacrity* and *Exploit* called at Jacmel,
Haiti, in late 1958, it marked the first time a U.S. Navy vessel had visited
that port since 1928.) During the cruise, the ocean minesweepers participated in amphibious exercises at Vieques Island and provided services for the Commander, Naval Base, Guantanamo Bay, Cuba.[27]
     Unfortunately, fleet maneuvers off Haiti did not signal the end of
Caribbean Contingency Operations in 1962. Yet to come was arguably
the most famous confrontation between the United States and the USSR
during the Cold War. The Cuban missile crisis resulted from Soviet
placement in 1962 of offensive ballistic missiles in Cuba, lying just a
hundred miles from the southern tip of Florida. This aggressive Soviet
act had been preceded by the embarrassing failure in April 1961 of the
U.S.-backed Bay of Pigs invasion by Cuban exiles to overthrow the Cuban
leader, Fidel Castro. A revolutionary, Castro had seized power in 1959

Map 4-13

Antigua: USS *Detector* (MSO 429) visited Antigua to represent the United States at the formal reopening of Nelson's Dockyard in English Harbour. The harbor served as the headquarters of the fleet of the Leeward Islands in the late eighteenth century.

when his forces overthrew the dictator Fulgencio Batista. Although he promised reform and a better way of life for his people, he installed a leftist regime and developed close ties with the Soviet Union, from which he received military aid. The Cuban alliance with the USSR precipitated the most serious U.S.-Soviet confrontation of the Cold War.[28]

As Castro aligned his country with the communist bloc, the United States led efforts to isolate its Caribbean neighbor, instigating its expulsion from the Organization of American States (OAS) in January 1962. However, the alienation of Cuba from neighboring countries was offset by increased military and economic aid from the Soviet Union. By the summer of 1962, the Soviet Union had begun a major arms buildup in Cuba. American intelligence knew that conventional weapons, including MiG-21 jet fighters and surface-to-air missiles, were being stationed on the island. However, unbeknownst to U.S. officials, the USSR had decided to place ballistic missiles on the island. In early September, the first missiles arrived in Cuba and were transported to secret launch sites under construction around the island.[29]

During the arms buildup, the Soviet government assured President John F. Kennedy that its military assistance to Cuba was strictly defensive. However, CIA director John A. McCone was not convinced; he urged that greater consideration be given to a possible ballistic missile threat. His fears were confirmed on 14 October when an American U-2 reconnaissance aircraft photographed a Soviet medium-range-ballistic-missile (MRBM) site in western Cuba, near San Cristobal. Kennedy was briefed on the discovery on 16 October and immediately convened a meeting of his top civilian and military advisers. The group faced a grave situation. Aerial reconnaissance over Cuba now revealed another MRBM site and two sites for more powerful, intermediate-range ballistic missiles, which intelligence reports indicated were close to completion.[30]

Kennedy and his advisers considered three options to remove the missiles from Cuba: a naval blockade, an invasion or direct air strike, or a settlement through the United Nations. By 21 October, the president had opted for a naval "quarantine," holding in reserve the option of direct military action. The next day, in a televised speech, Kennedy announced that the USSR had erected bases in Cuba to establish a nuclear strike capability against the Western Hemisphere. He declared that the United States was imposing a naval quarantine on all offensive military equipment en route to Cuba, and he appealed to the Soviet premier, Nikita

S. Khrushchev, to recall the weapons. In a separate action, Kennedy also placed U.S. military forces on alert and ordered a force readied for a possible invasion on 30 October.[31]

At the time, *Agile* and *Aggressive* were near Cuba, on station about five miles off Cape Maisi, the eastern point of Cuba. A crewmember of *Aggressive* recalls hearing Kennedy's "blockade" speech over the radio on 22 October:

> We were more than a little nervous with our single barrel 40mm [gunmount] on the foc'sle, but were relieved the next day by a DD [destroyer]. We went back to GTMO [U.S. Naval base at Guantanamo, Cuba] and were assigned to harbor patrol.[32]

The tense situation also affected Navy ships far from Cuba. An officer assigned to the coastal minesweeper USS *Warbler* (MSC 206) remembers the sortie of U.S. Navy ships from port in Hong Kong during this period:

> We saw all of the heavies (large Navy ships) putting out to sea without any ceremony or notice. I went up to the radio room to look at the Fox Schedules (radio messages) and found out that we were blockading Cuba. After all of the heavies had left, three, or maybe four sweeps were the only U.S. Navy ships still in Hong Kong. Our commanding officer, a lieutenant, was then the senior officer present afloat (SOPA) but not very happy about it. We radioed Sasebo asking for instructions and reminded them that we were there. They said OOPS! Get the hell underway and get out of there. I was on the bridge monitoring the Special Sea and Anchor detail and looked through the ship's telescope at the top of the hills above Kowloon to see what appeared to be several very large guns pointed right at us. We did not have to be told twice to haul ass for Sasebo.[33]

Soviet diplomats denied the presence of missiles in Cuba and expressed shock at Kennedy's message. On October 25, 1962, Ambassador Adlai Stevenson proved the U.S. charges by disseminating the incriminating U-2 photographs at the United Nations. A day later, Khrushchev sent a letter to Kennedy, stating that the USSR would remove the missiles if the United States agreed not to invade Cuba. On 28 October, Khrushchev ordered the destruction of Cuban sites in return for a pledge of nonintervention in Cuban affairs.[34]

On 1 November 1962, Mine Division 85 ships—*Ability*, *Notable*, *Rival*, and *Salute*—departed Charleston for the Caribbean. For the remainder

Photo 4-3

Soviet freighter *Volgoles* carrying missiles away from Cuba on 9 November 1962, escorted by destroyer USS *Vesole* (DDR 878) and an SP-2 Neptune patrol aircraft (Official U.S. Navy Photograph from the National Archives)

of the year, the minesweepers supported the quarantine of Cuba and participated with other U.S. military forces in the defense of the naval base at Guantanamo Bay. Duties included patrols of the Windward Passage, monitoring the actions of Soviet ships, and duty as harbor defense ships. The minesweepers were ideally positioned to sweep waters off Cuban beaches had pre-assault landing mine clearance been ordered or to perform other supporting tasks. Although amphibious assault was neither a desired nor the chosen option to induce the Soviets to dismantle the Cuban-based missile sites, the nearby U.S. naval base was an ideal location to stage the MSO ready force.[35]

During October and November, the Cuban situation also affected ships not directly involved in the naval blockade. Mine Division 82's pre-deployment training, which had begun on 15 October, was interrupted by Commander, Mine Force Atlantic's dispersal of the mine forces at Charleston, and the division remained at sea for the latter part of October and November.[36]

On 20 November, Kennedy stated that all known missile sites had been dismantled and ended the naval blockade of Cuba. In January 1963, in notes to the UN, the United States and Soviet Union announced a formal end to the crisis.[37]

SEARCH AND SALVAGE OPERATIONS

The term "shipwreck" invokes for many people a mental image of a site relatively permanent and mysterious in the ocean depths, perhaps unapproachable or inhabited by sharks. The loss of a ship is often a monumental event because of some vessels' cost and size and their personal relationship to the people who sailed aboard or were associated with them. Accordingly, there is great interest in vessels still lost and those recently found or recovered.

At sea, ships and small craft suffer fires, collisions, groundings, and storms that may damage or sink them. Vessels overdue their next port might prompt searches by aircraft or ships, including minesweepers if they were in the area or nearby. MSOs were often dispatched to look for recently sunk ships, and those that had disappeared long ago, some mysteriously.

Stateside, *Adroit* and *Venture* were ordered in early March 1963 to report to Commander, Key West Naval Base and to search with other Mine Force units for the steamship SS *Marine Sulfur Queen*. The sulfur carrier had mysteriously disappeared in the Gulf of Mexico off the Florida Keys. The 523-foot tanker departed Beaumont, Texas, on 3 February 1963 with a cargo of molten sulfur, but did not arrive as expected at Norfolk, Virginia, at noon on February 7th. There were no communications or sightings of the vessel and she disappeared, without a trace, with the loss of the thirty-nine people on board. During an extensive search in February and March, searchers found flotsam identified with the missing ship in the waters off the coast of Florida. Evidence of the tragedy included "an eight-foot piece of the quarterboard, eight lifejackets, some torn by sharks, five life rings, one shirt, an oil can, a gasoline can, a cone buoy, and a fog horn." *Direct*'s unsuccessful search ended on 13 March.[38]

OPERATIONS IN THE CARIBBEAN

In April 1965, the smoldering internal problems in the Dominican Republic flared up into civil war, resulting in the deployment of U.S.

forces and loss of American lives during ensuing military operations. On 25 February, Mine Division 45 ships—*Affray, Alacrity, Exploit*, and *Observer*—left Charleston on a regular deployment for blue Caribbean waters. Visions of picturesque seas would wait, however, as the rough seas encountered en route during the next four days forced many sailors to "man the rail." After their arrival at Guantanamo Bay, the ships engaged in local operations that included patrols of the Windward Passage, which separates the southeastern tip of Cuba from the nation of Haiti.[39]

Windward Passage patrols were tough on crews and engines, as MSO evaporators just could not make enough water. To compensate, minesweepers normally packed all available space on the fantail with empty lube oil drums lined with plastic and filled with fresh water for the engines. Open air showers during rainsqualls also provided crewmembers some relief from the heat and shortage of water. Moreover, during this period, no such thing as a ship's laundry existed aboard MSOs and soiled uniforms were another unpleasant fact of life. Water rationing began the minute a ship disconnected from shore fresh water to get under way so that fresh water was conserved for the ship's engines (augmented by that stored in drums on the fantail) and for drinking water. In the Windward Passage, when a rainsquall was spotted visually or on radar, the word was passed around the ship and everyone not on watch would lay to the main deck with towel and soap in hand. Because Caribbean rain squalls can be intense and brief, many times the squall would pass before the men could finish, leaving everyone standing in the sun with soap all over and no way to wash it off except with salt water. Only those who have experienced it know the feeling of being covered with salt when the temperature is ninety degrees or higher.[40]

In late March, *Observer* called at the port of Kingston, the capital of Jamaica. For the first two weeks in April, the division participated in an amphibious exercise at Vieques Island. On 28 April, *Alacrity* and *Observer* departed Guantanamo Bay for what was intended to be a two-month period of "island hopping." It was not to be. Civil war erupted in the Dominican Republic in late April, as supporters of exiled President Juan Bosch incited a military uprising to seize power from the ruling civilian junta. During the resultant strife, the city of Santo Domingo became a battleground, leading the United States to commit Marines and paratroopers after President Lyndon B. Johnson proclaimed, "The American nations cannot, must not and will not permit the establishment of another Communist government in the Western Hemisphere." First on the scene was the U.S. Navy's Caribbean Ready Group, designated Naval Task Group 44.9, composed of the amphibious ships *Boxer* (LPH 4), *Fort Snelling* (LSD 30), *Raleigh* (LPD 1), *Rankin* (LKA 103), *Ruchamkind* (LPR 89), and *Wood County* (LST 1178). On board the vessels were 1,702 Marines of the 6th Marine Expeditionary Unit.[41]

In late 1962, following the assassination of Trujillo and associated political upheaval, the Dominican Republic held its first free election in thirty-eight years. The winner, Juan Bosch, a writer and professor, was elected primarily by the farmers and urban middle class, who supported an independent government dedicated to political freedom and social reform. His administration lasted barely seven months. Unrest among the urban unemployed provided an excuse for upper class and military elements to stage a bloodless coup in September 1963, and install a civilian junta headed by Donald Reid Cabral.[42]

The new government was not successful in quelling national unrest, and on April 24, 1965, Bosch supporters, junior military officers and other opponents of the Cabral regime precipitated a civil war. On April 28, President Lyndon B. Johnson sent five hundred U.S. Marines into Santo Domingo for the purpose of protecting Americans and other foreign nationals. Soon, however, alarmed at reports from the U.S. embassy of communist influence among the rebels and worried about the establishment of a "second Cuba," Johnson dispatched thousands of additional troops to the country. Declaring, "Where American citizens go that flag goes with them to protect them," Johnson deployed U.S. troops under the code name Operation POWER PACK, which involved at its peak on 17 May 12,439 soldiers, 6,924 Marines, 1,100 airmen, and 10,059 sailors offshore. The U.S. Air Force transported army personnel, including the 82nd Airborne Division, the "fire brigade" of the nation's strategic reserve, to the island. American ground troops were able to separate the warring Dominican factions and effect a cease-fire in the capital. During the intervention, twenty-seven U.S. servicemen were killed in action (nine of them Marines) and one hundred and seventy-two wounded (including thirty Marines). One rifleman described fighting on the island as "just like Dodge City." A Marine corporal noted the confusion troops faced:

You're giving food out one minute, ducking sniper fire the next, fighting to reopen the corridor the next, then water distribution, then more fighting, and all of a sudden you're calling "Cease-fire! Cease fire! Those are our guys!"

On 6 May, OAS ministers authorized an Inter-American Peace Force (IAPF), composed of troops from the United States and five Latin American nations. This force was deployed on 23 May when other U.S. forces were withdrawn.[43]

Observer and *Alacrity*, part of some 40 vessels comprising Task Force 124, which replaced TG 44.9, spent almost the entire month of May helping to evacuate foreign nationals and supporting the inter-American force sent to restore order. Task Force 124 ships, which included the amphibious assault ship USS *Okinawa* (LPH 3), cordoned off the island. For her part, *Alacrity* assisted in the evacuation of twenty-one people of various nationalities. As they patrolled a coastline of about a hundred miles, Commander, Task Force 124 dubbed the two minesweepers the "Fingertips of the Fleet" for their ability to conduct surveillance close to shore.[44]

In September 1965, as order was gradually restored in the Dominican Republic, a provisional government was set up. Task Force 124 remained on station until September, when the Dominican navy assumed responsibility for patrolling coastal waters. On 4 October, *Dash*, *Detector*, *Direct*, and *Dominant* departed Little Creek to join Amphibious Squadron 8, the Ready Caribbean Squadron. *Dominant* proceeded to Guantanamo Bay and was employed during the next six weeks collecting intelligence data in the vicinity, while *Direct* performed patrol duties from 21 to 26 October. *Dash* operated from 20 to 26 October with units of Amphibious Squadron 8 as a force in readiness off the Dominican Republic.[45]

During the deployment, Mine Division 43 also took part in several land exercise operations and both an amphibious anti-submarine warfare exercise and a Marine expeditionary brigade amphibious landing exercise off the island of Vieques. It was joined by Mine Division 82, which, in company with the mine countermeasures support ship USS *Orleans Parish* (MCS 6) and the net layer USS *Nahant* (AN 83), had sailed from Charleston on 29 November under the tactical command of Commander Mine Squadron 8. A converted flatbottom World War II era tank landing ship (LST), *Orleans Parish* carried spare minesweeping equipment, repair parts, and supplies for the minesweepers. It also provided repair support, astern refueling, and "magtails" stored on reels below deck, as well as food and water.[46]

Nahant was a very well equipped utility vessel, originally designed to place and maintain heavy cable nets used to protect harbors and ships from submarines and torpedoes. Nets and booms were a part of harbor defenses used during World War II. The former guarded against underwater attack, and the latter, surface ship attack. Submarine nets were not new. The U.S. mine force had used British-designed nets in major Atlantic ports during World War I, the largest being a five-mile-long net across Long Island Sound. The wartime netlayer crews had an even more unglamorous life than minesweep sailors did. They never fired any guns, sank ships, went anywhere, or won any medals. Commissioned on 24 August 1945, Nahant was fitted in 1954 with permanent diving equipment and a decompression chamber to reconfigure her for a dual role as net tender and salvage ship. Following reassignment on 17 June 1962 to Commander Mine Force, U.S. Atlantic Fleet and installation of mine tracks, she gained the capacity to lay moored and bottom mines. Spanning only 166 feet, her length less than that of an ocean minesweeper, Nahant performed a variety of duties for the mine force, including mining and mine hunting, harbor defense, harbor clearance, torpedo net laying and recovery, and experimental mine/net tests and evaluation exercises. This American Locomotive-engined, diesel-electric powered "work horse" was decommissioned on 30 September 1968.[47]

A national election, supervised by the OAS, was held in the Dominican Republic in June 1966. Bosch was defeated for the presidency by Joaquin Balaguer, a respected moderate-conservative who was to lead the government for the next twelve years. The last U.S. units left the island with the departure of the IAPF in September 1966.[48]

THE SEARCH FOR A HYDROGEN BOMB

To support the U.S. military's mission to be prepared to defend the nation, service research laboratories continuously develop and test new and more advanced munitions, while ships and aircraft carry, train with, and employ those issued for use in the fleet. The people who routinely handle and use ordnance do so with care, following extensive training and supported by detailed procedures. Nevertheless, loss of weapons occasionally happens due to human error or mechanical failure.

The most important search and salvage operation in which the MSOs participated occurred in early 1966 following the mid-air collision of two U.S. Air Force planes on 17 January off Palomares, Spain. This event triggered a nuclear weapons accident scenario termed "BROKEN ARROW" by the U.S. military. The accident occurred during a routine high altitude refueling operation as a B-52G, carrying four hydrogen bombs, was returning to Seymour Johnson Air Force Base in Goldsboro, North Carolina after flying the southern route of the Strategic Air Command air alert mission codenamed "CHROME DOME." The bomber was making its third refueling attempt with a KC-135A, temporarily assigned duty with the Spanish Tanker Task Force at Morón, Spain, when the nozzle of the tanker's boom struck the bomber, ripping open its skin and causing it to snap into pieces. Of the eleven airmen involved in the collision, only four, a portion of the seven-man bomber crew, survived. The entire tanker crew perished. Wreckage, debris, and nuclear weapons were scattered over the countryside and adjacent sea areas. Two of the aircraft's four H-bombs released radioactive materials on impact, including plutonium, over the fields of Palomares. A third nuclear weapon also fell on land; the fourth, a B28RI 1.4 megaton bomb, fell into the ocean. The U.S. government immediately made a commitment to Spain to return the area near Palomares to its original condition, as well as to locate and recover the missing weapon. An estimated 1,400 tons of slightly contaminated soil and tomato plants were excavated, packed in 55-gallon drums, and transported to the United States for disposal at the Savannah River Plant in South Carolina. The U.S. Department of Energy reportedly spent $50 million in cleanup costs. The Joint Committee on Atomic Energy noted in 1968 in an interoffice memorandum that the cost for the two lost planes, an extended search and recovery effort, waste disposal in the United States, and settlement claims totaled $182 million.[49]

Liberty in Barcelona for Mine Division 84 was cut short on 20 January 1966 when the *Sagacity* and *Pinnacle* were ordered to proceed to Palomares, a sleepy farming hamlet of about six hundred people located in the Mediterranean on Spain's southeast coast in the province of Almeria. Upon their arrival on 21 January, the minesweepers immediately began a random search using their sonar, and embarked divers began bringing up debris from a narrow offshore shelf beyond which the ocean dipped to depths beyond their reach. Helicopters patrolling above the shallows augmented sonar contacts with visual sightings to help guide the divers. The following day, local fisherman Simo Orts, who had sighted an object suspended beneath a white parachute fall into the sea, was brought aboard *Pinnacle* to assist in positioning the minesweeper with "seaman's eye" over the estimated splashdown point. A sonar search of the area identified two promising contacts at a depth of 2,040 feet that unfortunately, in the absence of deep diving submersibles, could not be reached. The two minesweepers were joined two days later by *Nimble* and *Skill*, which had remained behind in Barcelona over the weekend to permit the division commander to assume duties as the senior officer present afloat and to exchange calls with local officials. On 22 January, *Skill* and *Nimble* sailed for Palomares, reporting to Rear Admiral William S. Guest, Commander Task Force 65 for duty. Task Force 65 (Aircraft Salvage Operations, Mediterranean) was formed on 23 January from assets of the 6th Fleet to conduct the at-sea phase of the operation. It comprised thirty vessels (not including ships, planes, and people used to transport equipment to the site) and a group of civilian underwater specialists engaged by the Department of the Navy to aid in the search, which took about eighty days and employed some three thousand Navy personnel. On 1 March, the submersible *Alvin* located the furrow made by the bomb as it slid down an underwater ridge into a deep submarine canyon, near the spot Orts had previously identified. The bomb itself was located on 15 March and recovered on 7 April. (In an unsuccessful attempt on 24 March by the oceanographic research ship USS *Mizar* (AGOR 11) to retrieve the bomb using her winch to lift it from a depth of 2520 feet, the nylon recovery line attached to the canopy parted, dropping the bomb once more into the abyss below.) The search had been very difficult because of the challenges presented searchers by the almost daily false clues and false alarms occasioned by the rugged deep ocean terrain. Admiral Guest described operational conditions thus: "It isn't like looking for a needle in a haystack. It's like looking for the eye of a needle in a field full of haystacks in the dark."[50]

During the thirty-five days of search and salvage operations, the division refined standard operating procedures and mastered new search methods. Vectoring submersibles was one of the innovations employed, and the *Deep Jeep*, *Cubmarine*, *Aluminaut*, and *Alvin*, underwater search vehicles utilizing the latest technology developed by military

Photo 4-4

The deep diving submersible *Alvin* secured in the well deck of the dock landing ship USS *Fort Snelling* (LSD 30) (Naval Historical Center)

laboratories and oceanographic research facilities, were baptized in actual search operations. *Deep Jeep*, obtained from the naval research station at Pasadena, was good for scrambling down into shallow waters to investigate contacts gained by surface sonar, but was an inadequate search vehicle for a variety of reasons, including poor mobility, lack of sonar, and propulsion motors inadequate to hold it in position against the strong current. The *Cubmarine*, a 22-foot-long two-man submersible (fitted with 14 portholes for visual search) developed by Perry Ocean Systems, Inc., was extremely valuable in working at depths between 200 and 400 feet. The larger 51-foot-long *Aluminaut*, a Reynolds Aluminum Company development designed to have four times the endurance of *Alvin*, could carry six men and dive to 15,000 feet. However, the submersible was ineffective in rugged canyons and ravines because of limitations of her ballasting system that precluded her from readily avoiding terrain features while still operating within the short distances from the bottom required by the prevailing visibility. The minuscule 22-foot-long *Alvin*, with an unusual ballast system, was able to squirm through bad terrain at depths, making her the most effective submersible for surveying deep, narrow underwater canyons. *Skill* was assigned as the mother ship for *Alvin*, operated by the Woods Hole Oceanographic Institute. The division continued the search until 23 February, when it was relieved at Palomares by Mine Division 85.[51]

When Mine Division 85, with *Ability*, *Notable*, *Rival*, and *Salute*, left Charleston for the Mediterranean on 24 January, only the briefest mention of the Palomares incident had been made in the local news and crewmembers were really not aware of what was happening off the Spanish coast. A day out of Hamilton, Bermuda, after a week in port, the division, escorted by the salvage ship USS *Hoist* (ARS 10), received a change of orders directing it to relieve the sweeps on station at Palomares. The four minesweepers arrived at Rota, Spain on 21 February after a brief layover in the Azores. (*Hoist* was detached before arrival in the Azores to proceed independently to Rota.) The next day, the division commander assumed duties as Commander, Task Force 68 (Commander 6th Fleet Mine Countermeasures Force) and reported to Commander, Task Force 65 for duty. The ensuing three weeks were spent searching for the nuclear device, which was suspected to be within a ten-square-mile area off the coast of Palomares. A former *Rival* crewmember recalls:

> After viewing on the sonar the jagged sea bottom and the proximity of the search area to the edge of the continental shelf, none of us thought the bomb would ever be found, or that we would ever leave the area, because we knew the Soviets were just waiting for an opportunity to try to salvage the weapon. (The Soviet effort included observation of the operation by the Soviet intelligence-gathering trawler *Lotsman*.)[52]

To equip *Notable* and *Salute* for the search, the Navy removed much of their minesweeping gear and replaced it with Westinghouse ocean-bottom-search-sonars (OBSS), experimental, short-range, towed acoustic devices. A high-speed winch and derrick were installed to hoist the device in and out of the water, along with a DECCA high-fix navigation system to increase the accuracy of plotted contacts. A half-dozen civilians embarked in *Salute* to operate the equipment. The torpedo-shaped device was towed about three feet off the bottom (hence the high-speed winch to expedite recovery), and it presented images so clearly defined that operators could often identify an object by its shape. However, there was no way of skimming the rugged bottom terrain, and of the five expensive "acoustic fish" sent by Westinghouse, three bumped into underwater peaks and ridges and two were permanently lost. *Notable* was assigned to search the deep underwater valleys off the Palomares coast, utilizing her new capabilities. When not thus occupied from 21 February to 29 March, she was assigned as outer barrier patrol ship to ensure that local fishermen and Soviet trawlers did not enter the search area. For a period, liaison with the *Cubmarine* (a privately owned two-man submersible from Fort Lauderdale chartered by the Navy for a reported $5,000 per day) was passed to *Notable* from *Rival* while the latter was fitted for a high-speed winch used to tow one of the earliest OBSS units.[53]

Rival participated in the salvage operations from 22 February to 10 March, when she left Palomares for Cartagena to load OBSS gear, returning to Palomares the following day. *Rival* was fitted with the UQS-1B underwater search equipment used in conjunction with the Cubmarine and the Westinghouse OBSS. The Cubmarine could work in depths up to 600 feet; however, *Rival* focused its search on areas averaging 300 feet so that an embarked UDT team could "bounce-dive" to pieces of wreckage and attach recovery lines. Because visibility near the bottom was only three to six feet, the sweep had to direct the Cubmarine crew through a series of very narrow corridors, multiple times, to ensure an adequate search.[54]

To steer the submersible to the B-52 wreckage identified by sonar, *Rival* sonar operators relayed course changes (in magnetic headings) to the Cubmarine via support crewmembers aboard the minesweeper. New headings were calculated after watchstanders simultaneously obtained range and bearing to the submersible, ship's position, and sonar position of any debris. *Rival*'s watch team made these calculations every two minutes for several hours a day, depending on the Cubmarine's battery reserves and the weather. The Cubmarine could not surface in rough seas for fear of flooding after broaching and opening the hatch, so at any sign of bad weather—which could appear in minutes along the unprotected coast—the Cubmarine returned to the mother ship for recovery. *Rival* crewmembers not involved in the operation found most of the time that the Cubmarine was submerged extremely boring; the ship just barely made headway while trying to keep the bow pointed toward a float streamed from the submersible so that propeller noise would not interfere with the sonar operations. However, this tedium was disturbed occasionally by Soviet naval vessels or Spanish fishing boats.[55] Several times while the *Cubmarine* was submerged, a Soviet frigate steamed at high speed through the five-square-mile search area trying to gather whatever information it could on the recovery operations, while flanked closely by a U.S. destroyer. The sight of the large ships, so close and moving so fast, was unnerving to some crewmembers. Also, the possibility of the *Cubmarine*'s float line being snagged by one of the larger ship's screws was worrisome. Each evening after working with the submersible, *Rival* would join the other ships patrolling the perimeter to keep out fishing vessels. Naturally, the local fishermen were certain that all of the best fish had retreated within the search area boundaries, and they wanted inside very badly. Many times, as *Rival* reached the end of its five-mile patrol, a fishing boat would rush as far as possible into the search area. After the sweep caught up to the boat and angry words had been exchanged, it would lower its nets and fish all the way out of the area. Once a fishing boat captain tried to board the *Rival* and was deterred only by the threat of charged fire hoses, which members of the deck division had hurriedly brought to bear.[56]

Salute conducted aircraft salvage operations off the coast from 24 February until 7 April, when the bomb was brought to the surface. The only rest the crew received during this period was time spent alongside a tender and one overnight visit to Cartagena. Portions of some minesweeper crews would occasionally go aboard the flagship USS *Albany* (CG 10) for "liberty" as weeks went by without shore leave. Time aboard the cruiser, which provided sailors the chance to visit the ship's store, use its library, and stretch their legs on deck, took the place of a day off. *Salute* towed the OBSS from her acoustic cable reel in assigned sectors, using DECCA and her fathometer to navigate the rugged sea floor. Because there was no navigation system like LORAN in the area, and it would not have been accurate enough in any case, a British DECCA system was used. Like LORAN, the DECCA system consisted of two widely-spaced radio towers broadcasting on different frequencies. Unlike LORAN, the DECCA system allowed navigators to directly obtain the time lapse between the emission and receipt of a signal, providing in just seconds the ship's position. Difficulties encountered included keeping the OBSS the correct distance off the bottom and limitations of its battery charge. When the OBSS was retrieved for maintenance, *Salute* conducted shallow-water sonar searches or moored alongside a tender.[57]

Photo 4-5

Sagacity (MSO 469) nested with another minesweeper inboard her alongside the destroyer tender USS *Cascade* (AD 16) (Naval Historical Center)

On 15 March, while *Salute* was assigned barrier patrol duties to keep fishing boats and small craft from the recovery area, the two-man deep-diving submersible *Alvin*, now under the control of *Ability* (following the departure of *Skill* and Mine Division 84), located the missing device in 2,850 feet of water. *Rival* crewmembers learned of this feat when someone shouted over the radio, "They found it! They found the Goddamned bomb!" The code for reporting that the bomb had been found was "I have located the instrument panel." (When *Rival* did locate the B-52 instrument panel, it didn't know what to call it in the ship's daily report.) A day later the bomb was aboard the submarine rescue vessel USS *Petrel* (ARS 14), brought to the surface by the experimental CURV (Cable-controlled Underwater Recovery Vehicle). Developed by the Naval Ordnance Test Station at Pasadena, California, to recover test-fired torpedoes, its great advantage was that it could be controlled from the surface without exposing men to the depths.

Although tethered to a mother ship, it combined the features of sonar, closed-circuit television cameras, and lighting with the ability to maneuver and recover relatively heavy objects from the ocean's floor to a depth of approximately 2,900 feet. The recovered bomb was carefully packed and transferred aboard the destroyer tender USS *Cascade* (AD 16) for return to the United States.[58]

Photo 4-6

Onboard the submarine rescue ship USS *Petrel* (ASR 14), Maj. Gen. Delmar E. Wilson, Commander, U.S. 16th Air Force, and Rear Adm. William S. Guest, Commander Navy Task Force 65, observe the hydrogen bomb recovered from the sea floor (Naval Historical Center)

The task force commander released *Notable* and *Ability*, with Commander, Mine Division 85 embarked, on 29 March. *Notable* arrived at Cartagena to offload the OBSS search equipment and to retrieve her minesweeping gear; the following day she pulled into Valencia for a week. *Rival* and *Salute* remained with the task force until 9 April, two days after the nuclear device was recovered by the *Petrel*. *Rival* and *Salute* also entered Cartagena to offload OBSS equipment and retrieve their gear before departing on 10 April for liberty in Palma de Mallorca.[59]

Three months later in the Caribbean, Mine Divisions 44 and 83 took part during July and August 1966 in search and recovery operations for a practice weapon lost off Vieques, Puerto Rico. Mine Division 44 ships *Adroit*, *Stalwart*, *Sturdy*, and *Swerve* were on the scene, having left Charleston on 28 March for a five-month tour with the Ready Amphibious Group in the Caribbean. Three of the ships participated in the search between 1 July and 20 August. *Sturdy* was detached from its Windward Passage Patrol duties near Cuba on 1 July and was joined by *Swerve*. *Adroit*'s patrol duties were terminated on 3 July. During the deployment, *Adroit* had also patrolled south of the island of Hispaniola (meaning "Little Spain," the name given it by Christopher Columbus upon his arrival there in 1492) to assist, as needed, in the tense national situation in that area. In addition, she made port visits to Charlotte Amalie, St. Thomas, Virgin Islands; San Juan, Puerto Rico; and Cap-Haitien, Haiti.[60]

INTELLIGENCE COLLECTION

Due to their innocuous appearance and shallow draft, minesweepers were also, if infrequently, ordered to perform such tasks as shadowing foreign intelligence-gathering ships to observe and, perhaps, inhibit their actions, or were sent in turn to collect intelligence on enemy ships or fleet operations. *Bold* and *Bulwark* surveyed units at a Soviet anchorage while deployed with Mine Division 83 to the Mediterranean in 1967, with, to put it mildly, unexpected results.

Early in the deployment, the minesweepers took part in exercise PHIBLEX 10-67 at Aranci Bay, Sardinia, and a fleet service mine test near Naples, Italy. During June, the ships were assigned surveillance duty to observe Soviet units at the Kithira Anchorage north of Crete. A former *Bold* crewman describes the operation and the shock of finding a Russian seaman, a defector, aboard his ship:

> Prior to steaming to the Kithira Anchorage we had been anchored at Souda Bay, Crete. There were a lot of ships present, including the USS *Galveston* and a submarine repair ship along with various warships. The aircraft carrier USS *America* and her task force were in the Med, but I did not have any knowledge as to her whereabouts.
>
> We steamed out of Souda Bay in the morning and were told that the Russian Navy was in the area some eight hours away. The normal steaming speed with four engines was 8 knots with a top speed of 13.6 if I was running the engine room. We were going to observe them

along with the *Bulwark*. She was our sister ship of the four in our division. We arrived on station late in the afternoon a little before dusk. I came topside after my watch in main control ended and was amazed at all the Russian ships around us. There were cruisers, destroyers, submarines, trawlers, and several merchant ships all either at anchor or steaming slowly in the area. The numbers kept increasing and decreasing as they completed whatever they were doing. Several times the merchants would pull alongside or bow-to-bow with a warship and the lifelines would be dropped and men would carry boxes of supplies over to the warship. Hoses were run along decks to pump fuel, oil, water, or all three to the warship. They did not practice underway replenishment as the U.S. Navy does.

Our job was to observe the Russians and send intelligence back to someone. The USS *America* had a plane flying overhead almost constantly and I was told that in the case the Russians fired on us the plane would record the incident and perhaps fire back. That gave me a warm fuzzy feeling. The Russians kept their deck guns trained on us as well as their missile launchers whenever we moved around the area. Our 40mm cannon was really impressive, let me tell you. Other than small arms and a BAR the only thing we could do would be to throw potatoes at them. At dark, we dropped anchor. Petty Officer —— ran the main engine room. He told me his orders were to run generators and that the main engines would be secured until 0500 the next morning. I set up a watch schedule, had supper, wrote a letter to my wife and hit the rack. At approximately 0200, I was shaken awake by the roving watch and told we had an emergency and to go to the main engine room and help get us underway. I did just that. Petty Officer —— had everything under control so I manned the sound powered telephones and communicated the status of the engine room to the bridge.

We were ordered to start the engines without the usual procedure, i.e., no blow-down or warm-up. The engines were Packard V-12's and very prone to water jacket leaks that allowed water to gather at the top of the piston. Without a blow-down, you took the chance of hydrolocking the cylinder, bending the connecting rod, and risking other horrible things that render the engine useless. We followed instructions and put the engines online at full rpm and filled the clutches. All of this took about fifteen to twenty minutes. I reported that the engine room was ready to answer all bells and the order was given on the bridge to go to six feet of pitch (we had variable pitch propellers and the clutches made the connection between the engines and the reduction gear to the shafts). As the pitch indicator moved forward, the (engine exhaust) manifold pressures started moving up into the danger area. Petty Officer—told me to tell the bridge that if they continued to add pitch, the engines would be overloaded and we would experience a casualty and have to take control back in the engine room and allow them to cool down and to discover why they were so overloaded. The bridge acknowledged our situation and reduced the pitch to three feet forward. This helped somewhat.

After steaming a few hundred feet with the engines almost in overheat, it was discovered that the anchor had not been brought aboard. Naturally, we stopped and brought the anchor in and then continued steaming away from the Russian Fleet while the *Bulwark* stayed on station. At the time, none of us below decks knew why we were getting underway so fast or where we were going. I told the guys in the engine room what I was hearing on the phones and that we were being followed by Russian subs. Two subs were steaming along with us on each side at about fifty yards distance. I often wondered if our dragging the anchor confused them about our sound profile. Later on, I heard that the captain had ordered a quiet underway, but that did not happen.

As we settled down into an underway routine, I left the engine room and proceeded to the messdecks. As I entered the messdecks, I saw the Chief Engineer and several other crewmembers staring at a guy in a dark blue bathing suit sitting at one of the tables. I did not recognize him as a *Bold* crewmember but thought he might be off the *Bulwark*. I asked the Chief Engineer who this guy was and why was he sitting there in his bathing suit? He stated that the man was a Russian defector who had climbed up our anchor chain and was found on the messdecks trying to get milk out of the milk machine. He was found by the roving patrol. Suffice to say, the guy wanted asylum and was not loaded with explosives to do us in.

You can imagine my surprise to learn that this guy represented a sworn enemy of the United States and he was sitting there drinking coffee on a U.S. Navy ship. The Chief Engineer told me that the man spoke broken English and that I was to get another man and "stand watch over him." They were trying to locate some clothes for him and let him take a shower to get the salt water off since he was experiencing some discomfort. After the clothes were found and he showered, we went back to the messdecks area and waited for the cooks to start serving breakfast. During this time, I tried to communicate with the Russian and was surprised to see that as time went on he became more fluent in English. He told me his name and that he was a seaman on the big cruiser we had been anchored about one hundred yards from. He said his duties were ship's librarian and captain's bartender. Those were his main duties but like all seamen he did whatever else he was told to do and that included a lot of swabbing the decks and hauling boxes to the storerooms. Not any different from a U.S. Navy seaman.

During the next six hours, I learned more from our Russian friend. He gave me his wallet, which he had wrapped in a plastic bag and shoved in his bathing suit before diving out a porthole into the sea. He had a picture of his girlfriend and family along with various cards from different places in Russia and Europe. I did not recognize anything in the wallet except that he bore some resemblance to the family that he said were his. The family consisted of his parents and two siblings, a boy and girl. They were smiling and looked like at the time of the picture they were having fun. The girlfriend's picture was of a young woman smiling at the camera and whoever was taking the picture. He said that they had talked about getting married when he returned from this trip, but who knew now what would happen?

His story was he had heard that two U.S. Navy ships were in the area but "they were too small to cause us any worry." After midnight, he went up to the captain's cabin and opened the liquor cabinet. He was taking a drink when the captain came in and caught him. The captain grabbed him by the collar and slapped him and was screaming at him. He said he hit the captain with his fist in the left eye and the captain let him go and staggered backward, tripped on a small table and fell over the couch. He did not help the captain up but just ran out of there down to his bunk and locker. He stripped off his clothes, pulled on his bathing suit, put his wallet in a plastic bag and went out a porthole that was in the living compartment on the starboard side of the ship. He never thought about staying around since he knew he would either be killed or spend the rest of his life in prison for striking his commanding officer.

The water was very cold and since he had jumped off the starboard side and we were on the port side he had to swim around his ship and the hundred yards to the *Bold* and then climb the anchor chain. He said he was very scared when the captain found him in the liquor and that the swim and climb had been very easy. Later on that week, several of our crew tried to climb the anchor chain while we were anchored for swim call. All of these guys were in good physical shape and none of them could climb more than halfway before having to give up. I figured if the circumstances had been the same for them as the Russian then they could have climbed on board very easily.

We arrived in Souda Bay mid-morning to meet a small boat from the USS *Galveston*. I was told the boat contained Office of Naval Intelligence and CIA officers and they were taking the Russian to the submarine repair ship. We put a ladder over the side and the Russian climbed down into the small boat which they turned and steamed toward the entrance to the bay and I never saw him again.

Much to our surprise, we turned around and went back on station to observe the Russian Navy again. Nothing untoward happened to us on the trip back or during the next day of observing them. The big cruiser was still on station and we pulled up next to her. The guns followed us around and when we went on the port side of the cruiser, I noticed a small boat in the forward davit. It was white with a lot of chrome and canvas and I saw the manufacturer's name on it. Chris Craft. Guess the captain had some pull to get that boat. I suppose someone got it overseas and transported it to Russia.

Around 1600 that afternoon the cruiser belched black smoke, the stern settled down in the water and within a half hour she was a dot on the horizon. All the other ships got underway and the subs went under. We were left by ourselves so we turned back to Souda Bay.

About a year after we returned from the Med I asked my buddy Petty Officer —— about our Russian friend. He said that he found out that the man had been killed in New York City during the robbery of a cab driver. Petty Officer —— said that the man had been interrogated overseas and then transported to [Washington] D.C. and settled in New York City to live a long and happy life. Apparently, life was not so happy since he participated in the attempted robbery and was shot in the back for his efforts.[61]

   The division participated during the latter part of the deployment in exercise PHIBLEX 1-68 at Timbakian, Crete, and joined British and Greek minesweepers in MEDSWEEPEX 60 near Piraeus, Greece. It returned on 16 September to Charleston.[62]

SEARCH AND SALVAGE OPERATIONS

The periodic loss of aircraft and more infrequent loss of vessels and craft demanded the services of minesweepers to probe the sea floor with their sonars. Because of the vastness of the sea, the MSOs were not always successful in finding the objectives of their searches, and the best results, obviously, were finding out that the plane or craft in question wasn't lost at all. Finding lost ordnance, however, was always good. Following are descriptions of representative operations in the late 1960s.

While deployed with Mine Division 45 to the Caribbean in 1967 and taking part in an amphibious landing exercise off Vieques Island, *Alacrity* received orders on 21 August to conduct a search and rescue mission for a downed Navy pilot. Detached from her duties as a helicopter guard ship supporting the airlift of Marines from the amphibious assault ship USS *Guadalcanal* (LPH 7), *Alacrity* steamed north to where the F8 Crusader jet had gone down in the waters between Culebra and Culebrita Islands.[63]

The fighter aircraft, operating from the nearby U.S. Navy base at Roosevelt Roads, had crashed about 8:30 a.m. that day. H46 Sea Knight and UH1N "Huey" helicopters from the amphibious force were at the scene within minutes. The helicopters located many parts of the aircraft, transported underwater demolition team personnel and equipment to the scene, and maintained visual contact until released by the on-scene commander eight hours after the crash.[64]

Both *Alacrity* and *Guadalcanal* proceeded immediately to the scene from Vieques. *Alacrity*'s shallow draft enabled her to enter the passage between Culebra and Culebrita and bring her EOD team and sonar capabilities to the site of the crash, where many parts of the plane could be seen on the bottom. The subsequent search had a sobering consequence when swimmers located the pilot's body. Salvage teams included UDT and EOD personnel, Roosevelt Roads swimmers, and a Marine Corps salvage team operating ashore at nearby Culebrita Island.[65]

Alacrity provided support to swimmers and rescue and salvage personnel throughout 21 and 22 August. On 22 August, H46 Sea Knight helicopters hauled heavy wing sections from the shallows to Culebrita for salvage. The covered lighter (self-propelled refueling barge) YF 852 arrived on 22 August and began recovery of sections of the aircraft, directed by the base diving officer, who was on board. Commander, Mine Division 45 assumed duties as on-scene commander the same day and completed the initial salvage efforts. After assisting in the recovery of the aircraft and the deceased pilot, *Alacrity* was released and proceeded to San Juan, Puerto Rico.[66] Later that same year, while deployed to the Mediterranean and at Timbakion, Crete, *Fidelity* was instrumental in September in the discovery and safe disposal of explosive charges aboard a sunken German fighter aircraft, presumably downed during World War II.[67]

While returning home from the Mediterranean in late spring 1968, Mine Division 84 ships *Skill* and *Sagacity* and their escort, the tank landing ship USS *Walworth County* (LST 1164), participated in the unsuccessful search for the nuclear attack submarine USS *Scorpion* (SSN 589), which had been lost on 24 May 1968. Leaving Rota, Spain, the minesweepers were joined by *Walworth County*. The formation was diverted to the north to search for debris along the track of *Scorpion*. The ships arrived in the search area at first light on 29 May and commenced searching. A considerable amount of flotsam was found, but nothing could be identified as originating from a submarine. The search was abandoned on 31 May, and the ships once again set out for Charleston, following from 1 to 6 June the submarine's planned transit route and arriving at Charleston on 9 June.[68]

The United States initially suspected that the Soviet Union was somehow involved in the loss of the submarine. These suspicions were allayed later in the year, when *Scorpion* was found crushed on the bottom of the sea at a depth of ten thousand feet, about four hundred miles southwest of the Azores. The naval research ship USS *Mizar* (T-AGOR 11) photographed a piece of wreckage on the seabed on 27 June; the wreck proper was found nearby on 29 October. The Navy court of inquiry found "no evidence of any kind to suggest foul play or sabotage," but could not establish the cause of the tragic loss. There has been much speculation about the case of her demise in the decades since this finding, within both the Navy and the press, but the loss of *Scorpion*, at least in "open sources," remains a mystery.

For three days, from 31 July to 2 August 1968, *Bold* conducted a surface and extensive underwater search for the missing shrimp boat *Eugenie*, believed to have sunk in a storm off the coast of Georgetown, South Carolina. She was unsuccessful. *Affray* looked for the trawler on 28 October; an expanding-square sonar search using the "classify" capability of the sonar proved to be futile. After a difficult underway period for the crew of *Bold*, it turned out that *Eugenie* was not lost after all. A former crewmember recalls:

We were ordered to search a grid off the coast of South Carolina. We left Charleston under overcast skies and things got worse as we put out past the sea buoy.

It became apparent the second day that we were not going to make very much water since we were running in eight to ten foot swells. The vapor compressor kept "tripping off the line" due to loss of vacuum and water pressure. The flash [evaporator] system tripped off the line because of the interruption in sea suction. It took us two days to get on station and two days to search our area, but by that time, even though we were making a lot of water, we were still so far behind [there was so little water on board] that showers were still secured.

We started on water hours about an hour after passing the sea buoy. All the piping for the fresh water distribution throughout the ship was located in the main engine room. We cut off water to all topside areas except the galley and sickbay. Naturally, we had cooling water for the engines, which was the higher priority. The crew did not get showers even while we were in the search area.

After searching our area, we headed back to Charleston. Naturally, we ran into the same seas as on the trip up. No water production on this leg either. When we arrived in Charleston, it was late afternoon and we had been six days without showers and had eaten a lot of soup and sandwiches. Needless to say, the showers were full once we were alongside the pier and hooked up to shore water. I heard later that the shrimp boat was found in Nags Head. The crew was holed up in a bar, drunk, and did not call their wives to let them know they were all right. If this is true or not I have no idea and figured if it was then that would be a typical event in the life of a sweep sailor.[69]

OPERATIONS IN THE CARIBBEAN

In addition to Windward Passage patrols and presence and contingency operations, Atlantic fleet minesweepers also journeyed south for exercises or cruises with Latin American navies. On 1 May 1969, *Agile* and *Bold* left Charleston for the Caribbean, with Commander Mine Division 83 embarked in *Agile*, to participate in a joint exercise involving U.S. and Latin American military units. After an overnight fuel stop on 6 May at Guantanamo Bay, the ships set a course for the Coco Solo Annex, U.S. Naval Base, Panama. Following a weekend in Coco Solo and nearby Colon (see map 4-14), the sweeps sailed through the fifty-one-mile Panama Canal and into the Pacific Ocean, bound for the

Nicaraguan coast to patrol their areas and intercept vessels posing as smugglers.[70]

The Panama Canal not only enables the movement of merchant shipping between the Atlantic and Pacific Oceans, for the U.S. Navy it provides an easy means by which to transfer ships between fleets. In recognition that enemy mining in its approaches or the canal itself would deny use of the passage, minesweepers occasionally surveyed them. *Prestige* and *Force* left Long Beach in 1957 for operations in the Canal Zone, under the control of COM 15. Such work was not performed exclusively by MSOs. On 12 February 1959, the coastal minesweeper USS *Falcon* (MSC 190) changed homeport from Little Creek, Virginia, to Rodman, Panama, on the Pacific side of the canal. Late that summer, in August, USS *Thrush* (MSC 204) arrived from Key West at Coco Solo, her new base on the Atlantic entrance. Thereafter, the coastal minesweepers conducted operations in waters on both sides of the canal.[71]

During the ensuing operations off Central America, a *Bold* crewmember recalls serene days at sea:

> The purpose of the exercise was to search an area to try to find a small boat that was going to try to make landfall somewhere, sometime, acting as a gunrunner. A retired Chief Boatswain Mate and a crew of two

Map 4-14

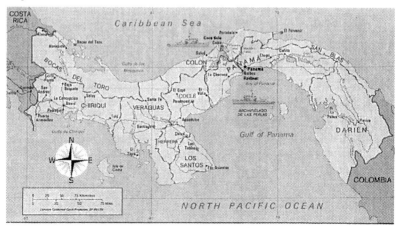

Panama: Ocean and coastal minesweepers conducted sonar surveys of the approaches to the Panama Canal as well as the canal itself.

manned the small boat. The boat was wood with a cabin and around the twenty-eight to thirty-foot range. Armed Forces units from Guatemala, El Salvador, Nicaragua, Columbia and Venezuela took part in the exercise. A few countries had ships in the area and some had ground forces available to meet the boat when it made landfall.

The operation area for *Bold* was off the coast of El Salvador and Guatemala. One of the advantages of a minesweeper was that its fantail was about six feet above the water's surface. That made for excellent fishing even if the ride was rough. The zone we were operating in was a prime fishing area and we took advantage of it. While running our search area we were able to secure two engines and operate on the remaining two, and with about one-foot forward pitch, just enough speed to maintain steerage way. The Captain approved fishing by the off-watch section and when a fish "got on" he would come to "all stop" and allow the fisherman to land his catch.

This was an exciting and relaxing time for the crew. We were fishing, making plenty of water, working tropical hours, wearing tropical work uniforms, and enjoying very calm seas. This was such a change from our usual routine that it seemed surreal. The crew would get up in the morning, take showers, eat breakfast, work or fish, have lunch and knock off for a movie by early afternoon. Talk about heaven! I personally enjoyed myself by fishing, getting some much-needed work done that could only be done underway, and relaxing with the crew. It was almost like a Caribbean cruise. The sunrises and sunsets were spectacular. Nights were cool and many of the crew stayed up most of the night just to savor the night sky. You could see forever with no ambient light to distort your view. The heavens seemed to open up and reveal sights never seen by humans. It was hard to count the number of falling stars and moving objects in the night sky. It was a sight to behold.

We made port after locating the target small boat on radar and tracking it to shore. We visited Columbia and enjoyed all the sites; this was before the current drug problems. The trip back was uneventful and the weather cooperated all the way to Charleston.[72]

Bold and *Agile* returned to Coco Solo, with the experience of their previous liberty to guide sailors in the pursuit of some relaxation. Departing Panama, the minesweepers conducted patrol surveillance operations off the coast of Colombia before mooring on 22 May at the Columbia Naval Base at Cartagena. The port on the Caribbean is very old, and the walls built in the 1600s to surround the city still stand. During the next four days, the crewmen of both ships took full advantage of sightseeing opportunities and entertainment spots, including Fort St. Phillip, El Principe, Juan Rubio's, and the old city itself. The MSOs left Cartagena on 25 May for their homeports (see map 4-15).[73]

OPERATIONS IN NORTHERN EUROPE AND THE MEDITERRANEAN

For three decades, from the late 1950s through the late 1980s, the small wooden ships deployed routinely to the Mediterranean and North Atlantic for operations with the 6th Fleet as components in the NATO force structure designed to confront the Soviets. The initial portion of one such deployment in 1970 was largely devoted to participation with allies in NATO exercises and showing the flag. The activities of the mine countermeasures vessels of participating countries were similar to those that would be conducted following the establishment of Standing Naval Force Channel (StaNavForChan) three years later. The deployment was unique for the U.S. minesweepers, as most of it was spent in Northern Europe. Remaining operations in the Med were standard fare, with the exception of participation of the minesweepers in a pass in review for President Nixon.

The ships of Mine Division 43—*Dash*, *Detector*, *Direct*, and *Dominant*—stood out to sea from Charleston on 10 June 1970 for northern Europe and the Mediterranean, initially setting a course for Halifax, Nova Scotia. Following the arrival of the sweeps fourteen days later, the Royal Canadian Navy entertained the Americans on board the destroyer HMS *Ottawa*. After a two-day visit, the MSOs left for St. John's, Newfoundland for a memorable visit to the picturesque capital city. The division took its leave of St. John's on 21 June. Plagued by fog, heavy weather, and reports of icebergs (which forced the ships to sail south of their intended route), they arrived in Campbeltown, Scotland on 30 June, having steamed two thousand miles. *Dash* entered port with less than one day's fuel remaining (see map 4-16).[74]

The division got under way for Bergen, Norway only to be forced back to Campbeltown on 1 July by a severe storm. A visit to Her Majesty's Station (HMS) Neptune, the British Polaris submarine base on Faslane Bay, Scotland was arranged and the minesweeps left Campbeltown on 3 July to make the short transit through the lochs and

Map 4-15

Colombia: In 1969, ocean minesweepers *Bold* and *Agile* visited Cartagena, Colombia, following joint exercises with Latin American naval units.

up the River Clyde. Upon arrival, the submarine officers hosted a warm reception for the division officers; the Americans reciprocated by holding a special Fourth of July party. The division then left the bay for Port Edgar on the east coast of Scotland.[75]

Map 4-16

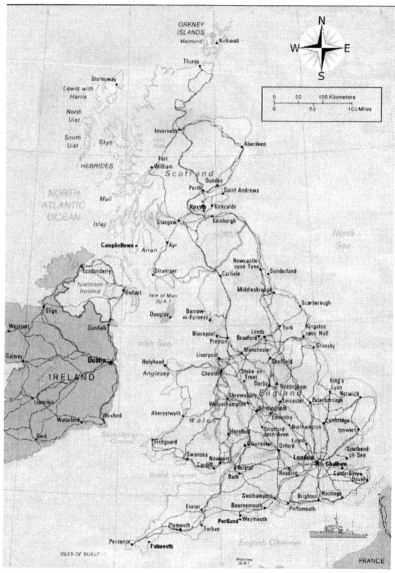

United Kingdom: MSOs visited the United Kingdom during Northern Europe deployments and operations with Standing Naval Force Channel (StaNavForChan).

Although Port Edgar is only sixty miles from Faslane Bay by land, the sea route required a two-day transit around Scotland's northern end ("the British Horn") and through the Pentland Firth. Though known for vicious currents and tides, the firth was calm during the trip. The port's proximity to Edinburgh ensured four days of excellent liberty and British hospitality was unequaled. British minesweepers and minehunters hosted parties for the American officers and crews. The division left Port Edgar on 13 July, accompanied by the British MCM force, to participate in LOVESONG, a NATO amphibious exercise.[76]

Upon arrival in the operations area, the joint U.S.-British MCM force searched the waters off Jutland Peninsula for old mines until 17 July, when, led by the British minelayer *Abdiel*, the ships entered Esbjerg, Denmark, a port city in southwest Jutland on the North Sea. The pleasurable three-day visit afforded tired sailors an opportunity to enjoy the Danish cuisine and scenic countryside. Highlights included tours of the ancient town of Ribe and the island of Fano and a cocktail party on board *Abdiel*. The force then got under way for LOVESONG; during the transit, the MSOs performed mine hunting, minesweeping, and escort duties.[77]

After exercise LOVESONG, the division headed south and up the Weser River to the bustling port of Bremerhaven, West Germany (see map 4-17), arriving on 25 July after an unusually long six-hour sea detail. This was the first of a series of "friendship" stops, and showing the flag proved pleasant. The MSOs left Bremerhaven on the 29th and entered Vlissingen (pronounced "Flushing"), the Netherlands, on the following day for a three-day visit. The attractive Dutch resort town offered beaches and local attractions, and some crewmembers took tours of the city of Amsterdam (see map 4-18).[78]

On 3 August, the ships made the thirty-two-mile trip to Ostende, Belgium (see map 4-19). Although the two ports were only a short distance apart, there was a striking contrast between the small, tranquil town they had left and the large, active city at which they arrived. *Direct* gave a demonstration of the operation and capabilities of the SQQ-14 sonar for officers of the Belgian navy, and the officers of HMS *Godetia* entertained their counterparts. The division bid adieu on 6 August and arrived in Plymouth the following day during the historic seaside town's celebration of the 350th anniversary of the *Mayflower*'s sailing.[79]

From Plymouth the division split up, with MSOs calling at both La Rochelle and Bayonne, France for two-day visits (see map 4-20). The

Map 4-17

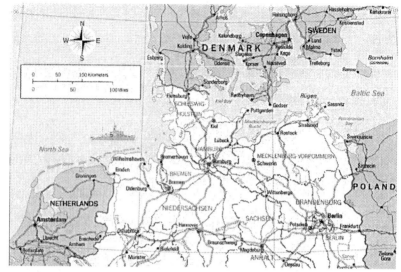

Germany: During their service, MSOs visited German port cities including Kiel and Bremerhaven. In 1978, *Leader* became the first U.S. Navy ship to call at Borkum, East Frisian Islands, since World War II.

ships left their respective ports and made the three-day transit around the northern and western Spanish coasts to Rota. This stop marked the first time that the ships had received direct U.S. naval supply support for over two months.[80]

From Rota, *Dash* towed a non-self-propelled open lighter to Cartagena, Spain, dropping it off to a tug at the mouth of the harbor; she then continued on to Naples, Italy, for a tender availability. Upon completion of the maintenance period, she proceeded to Toulon, France. *Direct* left Rota on 21 August and, en route to Naples for an availability with the destroyer tender USS *Shenandoah* (AD 26), participated in a surveillance mission of the Soviet research ship *Lomonosov*. *Direct* left Naples for Toulon, arriving via the Straits of Bonafacio on 17 September for a two-day visit.[81]

The division operated near La Spezia, Italy from 16 to 23 September, spending several evenings in port at La Spezia during the weeklong exercise MEDSWEEPEX 71. The MSOs joined units of the British and Italian navies in various mine hunting and minesweeping tasks. On 24 September the division left La Spezia and sailed south into the

Map 4-18

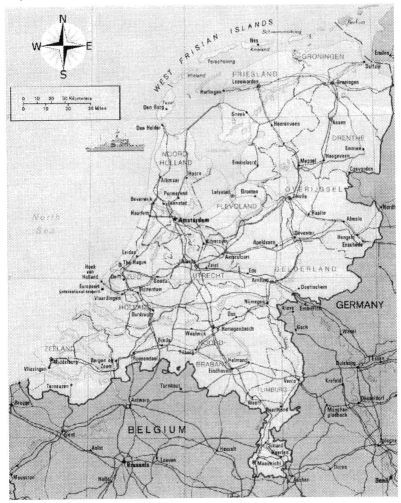

Netherlands: Ocean minesweepers often entered Den Helder, Holland's most important naval base and port, for logistics support and liberty, and frequently called at Amsterdam, Rotterdam, and the Dutch resort town of Vlissingen.

Tyrrhenian Sea in preparation for a 6th Fleet naval power demonstration for President Richard Nixon.[82]

The MSOs rendezvoused with other units of the 6th Fleet to practice for the pass in review, the actual review taking place on 28 September. Participants included the surface combatants USS *Springfield* (CG 7),

Map 4-19

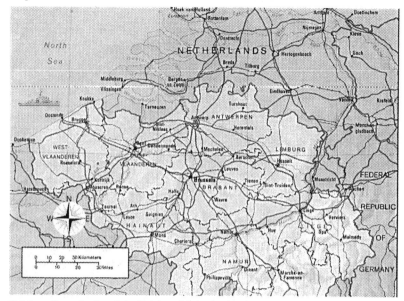

Belgium: Ostende, site of the Belgium/Netherlands mine countermeasures school, was a frequent destination of MSOs, which less frequently visited other ports such as Ghent and the medieval city of Brugge.

USS *Dahlgren* (DDG 43), USS *Vanvoorhis* (DE 1028), USS *Hammerburg* (DE 1015), and USS *Courtney* (DE 1021), the surveying ship USS *Sumner* (AGS 61), the fast combat support ship USS *Seattle* (AOE 3), and the submarine USS *Threadfin* (SS 410). As the formation passed the aircraft carrier USS *Saratoga* (CVA 60) (with the president and members of his cabinet aboard), the MSOs gave a minesweeping demonstration. Keeping up with the big boys, with gear streamed, was tricky business, but the ships came though with flying colors.[83]

Returning to Naples on 29 September for fuel and food, *Direct* left the following day for a maintenance period with *Shenandoah*, now in Souda Bay, Crete. *Direct* rejoined the division in Piraeus, Greece, the port of Athens. The division got under way on 13 October and participated off the coast of Alexandroupolis in a week-long NATO exercise, DEEP EXPRESS—which included the usual fare of mine hunting, minesweeping, and barrier-patrol duties.[84]

Upon completion of the exercise, *Direct* returned to Athens with the rest of the fleet, intending to anchor in Ormos Falirou, but sea

Map 4-20

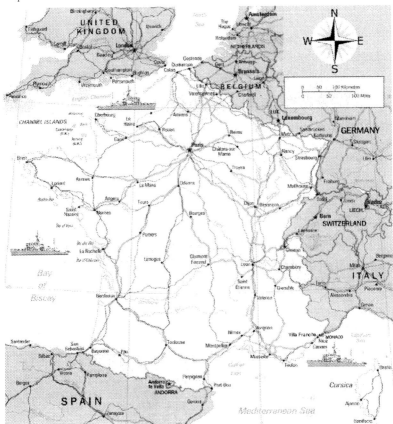

France: Calls at French sea ports often preceded or followed operations in the Mediterranean, Bay of Biscay, or English Channel.

conditions and bad holding ground prevented her from anchoring at her assigned location. While *Direct* was maneuvering on 23 October among the anchored "heavies," a minelike object was sighted floating in the water. An EOD team working from a utility boat managed to put a line on the shell-encrusted object. *Direct* then escorted the utility boat as it towed the object well clear of the anchored vessels so she could sink it with .50-caliber machine-gun fire. Following this exciting episode, she found an adequate anchorage; however, sea conditions prevented boating and liberty was not granted for the crew. Because liberty, replenishment, and fuel were lacking, MinDiv 43 sailed for

Augusta Bay on 24 October. It arrived three days later following a rough transit and, to avoid even higher seas, a diversion toward Taranto, a port city located in southeast Italy on the inlet to the Ionian Sea.[85]

Augusta Bay was only a brief stop for fuel; the division sailed the same day for the Straits of Sicily for 6th Fleet operations. At completion of this task, the MSOs entered Palma de Mallorca for a welcome break and to prepare for the return transit home. In anticipation of "outchop" from 6th Fleet, the division left Palma on 6 November for Rota, Spain. However, within a few hours MinDiv 43 received orders to return to the Straits of Sicily to continue 6th Fleet operations. The ships completed the assignment on 11 November and arrived again at Augusta Bay for an overnight fuel stop, departing the next day for Rota.[86]

Arriving in Rota on 17 November, the ships took stores on board and then headed west across the Atlantic the following day in company with *Shenandoah*. During the first half of the transit, the division encountered rough weather (with seas up to twenty feet) and conducted two astern refuelings. Taking its leave of the tender, the division proceeded to the naval station in Bermuda, remaining overnight to rest. The seas during the final leg of the voyage were unusually calm, and the ships entered Charleston on 4 December—to be greeted by hundreds of wives, children, friends, and mine force sailors.[87]

SEARCH AND SALVAGE OPERATIONS

The infrequent but very important tasking for minesweepers to search for lost ordnance, aircraft, and ships continued. *Vital* received orders on 8 December 1971 to proceed to Cape Canaveral and assist the Air Force Eastern Test Range in locating debris from an Atlas Rocket, and the classified payload it carried, scattered on the sea floor. She was initially the primary search vehicle, and four additional minesweepers were subsequently sent to the Cape to continue to hunt for pieces of the rocket.[88]

Alacrity was ordered on 15 December to conduct special underwater search operations off the coast of Cape Canaveral. She left port the following day, after borrowing personnel from other ships to replace a few key men on leave. She operated for a week before returning home on Christmas Eve so that crewmembers might enjoy the holiday with their families.[89]

Vigor arrived at Port Canaveral, Florida, on 28 December to provide underwater search services. After an exhaustive hunt and location of the important parts of the rocket, she returned on 17 January 1972 to Charleston. *Fidelity* left Charleston for Cape Canaveral on 10 January, arriving the next day. She completed her mission on 31 January. *Fearless* stood out from Charleston on 28 January for Cape Kennedy, and participated in the operation until 22 February 1972.[90] Two years later, the U.S. Air Force awarded the five minesweepers the Air Force Outstanding Unit Award for exceptionally meritorious achievement in support of U.S. Air Force operations during the period 9 December to 22 January 1972.[91]

In January 1973, when an aircraft carrying baseball star Roberto Clemente was lost off Puerto Rico, *Affray* was ordered to the Caribbean to assist in locating the wreckage of the prop-driven DC-7 aircraft, bound for Nicaragua. Earlier, while many of his friends and teammates had been celebrating New Year's Eve, Clemente had been at the airport in San Juan, Puerto Rico, loading supplies intended for the survivors of an earthquake that had caused the deaths of three thousand people. The flight had been delayed sixteen hours, and Clemente, knowing how desperately the people needed help, did not want to wait longer for a replacement plane. So, five men took off in a plane with a history of problems, overloaded with sixteen thousand pounds of supplies. Shortly after *Affray* arrived from Charleston at the crash site, the wreckage was located and portions of the plane recovered.[92]

In July 1974, *Exploit* attempted to locate the wreck of USS *Cyclops*, lost at sea in 1918. Designed to keep a battle fleet supplied with fuel, the 19,360-ton collier had been built in 1910 and supported wartime operations after being commissioned in 1917. In early March 1918, on the way home from a voyage to Brazil, she disappeared without a trace with 309 persons on board, including the ship's officers and crewmen, 73 sailors and marines from the South Seas Fleet who were returning home, and the U.S. Consul General at Rio de Janeiro. Prior to the ship's being cleared to depart Rio on 16 February, three military prisoners were escorted aboard in chains, having been found guilty of charges ranging from murder to perjury surrounding the beating death of a man. They were being returned to the United States to serve 50–99 years imprisonment, 15 years confinement, and to be hanged, respectively. Following her ensuing mysterious loss, President Woodrow Wilson observed, "only God and the Sea know where the great ship has gone." After the collier was reportedly discovered by a retired navy diver, *Exploit* located a sunken vessel at the estimated location and reported the possible finding of *Cyclops*. Further investigation by divers from the *Recovery* revealed that it was not the *Cyclops* but a Greek freighter of WWII vintage. To date, the wreck has not been found, and the cause of her loss remains unknown.[93]

DUTY WITH THE STANDING NAVAL FORCE CHANNEL

Exactly twenty-five years to the day after *Dash*, the first ocean minesweeper, was commissioned, *Illusive* and *Leader* put to sea from Charleston on 14 August 1978 for a yearlong deployment to Europe. This event also marked the first time MSOs had deployed to that area of the world since 1971. The seas in the North Atlantic in the winter are no picnic for large steel-hulled ships, let alone small, wooden, "mature" minesweepers. En route to Portsmouth, United Kingdom, the minesweepers were accompanied by the salvage ship USS *Edenton* (ARS 2). The ships arrived in Portsmouth on 15 September.[94]

The Standing Naval Force Channel (StaNavForChan), or "Stan's Navy" as the British commonly referred to it, was a permanently constituted multinational mine countermeasures squadron, formed on 11 May 1973 at Ostende, Belgium. Germany, the United Kingdom, the Netherlands, and Belgium typically provided ships continuously to the squadron of nominally seven vessels, including a dedicated command ship. Norway and Denmark allocated ships less frequently and the United States only occasionally. In 1998, the title of StaNavForChan was changed to Mine Countermeasures Force Northern Europe (MCMForNorth). In addition to the obvious benefits to all participants of having a standing NATO mine countermeasures squadron, including greater deterrence of enemy use of mines and improved interoperability between ships, the squadron also hunted down mines remaining from World War II and other munitions in the waters around Europe. American sailors considered temporary assignment to the Force as choice duty and, because of the multitude of frequently scheduled liberty ports, often referred to it as a "cocktail cruise." Of course, in many instances they had to weather high winds and heavy seas to reach the much anticipated good times ashore, particularly during winter months.

After the thirty-three-day voyage, *Illusive* entered H.M. Dockyard for two weeks of repair work, including the replacement of two of four main engines. *Illusive* and *Leader* sailed in late September for Ostende, Belgium to join the Standing Naval Force Channel. The NATO mine countermeasures squadron operates in the English Channel area, which has some of the densest shipping in the world and through which the reinforcement of Western Europe would have gone. Its proven vulnerability to mines underscores the vital importance of mine countermeasures vessels in the area. After the U.S. vessels' arrival, the squadron was composed of seven ships: two Dutch minesweepers, one British minehunter, one German and one Belgian minesweeper, and the two American ocean minesweepers.[95]

The NATO ships entered Ostende on 29 September and remained until 7 October. During this period, the officers and some crewmembers of the U.S. ships attended Eiguermin, the Belgian and Dutch mine countermeasures school, to become familiar with StaNavForChan NATO procedures. The ships participated from 8 to 18 October in the Dutch mine exercise SWEETWATER 78, which began in Den Helder, a port city in Holland. At completion, the squadron set a course south by southwest for Rotterdam, mooring in the heart of the Europort for liberty.[96]

The squadron put to sea on the 24th for StaNavForChan NATO exercises. *Leader* and *Illusive* arrived in Flushing, Holland on 26 and 27 October, respectively, for a ten-day visit. Located just north of Belgium, Flushing (also known as Vlissingen) is a port city on Walcheren Island in the southwestern part of the Netherlands.[97]

In early November, the MSOs participated in the Belgian mine exercise FLEXEX 78 and then entered port at Ostende for a two-day post-exercise debrief. The ships departed on 13 November for Wilhelmshaven, a German city on the North Sea located at the entrance to the Weser River. The force participated from 28 to 29 November in the German mine exercise SEFEX 78. However, severe weather limited the squadron's ability either to sweep or to mine hunt.[98]

Following the exercise, *Leader* sailed for Borkum, an East Frisian Island belonging to West Germany. The low-lying Frisian Islands off the coasts of the Netherlands and Germany are owned by the Netherlands, Germany, and Denmark. Separated from the mainland by shallows, dikes and artificial embankments protect them from the North Sea. Arriving on 1 December, *Leader* was the first U.S. Navy ship to visit the island since World War II.[99]

Leader put to sea on 4 December for Ghent on the Scheldt River in northwest-central Belgium. While in port, *Leader* hosted the squadron officers and their guests for a Christmas breakfast. *Leader* left Ghent for Portsmouth on 12 December, remaining through the end of 1978 while her crew stood down for the holidays. *Illusive* quit Wilhelmshaven on 5 December for Portsmouth for an upkeep period at H.M. Dockyard.[100]

As 1979 began, *Illusive* and *Leader* were attached to the StaNavForChan, which now represented nine nations, the composition of the force having changed as allied ships were rotated. *Leader* left Portsmouth to rendezvous with the MCM force off Belgium for training and exercises, entering Den Helder due to possible damage to her sonar towed body. Divers from HMS *Hubbertson* inspected *Leader*'s hull, finding no damage. While in port, she participated in an exercise in which her crew repelled hostile boarders and underwater swimmers of the Royal Dutch Marines.[101]

On the morning of 18 January, *Leader* left port to conduct minesweeping operations with Danish ships *Omoesund* and *Ulvsund*. At the completion of the exercise, *Leader* entered Den Helder to embark the commander of the Standing Naval Force Channel and his staff operations officer. After a night transit, *Leader* conducted operations off Ostende with the *Omoesund* and entered port for the weekend. The following week HNLMS *Sittard* departed the force. As she passed the moored Standing Naval Force Channel ships, she was besieged with thrown garbage, flares, thunderflashes, and streams of water from fire hoses, the traditional ceremony for detaching ships. It would be repeated in June when *Leader* and *Illusive* departed the force.[102]

Due to difficulties encountered with the replacement of two main engines, *Illusive* remained at Portsmouth through 25 January; she rejoined the Standing Force at Ostende on the 27th. Upon arrival, however, two of her three fire pumps failed; once again, she was stuck in port waiting for repair parts. The force left Ostende for exercises, and on 31 January, *Leader* entered the Firth of Forth in southeast Scotland, anchoring off Edinburgh, the capital city and a burgh of Midlothian on the Firth of Forth. After two days of exercises, *Leader* entered nearby Rosyth, Scotland for a weekend of official receptions and liberty for the crew.[103]

After joining the force on 4 February at Rosyth, *Illusive* participated with *Leader* in a joint British and Channel Force exercise in the Firth of Forth. At completion, the ships sailed from Rosyth in a force-10 gale, bound for Den Helder, Holland. (A ten on the Beaufort wind scale describes 48- to 55-knot winds and 18- to 27-foot waves.) During the transit, a large wave crashed down on the German minesweeper FGS *Paderborn*, damaging her bridge and mast guidewires. The ships continued through the night, and in early morning after receiving word that Den Helder was closed due to ice, altered course for Flushing, Holland. The MCM force left Flushing on the 26th for a week of exercises, with Commander Mine Squadron 12 embarked in *Leader*. On the first of March, the ships entered Den Helder for liberty.[104]

Illusive visited Den Helder before participating in a StaNavForChan exercise in the North Sea, followed by a call at Hamburg. From 12 to 15 March, the German Naval Force hosted the last mine exercise of the winter, Exercise JAGUAR, in the North Sea.[105]

On 16 March, the force entered the Thames River from the North Sea and berthed in late afternoon near the Tower of London. While in port, the force's officers attended a reception with the Lord Mayor of London, the Belgian ambassador, and others. On 27 March, all Standing Naval Force Channel ships dispersed to their homeports for a spring stand-down. Earlier, *Leader* had entered H.M. Naval Base at Chatham, in southeast England, and *Illusive* underwent a similar upkeep at Portsmouth, on the English Channel near the Isle of Wight.[106]

At completion of these upkeep periods on 17 April, the U.S. minesweepers left their respective ports and joined up to proceed to Portsmouth, conducting sea trials and training while en route. Arriving on 23 April, *Leader* received a visit from Rear Adm. A. J. Whitsone, RN, the Flag Officer for Sea Training. *Leader* headed to nearby Lyme Bay on 27 April to perform an electromagnetic survey of the bay, returning to Portsmouth the next day for upkeep.[107]

The Standing Force arrived in French waters in early May for mine exercises and made two visits to Brest, a port in Brittany. *Leader* put to sea on 8 May to conduct a bottom-depth survey in preparation for a deep-moored sweep demonstration in the Bay of Biscay. The following day, *Leader* entered Brest to embark six French naval officers to observe a deep-moored sweep on the 10th. Returning to port, *Leader's* officers toured the French Mine Warfare School, while the crew enjoyed a bus tour of the French countryside.[108]

Departing Brest, *Illusive* and *Leader* arrived at Portsmouth after a night transit. For the next six days, the force remained in port while a Standing Naval Force Channel change of command took place in which Commodore Marin, Belgian Navy, was relieved by Commodore Willis, Royal Navy. With the ceremonial ended, the force put to sea on 21 May to call at La Rochelle, France, an important base for Atlantic fishing boats on an inlet of the Bay of Biscay. Putting to sea, the ships stopped the following day in Brest. *Leader* embarked an Explosive Ordnance Disposal team and traded the previous pageantry and good times for seventeen days of fast-paced work during a large-scale NATO exercise. From 28 May to 8 June, the force and the French Navy participated in mine exercise NORMINEX 79 off the French coast. The ships visited Brest during the exercise to restock and refuel, and upon completion entered Lorient, in northwest France on the Bay of Biscay, for maintenance and well-deserved rest.[109]

On the 15th, the force sailed for Lisbon, the last port for the U.S. ocean minesweepers as members of StaNavForChan. Lisbon, the capital city of Portugal, is in the hills above an estuary of the Tagus River, which divides the mountainous northern country from the rolling plains and plateaus to the south. En route, a kite-flying contest was held; *Leader* and *Illusive* earned awards for the highest and best-sustained flights in the squadron. Following their arrival on 18 June, *Illusive* and *Leader* conducted a deep-moored sweep for the Portuguese navy, their final operation with the force. The two sister ships detached from StaNavForChan on 25 June, undergoing the traditional barrage, and set a course for Rota, Spain, arriving the following day. In Rota, *Leader* demonstrated deep-moored sweep techniques for the Spanish navy. The remaining time was spent in port preparing for the return transit of the Atlantic.[110]

Photo 4-7

Illusive (MSO 448) commences an approach for a deep sweep (courtesy of Joe Treat)

Departing Rota, the minesweepers set sail for Ponta Delgada in the Azores, arriving on 20 July. They put to sea two days later for Hamilton, Bermuda. Logistics support was provided en route by the dock landing ship USS *Plymouth Rock* (LSD 29). The ships began their final journey home on 2 August but were ordered to return to Hamilton due to bad weather. *Leader* and *Illusive* set sail on the 5th and arrived in Charleston three days later. A well-earned stand-down period allowed the crews to spend time with their families and friends, whom they had not seen since departing nearly a year earlier, on 14 August 1978.[111]

THE CUBAN BOATLIFT OF 1980

Search and rescue operations do not normally last very long; seamen are normally found relatively quickly or they perish. Both the law of the sea and humanity require ships (except submarines) to assist those in peril upon the sea. Minesweepers operating in the same inshore and coastal waters as small pleasure craft occasionally found such vessels and assisted them. All too often, the fate of mariners in difficulties (particularly those without the ability to transmit a distress call, or those for whom tasked aircraft or surface craft cannot provide help in sufficient time) is determined by the chance appearance of a ship or boat. Because of the MSOs' relatively slow maximum speed, they were not routinely tasked to provide assistance outside of their immediate area. Flotation devices and weather conditions aside, survival time is closely linked to water temperature. Hypothermia, the loss of body temperature, and ensuing death might occur within minutes after immersion in frigid Arctic waters, whereas a few hours in warm equatorial waters (absent sharks, sea snakes, or abrasive coral) is rarely life threatening.

Coast Guard and Navy ships may participate in humanitarian operations of a longer duration than a single rescue at sea, and minesweepers, if speed was not a requirement, were sometimes chosen for these missions because they were relatively inexpensive to operate or because enough steel hulls were simply not available. In 1980, Atlantic Fleet minesweepers participated in one such operation, involving the resettlement of native Cubans to the United States, termed the "Cuban Boatlift."

The mass exodus of people from Cuba began on 21 April 1980 and 125,698 Cuban refugees eventually arrived in the United States by boat, requiring massive efforts by the U.S. sea services in both search and rescue and law enforcement. Many of the vessels arriving from Cuba were twenty feet in length or less, some barely seaworthy. In support of President Carter's desire for orderly immigration of the Cuban refugees, the Navy formed Task Group 140. Navy ships, part of a joint Navy and Coast Guard task force, were directed to conduct search and rescue operations in support of the U.S. Coast Guard rescue and surveillance mission in the Straits of Florida between Mariel Bay, Cuba and Key West, Florida (see map 4-10).[112]

Fidelity, Illusive, Leader, Dominant, Engage, and *Exultant* participated from May to June in the humanitarian operation involving the resettlement of native Cubans to the United States. A total of 1,419 boats received search and rescue assistance during the operation. Three of the ocean minesweepers, *Fidelity, Illusive,* and *Leader,* were active ships and the remaining three, Naval Reserve Force ships. Because her reserve crew was unavailable, *Exultant* took part in the operation with only her nucleus crew, forty-three men and four officers, aboard.[113]

The ships assisted in all aspects of search and rescue, from directing refugees toward safe landfall to aiding sinking vessels, and made daily reports of vessels sighted to the U.S. Coast Guard. *Illusive* aided thirty-six refugee vessels, twenty-one of which required towing. Altogether, the minesweeper rescued 454 refugees from overloaded, unseaworthy, and sinking vessels. At one time *Illusive* was approached by nine small vessels that were either sinking or had engine problems. Crewmembers rigged the disabled boats for tow and embarked 228 refugees, many of whom required medical treatment, including several heart-attack victims. After delivering the survivors to Coast Guard authorities at Key West, the *Illusive* resumed her search and rescue station.[114]

The ship's most exhausting and frustrating rescue occurred on 3 June. The motor vessel *Solana,* 120-foot sister ship of the presidential yacht *Sequoia,* was being used to augment search and rescue operations when, on her way back to Key West with refugees, she experienced mechanical difficulties. *Illusive* came alongside and sent a boarding team to investigate her condition; they found her engineering and berthing compartments flooded. After embarking 166 people, *Illusive* took *Solana* under tow, while a salvage team on board tried to control damage and save her. After being towed for sixteen miles, the stately craft began to sink a mile seaward of the Key West sea buoy, and *Illusive* radioed the Coast Guard patrol boat *Point Spencer* for help. After hours of tireless effort to save the ship, *Illusive*'s exhausted repair party finally had to abandon *Solana*, just as she slipped beneath the waves. The minesweeper arrived at Key West on 1 June for some well-deserved rest and liberty before returning to Charleston.[1154]

In response to a Coast Guard request for assistance in the face of a growing number of Cuban refugees arriving on American shores, *Dominant* and *Engage* arrived on 5 June off the Straits of Florida. At one point during ensuring operations, a Cuban gunboat close off *Dominant*'s port beam ordered her to return an important refugee; she declined, and the gunboat withdrew. In a separate operation, *Engage* took two small craft in tow, transferring them six hours later to the U.S. Coast Guard cutter *Cape Star*. Two days later, she received on board eleven refugees from one boat and took another boat in tow; she transferred both the boat and the refugees to USCG *Point Hannon*. *Engage* put into Key West the following day to discharge the Marine detachment she had embarked eight days earlier. Ordered home on 11 June, *Dominant* and *Engage* left Florida for Perth Amboy, New Jersey and St. Petersburg, Florida, respectively.[116]

In early September, *Dash, Leader*, and *Illusive* made a second trip to Key West, Florida to assist U.S. Coast Guard units during the Cuban sealift. Joined by *Fearless*, they were tasked not to aid fleeing refugees but to assist the Coast Guard in stopping vessels en route from the United States for Cuba to embark more refugees and to rescue and assist refugee boats bound for Key West. The minesweepers also assisted into port boats that had already left Cuba.[117]

During a patrol, *Dash* made contact with a southbound boat, the *Scandia Nancy*. After a seven-hour chase, which included ramming attempts, the vessel came alongside and *Dash* took her occupants into custody for eventual transfer to the Coast Guard. (The reason for the boat's action is not clear. However, among the multitude of refugees were people Fidel Castro had imprisoned for their political views as well as criminals he had purged from his prisons, some of whom may have understandably wished to avoid the authorities.) The seizure occurred just a few miles outside Cuban territorial waters. For the remainder of the month *Dash* provided assistance to freedom-bound vessels.[118]

Leader, with a Coast Guard officer embarked, boarded several vessels and reported others to the Coast Guard for interception and investigation. *Fearless* and *Illusive* also assisted the Coast Guard in September.

Fearless escorted two fishing trawlers back to Key West, turning over approximately 350 refugees to immigration officials. *Illusive* conducted search and rescue operations in the western Atlantic.[119]

Direct, *Exultant*, and *Impervious* assisted the Coast Guard during the waning days of the operation in handling refugees fleeing Cuba on the "Freedom Flotilla." The Mine Division 126 ships escorted vessels in distress and prevented unauthorized vessels from entering U.S. territorial waters. After only a few days of operations, the task force was disbanded, marking the end of the largest and longest humanitarian operation in which ocean minesweepers participated during their service.[120]

5 Participation in the Space Program

One small step for [a] man, a giant leap for mankind.
Neil A. Armstrong, 20 July 1969

During the 1960s and 1970s, Atlantic Fleet surface units, including aircraft carriers, destroyers, amphibious ships, salvage ships, and minesweepers sailed frequently to Cape Canaveral (for ten years known as Cape Kennedy), Florida to support the U.S. space program. Seven days after President John F. Kennedy's assassination in 1963, the names of NASA and Air Force facilities in Florida were changed to honor the slain leader. However, by 1973 public sentiment in central Florida prompted Congress to change some of the names back. Today, NASA flies space shuttles from the JFK Space Center on Merritt Island, while the Air Force operates the Cape Canaveral Air Station on Cape Canaveral, located south by southeast of the Kennedy Space Center. (For continuity, the name Cape Canaveral is used herein to describe the geographic feature, referred to at various times as either Cape Canaveral or Cape Kennedy.)

For each manned space mission, the Navy assigned a recovery force that included principal recovery ships, either an antisubmarine-warfare support aircraft carrier (CVS) or a helicopter amphibious assault ship (LPH), because they carried the helicopters required to lift the recovered astronauts and spacecraft aboard. Navy Underwater Demolition Team (UDT) swimmers were dropped into the water by helicopters to assist with the recovery operations. Minesweepers and salvage ships were stationed in the coastal areas near Cape Canaveral to serve as close-recovery or backup vessels for retrieval of astronauts and spacecraft (nose cones) in the event of an aborted launch. MSOs also gathered sonic boom data during space shots. Remaining recovery force ships, mostly destroyers, were positioned along the flight path to retrieve spacecraft failing to land near their planned positions. The destroyers USS *Noa* (DD 841), USS *John R. Pierce* (DD 753), and USS *Leonard F. Mason* (DD 852) recovered astronauts and spacecraft.

Photo 5-1

Navy Underwater Demolition Team swimmers assist in the recovery of astronauts and their space capsule (Official NASA Photograph, Johnson Space Center)

PROJECT MERCURY

In 1962, President Kennedy made beating the Soviets to the moon (in a contest commonly referred to as the "space race") a national goal to be accomplished before the end of the decade. The program that successfully completed this mission was codenamed "Apollo." Its precursors were the Mercury and Gemini programs, which extended over a period of five and a half years and sixteen manned flights.[1]

Project Mercury, initiated on 7 October 1958 and completed on 12 June 1963, was the first U.S. man-in-space program. There were twenty-five launches, six manned flights, and no fatalities. The objectives of the program were to orbit a manned spacecraft around Earth, investigate man's ability to function in space, and recover both man and spacecraft safely.[2]

The first U.S. spaceship was a cone-shaped, one-man capsule
equipped with an escape tower and a retrorocket capable of bringing
the spacecraft out of orbit. The Mercury program used two types of
launch vehicles, a Redstone for the suborbital flight and an Atlas
booster for the orbital. Unmanned flights of the booster and capsule,
carrying a chimpanzee in lieu of a man to test the safety of the Mercury
capsules, were made prior to the six manned flights of 1961 to 1963.[3]
   For the manned flights, each astronaut named his own mission
capsule, to which all added the numeral 7 to remember the teamwork
of the seven original astronauts. From over four hundred original ap-
plicants, thirty-six men were chosen for the initial astronaut testing, of
which twelve continued through the rigorous training until finally
seven, all military officers and test pilots, were selected to be a part of
the Mercury Development Program. The original astronauts, who
came to be known to the world as the "Mercury 7," were Lieutenant
Malcolm Scott Carpenter, USN; Captain Leroy Gordon Cooper, Jr.,
USAF; Lieutenant Colonel John Herschel Glenn, Jr., USMC; Captain
Virgil I. "Gus" Grissom, USAF; Lieutenant Commander Walter Marty
Schirra, Jr., USN; Lieutenant Commander Alan Bartlett Shepard, Jr.,
USN; and Captain Donald Kent "Deke" Slayton, USAF.[4]
   On 5 May 1961, Lieutenant Commander Alan B. Shepard, Jr. com-
pleted the first manned mission, a fifteen-minute, twenty-eight-second
suborbital flight that reached 116 miles above the Atlantic Ocean, in
Freedom 7. *Ability* and *Notable* were assigned as recovery vessels in the
inshore waters off Cape Canaveral for the launching of America's first
man in space.[5]
   Arriving on 29 April, both ships Med-moored at the Pan American
Pier in the inner harbor of the missile test facility. The sight was so unusual in the United States that the U.S. Air Force sent a helicopter from
Patrick Air Force Base to take aerial photographs of the two ships. The
term "Mediterranean moor" refers to the practice of mooring the
stern of a ship to a mole or pier and putting out two anchors, one off
each bow. This method, used infrequently except in congested ports,
allows more ships to tie up within a given amount of dock space. This
arrangement also looks unusual because of the way the mooring lines
are made up; the stern is secured to the mole with a stern line and two
quarter lines crossed under the stern. While awaiting the launch date,
both sweeps helped hunt for Titan missile parts that had been lost

offshore. Using its sonar, *Ability* successfully located the sunken missile parts for the Air Force.[6]

At 9:34 a.m. on 5 May, *Ability* and *Notable* witnessed the liftoff of Project Mercury, Redstone 3, capsule *Freedom 7*, from launch pad number 5. Alan Shepard splashed down fifteen minutes later about 150 miles downrange, where he was recovered by a HUS1 helicopter of Marine Helicopter Squadron Light 262, which transferred both the space capsule and Commander Shepard to the aircraft carrier USS *Lake Champlain* (CVS 38).[7]

The location and disposition along the flight path of the ships and aircraft comprising the Mercury Redstone MR3 Recovery Force are shown in diagram 5-1. *Ability* and *Notable* were at Cape Canaveral, close to shore. To seaward were the salvage ship USS *Recovery* (ARS 43); the destroyers USS *Rooks* (DD 804), USS *Abbot* (DD 629), USS *The Sullivans* (DD 537), USS *Wadleigh* (DD 689), USS *Newman K. Perry* (DD 883), and USS *Decatur* (DDG 31); the carrier *Lake Champlain*; and, in

Diagram 5-1

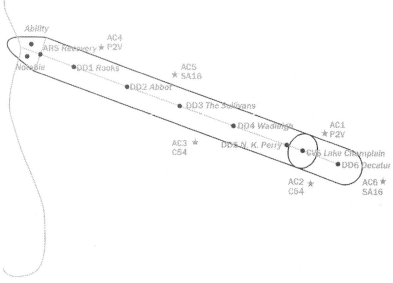

Minesweepers *Ability* and *Notable* stationed with other forces for the recovery of the Mercury *Freedom 7* capsule

aircraft stations 1 through 6, two P2V patrol aircraft, two C54 cargo aircraft, and two SA16 amphibious aircraft.

On 21 July, *Exploit* supported Mercury-Redstone 4, the second manned suborbital flight, by Captain Virgil I. Grissom in *Liberty Bell 7*. The fifteen-minute, thirty-seven-second flight was successful; however, premature blowoff of the hatch cover caused flooding of the spacecraft and made its recovery impossible. It sank shortly after splashdown, 303 miles down the Atlantic Missile Range, and would be the only U.S. space capsule not recovered. A helicopter picked Grissom out of the water and delivered him safely to the aircraft carrier USS *Randolph* (CVS 15).[8]

On 6 December 1961, in recognition of the accomplishments of America's first astronauts, a joint Navy–Air Force ceremony was held to pin new wings on now-Commander Alan B. Shepard and Captain Virgil I. Grissom. The new insignia displayed a shooting star superimposed on the traditional aviator wings of the respective services.[9]

During October and November 1961, *Avenge* and *Fidelity* participated in the Project Mercury program as units of the Contingency Recovery Forces. Early the next year, on 21 and 22 January 1962 respectively, *Pinnacle* and *Sagacity* left Charleston, South Carolina, for Cape Canaveral to assist with the Mercury-Atlas 6 flight. *Sagacity* was to be part of the recovery force for the unmanned flight, while *Pinnacle* was a backup ship for the launch. Following a delay in the launch, the ships returned home, to be replaced by *Exploit* and *Observer*. Lieutenant Colonel John Glenn became the first American to orbit the earth when, on 20 February, he completed three circuits in four hours and fifty-five minutes in Mercury spacecraft *Friendship 7*. He was recovered some 166 miles east of Grand Turk Island in the Bahamas by the *Noa* and delivered by helicopter to the *Randolph*.[10]

Three months later, on 24 May 1962, Lieutenant Commander Scott Carpenter completed three orbits of the earth in four hours fifty-six minutes in the Mercury-Atlas 7 space capsule *Aurora 7*. On station, as part of the recovery forces for America's second orbital space shot, were *Sturdy* and *Swerve*. The sweeps stood by vigilantly as the mission confirmed the success of Mercury-Atlas 6 by duplicating the previous flight. Carpenter's recovery became a joint operation when his capsule landed two hundred miles beyond the planned impact area in the Atlantic. He was located by a Navy P2V Neptune patrol aircraft, assisted by pararescue men dropped from an Air Force RC54 and, after almost three hours in the water, picked up by an HSS helicopter from the aircraft carrier USS *Intrepid* (CVS 11) and brought safely aboard. (*Intrepid* was later selected, in the early 1960s, as the primary recovery ship for the Gemini and Mercury Space Programs.) The *John R. Pierce* retrieved the capsule.[11]

Alacrity and *Affray* were on hand on 3 October 1962 to support Walter Schirra as he completed a six-orbit engineering test flight in Mercury-Atlas 8 capsule *Sigma 7* in nine hours thirteen minutes. The space capsule actually landed in the Pacific Ocean, 275 miles northeast of Midway Island, at the completion of a flight of over 160,000 miles. Helicopters dropped U.S. Navy UDT swimmers nearby, and the capsule and Commander Schirra were hoisted aboard the carrier USS *Kearsarge* (CVS 33).[12]

In mid-May 1963, *Adroit* and *Stalwart* were a part of the vast recovery force of ships distributed along the flight path of the last Project Mercury space shot, Mercury-Atlas 9. Only seven miles off the Cape, *Stalwart* was ready for immediate action if the Mercury "shot" had to be aborted on liftoff. Minesweepers, with their high-resolution sonar gear, were ideally suited for locating a submerged rocket or debris in the shallow waters offshore. Astronaut L. Gordon Cooper, Jr., completed twenty-two orbits of the earth on 15 and 16 May 1963 to evaluate the effects of a whole day in space. The flight time of capsule *Faith 7* was thirty-four hours nineteen minutes. Like *Sigma 7*, it splashed down in the Pacific, eighty miles southeast of Midway Island, and was recovered by the aircraft carrier *Kearsage*.[13]

On 18 October 1963, NASA announced the selection of fourteen men for a new astronautic team; among those chosen were a marine and four naval aviators.[14]

PROJECT GEMINI

The Gemini program was conceived when it became evident to NASA officials that an intermediate step was required between Projects Mercury and Apollo. The major objectives of Gemini were

- Subject two men and supporting equipment to long-duration flights—a requirement for projected later trips to the moon or deeper space;
- Effect rendezvous and docking with other orbiting vehicles and maneuver the docked vehicles in space, using the propulsion system of the target vehicle;

- Perfect methods of reentry and landing the spacecraft at a preselected land-landing point; and
- Gain additional information concerning the effects of weightlessness on crewmembers and record the physiological reactions of crewmembers during long-duration flights.[15]

The Gemini vehicles, larger and more complex than the Mercury craft, were designed to carry two astronauts instead of one. There were a total of ten manned Gemini flights, Gemini 3 through 12. Gemini 3 was conducted on 23 March 1965 and the last flight, Gemini 12, took place 11–15 November 1966.[16]

On 4 April 1964, *Bold* and *Bulwark* departed Charleston for Cape Canaveral to be recovery and backup ships for Gemini 1, the first of two Project Gemini unmanned flight tests of equipment. The launch took place on schedule and without a hitch.[17]

Observer was at Port Canaveral in early December to participate in Gemini 2, the second unmanned rocket launch, as alternate recovery ship. The first attempt was unsuccessful. Her replacement, *Agile*, was on station for the successful suborbital launch of Gemini 2 on 19 January 1965. *Lake Champlain* recovered the unmanned space capsule 1,879 miles down the Atlantic Missile Range and within twenty-three miles of the aircraft carrier.[18]

The second phase of the Apollo program began with the first manned flight, Gemini 3, on 23 March 1965. Virgil I. Grissom and John W. Young completed three orbits of the earth in four hours and fifty-two minutes. *Sturdy* and *Swerve* were off Cape Canaveral on that date as part of the recovery forces. The space capsule landed in the ocean east of Bermuda. A Coast Guard helicopter spotted the craft about twenty minutes after the landing and, within an hour, the astronauts were picked up and delivered to the *Intrepid*.[19]

The second manned flight, Gemini 4, flown by James A. McDivitt and Edward H. White, took place from 3 to 7 June 1965. The mission, which lasted four days, two hours, fifty-six minutes, included the first extravehicular activity (EVA) by an American, a twenty-two minute "space walk" by White. *Nimble*, *Pinnacle*, and *Skill* supported the space orbit, *Skill* as a member of the inshore recovery force. Minutes after the spacecraft splashed down in the Atlantic about forty miles off target, Navy divers dropped from a helicopter and attached a flotation collar to increase the spacecraft's buoyancy. Less than an hour after water entry, the astronauts were landed by helicopter aboard the USS *Wasp* (CVS 18).[20]

Avenge and *Exultant* were at Port Canaveral during the launch of the 21–29 August 1965 Gemini 5 mission. The flight of L. Gordon Cooper, Jr., and Charles Conrad, Jr., lasted seven days, twenty-two hours, fifty-five minutes, and marked the first use of fuel cells for electrical power. It also evaluated the guidance and navigation system for future rendezvous missions. Forty-five minutes after Cooper and Conrad entered the Atlantic, Navy divers helped the astronauts out of their spacecraft and aboard a helicopter for flight to the primary recovery ship, *Lake Champlain*.[21]

Fearless and *Fidelity* were teamed for participation in the Gemini 6 space shot. They sailed from Charleston on 22 October 1965 for Cape Canaveral and reported as members of the inshore recovery group. However, the space shot was rescheduled and the two ships were released to proceed to West Palm Beach, Florida, for a liberty visit.[22]

Minesweeper *Ability* provided support for the *Gemini 7* space shot in December 1965. When the Agena target for rendezvous and docking of Gemini 6 failed, the 6 mission was scrubbed and 7 was used for the rendezvous instead. From 4 to 18 December, Frank Borman and James A. Lovell, Jr., completed 220 orbits of the Earth (thirteen days, eighteen hours, thirty-five minutes). The objective of the mission was to determine whether humans could live for two weeks in space without any adverse effects. Astronauts Walter M. Schirra, Jr., and Thomas P. Stafford subsequently made history when, after lifting off 15 December 1965 in Gemini 6, they rendezvoused with Gemini 7. During this mission they orbited the earth seventeen times in one day, one hour, fifty-one minutes.[23]

Wasp recovered Schirra and Stafford after they had landed their spacecraft in the Western Atlantic about three hundred miles north of Puerto Rico. *Gemini 7* splashed down on 18 December in the Western Atlantic about 250 miles north of Grand Turk Island. Members of Helicopter Squadron 11 recovered Lieutenant Colonel Frank Borman, USAF and Commander James A. Lovell, delivering them to the *Wasp*. In addition to successful station-keeping with Gemini 6, the astronauts also established a new duration record for manned space flight.[24]

On 16 March 1966, Neil A. Armstrong and David R. Scott in Gemini 8 accomplished the first docking with another space vehicle, an unmanned Agena stage. When a malfunction caused uncontrollable spinning of the craft, the crew undocked and effected the first emergency landing of a manned U.S. space mission, which lasted ten hours forty-one minutes. The destroyer *Leonard F. Mason* (DD 852) recovered the astronauts five hundred miles east of Okinawa in the Pacific. *Fidelity*, *Fearless*, and *Avenge* had been assigned to the coastal area of Cape Canaveral during the Gemini space shot in the event of an aborted launch.[25]

On 4 April, NASA announced selection of nineteen men for the Astronaut team, among whom eleven were current or former Navy or Marine Corps aviators.[26]

Nimble was the inshore recovery ship for the Gemini 9 space shot, flown 3–6 June 1966 by Thomas P. Stafford and Eugene A. Cernan. The spacecraft completed three different types of rendezvous, two hours of EVA, and forty-four orbits, during which Cernan spent well over an hour outside the capsule. The astronauts elected to remain in the spacecraft after splashing down 345 miles east of Cape Canaveral and were hoisted aboard the carrier *Wasp*.[27]

The following month, John W. Young and Michael Collins flew the Gemini 10 mission from 18 to 21 July 1966. During forty-three orbits, in two days, twenty-two hours, and forty-six minutes, the spacecraft rendezvoused with the Gemini 8 target vehicle, an Agena. Collins performed forty-nine minutes of EVA standing in the hatch and another thirty-nine minutes retrieving an experiment from the Agena stage. This flight also marked the first use of the Agena target vehicle's propulsion systems and a space walk by Collins. The astronauts landed in the Atlantic 460 miles east of Cape Canaveral and were recovered by a helicopter from HS 3 aboard the amphibious ship USS *Guadalcanal* (LPH 7).[28]

Using the Agena's propulsion system, the Gemini 11 spacecraft reached a record altitude of 739 miles. During the forty-four orbits by Charles Conrad, Jr., and Richard F. Gordon, Jr., Gordon performed two hours and thirty-three minutes of EVA. The mission, two days, twenty-three hours, and seventeen minutes long, took place between 12 and 15 September 1966. Helicopters from HS 3, this time aboard the amphibious assault ship USS *Guam* (LPH 9), recovered the astronauts at sea seven hundred miles off Cape Canaveral.[29]

During the final Gemini mission, from 11 to 15 November 1966, Gemini 12 rendezvoused and docked with its target Agena and kept station with it during extravehicular activity. During the three-day,

twenty-two hour, and thirty-four minute mission, Edwin A. Aldrin, Jr.,
set an EVA record of five hours, thirty minutes of operating time,
completing one space walk and two stand-up exercises. The *Wasp* made
the last recovery of the Gemini program. James A. Lovell, Jr., and
"Buzz" Aldrin were lifted from their spacecraft to the ship by an SH3A
Sea King helicopter of HS 11.[30]

THE APOLLO PROGRAM

The goals of Project Apollo went beyond landing men on the moon
and returning them safely to earth. They included
- Establishing the technology to meet other national interests in space;
- Achieving preeminence in space for the United States;
- Carrying out a program of scientific exploration of the Moon; and
- Developing man's capability to work in the lunar environment.[31]

Three Apollo modules were designed and built: a command module to carry three astronauts to and from the moon; a service module to
house the propulsion, power, and life-support systems needed for the
flight; and the lunar module that would actually land two of the three
astronauts on the moon.[32]

The Navy supported Apollo manned space-flight operations in the
Pacific and Atlantic areas from 1 July 1967 to 26 July 1969, with
Manned Spacecraft Recovery Force Pacific (TF 130) and Manned
Spacecraft Recovery Force Atlantic (TF 140). The task forces coordi-
nated operational employment of numerous Navy, Air Force, Marine,
and Army units as well as civil agencies.[33]

In February 1966, *Avenge* was a member of the recovery force off
Cape Canaveral for the first of three tests of the Apollo rocket, which
was to be used in future manned moon shots. The first (suborbital)
launch of the Saturn IB AS-201 rocket was conducted on 26 February.
Subsequent tests were conducted on 5 July and 25 August 1966.[34]

There were a total of fourteen Apollo missions. The first three,
Apollo 3, 4, and 5, were unmanned tests of the spacecraft, using first
the Saturn 1B booster and later the Saturn 5, which was the model used
for the lunar landing missions. These took place on 9 November 1967
and 22 January and 4 April 1968. Apollo 7, the first manned mission,
left the launch pad on 11 October 1968. At the end of the eleven-day
mission, helicopters from USS *Essex* (CVS 9) located and recovered,
with assistance from UDT 21 swimmers, Walter M. Schirra, Don F.

Eisele, and R. Walter Cunningham about 285 miles south of Bermuda and delivered them safely to the ASW support aircraft carrier.[35]

Apollo 8, the first mission to circle the moon, blasted off on 21 December 1968. Helicopters of HS 4 hovered over the capsule as it ended its historic flight with a predawn splashdown in the Pacific within three miles of USS *Yorktown* (CVS 10). At first light on 27 December, astronauts Frank Borman, James A. Lovell, and William A. Anders were picked up by helicopters and carried to the aircraft carrier. UDT 12 swimmers assisted.[36]

A preliminary test of the lunar module in earth orbit was conducted by Apollo 9. James A. McDivitt, David R. Scott, and Russell L. Schweickart were recovered by helicopters from HS 3 off *Guadalcanal* on 13 March 1969 after completing a ten-day orbit of the earth. UDT 22 swimmers assisted.[37]

During an eight-day orbit of the earth, Apollo 10 combined Apollo 8's mission with the lunar module maneuvers of Apollo 9. Following splashdown on 26 May 1969, Thomas P. Stafford, John W. Young, and Eugene A. Cernan were recovered by HS 4 helicopters from the amphibious assault ship USS *Princeton* (LPH 5). UDT 11 swimmers assisted.[38]

During the historic Apollo 11 mission on 20 July 1969, Neil A. Armstrong and Edwin E. Aldrin became the first men to walk on the moon. Charles Conrad, Jr., and Alan L. Bean were the third and fourth men to walk on the moon, on 19 November 1969, when their lunar module landed during the Apollo 12 shot. The all-naval aviator crew, which included Richard F. Gordon, Jr., was recovered on 24 November by HS 4 helicopters off the aircraft carrier USS *Hornet* (CVS 12).[39]

The Apollo 13 lunar landing mission, launched 11 April 1970, was aborted after an oxygen tank exploded; heroic measures by both crew and ground control were required to bring the astronauts safely to earth, six hundred miles south of Pago Pago. The successful Apollo 14 and 15 lunar landing missions blasted off on 31 January and 26 July 1971, respectively.[40]

On 16 April 1972, the Apollo 16 lunar landing mission was launched with veteran John W. Young, who had already orbited the moon, and two rookies, Charles M. Duke, Jr., and Thomas Mattingly II. *Alacrity* and *Exploit* were on station 15–16 April for observation duties and, if necessary, underwater search operations. *Exploit*, under the operational control of CTF 140, was responsible for sonic-boom measurements and served as a standby rescue ship during the Apollo 16 mission launch.[41]

The target of Apollo 16 was the Descartes region of the Moon, a highland area in the south central sector of the visible side. Young and Duke landed on the Moon on 20 April, made three lunar excursions, and splashed down at 2:45 p.m. on 27 April, 215 miles southeast of Christmas Island.[42]

The last moon landing mission of the Apollo program, Apollo 17, took place on 7 December 1972 when, after a delay of almost three hours, astronauts Eugene A. Cernan, Ronald E. Evans, and Harrison H. Schmitt blasted off. Four minesweepers, assigned as units of Task Force 140 for the launch, arrived at Port Canaveral on Saturday, 2 December. Assignment to the task force was considered very prestigious, and crewmembers of ships received a TF 140 certificate with seals commemorating the event. *Alacrity*, *Assurance*, *Adroit*, and *Fidelity* got under way the following Tuesday to arrive 6 December off Cape Canaveral, joining the tank landing ship USS *Saginaw* (LST 1188) and the *Recovery*.[43]

The minesweepers were present to provide platforms for sonic-boom measurement equipment and record associated data, and at about 1:30 a.m. on 7 December, they witnessed the spectacular launch of the spacecraft. Although it was a cloudy night, the sailors were able to see from about twelve miles offshore the huge fireball created by rocket liftoff. The launch had been delayed several times. Following each delay, the MSOs had to reposition themselves to adjust for the new spacecraft launch azimuth—and thereby be located under the projected flight path. The Executive Officer of the *Assurance* recalls the event:

> *Assurance* was assigned as a down range test ship. . . . Along with a string of others, we were to record the sonic boom created by the Saturn V as it passed over. We made the trip from Charleston to Port Canaveral where we were outfitted with microphones and recording gear on the forecastle and fantail. We were given tours of the Cape, visiting the VAB and the Saturn transporter, the original launch pads from the early 1960s, and the museum.

> When the big evening arrived (this was a night shot), we headed out to sea. Our launch position kept changing as the countdown was delayed and the rocket's trajectory got modified. Eventually, the Cape and *Assurance* were ready. Our location was such that *America* and *Challenger*,

Photo 5-2

Launch of Apollo 17 from the Kennedy Space Center (Official NASA Photograph, Johnson Space Center)

the Lunar Orbiter and Lander atop the Saturn, were just below the horizon to the northwest. As launch time neared, we shut down our main engines and reduced ship's noise to a bare minimum. Even speaking above a whisper was prohibited. The countdown was broadcast over the 1MC (public announcing system), and all eyes looked toward the

beams of crossed searchlights that shone on the Apollo modules just
out of sight on the launch pad.

The countdown reached zero and at first nothing happened. Then the
horizon lit up like a very bright sunrise. Moments later, we saw the
rocket slowly rising up through the orange glow. There was a band of
clouds a few degrees up. When the Saturn entered it, things again went
black until orange beams of light started radiating from the top of the
clouds, vertical at first, slowly flattening toward the horizon as the Saturn V again broke into the clear. As it rose, the fire from its nozzles
changed color from orange through yellow to eventually a bluish
white streaked with lavender and green. I also remember that the visible flames were perhaps ten times as long as the rocket, making them
nearly a mile long. It was dazzling.

When the rocket approached zenith, the radio from the Cape indicated first stage separation was imminent. The main engines went
dark. Moments later there was a flash directly above us, and we could
see the huge booster falling away. The second stage ignited and sped
the astronauts toward their destination. The radio was constantly up-
dating the time since launch and the altitude and distance downrange.
It may sound unbelievable, but we could still see the second stage
rocket exhaust when it was 10,000 miles away.

Until the rocket was nearly overhead, there was no sound but the
voices from the radio and the lapping of the sea on the side of the ship.
Then we started to feel and shortly afterward hear a low rumble. It
built, increasing in intensity to a crescendo as loud as a freight train.
There were two loud bangs, the sonic booms from the nose and the
tail of the rocket. The rumble then decreased like it had built up until
all we heard was silence. We all stood slack jawed.

Apollo 17 was our last Saturn launch and the only one that took place
at night. It marked man's last visit to the moon. As such, it was an historical event, and we on *Assurance* were proud to have had some small
part in it.[44]

The spacecraft entered lunar orbit on 10 December. The next day,
Cernan and Schmitt landed the lunar module *Challenger* in the
Taurus-Littrow Valley, the planned target, where they hoped to find a
form of volcanic ash. While the two explored the lunar surface, on foot
and in the lunar rover vehicle, Evans remained in the command module *America* and made moon observations. The most startling discovery
of the mission was made by Schmitt, who found a layer of orange-colored

soil that, he suggested, might be evidence of past volcanism on the moon. On 14 December, Cernan and Schmitt rose from the lunar surface in *Challenger* and rejoined Evans and *America* in lunar orbit. They then set off for earth, taking about 275 pounds of lunar rocks and soil with them. The three astronauts splashed down in the Pacific on 19 December 1972.[45]

The launch of Apollo 17 marked the end of direct involvement of Atlantic Fleet ocean minesweepers with the U.S. Space Program. That involvement began on 5 May 1961 and ended eleven and one-half years later on 7 December 1972. During this period, small groups of MSOs, normally two-ship subdivisions, from Mine Divisions 44, 45, 82, 83, 84, 85, and 24 (former Mine Division 45), homeported at Charleston, routinely sailed to Cape Canaveral. When not engaged in supporting the U.S. Space Program, they assisted the Air Force Atlantic missile test facility at the Cape in locating ordnance lost offshore and provided services to the Naval Ordnance Laboratory at Fort Lauderdale.

6 Pacific Fleet Operations

MINESWEEPERS IN ASIA

Although this book is devoted to the service of ocean minesweepers, it is appropriate to highlight the important contributions made by the smaller coastal minesweepers, minesweeping boats, and mine craft, as well as their support ships, that served in Southeast Asia. Their rich story and that of the ships and craft that served in the Atlantic Fleet will undoubtedly one day be published.

From the initial deployment in 1955 of ocean minesweepers to the Far East to the return to the U.S. in September 1973 of the last of the MSOs that participated in Operation END SWEEP (the clearance of mines from Haiphong Harbor near the end of the Vietnam War), divisions of the ships made some fifty deployments to the Western Pacific. During the intervening years, many things had changed within the Navy, including terminology and common phrases, duties performed, and the ports visited by the ships, as well as the perspectives and attitudes of sailors regarding deployments to "Westpac." Sailing on a deployment from Naval Station Long Beach, California, homeport of the West Coast MSOs, was initially referred to as a deployment to the Far East for duty with the 7th Fleet. The term "Far East" in the late 1950s and early 1960s meant for many young sailors exotic ports with foods, cultures, and practices not experienced in the United States, and the opportunity to purchase low-cost tailor-made clothing, stereo gear, and other bargains. Departure from the West Coast of the U.S. would later be termed deployment to the Western Pacific (commonly called "Westpac") and not the Far East, and as the protracted war in Southeast Asia continued, less formally became just "another tour of duty in Vietnam."

Initially the hub of the U.S. mine force in Asia (and site of the commander to which deployed MSOs reported) was Sasebo, Japan, the location of Commander Mine Flotilla 1, his staff, and ships. The flotilla was composed of ten 144-foot coastal minesweepers (assigned to either

Mine Division 31 or 32), ten 36-foot minesweeping launches (Mine Division 33), and the mine countermeasures support ship USS *Epping Forest* (MCS 7), which carried the launches and doubled as the flagship of the flotilla commander, a Navy captain. While deployed and serving as part of the 7th fleet, the ocean minesweepers greatly enhanced the operational capabilities of this permanently constituted mine countermeasures force.

Photo 6-1

India Basin, Sasebo, Japan (courtesy of Mike Goss)

The first coastal minesweepers to be based in the Far East, USS *Cormorant* (MSC 122) and USS *Peacock* (MSC 198), departed Long Beach for Sasebo on 4 January 1956, sailing in company with Mine Division 93, composed of ocean minesweepers *Conflict, Constant, Energy, Pivot, Pluck,* and *Prestige.* Thereafter, ocean and coastal minesweepers frequently operated together in the 7th Fleet area of responsibility, and during the Vietnam War commonly relieved one another on patrol, with the MSOs deploying from and returning to Long Beach and the MSCs and minesweeping launches to Sasebo, thereby providing a permanent U.S. mine countermeasure capability in Asia. Although the smaller coastal minesweepers had fewer capabilities and were less seaworthy than the ocean minesweepers, they very capably performed missions never envisioned by their designers, including, like the MSOs, combat operations, and had the added advantage of being able to operate in waters too shallow for the larger minesweepers. However, the repeated extended periods at sea drained life from the small ships designed for coastal operations of only a few days' duration.

In the early 1970s, eight of the ten coastal minesweepers returned to the United States for immediate decommissioning and transfer to the naval reserve. The other two, USS *Albatross* (MSC 289) and USS *Gannet* (MSC 290), the first two of the *Albatross* class and the only such minesweepers serving in the U.S. Navy, had suffered throughout their short service long-standing engineering and reliability problems and were accordingly decommissioned at Sasebo on 1 April 1970 and sold locally for scrap. The surviving Pacific Fleet MSCs spent the bulk of their remaining service (until the last ships were struck in 1975) alongside piers in their West Coast homeports, getting under way only occasionally for reserve drill weekends—with the ribbon boards on their deckhouses as reminders of their former service. The return to the United States in 1973 of the five MSOs homeported at Guam in October 1971 marked the first time since World War II that no U.S. minesweepers were based in the Western Pacific. (USS *Guardian* [MCM 5] and USS *Patriot* [MCM 7] were subsequently sited at Sasebo, Japan, where they currently serve.)

PEACETIME COLD WAR OPERATIONS

The first deployment of Pacific Fleet MSOs to the Western Pacific occurred on 1 July 1955, when Mine Division 92—*Engage, Fortify, Impervious, Inflict,* and *Loyalty*—departed Long Beach on a Friday morning for Sasebo, via stops at Pearl Harbor, Midway Island, and Yokosuka, Japan. While in the Hawaiian Islands, *Fortify* also visited the island of Oahu. Arriving at Sasebo (see map 6-1) on 5 August, the MSOs became the first ships of their type to serve in the Far East, reporting for duty to Commander Naval Forces Far East and Commander Mine Flotilla 1, and thereafter participating in local exercises with Japanese minesweepers and visiting Nagasaki. The division left on 22 August for Kobe for a five-day goodwill visit, transiting the Inland Sea of Japan via the Shimonoseki Straits on both the trip from Sasebo to Kobe and on the return. It departed on 30 October for Kaohsiung, Formosa (now called Taiwan), taking part there in exercises with Chinese Nationalist minesweeping units. The MSOs arrived

Map 6-1

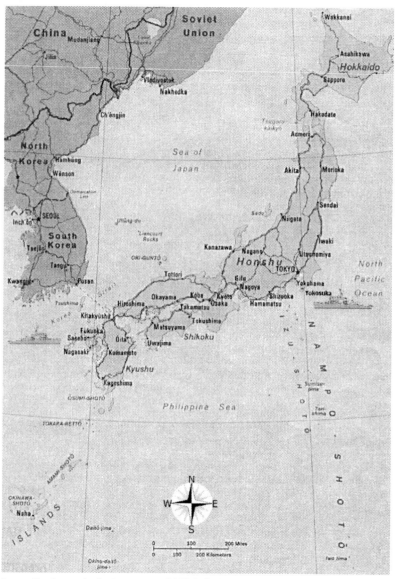

Japan: During early deployments of MSO divisions to the Far East, the ships first touched Japan at Yokosuka for needed voyage repairs and logistics support before reporting to Commander, Mine Flotilla 1 at Sasebo for duty.

on 7 November at Hong Kong, British Crown Colony, for a seven-day visit before returning to Sasebo. Following upkeep, the ships journeyed to Okinawa for an amphibious exercise directed by the Commander, Amphibious Squadron 1. Upon completion of the exercise on 6 December, the division left for Sasebo to stand down for the Christmas holidays.[1]

On 9 January 1956, the MSOs bid "Sayonara" to Sasebo and proceeded to Korea for their last joint exercise, joining Republic of Korea minesweepers at Koje Do (see map 2-1). Upon completion, the division detached from the control of Commander Mine Flotilla 1 and set a course for the ship repair facility at Yokosuka to receive the repair work, maintenance, and upkeep necessary to prepare it for the return transit to the United States. Mine Division 92 departed Yokosuka on 21 January for Long Beach, arriving nearly a month later on 18 February 1956, following stops at Midway Island and Pearl Harbor, Hawaii.[2]

These were the Eisenhower "show the flag" years, during which minesweepers made frequent goodwill cruises to support the People to People Program, entering small ports as the Commander Seventh Fleet representative, some of which the Navy had not visited since World War II. However, the agreeable peacetime routine of the minesweepers was occasionally broken by reminders of Cold War realities. In the late 1950s and early 1960s, the U.S. Navy transferred mine craft to Formosa and routinely participated with Chinese Nationalist Navy units in minesweeping exercises. American support of Chiang Kai-shek, the head of the Nationalist Chinese government, located on the island, included the provision of military aid and also resulted between August 1958 and June 1963 in 7th Fleet units (including MSOs and MSCs) periodically coming face to face with opposing Chinese Communist forces off the Quemoy and Matsu islands and in the Taiwan Straits (see map 6-2).

The first MSO division to be involved in the conflict was MinDiv 71—*Engage, Fortify, Inflict, Impervious,* and *Loyalty*—which left Long Beach on 3 January 1958 for the Far East. During the early part of the deployment, as part of the 7th Fleet off Taiwan to demonstrate American resolve, the division trained Chinese Nationalist mine forces, participating from 22 February to 2 March in a bilateral exercise at Kaohsiung, Taiwan. MSOs also helped train and exercise the crews of Nationalist Chinese minesweepers in April and May.[3]

In August 1958, as Communist China resumed its shelling of Quemoy and Matsu, the Eisenhower administration declared its readiness to defend the island groups. When Eisenhower reinforced the 7th

Photo 6-2

Coastal minesweepers *Warbler* and *Whippoorwill* in port to support the People to People Program (courtesy of Capt. Richard R. Tarbuck, USN [Ret.])

Fleet and authorized it to escort Nationalist supply ships to the islands, Pacific Fleet minesweepers supported the effort.[4]

Mine Division 92 ships—*Constant, Energy, Pivot,* and *Pluck*—participated in the Quemoy Crisis in late summer and early fall. Between 2 September and 27 October, *Constant* operated at wartime readiness conditions in the Taiwan area, including the ports of Boko Ko, Pescadores Island, and Keelung and Kaohsiung, Taiwan. *Pluck* and *Energy* stood by off Taiwan during the second week of September as units of the Taiwan Readiness Defense Force. *Pivot* reported on 8 October as one of the "ready" ships off Taiwan, under the operational control of Mine Flotilla 1. She joined the other division ships during the week of 20 October in a minesweeping exercise off Kaohsiung, with Mine Flotilla 1 and six Chinese Nationalist minesweepers. *Pluck* returned for additional duty with the Taiwan Readiness Defense Force on 24 October and operated out of various Taiwanese ports until 19 November. *Constant* was assigned similar duties from 4 to 15 November.[5]

In an effort to resolve the crisis, ambassadors from the United States and Communist China met on September 15 in Warsaw, Poland. In October, U.S. Secretary of State John Foster Dulles traveled to Taiwan to discuss with Chiang the U.S. desire to lessen Nationalist-Communist tensions. In a written statement released October 23, Chiang announced

Map 6-2

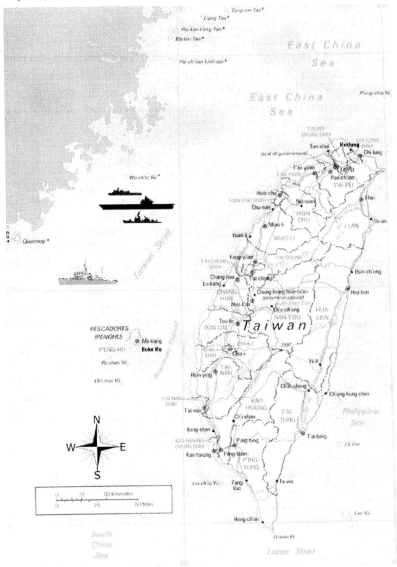

Taiwan: In 1958, in response to Communist Chinese shelling of the Quemoy and Matsu Islands, ocean and coastal minesweepers participated in 7th Fleet operations as units of the Taiwan Readiness Defense Force.

a reduction in Nationalist military presence on the offshore islands and an end to Nationalist attempts to return to the mainland by force. Peking responded by curtailing the shelling of the islands, effectively bringing the crisis to a halt.[6]

The division left Yokosuka on 12 December 1958 for Long Beach. However, its return home did not signal an end to naval operations and the presence of MSOs off Taiwan. In response to later communist acts of aggression against Taiwan, 7th Fleet operations off Quemoy and Matsu and in the Taiwan Straits, which began in August 1958, continued until June 1963. Thereafter, during the Vietnam War, a collateral duty of minesweepers in the Western Pacific was to act as units of the Taiwan Straits Patrol Force while transiting areas around Taiwan.[7]

Patrol operations in potentially hostile waters often offer some interesting experiences, and such was the case in 1959 when *Leader* rescued a Nationalist Chinese pilot in the Taiwan Straits while en route to Kaohsiung, a major naval port located on the southwest coast of Taiwan. An officer standing watch at the time recalls the event:

> We were steaming in moderately calm seas in the Straits of Formosa, outward bound from Keelung, near the north end of the island of Formosa [Taiwan]. One of our lookouts spotted a large plume of water about two miles off the starboard beam. Wondering what could have caused such a large "splash" in the middle of the Straits, the bridge watch team concentrated its attention in that direction. Continuing to scan the area around the splash, one of the lookouts spotted a parachute about 500 feet above the water.
>
> Captain Vasse immediately sounded "Man Overboard" and told me to come right to a course that would intersect the point where the parachute would enter the water. The Commodore ordered the rest of MinDiv 93 to proceed on the previous course toward Kaohsiung. We saw the parachute enter the water about one mile ahead of us. When we were about 500 yards from the man in the water, Captain Vasse ordered BM1 DeWitt to launch the motor whaleboat and recover the man floating in the life raft. BM2 Weiss assumed coxswain of the MWB with EN3 Carl Haynes as Engineer, and proceeded to pick up the man who had, literally, fallen from the skies. The biggest difficulty in the recovery was the parachute, which did not want to get into the motor whaleboat. The man said that he had to recover the parachute or he would not be allowed to fly any more.

When the man was brought to the bridge, he informed us, in rather well-spoken English, that he was a Nationalist Chinese pilot who had been on a flight over Communist China, had been attacked by the mainland Chinese Air Force, and his Saber Jet had been damaged in a dogfight. He had limped as far towards home as he could and then fire in the cockpit had forced him to bail out before he could reach the coast of Formosa. In the tradition of pilots rescued at sea, he presented his sidearm (an S&W 38 Special) to BM2 Weiss and the life raft to BM1 DeWitt. He said that he had to keep his flight suit to show the flame-singed leg of it to his superiors as proof that the plane had been on fire. Some members of the Nationalist Chinese military had purposely damaged equipment out of loyalty to the Communist Chinese and he needed to prove that the bailout had been necessary.[8]

1962 PACIFIC NUCLEAR TEST PROGRAM

Another reminder of the Cold War was the participation in 1962 of ocean minesweepers, with other military and civilian aircraft and vessels, in nuclear weapons tests in the Pacific. While using both diplomatic and conventional military means to deter and slow the spread of Soviet domination of other countries, the U.S. government was prepared, if necessary, to employ nuclear weapons against its Communist foe. This doctrine mandated an associated weapons research, development, and test program. In 1962, Mine Division 71—*Loyalty, Inflict, Engage, Impervious,* and *Fortify*—participated in Operation DOMINIC, the Pacific nuclear test program conducted at Christmas Island and Johnston Atoll in the Central Pacific and off San Diego, California (one test only). On hand primarily to use their sonar to locate ordnance dropped into the ocean during or after tests, the MSOs were also pressed into supporting duties.

DOMINIC included thirty-six successful weapons development tests, of which twenty-nine involved airdropped weapons. In the remaining tests, five nuclear-tipped rockets were launched to gather weapons effects data on high-altitude phenomena, and two operational weapons systems were tested: a Polaris submarine ballistic missile and an ASROC (antisubmarine rocket). The ballistic missile submarine USS *Ethan Allen* (SSBN 609) launched a Polaris A2 missile on 6 May from fifteen hundred miles east-northeast of Christmas Island. The submarines USS *Carboneo* (SS 337) and USS *Medregal* (SS 480) were positioned within thirty miles of the burst point, and an image of the DOMINIC "Frigate Bird" mushroom cloud was taken through the

Photo 6-3

Detonation Cloud, Christmas Island
(courtesy of Bill Vaughn)

Carboneo's periscope. On 11 May, 400 miles west of San Diego, California, the destroyer USS *Agerholm* (DD 826) fired an antisubmarine rocket at a target raft 4,348 yards away. The rocket exploded at a depth of 650 feet in water that was 17,140 feet deep.[9]

The first phase of Operation DOMINIC occurred from 25 April through 11 July 1962, during which twenty-four nuclear weapons were dropped from aircraft for airbursts in the vicinity of Christmas Island, and one warhead was sent aloft by rocket from Johnston Atoll for high altitude detonation. Johnson Atoll, located between the Marshall Islands and Hawaii, is known as Kalama Island to the Kanaka Maoli, indigenous people of the Hawaiian Archipelago. The atoll was annexed by both the United States and the Kingdom of Hawaii in 1858. It was taken over by the U.S. Navy in 1934, transferred to the U.S. Air Force in 1948, and used in the 1950s and 1960s for high altitude nuclear tests. Ocean minesweepers routinely stopped at the atoll in the 1960s and early 1970s for fuel en route and returning from the Western Pacific. During the second test phase, from 2 October through 3 November 1962, four warheads were launched from Johnston Atoll for high altitude detonation and five weapons were dropped from aircraft for airbursts. Three attempted rocket launches during phase one were failures and one launch during the second phase.[10]

The series of high altitude tests was known as Operation FISHBOWL, consisting of Thor-missile-launched warheads detonated at very high altitudes (30–248 miles) to evaluate the destructive mechanisms and effects of high yield explosions against Soviet ballistic missile reentry vehicles. Several codenamed tests failed (and range safety officers destroyed missiles in flight) due to electronics failure (BLUE-GILL), rocket motor malfunctions (STARFISH and BLUEGILL PRIME), and the missile's veering out of control (BLUEGILL DOUBLE PRIME). On 4 June, during the first U.S. attempt at conducting a high-altitude test, the nuclear device fell into the Pacific Ocean near Johnston Atoll when the Thor rocket booster malfunctioned within minutes after lift-off and was destroyed. In the Starfish test on 20 June, the launch of a Thor missile carrying a nuclear warhead was aborted one minute into the flight and a self-destruct order blew the missile apart, dropping large pieces of radioactive missile back onto the atoll. BLUEGILL PRIME on 25 July was particularly disastrous. The Thor missile was carrying one pod, two reentry vehicles, and the warhead. The missile engine malfunctioned immediately after ignition, and the range safety officer destroyed the missile while it was still on the launch pad. The explosion of the Thor missile scattered debris throughout the launch pad area, and the Johnston Atoll Thor launch complex was destroyed and heavily contaminated with plutonium, requiring reconstruction of the facility before launches could resume. On 15 October in the BLUEGILL DOUBLE PRIME test, the rocket was destroyed after it malfunctioned 90 seconds into the flight. It also contributed to radioactive pollution on the atoll.[11]

Mine Division 71 left Long Beach on 7 April for Pearl Harbor, where *Loyalty* and *Inflict* remained when the balance of the division continued to the Far East. The two minesweepers came under the operational control of Commander, Navy Task Unit 8.3 on 26 April and were employed for the next four months in and around Hawaiian waters gathering electronic data from the air burst blasts above Johnston Atoll. *Inflict* observed Starfish Prime from a distance and collected background readings for recovery operations. *Loyalty*, assisted by five civilian engineers on board, was to determine the effects of the blast on her radar and communications equipment. A former crewmember recalls:

> When the blast occurred, although we weren't supposed to, just about everybody on board watched the light in the sky. We were each given a small canister (a film-type dosimeter) that we wore on our dog tag chain during the test. Afterwards, the canisters were collected by a civilian engineer and that was the last we ever heard of them. I had a small photo lab where I processed film for myself and others. A roll of Ektachrome that was in my camera when the blast occurred was totally exposed. I showed it to one of the engineers and he took it as part of the data he collected.

The two minesweepers departed Hawaii on 8 August in company with Mine Division 91, arriving at Long Beach on 17 August.[12]

Returning from the Western Pacific, *Engage, Impervious,* and *Fortify* also participated in the observation of atomic tests. *Engage* was positioned at Johnston Atoll with other naval vessels between 18 October and 4 November (see diagram 6-3) to observe the rocket-launches KINGFISH, BLUEGILL TRIPLE PRIME, CHECKMATE, and TIGHTROPE as well as airdrops CALAMITY, CHAMA, and HOUSATOMIC. *Impervious* arrived at Pearl Harbor on 8 September. She was offshore

Diagram 6-3

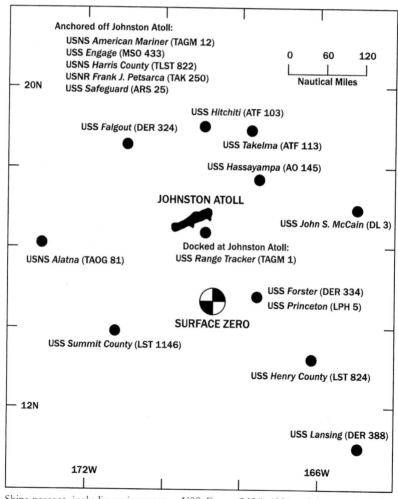

Ships present, including minesweeper USS *Engage* (MSO 433), at Johnston Atoll for nuclear weapons test CHAMA.

Kauai Island in late October during the rocket shot CHECKMATE and in early November participated in Operation DOMINIC. Visual effects of BLUEGILL TRIPLE PRIME and KINGFISH, both conducted forty-three miles from Johnston Atoll, were seen by observers in Hawaii. Viewers on Maui saw a fireball from the first test and brilliant streamers (beta particle auroras) from the second. Those on Oahu observed a bright flash and, after about ten seconds, a great white ball that appeared to rise slowly from the sea and remained visible for several minutes.[13]

In October, *Fortify* also joined Operation DOMINIC as a unit of Task Element 8.3.2.4, Surface Recovery. Her primary mission was to recover instrumented nose cones in the Kauai operating area. The recovery forces normally included four to six P2V patrol aircraft, four to six HUS helicopters, and two recovery ships, usually fleet tugs, salvage ships, or ocean minesweepers. *Fortify* participated as a surveillance unit during the airdrop CALAMITY, patrolling a designated area to detect, warn, and track ships, submarines, and aircraft operating within the limits of established danger areas. Mine Division 71 ships departed Hawaii on 9 November.[14]

INITIAL MINESWEEPER INVOLVEMENT IN THE VIETNAM WAR

During the late 1950s and early 1960s, divisions of ocean minesweepers continued to deploy regularly from Long Beach to the Far East. It was unusual for an "escort" ship to accompany a division across the Pacific, although one might if deploying itself, and the sweeps were thus normally on their own after departing Long Beach, making routine brief stops at Pearl Harbor and Midway Island for fuel and other logistical support both en route Westpac and returning home. After leaving the naval station on one such deployment on 3 May 1960, Mine Division 71 took ten days to get to Hawaii, with engineers aboard *Inflict* hand-cranking diesel fuel into the fuel storage tanks out of the fifty-some 55-gallon drums deckloaded on the fantail. (In later years, MSOs would deploy with a fuel bladder strapped down on their fantails to extend their range.) Aboard the accompanying dock landing ship was a doctor to handle any major medical emergencies requiring care and facilities beyond those available aboard the small vessels. There were at the time no long-range helicopters that could rescue an injured or sick member of the crew aboard a ship in the mid-Pacific.[15]

Photo 6-4

Gallant between Midway Island and Pearl Harbor; homeward bound with Mine Division 73 (courtesy of Lt. jg. S. H. Cochran, USNR—1957)

As the United States continued to try to prevent a Communist takeover of South Vietnam, its involvement in Southeast Asia and commitment of military forces continued to increase as did the associated requirement to "show the flag" in an effort to demonstrate American resolve and to create or improve alliances with regional countries. In 1961, as part of the larger effort to establish an American presence in Indochina, Mine Division 93 units *Leader* and *Excel* became the first ships of the U.S. Navy to pay an official call at Phnom Penh, Cambodia. To reach the capital city, the minesweepers navigated from the South China Sea 180 miles up the Mekong River through South Vietnam (see map 1-1). Sailing through shallow water at the mouth of the river, the ships were not certain they would clear the delta, but in the event had no trouble. On hand to meet *Leader* and *Excel* as they entered Cambodian waters were Royal Cambodian Navy gun ships. These vessels, about the size of large dugouts with an old tank gun mounted forward, escorted them up the Mekong to Phnom Penh, where they were accorded a very cordial diplomatic welcome upon arrival. No less a personage than General Lon Nol, the minister of national defense, greeted the visiting Americans and told them he was "most happy that the two vessels could visit Cambodia."[16]

During the visit, from 27 to 30 August 1961, the officers and men of *Excel* and *Leader* welcomed aboard their ships officials of the royal government and members of the staff of the Palais Royal and Jeunesse Royale Socialiste Khmere. Other guests included students of the Centre de Preparation Pedagogique, the Ecole National des Arts et Metiers, and other schools in the capital. Commander, Mine Division 93, embarked in *Leader*, and the commanding officers of *Excel* and *Leader* paid courtesy calls on government officials, local dignitaries, and members of the

Photo 6-5

Use of a fuel bladder ("the Blob") and fuel deckloaded in drums enabled *Endurance* to make ocean crossings during deployments. As the ships aged, they also carried additional deckloaded lube oil for use in machinery (courtesy of Michael Wark).

Cambodian and U.S. military, including the chief of the U.S. Military Assistance Advisory Group, a brigadier general. The resounding success of the visit was later recognized by the Chief of Naval Operations, Commander in Chief, Pacific, Commander in Chief, Pacific Fleet, Commander, 7th Fleet, and the American consulate in Cambodia, who sent congratulatory messages praising the performance of *Leader* and *Excel* sailors.[17]

King Norodom Sihanouk subsequently, under pressure from leftists, refused further U.S. aid and in 1965 broke diplomatic relations with the United States. However, later in the decade he became angry with the Khmer communist party (commonly referred to as the Khmer Rouge) and restored normal relationships with Washington. In the spring of 1970, while Sihanouk was abroad receiving medical treatment, civilian bureaucrats and military officers overthrew his regime and established the Khmer Republic, led by General Lon Nol, the new president.[18]

The year 1961 also marked the first involvement of minesweepers in the Vietnam War, when MSOs began to train units of the South Vietnamese Navy in how to conduct patrols and to assist them in patrolling the 17th parallel, the boundary between North and South Vietnam, to stop Viet Cong infiltration of war material and men into South Vietnam.

The first minesweepers to participate in these operations were those of Mine Division 73, *Conquest, Esteem, Gallant, Illusive,* and *Pledge.* The division had departed Long Beach for a regularly scheduled Western Pacific cruise on 24 August 1961. After a brief reprise in Guam for six days of upkeep and rest and relaxation, it set a course for Subic Bay; however, three hundred miles from Guam, *Pledge* suffered a casualty that rendered her starboard shaft inoperative and, with a typhoon approaching, was ordered back to Guam, arriving on 2 October for repairs. The rest of the division continued westward; it arrived on the 5th of October at Subic Bay and remained in the area for almost a month, rejoined by *Pledge* on 29 October.[19]

Upon arrival in P.I., the division began a schedule of normal deployment activities, making a goodwill cruise to Manila and then participating in a combined U.S.-Philippine mine exercise off Corregidor Island in Manila Bay. Units of the division were similarly engaged in November and early December, taking part in a mine exercise off Kaohsiung with units of the Chinese Nationalist Navy, and, following their arrival at Sattahip, in a minesweeping exercise, EXPERIENCE FOUR, in the Gulf of Thailand. The latter exercise, with Royal Navy and Royal Thailand Navy units, was conducted from 27 November to 2 December. Upon completion, the division made a trip up the Bangkok River for a port call at Bangkok.[20]

The schedule for the division's remaining duty with 7th Fleet was interrupted by the build-up of U.S. aid to strife-torn South Vietnam, and Mine Division 73 was assigned to Da Nang, South Vietnam to train Vietnamese naval units in patrol techniques. Accordingly, after its visit to Bangkok, the division sailed for the capital city of South

Vietnam, reaching Saigon on 8 December. *Esteem* received six Vietnamese midshipmen on board and left port on 10 December for a mine exercise with two South Vietnamese patrol craft, during which *Conquest*, *Esteem*, *Pledge*, and *Gallant* trained South Vietnamese officers and men. Following the exercise, *Esteem* returned to Saigon before sailing on 18 December for the South China Sea to patrol the coast of South Vietnam with division mates and the South Vietnamese Navy. *Illusive* remained in readiness at Da Nang, South Vietnam, and was at year's end at Subic Bay undergoing a much needed maintenance availability.[21]

The ocean minesweepers began operating off the coast of Vietnam on 22 December, five miles south of the 17th parallel. This action, following issuance of CincPacFlt Operation Plan 75-61 on 14 December, marked the first time that major units of the 7th Fleet had participated directly in the Vietnam conflict. The division conducted patrol, surveillance and training operations in the coastal waters off South Vietnam to assist CHMAAG (Chief, Military Assistance Advisory Group) Vietnam and South Vietnamese naval forces in preventing infiltration. The MSOs themselves were not permitted to stop any ships, but, through the use of radar and visual surveillance, were allowed to locate suspicious vessels and direct the South Vietnamese Navy ships to intercept them.[22]

The minesweepers continued to detect surface contacts and vector South Vietnamese Navy forces through 17 February 1962, when Mine Division 73 was relieved of these duties by the destroyer escorts USS *Edmonds* (DE 406) and USS *Walton* (DE 361). *Illusive* left Subic Bay on 2 January for Da Nang to join the operations, until returning to Subic Bay in February for upkeep. *Pledge* participated from early February until departure from Da Nang on 17 February. Relieved of her patrol duties on 5 February, *Gallant* proceeded to Subic Bay for maintenance. *Conquest*, *Esteem*, and *Gallant* sailed following these operations for Victoria, Hong Kong, British Crown Colony, for rest and relaxation while moored at HMS (Her Majesty's Station) Tamar.[23]

Departing Hong Kong, *Conquest* and *Gallant* stopped at Subic Bay before leaving with *Illusive* en route to Guam for voyage repairs. *Conquest*, *Esteem*, *Gallant*, and *Illusive* left Guam on 16 March when all available ships were ordered to sea to participate in a search and rescue mission for a missing chartered Flying Tiger Airlines plane supposedly down somewhere between Guam and the Philippine Islands. The unsuccessful search was terminated on 23 March. Three days later, after being relieved of all duties with the 7th Fleet, the division set a course for Long Beach, arriving home to a large welcome as the first U.S. naval units to return from actual duty in South Vietnam, with the homecoming recorded by local and national news.[24]

FORMAL MINESWEEPER ENTRY INTO THE VIETNAM WAR

In 1965, U.S. Navy ships were directed formally to assist the South Vietnamese Navy in its coastal surveillance and anti-infiltration patrol efforts. Operation MARKET TIME, a massive combined U.S. Navy and South Vietnamese Navy effort to stop Viet Cong infiltration of weapons and supplies into South Vietnam, was inaugurated on 11 March 1965. General William C. Westmoreland, the U.S. commander (of the Military Assistance Command in Vietnam) at the time, estimated that prior to 1965 Viet Cong enemy forces in South Vietnam received about seventy percent of their supplies by sea, a percentage which by the end of 1966 had been reduced to less than ten percent. In *A Soldier Reports*, Westmoreland states, "I decided to institute MARKET TIME after South Vietnamese planes during the first two months of 1965 found two big trawlers unloading arms and ammunition along the coast, clear evidence that screening by a fleet of South Vietnamese junks was inadequate."

On 31 July, the Coastal Surveillance Force (Task Force 115) was formed, with headquarters at Cam Ranh Bay. Three zones of interdiction were established. Farthest out to sea, 100 to 150 miles from shore, was an air surveillance zone in which Navy maritime patrol aircraft, operating from bases in the Philippines and Vietnam itself, searched for mother ships that might be supplying the coastal smugglers. Closer in was an outer surface barrier, patrolled initially by fifteen destroyers or minesweepers and later by radar picket escorts (DER). In May 1965, U.S. Coast Guard Squadron 3, equipped with 82-foot cutters, arrived on station to patrol this barrier, and by February 1966, 26 cutters were in operation. Between 1967 and 1971, the force would be augmented by three Royal Australian Navy guided-missile destroyers. Nearest to shore was an inner or shallow-water barrier. Here, in addition to the South Vietnamese Junk Force (later renamed the Coastal Force), the Navy deployed 84 Swift boats, 50-foot vessels armed with .50-caliber machine guns and mortars, which darted among the hundreds of shallow coves and inlets that dot South Vietnam's extensive coastline.

From the Gulf of Tonkin, all the way down the South China Sea to the Cambodian border, a picket line of minesweepers, Coast Guard cutters, destroyer escorts, Swift boats, and patrol aircraft roamed off shore on "Operation MARKET TIME" duty. Assisted by airborne spotters, the surface units challenged unidentified ships and searched passing suspect junks and stationary fishing fleets for caches of ammunition and grenades and uniforms, in addition to keeping a constant lookout for supplies being smuggled to the enemy by junk, sampan, or freighter. Captain Ho Tan Quyen, South Vietnamese Chief of Naval Operations (1960-1963), when asked to describe the most numerous indigenous vessels plying Vietnamese waters, replied: "Junks may be defined as any craft large enough to carry a water buffalo standing athwartships."

The assignment of divisions of ocean minesweepers to Operation MARKET TIME resulted in a change to the "navigation tracks" commonly used by minesweepers en route and returning from operations with the 7th Fleet in the Western Pacific. Formerly, ships outbound from Long Beach touched first at Pearl Harbor and then Midway and Guam en route the Far East. Now, deploying to waters off Vietnam, they received en route fuel and other logistics at Kwajalein and Johnston atolls in lieu of Midway before more lengthy stays at Guam for needed maintenance en route Subic Bay, the base from which they would conduct operations in Vietnam.

Patrol Procedures

Throughout the war, divisions of minesweepers departed the West Coast of the United States every four months, headed west to relieve a division on station that was rotating home, often proceeding with lights darkened and emissions control set (the restricted use of radar and communications equipment to avoid detection), preparing for combat duty. In a representative deployment, Mine Division 73—*Conquest, Enhance, Illusive,* and *Leader*—bid farewell to friends and loved ones on 12 August 1968 and sailed from Long Beach for Vietnam, with stops en route at Pearl Harbor for voyage repairs, Johnston Atoll (probably the smallest inhabited "island" in the Pacific) for fuel (see map 6-4), and Kwajalein Atoll for fuel, stores, and mail before arriving at Guam. There sailors spent leisure hours swimming, playing softball, football, and tennis, diving in the coral reefs surrounding the atoll, and just plain relaxing while receiving materials and help from the ship repair facility.

Map 6-4

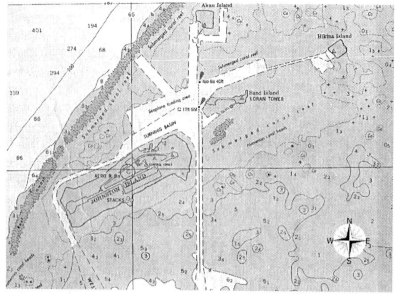

Johnston Atoll, perhaps the smallest inhabited island in the Pacific, was a fuel stop for divisions of MSOs during Pacific crossings and, in 1962, one of three sites at which the United States conducted Operation DOMINIC nuclear weapons tests.

With Packard propulsion engines humming again, the division departed Guam on 22 September for the Philippine Islands.[25]

En route Vietnam, minesweepers typically stopped at Subic Bay to receive, in addition to the 20mm or 40mm gun mount located on their foc'sles and the other small arms carried aboard, one or two .30-caliber machine guns to provide additional firepower. Following receipt of needed maintenance, food, fuel, ammunition, and other logistics support, the minesweepers stood out of Subic Bay, headed for the war zone. En route, they made final preparations for action, among them tests of all small arms and automatic weapons, including the gun mount, by gunner's mates.[26]

Arriving individually at one of eight patrol areas (designated area 1 through 8), the MSOs normally entered port at one of five coastal surveillance centers (Da Nang, Qui Nhon, Nha Trang, Vung Tau, or An Thoi), where they received operations and intelligence briefings for their area before taking up their MARKET TIME duties (see diagram 6-5). At the completion of a patrol or operation, the ships usually returned to

Diagram 6-5

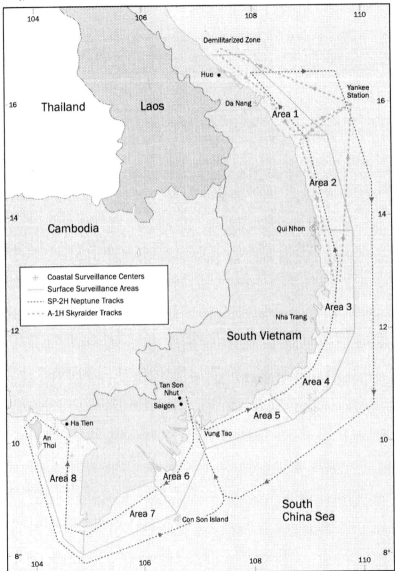

Market Time patrol areas.

the naval station at Subic Bay to receive necessary maintenance, provisioning, upkeep, and rest and relaxation for the crew prior to the next patrol.

During her second patrol of the deployment, *Endurance* was assigned from 1 through 12 January to area 8, off the extreme southeast coast of South Vietnam and south of area 7. A VNN liaison petty officer was assigned to assist her in the boarding and inspecting of junks. This addition proved to be a great aid in boarding vessels, although on several occasions medical assistance had to be rendered to suspects as a result of interrogation by the petty officer.[27]

Assigned to patrol a specific barrier line between two grid positions, *Endurance* was allowed to maneuver within five miles of the barrier to investigate and identify all detected contacts and craft. She interrogated merchant vessels with flashing light to determine identity, port of origin, destination, and cargo. Sampans, junks, and local steel-hulled cargo craft were usually intercepted and called alongside for boarding and inspection. On patrol, *Endurance* moved randomly through her assigned waters to prevent potential infiltrators from predicting her position along the barrier.[28]

Proceeding on a course and at a speed to put the wind and seas at about four knots, *Endurance* brought the craft alongside her starboard quarter, which was well-fended with old truck tires. When the craft were within one thousand yards, the officer of the deck called away the boarding party and ordered the starboard .50-caliber machine gun manned. The boarding party was armed and prepared to repel any hostile action by the craft. Normally, boats responded to calls by flashing light or by loudhailer and quickly came alongside. On two occasions when they did not, the use of .45-caliber pistol fire obtained prompt responses. A few fishing boats were contacted while they had gear

Photo 6-6

Boarding team inspecting a junk brought alongside an ocean minesweeper (courtesy of Charles Wymer)

streamed, in which cases the boarding party traveled to the craft via motor whaleboat while *Endurance* stood off and provided protection for the boat crew with a machine gun.[29]

Standard procedure, either alongside or via motor whaleboat, was to send a VNN liaison petty officer aboard the vessel first, followed by the boarding officer (normally the executive officer) and one or two other boarding party members (a Gunner's Mate and Signalman in most cases). While the boarding officer and VNN liaison PO inspected the ship's papers, cargo manifests, crew lists, and crew identity cards, the other boarders conducted a physical inspection of holds and storage compartments, engine spaces, topside stowage areas, and any other possible contraband stowage areas. On completion of the inspection, if everything was in order, *Endurance* rendered whatever assistance she could to the craft and its occupants. Her corpsman provided minor medical assistance, small packages of soap and rice, and frequently candy and cigarettes. The craft master was thanked for his assistance and given the reason for the boarding visit. "It was made necessary by Viet Cong and North Vietnamese infiltration efforts," was the standard explanation given as part of the psychological warfare program. *Endurance* was relieved by *Dynamic* and departed 12 January for Subic Bay.[30]

MARKET TIME patrol duties entailed many long, tedious, and hard hours of detection, interception, inspection, and boarding of vessel traffic in the South China Sea. Hour after hour, day after day, week after week, MSO crewmen manned the motor whaleboat or brought junks alongside their ships and clambered over heaving gunwales, across slippery decks through coiled fishing nets, and into rancid bilges, searching for any arms, ammunition, medicine, or food that might be headed for the Viet Cong ashore. This work was particularly exacting when coastal traffic was high and cargos of every imaginable item brought new odors and challenges to boarding and inspection teams. Moreover, avoiding "fish stakes" could be a challenge, and piloting skills and a sixth sense of where they might be located were very important to patrol success. The long wooden poles, which were driven vertically into the sea floor to provide Vietnamese fishing boats a moorage in fishing areas, could damage MSO propellers and running gear. In one such incident on 12 July 1966, the day started out on a negative note for *Constant*, when a few minutes after midnight something got tangled in and fouled the starboard screw. A subsequent investigation by divers at Da Nang revealed a bamboo pole used to hold boats along the twenty-fathom curve for squid fishing. The thirty-foot section of stake was removed in less than five minutes with luckily no resulting damage to the ship. Patrols in some parts were a nightmare during darkness, when the officers of the deck could not see the fish stakes.[31]

The routine of boarding and searching, and dodging fish stakes aside, occasionally a more humanitarian aspect of patrol presented itself.

On 19 September 1966 while deployed with Mine Division 92, *Pluck* was ordered to provide assistance to a disabled junk that a U.S. Navy patrol aircraft had spotted about seventy-five miles off the coast. The pilot described the vessel as a cargo junk about sixty feet long, drifting dead in the water, and reported that on his first pass overhead fifteen to twenty people had appeared on deck waving wildly. He had also sighted a sign from the air with the message, scrawled in English, "boat is accident." *Pluck* discovered, arriving alongside the junk *Chan Hung*, that it was indeed an accident, the vessel having lost its rudder four days earlier and having been adrift since that time. Another hand-written sign proclaimed "passenger is hungry," which was certainly true; the nineteen men, six women, and seven children aboard had been without food for three days and without water for almost two. The junk's crew and passengers were brought aboard *Pluck*, whose cooks prepared a meal for the hungry Vietnamese while the ship took the disabled vessel under tow and set a course for a South Vietnamese port. Following the meal, *Pluck* unfolded the wonders of Hollywood for her guests, who joined the crew in watching a movie on the fantail. There men, women, and children sat mesmerized by a DeMille epic in Technicolor until the strain of the past few days took its toll and one by one they fell asleep on the deck. Several hours later, a South Vietnamese Navy ship arrived to tow the junk to Saigon; the sleepy and well-fed crew and passengers were returned to their junk and it was turned over to the naval vessel. Following this short interlude of assistance, sharing, and friendship, *Pluck* returned the following day to the routine of board and inspect.[32]

Although the investigation of junks in the outer surface barrier was their primary duty, minesweepers were occasionally sent farther out to sea or to areas near shore, based on TF 115 requirements. Trying to investigate trawlers in deep waters proved to be difficult as, in addition to being reluctant to answer flashing light queries, many of the larger merchant ships also had a speed advantage over the minesweepers. The shallow-draft MSOs were also candidates to work near shore, providing such tasking did not expose them to unacceptable risk from enemy fire. Assigned from 10 January to 21 February 1966 in an area of the coast near Cam Rhan Bay and Nha Trang, *Persistent* operated close to shore, boarding and searching small fishing junks, with much of her work done inside the four-fathom curve and within five hundred yards of land. Suspect craft were either brought alongside her starboard quarter for boarding or boarded from her motor whaleboat. The latter method was used extensively at night when the ship inspected heavy concentrations of junks near villages and fishing grounds. Well utilized during the same deployment, division mate *Endurance* acted as the mother ship for smaller and faster Navy Swift boats and U.S. Coast Guard patrol boats that were assisting her with coastal surveillance. She functioned as a communications guard ship to provide radio message traffic to the smaller craft, a prisoner compound for detained Viet Cong suspects, and a logistics support ship. The best patrol coverage was obtained by letting the smaller and faster boats do the majority of active patrolling while *Endurance* provided logistic and gunfire support. In addition, she informed the smaller boats of changes in the weather and passed them important (radio) message traffic they were unable to "copy" themselves.[33]

In addition to boarding sampans and junks, minesweepers routinely distributed packages of psychological operations materials, treated children in Vietnamese villages under the Medical Civic Action Program (MedCap) and, at patrol end, turned over any detainees to the coastal surveillance center in their area before leaving for Subic Bay. Minesweepers assigned to patrol area 7 sometimes relieved the ship on station at the "sleepy lagoon" of Con Son Island. It was famous as a penal colony used by the French to imprison Vietnamese revolutionaries, and the United States similarly used it to house prisoners of war.[34]

Shipboard life during intense operations under arduous conditions was made worse by equipment casualties that degraded habitability beyond that normally found in a small cramped vessel. However, when hardship did not preclude a ship from performing its mission, it, in good Navy fashion, pressed on. A former *Leader* crewmember remembers one such patrol:

We had been on MARKET TIME patrol for many weeks, standing port and starboard watches of 8 [hours] on [watch] and 8 off. The evaporators had gone down and we were on water rationing and that meant salt-water showers, washing your clothes by dragging them behind the ship, and water hours on the drinking fountain, all in well over 100 degree heat. The radio shack was so hot that we had a "red devil" (blower) ducted (drawing air through a portable duct) from the escape hatch to the transmitters to keep the radios up. Your bunk never got dry and I slept in the 40mm gun tub at night on a pile of life jackets. All in all, it was a little slice of hell.

Because prolonged periods at sea can be difficult at any time and tend to be even more so under wartime conditions, the minesweepers normally received a few days of rest and relaxation following a patrol, either upon their arrival at Naval Station, Subic Bay or via a liberty port. However, sometimes R&R took place "in the field." The same crewmember recalls:

> The skipper knew the crew was tired but we were a long way from Subic and had more patrol time to do. So the captain found a seaplane tender in a cove with a white sandy beach. Two seaplanes were moored alongside her as we pulled into the small bay.

> The skipper made a deal with the tender and we used the lifeboat to pick up beer and put men on the beach to relax and drink. The bay was calm but we had seen several sharks and the jellyfish were as big as cars.

> The day wore on and the skeleton crew stayed on board as the whaleboat came and went. As dusk began to set in, it was time to bring all hands back on board and get under way. [35]

Additionally, although sailors were relieved to leave the combat zone for the last time following their final patrol during a deployment, the transit home was not always easy. The same crewmember remembers battling a typhoon en route the United States:

> Upon being relieved from patrol by another sweep division, *Leader* headed home from the Philippines in late 1965. Traveling north of the Philippines, we were in the classic "H" formation with *Leader* as flagship in the center and the *Lucid*, *Excel*, *Guide* and *Enhance* at the four outer points. We had reports of an incoming storm and right in the middle of the San Bernardino Straits we hit Typhoon Faye. For several days we experienced the most extreme conditions I had ever seen. We were taking water over the bridge and that was an open bridge. During an evening watch I had to take message traffic to the OOD [officer of the deck] on the bridge. As I finally got there, the OOD turned around and he was wearing a scuba diving mask. Almost in hysterics, I said to Lieutenant—, "What the hell are you wearing that for, sir"? About that time, one of the lookouts on the bridge called out "WAVE" and we all hit the deck with me and the lieutenant hanging on to the compass and we were all damn near swept overboard. As the bow came back up, Lieutenant— looked at me and said, "Now do you know why I am wearing this f—-ing thing? I can't see a damn thing without it." I asked him if he had another one.

Seas were so heavy that while on the bridge I watched the *Guide* in front of us heel over so far that both screws came out of the water. When it was all over, one sweep had its steel bow plate ripped off and another had its mast twisted some five or so degrees. When you ran next to her dead amidships you could see both the port and starboard green minesweeping task lights because the yardarms were twisted so far.

Sleeping at night in the bow-berthing compartment was nearly impossible. You had to strap yourself in the bunk and then hang on as the ship "went over one [wave] and under two." It was the only time on board the lady that I was not quite sure she would hold together.[36]

COMBAT ACTION

The tedium of patrol duty, with the seemingly endless chore of inspecting, boarding and searching junks, sampans, and larger vessels, and weariness associated with battling frequent storms was periodically broken by combat. The highest award that may be received by a Navy ship for extraordinary heroism is the Presidential Unit Citation, which is the unit equivalent of a Sailor or Marine's receiving the Navy Cross for extraordinary heroism not justifying the Medal of Honor. USS *Leader* (MSO 490) received this award for participation between 18 October and 5 December 1968 as a member of Task Group 194.0 in Operation SEA LORDS. Signed by President Richard Nixon, the citation reads:

> For extraordinary heroism and outstanding performance of duty from 18 October to 5 December 1968 while engaged in armed conflict against enemy forces in the Republic of Vietnam. Commander Task Group 194.0 initiated and prosecuted the first of several interdiction campaigns to sever enemy lines of communications and resupply and to establish the legal government in areas previously held by the enemy. The naval units engaged in Operations SEA LORDS consistently displayed the striking power and professionalism which were to mark this and following campaigns. Tasked with routing a myriad of enemy forces from their previous sanctuaries, personnel of Task Group 194.0 ventured courageously into little-known canals and back-water areas, fighting valiantly through countless intense enemy rocket and automatic weapons attacks. The naval units, through their persistent and aggressive strikes against enemy strongholds, were eminently successful in their campaign to interdict enemy resupply routes and base areas throughout the lower Mekong Delta region. The courage,

professionalism, and dedication displayed by the officers and men of Commander Task Group 194.0 reflected great credit upon themselves and were in keeping with the highest traditions of the United States Naval Service.

During the participation of ocean minesweepers in Operation MARKET TIME, other ships engaged in less-recognized dangerous combat operations including the courageous action of USS *Endurance* (MSO 435) in vigorously engaging a Viet Cong steel-hulled trawler in a sea battle, depicted in the opening chapter. Following are brief descriptions of other combat actions, in addition to Operation SEA LORDS, occurring during the deployments of Mine Divisions 91, 71, and 92 to Vietnam between 1965 and 1970.

The ships of Mine Division 91—*Conflict, Dynamic, Endurance, Implicit,* and *Persistent*—stood out of Long Beach on 21 September 1965, headed west. The division arrived at Subic Bay on 8 November, completing a fifty-day ocean transit. There, the ships received stores and two additional .30-caliber machine guns in preparation for MARKET TIME operations. During ensuing combat operations in Vietnam, units of the division either engaged directly with enemy forces or provided gunfire support to troops ashore.[37]

Conflict sailed from Subic Bay on 12 November 1965 for South Vietnam and area 6, and began her task of patrolling along the coast, intercepting junks, searching them, and checking their crewmen for proper identification. Continuing her patrol into December, she sharpened her gunnery on targets of opportunity but drew no enemy fire. On her last day on patrol, *Conflict* intercepted a call for assistance from VNN Junk Division 31 at Point Kega, which was under machine gun fire from enemy shore positions. *Conflict* arrived in the area just as a three-plane carrier strike group hit the position with bombs and rockets. Upon completion of the air strike, she began placing 40mm and machine gun fire on enemy spotted by an Army observer aircraft, reported as two Viet Cong companies. *Conflict* retired after an hour of firing with no casualties, having expended 560 rounds of 40mm and 1,200 rounds of machine gun fire in the target area. On the following day, she departed MARKET TIME operations bound for a Christmas holiday in Hong Kong.[38]

In the early morning of 22 March 1966, following receipt of a report from Junk Division 30 that its vessels were being fired upon by Viet Cong on the beach, *Implicit* silenced the enemy fire. From about eight hundred yards her guns unleashed 640 rounds of 40mm, 1,700 rounds of .50-caliber, and 2,500 rounds of .30-caliber ammunition against the shore. *Implicit* received no enemy hits, although two crewmembers of the junk division received superficial wounds, subsequently treated by the MSO's hospital corpsman. The following morning, *Implicit* again supported Junk Division 30, which had once more drawn fire from the beach, expending 40mm, .50-caliber, and .30-caliber ammunition upon the enemy. Upon completion of her patrol on 4 April, *Implicit* sailed for Subic Bay.[39]

After spending New Year's Day in Hong Kong, from 18 January to 24 February, *Endurance* resumed MARKET TIME patrol duties of "inspect, board, and search" as part of Task Force 115. Her patrol routine was broken by a gunfire support mission involving an attack by her motor whaleboat and a Vietnamese Coastal Group Patrol junk upon a Viet Cong position ashore, resulting in the award of the Bronze Star medal to her executive officer and Navy Commendation medals to members of the boat crew, all decorations awarded with combat distinguishing devices. At completion of the patrol, *Endurance* departed for Subic Bay.[40]

Persistent returned to Vietnam on 11 March 1966 for her third patrol, operating this time in the vicinity of Quang Ngai and Chu Lai. Other U.S. units were present in this area, including WPBs, PCF's, and coastal minesweepers. On 25 March, *Persistent* fired her 40mm and .50-caliber machine-guns at shore targets following attacks by Viet Cong units on Coastal Group junks. On five different nights, she provided illumination with her 24-inch searchlight to aid Coastal Group and Popular Forces bases in fighting off or preventing Viet Cong night attacks. She returned on 1 April to Subic Bay.[41]

USS *Loyalty*, deployed with Mine Division 71, left Subic Bay on 30 March 1966 to take position off the coast of Vietnam for MARKET TIME operations with Task Force 115. During her first two weeks on patrol, she fired 540 rounds of 40mm, 1,380 rounds of .50-caliber, and 835 rounds of .30-caliber gun ammunition at various targets. Her landing and search crews detected 914 junks, investigated 401, and physically boarded 239. During the deployment, her crew boarded 348 junks, detained two vessels and fifteen suspects, and killed three Viet Cong.[42]

On 6 April, inspecting junks approximately one mile off the beach, *Loyalty* signaled a vessel by flashing searchlight to heave to. When the

Photo 6-7

Loyalty's motor whaleboat moves toward a Vietnamese junk to inspect it for smuggled Viet Cong arms and ammunition (Official U.S. Navy Photograph from the National Archives)

junk failed to stop, the MSO fired 50-caliber warning shots that resulted in immediate hostile fire from an enemy position ashore, from what was believed to be a 37mm gun. *Loyalty* returned fire with her 40mm gun and one 50-caliber machinegun, pounding the beach for about twenty minutes and silencing the enemy gun.[43]

Two days later, *Loyalty* knocked out a Viet Cong emplacement that had been firing on a U.S. Army L-19 Bird Dog artillery spotter plane. She had received a call from the aircraft saying that it was under fire from four Viet Cong on the beach and requesting the ship's assistance. Upon her arrival at the scene twenty minutes later, the ship caught four of the enemy hiding behind some rocks at the water's edge beneath what appeared to be camouflage netting. *Loyalty* commenced firing. When her guns quieted, three Viet Cong soldiers were confirmed killed.[44]

While patrolling about two miles off the coast on 17 April, *Loyalty* signaled two junks of Republic of Vietnam Coastal Group 30 to come alongside to learn if they had any information about any Viet Cong activity in the area. When one junk came alongside, the MSO crew discovered a wounded American advisor onboard. The man was brought aboard *Loyalty* for medical treatment and then placed in the motor whaleboat for transfer to an Army helicopter, which hovered over the boat and then descended until its skids were resting on the gunnels (gunwales) of the craft. The wounded officer was taken to a nearby hospital for medical treatment. *Loyalty* completed her patrol eight days later.[45]

In a subsequent deployment, Mine Division 91 left Subic Bay on 29 November 1967 for rest and relaxation in Hong Kong, happy to make port as a foul sea from the northeast had made the journey uncomfortable. The sweeps sailed in company on 8 December but split up thereafter, each ship headed for its own patrol area. *Conflict* relieved *Esteem* at Qui Nhon and commenced patrol duties. On 22 and 23 December, she courageously helped defend the MARKET TIME base at Qui Nhon when it was attacked by hostile forces. Moored to the pier at the base, with her guns masked by friendly forces, her crew assisted local forces in repelling a Viet Cong unit that had penetrated the base. At 11:15 p.m., a command junk located about one hundred yards from *Conflict* was damaged by a Viet Cong charge, as a result of which the base and the minesweeper went to general quarters. A few hours later, *Conflict* secured from general quarters, only to return to battle stations at 2:30 a.m. when a second explosion occurred. During this GQ, she assisted the base commander by illuminating the area with her 24-inch searchlight, putting her landing party ashore to assist as stretcher-bearers and ammunition carriers, as well as providing other needed services. *Conflict* returned to MARKET TIME duties on 23 December. Relieved by *Impervious* at Qui Nhon on 12 January, she arrived three days later at Subic Bay.[46]

Mine Division 91 units were engaged on 29 February and 1 March in individual patrol periods, typified by bad weather and associated minimal junk activity, when four heavily-laden arms trawlers attempted to infiltrate South Vietnam. During the ensuing night action, U.S. forces destroyed three of the trawlers and turned back a fourth. The engagement began when *Conflict* received a radio message on 29 February from Commander, Coastal Surveillance Force, indicating that a probable infiltrator was in her area. Coast Guard cutter USCGC *Winona* (WHEC 65) was to maintain covert surveillance and, in the event of an attempted shore landing by the suspected trawler, become the primary action unit. *Conflict* was directed to remain in her present position and maintain the arms blockade.[47]

Conflict subsequently picked up the trawler on her radar and tracked her movements into the contiguous waters of the Republic of Vietnam. The Task Force 115 blockade force units were at "darken ship" condition and trawler 28F1 steamed headlong into the well-planned trap. *Conflict* and other units in area 7 cut off its escape and it was destroyed by *Winona*. The cutter had followed the unsuspecting vessel in past the twelve-mile limit and signaled her to "stop her engines." The infiltrator's reply was a spray of machine gun tracer. *Winona* answered by firing rounds from her 5-inch gun mount, and trawler 28F1 met its end in a huge fireball of orange flame, sinking seconds later with nothing but small pieces of debris and a few battered rifle stocks left afloat. Within hours after the explosion and sinking of the infiltrator, *Conflict* began a sonar search for the wreckage and her prompt action contributed significantly to subsequent salvage efforts.[48]

Persistent, in area 1, assisted in the effort to trap and destroy a second trawler, designated 29F2. When an electrical power failure in Da Nang disrupted communications between the engaged force and the Coastal Surveillance Center, *Persistent* assumed the function of communications-relay ship, directing the interception and destruction of the trawler.[49]

A third trawler, which had been headed toward the location in area 3 that *Endurance* was patrolling, turned back and escaped seaward after challenge by a Coast Guard cutter. *Endurance* subsequently took up a blocking position to prevent any escape effort by a fourth trawler, designated 29F3, which was later beached and destroyed in area 4.[50]

Within hours of the trawler incident, *Persistent* captured an abandoned Chinese Communist junk found anchored north of Bano Du Volta. Initially brought to Da Nang for intelligence exploitation, it was later transported to the United States for transfer to the Mine Force, U.S. Pacific Fleet museum at Long Beach. Relieved by *Fortify* on 12 March, *Persistent* left for Sasebo.[51]

Endurance was on patrol in area 3 the night of 3 March when the coastal group base and training camp at Tuy Hoa, South Vietnam was taken under attack. Proceeding rapidly to the area, she established upon arrival an inshore barrier seven-hundred to fourteen-hundred yards from the beach to prevent infiltration and exfiltration via the water, despite dangerous shoals and threat of attack from hostile forces ashore. At daybreak on the 4th, *Endurance* detected and intercepted two small craft that had been identified as "positively" hostile and were reported to contain enemy forces escaping from the beach. However, the craft were Vietnam Navy Junk Force units departing on a morning patrol. By holding her fire until the targets were clearly distinguishable and directing aircraft to refrain from further firing until positive identification had been made, *Endurance* averted the tragic destruction of friendly forces. On 4 March, *Endurance*'s patrol was shifted to area 4, where she remained on duty until her relief on 11 March by *Engage* in Nha Trang Harbor.[52]

Mine Division 91 sailed from Sasebo on 23 April for Long Beach. Blessed with beautiful weather, save for several days either side of Midway Island, the ships enjoyed a smooth transit. Four days prior to arrival in Guam, the division "chopped" to Commander, 1st Fleet, signifying the ships were getting closer to the West Coast, and arrived in homeport, following an absence of nine months, on 21 March.[53]

Operation SEA LORDS

In October 1968, Vice Adm. Elmo R. Zumwalt, Commander Naval Force Vietnam, launched Operation SEA LORDS (Southeast Asia Lake, Ocean, River, Delta Strategy), a combined effort by U.S. Navy, South Vietnamese Navy, and allied ground forces to cut the enemy's supply lines from Cambodia and disrupt operations originating from base areas deep in the delta. In the operation, the U.S. Navy's three major operating forces in Vietnam (Task Force 115, the Coastal Surveillance Force; 116, the River Patrol Force; and 117, the Mobile Riverine Force) were brought together for the first time to stop Vietcong infiltration into South Vietnam's Mekong Delta. Forces used included Navy "Swift boats" (PCF) and River Patrol Boats (PBR), Coast Guard WPBs, minesweeping boats, monitors, transports, and other armored craft, armed helicopters, fixed-wing OV-10 Bronco aircraft, and five SEAL platoons. Proving support for craft working the dangerous inland waterways were two Mobile Riverine Force support vessels, World War II tank landing ships USS *Hunterdon County* (LST 838) and USS *Jennings County* (LST 846), and two ships normally assigned to the Coastal Surveillance Force, the tank landing ship USS *Washoe County* (LST 1165) and ocean minesweeper USS *Leader* (MSO 490). Coast Guard high endurance cutters—*Bibb* (WHEC 31), *Ingham* (WHEC 35), and *Wachusset* (WHEC 44)—similarly served as motherships for WPBs and Navy Swift boats.[54]

Between 18 October and 5 December 1968, *Leader* participated in Operation SEA LORDS. A former crewmember recalls that generally while deployed the sweep was always involved in some operation, fired her weapons frequently, and afforded the crew little sleep since they were always at general quarters.

> We had eight PBRs we worked with who did most of the river combat; we were their support and helped them whenever we could. During one operation, we lost a couple of the PBRs and I remember transferring the bodies of the deceased crewmembers.[55]

The larger and more heavily armed *Washoe County*, assigned as a mothership from 27 October to 9 December, functioned as an emergency helicopter-landing pad in evacuating eight Navy and Coast Guardsmen wounded in action and the body of one Coast Guardsman who had been killed in action ashore. She also dispensed fuel, food, water, and ammunition to 134 patrol boats and fired 42 naval gunfire support missions.[56]

SEA LORDS began on 18 October 1968 when a Navy Swift boat (PCF) reconnoitered the entrance to the Cua Lon River on the Gulf of Thailand side of the Ca Mau Peninsula. Following this mission, Swift boats conducted a series of incursions along the southern rivers and canals, upsetting Viet Cong base camps and cutting supply and communication lines (see map 6-6).[57]

On 1 November, Vietnamese Marines from the 4th Battalion and elements of the 21st ARVN Division boarded Vietnamese and American riverine craft and the force swept through the Rach Gia-Long Xuyen Canals. The force worked with Kien Giang Province Regional Force and Popular Force troops during the sweeps and uncovered large quantities of enemy weapons and munitions. Fifteen days later, the Navy launched Operation TRAN HUNG DAO, performing a series of interdiction patrols on two waterways along the Cambodian border, from the town of Ha Tien on the entrance to the Giang Thanh River to the river city of Chau Doc located west of Saigon. Navy Swift boats patrolled the western end and river patrol boats (PBRs) the eastern end. In December, Operation GIANT SLINGSHOT, another part of SEA LORDS, commenced as River Patrol boats and river assault craft (RACs) of the U.S. and Vietnamese Navies began operations in the

Map 6-6

Operation SEA LORDS brought together U.S. Navy, South Vietnamese Navy, and allied group forces to cut the enemy's supply lines from Cambodia, and stop Viet Cong infiltration into South Vietnam's Mekong Delta.

Vam Co Dong and Vam Co Tay rivers, which form a boundary around the "Parrot's Beak" section of the Cambodian border protruding into Vietnam.[58]

During the ensuing two months, the U.S. Navy, working closely with the U.S. Army 1st Cavalry Division (Airmobile), uncovered numerous enemy caches of munitions, and thereafter the joint force became known locally as the "NavCav." In January 1969, the U.S. Navy moved a task force of PBRs and armored assault craft into a 56-mile-long canal complex across the Plain of Reeds, establishing the final link of a 250-mile-long naval blockade extending from Ha Tien to Tay Ninh City. Dubbed "BARRIER REEF," the operation successfully impeded enemy movement along the two canals.[59]

-o-o-o-o-o-o-o-o-o-o-o-o-

The participation of other minesweepers in combat action continued during and after Operation SEA LORDS. During the early hours of 29 October 1968, *Illusive* took part in shelling an enemy position after a spotter aircraft reported a group of approximately two hundred Viet Cong on the Mai Cong May Dong Peninsula (about thirty miles from *Illusive*), and the call went out to all units for gun fire support. The Viet Cong troops were reported to have taken refuge in the numerous caves in the mountainous terrain of the peninsula; two destroyers shelled the position, with additional gunfire from a LCMR (medium rocket landing ship) and *Illusive*, to seal up the caves in the area. *Illusive* patrolled near the beach during the night to prohibit escape of any VC by sampan. During the operation, she expended 521 rounds of 40mm and 300 rounds of .50-caliber ammunition.[60]

In 1970, USS *Guide*, deployed as part of Mine Division 92, departed Subic Bay on 5 May for Vietnam, calling at Da Nang three days later for a briefing by the Coastal Surveillance Center before relieving *Lucid* as Demilitarization Zone Patrol Ship. During the course of her patrol from 8 May to 9 June, she engaged in combat actions against enemy troops on the beach and was credited with fifty-two Viet Cong killed in action. Following her relief by *Pivot*, *Guide* left for liberty in Singapore.[61]

Minesweeping Operations

Employed primarily as patrol vessels during the Vietnam War, ocean minesweepers only infrequently performed their primary duties. In the early days of United States participation in the war, MSOs conducted an exploratory sweep off a beach north of Vung Tau, South Vietnam when it was believed families of U.S. personnel might be evacuated in the event of a Viet Cong assault on Saigon. In 1967, ocean minesweepers performed exploratory sweeping off a beach location in conjunction with a feint landing by an amphibious force. On 25 January 1968, units of Mine Division 91 departed Subic Bay for Da Nang to take up the third patrol of their deployment. Two days later the division received orders diverting it from MARKET TIME operations to clear what was believed to be the first live minefield encountered by the U.S. Navy since 1953, created when, under unexplained conditions, U.S. air forces lost a load of mines north of the 17th parallel in the Tonkin Gulf. *Endurance* made preparations for sweeping during the transit: the magnetic cable ("magtail") was streamed astern and "meggered" for possible electrical grounds (it had just been received in Subic Bay from the pre-positioned war reserve stocks); a new bridle was set for the port O-gear; and preparations for off-loading excessive magnetic material were completed. Mine Division 91 arrived at Da Nang to off-load its magnetic material (tools, canned goods, and other non-essential items normally carried aboard that might detonate a magnetic mine) in preparation for sweep operations.[62]

Before the offload could be conducted, Viet Cong forces launched the massive "Tet Offensive," causing the minesweepers to remain anchored in Da Nang Harbor throughout the first furious night of 29 January. On the following day, the ships went alongside the Naval Advisory Group pier to off load magnetic materials into Conex boxes for secure storage. After departure on 30 January, the division was engaged through 3 February sweeping two areas believed to contain Mk 36 destructors. These were Mk 80 low-drag aircraft bombs turned into magnetic mines by insertion of a mine-mechanism package instead of a fuse-mechanism. The United States used in excess of a quarter million destructors throughout the war, including 11,000 (as well as about 100 Mk 52 mines) toward the end to mine Haiphong Harbor in North Vietnam. At both sites, previous unexplained explosions had given reason to believe that the weapons were armed or had become armed on impact. Shortly after the ships began mine hunting in the first danger area, operations were halted and the minesweepers relocated to the second danger area, a higher priority as it interfered with the free maneuverability of the carrier forces at Yankee Station. Located off South Vietnam in the South China Sea (16 degrees north and 110 degrees east), it was the closest point from which the Navy launched air strikes against North Vietnam. After thirty straight hours of combat sweeping, the MSOs returned to the first danger area to conduct another thirty hours of sweeping, rendering both areas safe. During these extensive periods, sailors could not go below decks in order to prevent or minimize death or injury resulting from a mine explosion close aboard, and three days of rain and cold weather tested the endurance of all. Throughout the operation, the cruiser USS *Dale* (CG 19) provided defense for the division. At completion of operations on 4 February, the division returned to Da Nang to back load magnetic material that had been left ashore temporarily to help ensure the safety of the ships during mine clearance operations. The completion of minesweeping operations prompted a "Well Done message" from Commander Naval Force to the division.[63]

This "Bravo Zulu" aside, the degradation in the material condition of the minesweepers and lack of upgrades was highlighted by Commander 7th Fleet: "Minesweepers were spending too much time on patrol and were not maintaining their MCM proficiency; there was a lack of means to navigate accurately; and a lack of funds to accomplish needed alterations on the minesweepers." After years of deployments to the Western Pacific for operations with the 7th Fleet and more recently MARKET TIME duties off South Vietnam, these operations, in conjunction with the long transits to and from Long Beach, had brought the MSOs into disrepair. The vessels, constructed of wood and fitted with aluminum engines for protection against mines and not for durability, simply wore out. Unfortunately, the high cost of the war had precluded their replacement with a proposed 1965-1966 type designed to carry the Shadowgraph side-scan sonar and a wire-guided torpedo known as the Sea Nettle for mine disposal. Faced with the challenge of keeping the aging MSOs operational, the Navy began in Fiscal Year 1968 a rehabilitation program to extend their service life. However, cost growth, technical deficiencies, and diversion of funds to support East Asian operations resulted in only 13 of the planned 65 ships receiving a complete modernization, although additional minesweepers received some improvements. (In the early 1970s, confronted by continued diminishing resources, a failed MSO modernization program, and obsolescence of both its ocean minesweepers and coastal minesweepers, the Navy would place much greater emphasis on the use of minesweeping helicopters and begin a large-scale reduction of its force of mine countermeasures ships.)[64]

Between January 1966 and July 1967, MARKET TIME forces sank several North Vietnamese steel-hulled trawlers and visually inspected or boarded more than 700,000 vessels in South Vietnamese waters. In 1967, the destroyers USS *Walker* (DD 517) and USS *Wilhoite* (DER 397) captured a trawler with one million rounds of ammunition and two tons of TNT on board. Except for five enemy ships that were either sunk or turned back while attempting to resupply their forces in the aftermath of the 1968 Tet Offensive, no other enemy trawlers were spotted from July 1967 to August 1969.

Meanwhile, minesweepers continued to conduct patrol operations and only occasionally perform mine countermeasures duties, although on another occasion ocean minesweeper *Pluck* conducted a magnetic sweep at the mouth of the Cua Viet River, located ten miles south of the Demilitarized Zone, with negative results. On 11 and 12 July 1970, while operating as the sole U.S. MARKET TIME unit in "I" Corps, *Guide* engaged in actual minesweeping operations during a "check-sweep" for enemy mines in the vicinity of the DMZ in preparation for the repatriation of North Vietnamese prisoners of war carried aboard the Vietnamese tank landing ship VNN LST 503. The exchange took place as scheduled. *Guide* also conducted harassing fire missions and three "Medcaps" during the patrol. On 4 August, she engaged an enemy mortar near the DMZ and received return fire from both the mortar and a 152mm coastal defense gun farther north with no casualties.[65]

Of course, the use of MSOs for duties they were not designed for was inevitable. The Navy needed many patrol vessels to conduct Operation MARKET TIME duties, not all of which could be met by heavily taxed combatant ships, and there were few mines laid in the waters in which the ocean minesweepers operated. Beginning in 1965, while larger ocean and coastal minesweepers conducted patrol duties off the coast of Vietnam, smaller shallow-draft 65-foot U.S. Navy minesweeping boats (MSBs) began operating inland to keep the waterways leading into and out of Saigon clear of mines. The North Vietnamese used mines to attack tankers and ammunition ships of the MSTS (the Military Sea Transport Service, which later become a part of the Military Sealift Command) transporting materials to support U.S. and allied military operations, often in conjunction with attacks by rocket, rocket-grenade, or machinegun fire. The Viet Cong mines employed varied from the simple contact types to a few advanced Soviet influence mines. Most were homemade controlled mines, command-activated by watchers hidden in the foliage along waterways as unsuspecting ships passed nearby, drifting mines made of explosive-filled logs or disguised as garbage, or swimmer-delivered limpet mines that adhered directly, usually by suction cups, to vessel hulls.[66]

Following the commencement of U.S. inshore sweeping, the Viet Cong attacked the MSBs as well, resulting in the installation of additional armor and armament in the boats, and the assignment of PBRs to provide protection. The Navy also introduced specialized craft to keep the waterways open and support riverine warfare, amphibious landing craft (LCM-6) rigged with minesweeping gear and redesignated river minesweepers (MSM), 30-ton patrol minesweepers

(MSR), and, to a much lesser degree, experimental minesweeper drones (MSD). Other mine countermeasures craft, including a modified 50-foot motor launch, and the ten 36-foot minesweeping launches (MSLs) carried by *Epping Forest* swept for combination magnetic-acoustic influence mines in the Cua Viet River in 1968.[67]

Operation MARKET TIME succeeded in closing down North Vietnam's lines of supply by sea. Unfortunately, success at sea was over-shadowed by the failure of efforts to close down the landlines of supply along the Ho Chi Minh Trail through "neutral" Laos and by the overt transshipment of arms and equipment to the Viet Cong through the "neutral" Cambodian port of Sihanoukville. When this port was closed to Communist shipping in August 1969, the North Vietnamese made an attempt to resume trawler traffic. However, of the 15 trawlers detected moving south between August 1969 and late 1970, one was sunk, 13 were turned back, and only one got through. The destroyer USS *Wilhoite* (DER 397) drove an arms trawler ashore in 1969, thereby affecting capture of the largest arms cache during the entire war.[68]

As part of the "Vietnamization" of the war, the VNN took charge of the inner screen in September 1970, and the United States trans-ferred all Swift boats to South Vietnamese control. The combined op-erations continued into 1971 (when 10 out of 11 enemy trawlers were either sunk or turned back) as the Vietnamization of the outer barrier was enacted. Between 1971 and 1972, all 26 Coast Guard cutters from that screen were turned over to the VNN.

OPERATION END SWEEP

On 8 May 1972, three Marine A-6 Intruder and six Navy A-7 Corsair attack aircraft launched from the aircraft carrier USS *Coral Sea* (CVA 43), carrying mines bound for the river approaches to Haiphong Har-bor through which passed most of North Vietnam's imported war ma-terial and all of its fuel. The U.S. decision to mine was motivated by the need to deny North Vietnamese forces invading South Vietnam the lo-gistical means to sustain their offensive against the cities of Quang Tri, Pleiku, An Loc, Hue, and Da Nang, which had been attacked or were threatened. After laying their load of Mk 52 mines and Mk 36 destruc-tors, the planes returned to the carrier. In succeeding days and months, other carrier aircraft laid thousands more destructors in the six principal ports of Haiphong (Hon Gai, Cam Pha, Quang Khe, Thanh Hoa, Vinh, and Dong Hoi) and "reseeded" the Haiphong approaches to complete the operation. For the remainder of 1972, twenty-seven Sino-Soviet merchant ships remained trapped in Haiphong and none of the nations trading with Hanoi would risk steaming their ships through the American minefields to enter port. The offensive mining campaign, in conjunction with air attacks on North Vietnam's land supply lines, severely curtailed the supply of munitions to Communist forces mounting the "Easter Offensive" in South Vietnam. The subsequent U.S. LINEBACKER II or "Christmas bombing" campaign of Hanoi and North Vietnam, begun 18 December 1972, finally persuaded Hanoi to negotiate seriously an end to the prolonged conflict.[69]

With President Nixon's announcement of the mining of North Vietnamese ports by U.S. aircraft on 11 May 1972, followed by a report five days later in the *Washington Evening Star* that stated "Nixon says mines will go when POWs are free," minesweepers, low amongst Navy priorities, rapidly became a topic of vital concern. The Navy believed before it laid the mines that it might be ultimately responsible for clearing them as a provision of future peace negotiations, and this presumption proved valid. On 23 January 1973, Henry A. Kissinger and Le Duc Tho, acting on behalf of the United States and the Democratic Republic of Vietnam, initiated the 1973 Paris Agreement on Ending the War and Restoring Peace in Vietnam. At the conclusion of the talks, the United States became responsible for neutralizing the mines under the terms of the 1973 Peace Accords. Subsequent negotiations to discuss the details of the operation would take place in Haiphong, Saigon, and aboard a U.S. Navy ship in the Gulf of Tonkin. The follow-on activity of minesweeping helicopters and ocean minesweepers to render safe the approaches and harbors of North Vietnam was code-named Operation END SWEEP. Lasting from 6 February to 18 July 1973, the effort would be the U.S. Navy's largest mine countermeasures operation since October 1950, when 3,000 North Korean mines, spread over a 400-square mile field, had prevented an armada of allied ships from landing troops ashore at Wonsan for almost a week.[70]

The Navy had to scramble to put together an adequate force of ships and helicopters to deal with the mines, and it would not be ready to proceed until early 1973 because the ocean minesweepers were not in a state of readiness and the helicopters lacked experience in conducting mine clearance operations. Ocean minesweepers, the backbone of the large mine countermeasures force that had resulted from the somber experience of the Korean War, had suffered a gradual deterioration of numbers and material condition in the 1960s and early 1970s. Over a two-year period, the numbers of MSOs operating in the Western Pacific had declined from twenty in 1970 to five in May 1972, as all but the Mine Flotilla 1 ships had returned to the United States for planned transfer to the Naval Reserve, inactivation, or scrapping. Additionally, while the MSOs had been designed to be the most sophisticated mine countermeasures ships when built, control and monitoring of their magnetic condition had been relaxed through the years. Initial reports from Mine Flotilla 1 indicated that all Western Pacific MSOs had unsatisfactory magnetic signatures, a term referring to a ship's susceptibility to causing a disturbance in the Earth's magnetic field sufficient to detonate a mine. Constructed largely of non-magnetic materials that were more expensive and difficult to obtain, MSOs had over the years been repaired in ways that increased magnetic signatures. (Excessive signatures would continue to haunt the U.S. Navy. Almost twenty years later, in 1990-1991, the relatively high magnetic and acoustic signatures of U.S. mine countermeasures ships would primarily limit their use during Operation DESERT STORM to support of U.S. minesweeping helicopters performing precursor sweeps while a British MCM flotilla performed the bulk of the mine clearance.)[71]

In May 1972, the U.S. Navy surface mine countermeasures force consisted of thirty-nine ocean minesweepers (MSO), twenty coastal minesweepers (MSC), nineteen minesweeping boats (MSB), twelve minesweeping launches (MSL), and one special minesweeper (MSS). Five active MSOs were assigned to Mine Flotilla 1 at Guam. Fifteen active and reserve ocean minesweepers served on the East Coast as part of Mine Flotilla 2 at Charleston, and nineteen active and reserve ships as part of Mine Flotilla 3 on the West Coast. The coastal minesweepers, now all in either reserve or inactive status, were split between the East Coast (11 ships) and West Coast (9 ships). One squadron of nineteen 57-foot minesweeping boats and twelve 36-foot minesweeping launches was based at Charleston, as well as one special minesweeper vessel (MSS 1), a former *Liberty*-ship that had been converted specifically for use against pressure mines and which could perform magnetic and acoustic sweeping.[72]

In spite of these challenges, U.S. Navy persistence ultimately prevailed, perhaps to the future disadvantage of the service. While the ineffectiveness of mine countermeasures efforts at Wonsan had spurred a renaissance in mine warfare, the Navy's success at Haiphong in neutralizing its own mines probably presented a false picture of its future capabilities to rapidly locate and counter enemy mines for which it did not have complete knowledge of location and capabilities. Moreover, the extensive use of minesweeping helicopters seemed to validate a decision by the Navy in 1970 to reduce its numbers of minesweepers (and thereby avoid the increasing costs of maintaining and operating the Vietnam-era force of MSOs), and rely primarily on airborne mine countermeasures. The helicopters were required to conduct clearance efforts in shallow waters because of insufficient maneuvering room for ocean, coastal, or smaller minesweepers and the possibility that the sensitive Mk 36 destructors might damage the ships. Accordingly, the MSOs worked deeper areas (where the water column between the mines and their hulls would be more likely to absorb the force of any detonations induced by sweep gear) and provided the air control and navigation required by the helicopters conducting minesweeping operations.[73]

However, the future was unknown in fall 1972 as Navy and Marine Corp units received deployment orders. As Mine Flotilla 1 ships were en route Chinhae, South Korea to participate in an exercise, *Impervious* received orders recalling her to Guam to prepare for an immediate deployment to the Western Pacific. *Force* and *Inflict* continued onward, stopping briefly for fuel on 1 September at Buckner Bay, Okinawa. Two days out of port, *Force* suffered a casualty to a main engine and was rerouted to Sasebo for voyage repairs. Arriving at Chinhae, *Inflict* spent the next two weeks participating in the mine exercise and sailed at completion for a port call at Sasebo. While the ship was en route, though, the planned visit was cancelled and she set a course for Guam. However, a typhoon lying across her track caused her to divert to Kaohsiung and then to Subic Bay. *Force*, under way from Sasebo for Subic Bay, also had to divert to Kaohsiung for storm evasion. Arriving at Subic, *Inflict* joined the rest of the flotilla, which was preparing to undertake a possible sweep operation in the Gulf of Tonkin. Mine Flotilla 1 had been established on 1 October 1971 at Guam, Marianas Islands, with ships from Mine Divisions 31 and 35 based formerly in Pearl Harbor and Long Beach, California. Now sited much closer to Vietnam, flotilla units—*Engage, Force, Fortify, Impervious,* and *Inflict*—continued to operate there regularly.[74]

The end of October found *Inflict* lying off the North Vietnamese coastline, sent to hostile waters to conduct a magnetic environmental conditions survey of the "*Strauss-Warrington* area" to determine if conditions conducive to minesweeping existed. This area off Dong Hoi was so-called because in it on 4 June the destroyer USS *Joseph Strauss* (DDG 16) had been rocked by an underwater explosion and on 17 July the destroyer USS *Warrington* (DD 843) was seriously damaged by an explosion as they conducted naval shore bombardment missions. Navy experts believed that stray U.S. Mk 36 destructor mines, dropped due to a navigation error of an aircraft attempting to jettison its load of weapons, might be the source of the explosions. On 5 September, the Navy considered the possibility of sweeping the area with ocean minesweepers. Because it was located in the open sea, ten to twenty miles northeast of Dong Hoi with adequate water depths of sixty to eighty feet, MSOs pulsing electricity through their magnetic cables ("magtails") were considered the best method of clearance. However, the unintentional minefield was never cleared, except perhaps through self-destruction of the destructors. During the next three weeks, *Inflict* endured hostile shelling, a fire on board, and a typhoon; the latter she evaded, seeking safety first in Da Nang and then in Cam Ranh Bay, South Vietnam. Leaving Cam Ranh Bay in the middle of November, *Inflict* sailed for Subic Bay to join the other units of Mine Flotilla 1 in preparation for possible mine clearance operations off North Vietnam. Following her arrival at Subic, *Inflict* participated in the training of crews of minesweeping helicopters deployed from Norfolk, Virginia. Flotilla mate *Engage* spent the first two weeks of January 1973 at Subic, preparing for Operation END SWEEP by taking part in minesweeping exercises conducted in local waters. The latter part of the month she spent in port, engaged in last minute training, upkeep, and the offload of non-essential materials to reduce her magnetic signature.[75]

The preceding year had been a busy one for Mine Flotilla 1 ships. *Force, Fortify, Impervious,* and *Inflict* had participated from 2 March to 15 December 1972 as units of Task Force 115 in interdicting enemy supply lines into South Vietnam. During this period, task force units destroyed or captured large quantities of war materials, conducted gunfire support missions, completed search and rescue operations, carried out psychological warfare missions and medical civic action programs, and conducted training programs for Vietnamese naval personnel. These activities preceded the turnover of the Coastal

Surveillance System and the operational control of the inner and outer coastal barriers to the Vietnamese Navy.

On 8 November 1972, the day following the presidential election, three Mine Flotilla 3 units, *Leader*, *Enhance*, and *Illusive*, based at Long Beach, received verbal orders to make all preparations to sail to the Western Pacific to conduct minesweeping operations along the coast of North Vietnam. To prepare for this operation, which was classified Secret for the next several months, the three MSOs put to sea on 20 November for a condensed minesweeping exercise off Huntington Beach in southern California. Entering port after twenty-four hours of straight work, *Leader* on-loaded her magnetic material before standing down for the Thanksgiving holiday. She had earlier, on 15 November, off-loaded magnetic material and on-loaded ammunition at Long Beach Naval Station in preparation for making runs (passes) on the Long Beach degaussing range to "check range" and calibrate her degaussing system.[76]

Under special orders on 4 December 1972, Task Unit 10.5.1, composed of *Enhance*, *Illusive*, and *Leader*, left Long Beach for Pearl Harbor in a cold and lashing rainstorm. After weathering high seas and heavy rains for the first two days of the transit, the three ships settled down to an uneventful passage in calm weather and placid seas. The ships of the task unit refueled from the fleet ocean tug USS *Cocopa* (ATF 101) on 9 December and stood into Pearl Harbor at first light five days later. Originally planning to remain at Pearl Harbor only long enough to refuel and re-provision, the ships were forced by extensive engine repairs to *Enhance* and a temporary stalemate in the Vietnam peace talks to remain in port through year's end, awaiting sailing orders for continued transit to Westpac.[77]

On 10 January 1973, Rear Adm. Brian McCauley, Commander Mine Warfare Forces and Commander Task Force 78, met with key members of all mine warfare forces present in Subic Bay. The watchword at that time was still "wait" as negotiations in Paris continued to unfold. The ships were informed on the 25th that TF 78 would sail in three days for mine clearance operations off the coast of Vietnam, and the next three days were hectic as task force units readied themselves for the mission. Finally, on 28 January, following months of preparation and training, the initial units of the 7th Fleet's Mine Countermeasures Force, led by McCauley, departed Subic Bay for a staging area off Haiphong. During the ensuing six-month long operation, a total of ten ocean minesweepers, nine amphibious ships, six fleet tugs, three salvage ships, and nineteen destroyer-type ships would serve with Task Force 78. Included in the initial group of ships were four of the five Mine Flotilla 1 units, *Engage*, *Force*, *Impervious*, and *Fortify*, with the flotilla commander embarked, and the salvage ship USS *Safeguard* (ARS 33) as damage support contingency vessel. *Inflict* would join the operations on 16 April 1973. Two days later, the group reached a holding area about one hundred miles east of the DMZ, near Yankee Station, where it awaited further instruction. On 31 January, the cruiser USS *Worden* (DLG 18) and the destroyer USS *Epperson* (DD 716) joined the task group to provide force protection. On 2 February, the task group units replenished from the oiler USS *Ponchatoula* (AO 148).[78]

Also on 28 January, the Chief of Naval Operations ordered the activation of now reserve Mine Division 54 ships *Conquest* and *Esteem*, based in Pearl Harbor, for immediate deployment to participate in END SWEEP. The nucleus crews of the minesweepers, reduced to thirty-five men upon their transfer to the Naval Reserve Force, were augmented by officer and enlisted personnel from Charleston-based mine warfare forces, the ocean minesweepers *Assurance*, *Affray*, *Adroit*, *Fidelity*, and *Fearless*, and Mine Squadron 10. Upon their activation, the administrative and operational control of the two ships reverted to Commander Mine Flotilla 3, and on 22 February the two MSOs, in company with the fleet ocean tug USS *Moctobi* (ATF 105), departed Hawaii for Guam, arriving on 10 March for an indefinite period.[79]

On 5 February, the four Mine Flotilla 1 minesweepers in theater received orders to move north to begin minesweeping operations outside Haiphong Harbor to clear anchorage areas for the larger helicopter support ships of Task Force 78. Operation END SWEEP began formally on 6 February, the day after McCauley met with Col. Hoang Huu Thai, his North Vietnamese counterpart. The operation was historical and unique in that it was the first time in history that the U.S. Navy engaged in neutralizing U.S-laid mine fields with air and surface units in formerly hostile waters. Following arrival at Haiphong Harbor roadstead, the minesweepers laid master reference buoys (MRBs) in preparation for minesweeping. (The MSOs typically used an MRB as a point of reference while "driving up and down" adjacent lanes, laid out on a nautical chart with spacing based on the propagation of sonar in the water at that particular location.) *Fortify* and *Force* streamed their magnetic cables and acoustic noisemakers to perform a combination-influence sweep of the area where *Worden*, the support ship for local negotiations

Photo 6-8

Fortify, Impervious, Engage, and *Force* depart Subic Bay on their way to Operation END SWEEP (Official U.S. Navy Photograph from the National Archives)

between United States and Democratic Republic of Vietnam representatives, would anchor. (Both sides had agreed to meet on a rotating basis in Hanoi and on board the cruiser to discuss the details of how much and what type of mine clearance would be provided.) *Impervious* then laid Dan buoys to mark the boundaries of the safe area. Upon completion of the liaison area on the 6th, the minesweepers moved to the proposed amphibious ship anchorage area. In addition to sweeping the anchorages and marking them, the MSOs also laid buoys marking the boundaries of swept channels that led from one anchorage to another. On 8 February, the tank landing ship USS *Westchester County* (LST 1157) arrived in the area. She served as the primary minesweeper logistics support ship and the flagship for Commander, Mine Flotilla 1. For the MSOs, minesweeping and laying master reference buoys continued to be the mainstays of employment through the end of the month. Between 8 and 26 February, *Impervious* swept various seaward approaches to Haiphong, conducted oceanographic surveys, laid MRBs, and engaged in marking and recovery operations. *Fortify* performed similar tasks and, following the commencement of airborne operations, served twice as a search and rescue ship for crashed helicopters.[80]

By the end of February 1973, the amphibious ships *New Orleans* (LPH 11), *Dubuque* (LPD 8), *Ogdon* (LPD 5), *Cleveland* (LPD 7), and *Inchon* (LPH 12) had arrived off North Vietnam. Aboard the "gators" were the CH-53 Sea Stallion helicopters from Navy Helicopter Mine Countermeasures Squadron 12 and Marine Helicopter Squadrons HMM 165 and HMH 463. The first helicopter sweep in a live minefield, in the Haiphong main channel, took place on 27 February. During ensuring operations, the specialized aircraft towed minesweeping sleds and other devices to conduct mine countermeasures in the inland waterways and shallow port areas of North Vietnam. The basic sweep was the Mk 105 hydrofoil sled supporting an electrical generator, which powered a standard "magnetic tail" streamed astern. This unit, however, proved to be difficult to launch and tow compared with a magnetized iron pipe filled with Styrofoam for floatation. These pipes, painted orange for better visibility, were commonly known as MOPs (Magnetic Orange Pipe). To work against acoustic influence or combination magnetic acoustic triggered mines, the helicopters towed noisemakers independently or astern of either the Mk 105 sled or MOP. The MSOs continued to perform minesweeping or, while at anchor, provide air control and navigation for helicopters conducting mine countermeasures.[81]

On 28 February, Task Force 78 was ordered to sortie (withdraw) to a holding area in the southern portion of the Gulf of Tonkin, about fifty miles south of Haiphong, while United States representatives negotiated with Democratic Republic of Vietnam representatives concerning the release of U.S. prisoners of war held in North Vietnam.

Photo 6-9

A Marine Heavy Helicopter Squadron 463 CH-53D Sea Stallion helicopter with a magnetic orange pipe in tow sweeps Haiphong Bay during Operation END SWEEP (Official U.S. Navy Photograph from the National Archives)

The ships steamed in the Gulf of Tonkin until their return on 4 March to Haiphong Harbor after the POW release issue was resolved.[82]

On 6 March, minesweeping resumed in earnest and for the next six weeks helicopters and minesweepers worked the northern ports of Haiphong, Hon Gai, and Cam Pha; the former location included the Cua Cam and main channel to Haiphong. Aircraft also swept the Lach Huyen area and the Hon Gai approach to Passe Henriette. *Engage* spent a majority of her time between 5 and 30 March engaged in helicopter control operations. Minesweepers *Enhance*, *Illusive*, and *Leader* arrived on scene on 15 March from Long Beach. They had reached the Gulf of Tonkin six days earlier after having been in transit for over three months, delayed by voyage repairs, fuel stops, and political/diplomatic hold-ups. To help prepare for operations upon arrival, the three ships conducted training en route the Western Pacific.[83]

On 17 March, *Enhance* was operating in the Hon Gai area, providing air control for minesweeping helicopter operations. That night, fire broke out in her forward engine room at 9:50 p.m., caused by diesel from a leaking 185-kilowatt generator fuel line spraying onto the hot engine. The fire quickly raged out of control and spread into the area above the generator, causing the loss of electrical power, although not before an emergency message had been transmitted for help. Repair parties valiantly battled the flames using fire hoses spraying salt water supplied by portable gasoline pumps that also fed the installed aqueous-film-forming-foam sprinkler system, re-supplied with cans of gasoline (for the pumps) and foam concentrate by helicopter. *Illusive* and *Safeguard* rushed to the scene, transiting "unswept" waters, and *Safeguard* moored to *Enhance*'s starboard side to provide additional firefighting water and relief hose teams. *Engage*, arriving after weighing anchor, provided illumination to firefighters and supplied *Safeguard* with additional cans of gasoline. *Fortify* evacuated crewmembers from *Enhance* as *Safeguard* brought the blaze under control. By daybreak on the 18th, the fire was out and all but fifteen crewmembers had been transferred to an amphibious transport dock ship for transportation to Subic Bay. Rear Adm. McCauley boarded the ship later in the day for a first-hand assessment of the damage, and *Enhance* was then towed by the fleet ocean tug *Chowanoc* (ATF 100) to Subic Bay for repairs, removing her from service for the duration of END SWEEP.[84]

Engage refueled on 19 March from the amphibious transport dock USS *Cleveland* (LPD 7), which functioned as a helicopter carrier and provided limited fueling capabilities to the minesweepers. On the 27th of March, after again refueling from the *Cleveland*, *Engage* left with *Fortify* for upkeep in Subic Bay, arriving on 31 March following sixty-three days at sea. After two months, the initial TF 78 ships to arrive off North Vietnam required upkeep, maintenance, and rest and recuperation time, provisions for which had been made in END SWEEP scheduling.[85]

At month's end, as MSOs worked in the Cam Pha approaches and the helicopters swept in the Hon Gai and main Haiphong channels, *Impervious* controlled minesweeping helicopters while lying at anchor, vice conducting minesweeping herself. In April, airborne units swept in the Haiphong, Hon Gai, and Cam Pha channels as MSOs worked the Cam Pha approaches and the outer three miles of the main Haiphong channel. *Impervious* provided air control from 1-16 April for helicopters in the vicinity of the Hon Gai roadsteads. From 14 to 18 April, *Conquest* acted as both an air control ship for helicopter minesweeping and as a sonar search unit for the salvage ship USS *Bolster* (ARS 38).[86]

Earlier, on 6 April, the former tank landing ship USS *Washtenaw County* (LST 1166), now the newly converted Special Minesweeper (MSS 2), had arrived in the Haiphong area. The MSS 2 was used for pressure mine and check sweeping. It made several passages beginning on 14 April through the main Haiphong channel to demonstrate the effectiveness of mine clearance efforts, conducting the last runs on 20 June. The use of a "guinea pig" ship to demonstrate that previously mined waters were safe for shipping, following mine clearance efforts, was not a new idea. During post-World War II mine clearance operations in the Western Pacific, the U.S. Navy had dispatched large derelict ships to make high-speed runs through channels where pressure mines were supposed to have been sterilized. The first guinea pig ship was the attack transport USS *Marathon* (APA 200) which had been damaged by a kaiten (a one-man suicide Japanese submarine, launched by submarine I-53) at Buckner Bay, Okinawa; two others were damaged merchant cargo ships, SS *Joseph Holt* and SS *Pratt Victory*. LST 553 and LST 768 also worked as pigs. During operations in World War II, to minimize the possibility that the volunteer crewmembers might be injured or killed by a mine explosion, the modified ships were fitted with remotely operated gear in order that mine clearance could be conducted with all hands stationed topside, wearing helmets and standing on piles of mattresses.[87]

Inflict left Subic Bay on 12 April for the Gulf of Tonkin. Following her arrival, she conducted END SWEEP operations with Task Unit 78.2.0. On the night of 16 April, TG 78.2 was ordered to sortie from the Haiphong area, again due to a breakdown in the ongoing peace negotiations. *Engage* and *Fortify* joined the task group a few days later as it headed south to a holding area, where it remained until ordered on 23 April to proceed to Subic Bay; arriving two days later, the ships were put in a "ready group status" pending negotiations between North Vietnam and the Republic of South Vietnam. Tragically, the following day, *Force* sank approximately 770 miles west of Guam due to a fire originating in her aft engine room. Detached on 12 April from Task Force 78 to proceed independently to Guam for a regularly scheduled overhaul, she was en route after stopping at Subic for fuel. Fortunately, none of her crew suffered serious injuries and, forced to abandon ship, all hands were rescued by a merchant ship late on the same day. This was the second serious engine room fire in a task force minesweeper and the second fire *Force* had experienced since departing Subic for END SWEEP in January.[88]

Conquest, Esteem, Illusive, and *Inflict* departed Subic Bay on 9 June for a port visit to Kaohsiung, Taiwan before sailing on 15 June for Vinh, North Vietnam to resume END SWEEP operations. The remaining units of TG 78.2 left Subic Bay on 15 June for Haiphong. The task group was comprised of the *Westchester County* with Commander, Mine Flotilla 1 embarked, the *Washtenaw County,* the salvage ship USS *Grasp* (ARS 24), the ocean minesweepers *Engage, Impervious,* and *Leader,* and the *Moctobi.* The ships arrived at the Haiphong Harbor roadstead the following day. During End Sweep, the oiler USS *Guadalupe* (AO 32) anchored in Haiphong Harbor for a period and refueled the MSOs. Two of the stipulations of a joint U.S.–North Vietnamese mine clearance protocol were that the Democratic Republic of Vietnam would ensure the safety of U.S. personnel for the duration of mine clearance activities and that the U.S. personnel engaged in these operations would not conduct activities inconsistent with ending the war in Vietnam and restoring the peace. A *Guadalupe* crewmember recalled, "North Vietnamese gun boats were always around us and we had to keep our three-inch guns covered at all times."[89]

By June, all remaining U.S. mines were well past their self-destruct date, and considerable statistical data gave evidence that the vast majority of mines would have self-destructed and any remaining would be inert and totally deactivated. Therefore, all sweeping conducted after 18 June was "exploratory," less time consuming than check or clearance sweeping as it requires fewer passes through a suspected area. Task Force 78 units completed sweeping the northern ports on 26 June and departed for Vinh. *Impervious,* which had been engaged in providing helicopter control at Cam Pha Roadsteads, sailed with TG 78.1, comprised of the amphibious transport dock USS *Vancouver* (LPD 2), the amphibious assault ship USS *Inchon* (LPH 12), *Moctobi, Illusive,* and *Inflict.*[90]

On 28 June, sweeping in North Vietnamese waters resumed with helicopters located north of the Sot River and just off the entrance to the river near Vinh. The following day, helicopters swept in the Hon La coastal area and near Quang Khe, seventy-five miles to the southeast. Airborne sweeping continued in the Sot River and in the Hon La, Quang Khe, and Vinh areas through early July. U.S. planned sweeping in the ports of Thanh Hoa and Dong Hoi was never accomplished because negotiations with Democratic Republic of Vietnam representatives to approve this action proved futile. As completion of END SWEEP operations drew closer, the MSOs remained busy. *Esteem*, assigned to mine hunt in Haiphong Harbor during periods between 20 June and 12 July, alternately worked the harbor and moored for short periods alongside the *Westchester County*. Following her arrival at Vinh, *Impervious* controlled minesweeping helicopters in the area. On 3 July, a HM-53 minesweeping helicopter crashed into the sea about fifteen hundred yards off the coast of Vinh. *Impervious* located and marked the tail section of the lost aircraft while at the same time still controlling airborne helicopters. On 9 July, *Impervious* proceeded in company with *Moctobi* for Haiphong Harbor, arriving on 11 July. The following day *Esteem* departed Subic Bay under tow by *Moctobi*.[91]

The two vessels soon encountered difficulties. *Esteem* lost steering control on 16 July in the heavy seas of Typhoon Anita and slowly swung to port while the fleet ocean tug went to starboard. The helmsman in the pilothouse alerted the bridge by voice tube and sounded the loss of steering alarm to alert the watch teams on the minesweeper and tug, but to no avail due to the noise from wind and waves. Sounding the General Quarters alarm was also futile, as the MSO had veered too far to port out of the tug's hearing, and crewmembers could only watch as the towing line and then the anchor chain attached to it paid out. When the bitter end of the chain was reached, the chain laid over one side of the bull nose (through which it was led on the bow) and started tearing things up, ripping off the hatch leading to the paint locker and chain locker and tearing foc'sle stanchions from the deck like toothpicks, resulting in loss of railing forward. The chain itself ran out freely until it pulled the end-stop from its bulkhead mount in the chain locker and jammed it half way up the chain pipe. Deck force members "jury-rigged" a harness over the next few hours and *Esteem* headed into Olongapo, Philippine Islands under tow again to be put back together in the yards, arriving at Subic Bay on 17 July.[92]

From 21 June to 17 July, *Engage* was employed once more primarily as a helicopter control ship. On 7 July, she weighed anchor and got under way for Passé Henriette, a shelter anchorage, to avoid Typhoon Anita. After two days, the typhoon passed and the ship left for Haiphong Harbor. *Conquest* was similarly engaged in providing support for aviation mine countermeasures operations broken by typhoon evasion. *Inflict* spent two days evading the typhoon and another day steaming back to station.[93]

Task Group 78.2 departed Haiphong Harbor, North Vietnam on 18 July for Subic Bay, bringing Operation END SWEEP to a close. The task force itself was disestablished on 28 July. *Conquest, Engage, Enhance, Esteem, Illusive, Inflict, Impervious,* and *Leader* left Subic in company on 31 July for Guam, arriving at Apra Harbor on 7 August 1973. (*Fortify* had arrived there two months earlier to commence a regularly scheduled overhaul.) Bidding the Mine Flotilla 1 ships goodbye, *Conquest, Enhance, Esteem, Illusive,* and *Leader* departed Guam for Pearl Harbor on 13 August, accompanied by the oiler USS *Caliente* (AO 53), which detached from the group three days before the minesweepers arrived in port on 27 August. Here, the temporarily assigned personnel from mine warfare units in Charleston, which had arrived aboard *Esteem* in February to augment her nucleus crew during operations, departed. With the Pearl Harbor–based Mine Division 54 ships now in homeport, the Mine Flotilla 3 sweeps pressed onward to Long Beach; *Enhance* arrived home on 10 September.[94]

Operation END SWEEP presented the first opportunity for mine countermeasures ships and minesweeping helicopters to work together in a large-scale mine clearance operation, and helped identify how they might best complement one another. The mission demanded the use of all thirteen Navy CH-53D helicopters and an additional twenty-four Marine Corps CH-53s converted for minesweeping. The helicopters could be rapidly deployed overseas, were relatively immune to damage from exploding ordnance, and were able to operate in waters too shallow for minesweepers. However, the aircraft could only remain on task for limited periods, unless able to operate from and receive support from a "helicopter-carrier" positioned nearby. A large-deck ship, either an amphibious transport dock (LPD) or an amphibious assault ship (LPH) was an ideal platform for such a task. However, these ships represented the major troop carriers, were the only platforms for vertical assault, and comprised a significant portion of the well-deck battalion landing team capability that is vital to amphibious assault. (This shortcoming would resurface in 1990-1991 when, during Operation DESERT SHIELD/STORM, both Commander, U.S. Naval Forces, Central Command and his amphibious task force commander were loath initially to dedicate a major vessel, essential for the conduct of amphibious aerial assault, to the mine clearance mission.) Moreover, the helicopters could not operate during restricted visibility conditions and could not neutralize deep-moored or pressure mines. The minesweepers were able to remain on station, constrained only by crew fatigue and maintenance requirements that necessitated some time off-task for rest and particularly bad sea conditions that precluded minehunting and minesweeping. The MSOs were able to counter all types of mines, except those planted in shallow waters and those triggered by a change in water pressure caused by a passing vessel. For the latter type of ship killers, it was still necessary for a "guinea pig" to steam in harm's way in an effort to detonate them.[95]

A full six months of hard effort was required to sweep two types of simple magnetic mines of known settings and locations placed in the waters of North Vietnam by U.S. forces. The resources available to the Navy then (much fewer today) would have been inadequate to cope with a similar number of unknown mines. Success was achieved in END SWEEP primarily because the U.S. mines had known influence characteristics and could be swept efficiently by U.S. mine forces. Had moored mines been added to the minefields, the clearance efforts would have been considerably more complex and time consuming.[96]

7 Naval Reserve Force Duty

The reservist is twice the citizen.
Attributed to Winston Churchill (1874–1965)

The former British Prime Minister was no doubt referring in the above tribute to the continuous, albeit part-time, engagement of reservists in their country's military that directly enables the maintenance of (and if necessary, the wartime mobilization of) a larger and more capable force. Citizen-sailors also provide a very important link between the active-duty military and legislators and members of large and small communities all across the nation that collectively determine its size and level of support.

The tradition of a reserve militia to serve the United States dates back to colonial days. In 1887, the Navy Department prepared a plan of organization that gave the Secretary of the Navy authority to lend each state with a naval militia one of the Navy's older ships, as well as equipment, to "promote drills and instruction." In 1915, Congress formally created a "Federal Naval Reserve," the ancestor organization of today's Naval Surface Reserve Force.

The use of reservists to augment the crews of reserve ships allows the Navy to "husband" vessels that would otherwise be decommissioned because they are not affordable. A majority of total surface force funding is consumed by recapitalization (procurement) of new ships to replace those whose service lives have expired; the cost to operate, maintain, and repair existing ships; and the pay for the people who crew them. Faced with decreased funding—usually in post-war years—and a shrinking fleet, the Navy can reduce the costs to operate lower priority, but still important and necessary, vessels. This is accomplished by drawing down the number of active-duty crewmembers aboard ships and transferring them to the Naval Reserve (where part-time, and therefore less expensive, reservists comprise the balance of their crews), allocating less underway time and reducing funds for maintenance and training.

From a top-down perspective, the above practice is both long-standing and successful, and it enables the Navy to keep more ships afloat. However, the view from the deck plates is, not unsurprisingly, different. Maintaining high standards of readiness with fewer people and fewer resources for training, maintenance, and repair of equipment is challenging—even more so if ships are "mature" and in need of care when consigned to the reserves.

In 1970, the Navy began to reduce the number of ocean mine-sweepers. Some of the decommissioned ships were struck, transferred to foreign navies, or laid up as mobilization assets. Twenty-four MSOs were reassigned as Naval Reserve Force training ships, thirteen in the Atlantic Fleet and eleven in the Pacific Fleet.

Atlantic Fleet		Pacific Fleet	
Adroit	(MSO 509)	*Conquest*	(MSO 488)
Affray	(MSO 511)	*Constant*	(MSO 427)
Dash	(MSO 428)	*Embattle*	(MSO 434)
Detector	(MSO 429)	*Enhance*	(MSO 437)
Direct	(MSO 430)	*Esteem*	(MSO 438)
Dominant	(MSO 431)	*Excel*	(MSO 439)
Engage	(MSO 433)	*Gallant*	(MSO 489)
Exploit	(MSO 440)	*Implicit*	(MSO 455)
Exultant	(MSO 441)	*Pledge*	(MSO 492)
Fearless	(MSO 442)	*Pluck*	(MSO 464)
Fortify	(MSO 446)	*Reaper*	(MSO 467)
Inflict	(MSO 456)		
Impervious	(MSO 449)		

While active MSOs were manned by crews of seventy-two to seventy-six officers and enlisted men, the reserve training ships had a core crew of only three officers and thirty-six enlisted active-duty Navy personnel, plus a selected reserve component of two officers and twenty-nine enlisted men to round out the crew. The reservists trained aboard ship one weekend per month and during a two-week "active duty for training" period each summer. Qualified reservists were occasionally embarked for long deployments, sometimes of several months, when funding was made available. In the 1980s, as the Navy expanded toward a goal of six hundred ships and placed increased emphasis on mine warfare, the number of active-duty personnel assigned to the reserve ships increased. However, due to a scarcity of resources, the 1970s and early 1980s were the "dog days" in the service life of the reserve MSOs when legislators expected a "peace dividend" following the Vietnam War and funding for operations and maintenance was accordingly decreased.

There was also occasional conflict between active-duty and reserve crewmembers. For all but one weekend a month when the reservists making up the balance of the crew came aboard, the active-duty component worked extraordinarily hard to complete all of the ship's work, and they perceived the reserves with some resentment as civilians merely looking forward to a fun weekend away from the routine of their jobs. This sometimes love–sometimes hate relationship was described thus by a Captain in the Naval Reserve:

> The problem was the Mine Force never had enough resources. There was never enough money for maintenance and there was never enough money for training. Also, there were cultural differences between the regular crews and reservists. At the individual level, it was "I wouldn't get underway without Chief Smith" and not "those damn reservists," but at the organization level there was always some friction.

Although life aboard a reserve MSO was challenging, minesweeper duty, whether aboard an active or reserve ship, continued to attract those seeking the increased responsibility afforded by service aboard a small vessel. This experience is summarized well by a former crewmember of USS *Bold*:

> During all my time on the *Bold*, I had the sense of doing something important. Whether it was searching for a lost shrimp boat, a prototype gun barrel lost over the side, checking out the Russian Navy, tracking a small boat acting as a gunrunner, or just practicing mine sweeping it was all-important to the big scheme of things. There was never a dull moment aboard a sweep. The crew was pretty tight and acted as a unit to accomplish an assigned task. We knew each other's limitations and quirks and this allowed us to be ourselves with no pretensions. Sometimes I think that being a part of the crew of a minesweeper made one a better sailor. Extensive duties or responsibility at an early age or

junior pay grade contributed to learning and doing more than was required. Looking back, it was a real experience.[1]

Reserve minesweepers periodically got underway to provide training for their combined nucleus and selected reserve crew and other reservists performing their annual two weeks of active duty for training or monthly drill periods. Time at sea was devoted to mine warfare training in local waters to maintain proficiency, periodic visits to degaussing facilities for magnetic stray field tests and check ranging, participation in mine warfare exercises and two-week summer cruises, port visits for crew liberty, and support of community celebrations and Navy recruiting.

The minesweepers also operated at sea, with or without the reserves, preparing for inspections used to assess their operational prowess and material condition. The most important—and dreaded—of these was the Mine Readiness Certification Inspection conducted by a Charleston-based team led by a senior officer and composed mostly of Warrant Officers and Master Chief Petty Officers who examined every aspect of the operations and maintenance of the ship as well as supporting management programs. Success meant that the ship was certified to conduct mine clearance.

PACIFIC FLEET

Following the post–Vietnam War drawdown, all eleven remaining Pacific Fleet minesweepers were transferred to the Reserve Force and assigned to Mine Flotilla 3, the headquarters of which was located in Long Beach. Mine Flotilla 3 was redesignated on 30 June 1973 as Mine Squadron 5, and in August 1980, after having been based for more than thirty years in Long Beach (originally as Mine Flotilla 3), relocated to Naval Support Activity, Seattle, Washington, at Sand Point. In 1984, the designation of Mine Squadron 5 was changed to Mine Group 1.

Embattle and *Reaper* were decommissioned on 22 September 1972 and there were, during the 1970s, some redesignations of mine divisions and associated changes of homeports. However, after August 1980, the organization was set: Mine Division 51 ships *Enhance* and *Implicit* were homeported in Tacoma, Washington; MinDiv 52 ships *Excel* and *Gallant* in San Francisco; MinDiv 53, *Conquest*, *Esteem*, and *Pledge*, in Seattle; and MinDiv 54, *Constant* and *Pluck*, in San Diego.

A few coastal minesweepers (MSC) were also originally assigned to Mine Divisions 51, 52, and 53. After they were decommissioned on 1 July 1975, an associated movement of MSOs occurred between divisions to distribute more equitably the remaining mine warfare ships.

The nine ocean minesweepers were dispersed to support three West Coast areas of major naval fleet concentrations: Long Beach and San Diego, San Francisco, and Seattle. Five of the nine sweeps were based in the latter area due to the vast inland waterways leading to key ports and facilities. The role of the MSOs was defensive in nature. If a hostile country mined U.S. harbors, bays, or sea lanes, to bottle up or prevent the free passage of naval and merchant shipping, the MSOs were positioned to clear the mines.

In 1973, *Conquest*, *Enhance*, and *Esteem* deployed to the Western Pacific for participation in Operation END SWEEP, and *Implicit* made a three-week training cruise to Alaska. These operations marked the last time MSOs would engage in extended operations for the next ten years. In 1983, minesweepers made a summer cruise to Alaska, returning in 1984 and 1985. In the twilight of their service, three Pacific Fleet MSOs were forward deployed to the Persian Gulf from 1987 through 1990, supporting Operation EARNEST WILL. During this period, the remaining West Coast–based minesweepers trained crewmembers rotating to the Gulf to support the operation.

With no scheduled deployments and limited funding for operations and maintenance, the MSOs spent the decade between 1973 and 1983 in the doldrums. Manned by significantly reduced crews of active-duty members, the ships spent declining periods of time at sea. However, if anything, workload increased. With their wooden hulls crammed full of equipment and machinery, the MSOs were maintenance intensive and fewer crewmembers meant more work for those remaining. Doing the same with less became doing more with less, as funding shortfalls resulted in a shift of some work traditionally done by shipyards or other support activities to ship's force. These challenges were not obvious to everyone in the fleet. Some sailors, who sought duty on sweeps because they believed that since the ships did not deploy the duty would be "easy," found instead that they had to do more work than elsewhere. A small crew mandates a very thin layer of management, and everyone must do his or her share.

Staff planners endeavored to align reservist drill periods with participation in exercises or workups for required inspections, but they were not always able to do so. Consequently, the ships routinely operated shorthanded with only the active-duty members of the combined crew performing these and other tasks, including shipyard periods.

The minesweepers periodically entered dry dock for the replacement of hull sheathing and overhaul of equipment and machinery, and regularly visited degaussing ranges at the Canadian Forces' Base at Esquimalt, British Columbia or the Magnetic Silencing Facility in San Diego to validate their degaussing systems. This equipment was designed to prevent the detonation of, and associated damage to the ships from, magnetic mines.

The MSOs were often chosen to represent the U.S. Navy in festivals and community events. Ideal candidates for visits to localities with narrow channels or limited pier space at which to berth, the MSOs were economical to operate and had more flexible schedules than ships regularly deployed. Favorite celebrations included the Sea Festivals and Sea Fairs at Coos Bay, Oregon; Seattle, Washington; and Vancouver, British Columbia; Salty Sea Day Festivals at Everett, Washington; and Daffodil Festivals at Tacoma, Washington. Eureka, California and Port Townsend, Washington hosted Rhododendron Festivals; the latter city also had a Spanish Festival and a Wooden Boat Festival. Newport, on the Oregon coast, put on Loyalty Days Festivals and, inland, the city of Portland, Oregon hosted the Rose Festival, arguably the best liberty on the West Coast.

Minesweepers based in San Francisco were invited to act as the flagship and grandstand for the blessing of the fleet, conducted in Raccoon Strait. A bishop onboard *Excel*, anchored in 1975 off the Corinthian Yacht Club of Tiburon, California, blessed thousands of craft as they passed in review. The MSOs also made passage from San Francisco Bay up the San Joaquin River to the Port of Stockton for the Captain Weber Day Festival.

In addition to unique community celebrations, Pacific Fleet minesweepers attended many Fourth of July and Bicentennial festivities and also supported other events. Although the MSOs are now long gone from service, visitors to clubs and restaurants frequented by sailors in popular destinations and in small out-of-the-way ports and harbors may still find evidence that the minesweepers called there by the presence of ships' ball caps, plaques, and pictures displayed on the walls.

The next few pages are devoted to the more notable or interesting operations of the Pacific Fleet MSOs from their transfer to the reserves in the early 1970s to their end of service in the early 1990s.

Cape Flattery Surveillance Operations—1982

Surveillance of Soviet intelligence-gathering ships (AGIs) occupied many of the Pacific Fleet MSOs during the summer and fall of 1982. Tasking from Commander, 3rd Fleet had placed ships on call to assist—as necessary—with operations incident to the arrival of the first *Trident*-class submarine at the new submarine base at Bangor, Washington. On 31 July, the MSOs and other ships received orders to conduct surveillance on several AGIs operating off the coast of Washington in an effort to collect data associated with USS *Ohio*'s (SSBN 726) arrival in the Puget Sound area. During the summer and early fall, as many as five of the MSOs were at sea off Cape Flattery (see map 7-1) at one time. The minesweepers operated primarily from Port Angeles, Washington, which provided food, fuel, lube oil, and recreation. Eventually, the operation grew to encompass all nine of the Mine Squadron 5 ships and involved the entire West Coast.[2]

Conquest was on station from 31 July to 8 October, with only brief stops in port for fuel interrupting her surveillance of the AGIs shadowing the *Trident*. From 10 to 14 August, *Pledge* conducted mine countermeasures exercises off Cape Flattery and in Puget Sound, including a two-ship deep sweep, and then conducted surveillance operations off Cape Flattery in late August. Deep sweeps were used during the operation in an effort to render inoperative any deep-moored listening devices. Based on a chart obtained from a communist bloc fishing vessel, top Navy brass believed that several areas near Cape Flattery might contain bottom-tethered listening devices planted to gain acoustic information on the *Ohio* as she arrived and departed her homeport at Bangor, Washington. Any suspicious sonar contacts were to be swept with a deep-moored sweep.[3]

On 20 August, *Excel* and *Gallant* sailed from San Francisco to participate in the surveillance operation. *Gallant* operated in the Straits of Juan de Fuca and the Seattle area. To maintain continuous surveillance of the AGIs, *Esteem* and *Excel* operated alternately in the Cape Flattery area. Throughout the summer and late fall the minesweepers conducted surveillance and minesweeping operations, interrupted by brief reprieves for fuel, stores, and minor repair at Port Angeles, South Bend, and Seattle, Washington, and Esquimalt, British Columbia.[4]

Pluck was dispatched from San Diego in September for duties as a surveillance unit. She was off Cape Flattery from mid-September

Map 7-1

Washington State: During the summer and fall of 1982, Naval Reserve MSOs conducted surveillance of Soviet intelligence-gathering ships trying to collect data on the first *Trident*-class submarine to arrive at Bangor, Washington.

through early October, with rest periods at Port Angeles and at anchor in Neah Bay, Washington. *Implicit* operated off Cape Flattery from 21 September to 4 October, keeping watch on the Soviet intelligence ship AGI 468. Two ships, either MSOs or an MSO and a Coast Guard cutter, were to keep station on both sides of the AGI to observe the laying of any intelligence devices. *Implicit* made close passes along the vessel's sides to inspect her underwater hull characteristics. Her sonar display revealed, suspended beneath the Soviet ship, an array of two cables, running bow to stern, with three large, cylindrical objects supported by the cables forward, amidships, and aft.[5]

During this period, a submarine in the area, believed to be Soviet, made contact with two shrimp boats; it ensnared the nets of the first vessel and dragged it astern at four knots for about a mile before the gear parted. A submarine surfaced near a second shrimp boat, the *Howard M*, the following day and was observed on the surface for several minutes. *Implicit*'s operations officer boarded the shrimp boat to obtain sketches and a description of the submarine from her master, a former Navy cryptologist.[6]

With information obtained from the MSOs and other sources, the Navy began an antisubmarine operation utilizing Navy patrol P-3s from Pacific Northwest bases and MSOs as check-in points for relieving aircraft. In early October, AGI 468 departed the Cape Flattery area on a southwest heading, trailed by the frigate USS *Marvin Shields* (FF 1066). *Implicit* returned to Tacoma on 4 October upon completion of the operation. This was a heady time for the MSOs, which had been limited to Naval Reserve Force training during the past decade. Aboard *Excel*, crewmembers were still discussing the Cape Flattery operation a year later.[7]

Alaskan Cruise—1983

Seven of the nine Pacific Fleet minesweepers made a summer cruise in 1983 to Alaska to participate in mine countermeasures exercises in conjunction with the tank landing ship USS *Cayuga* (LST 1196) and the U.S. Coast Guard cutter *Sweetbriar* (WLB 405). The operation integrated U.S. Navy and Coast Guard forces for an open-ocean transit and port calls to various Alaskan cities, and for training reserve personnel aboard the ships during two weeks of active duty. As part of the exercises, the minesweepers employed their high-resolution sonar gear to conduct Q-route surveys. This term refers to the process of locating for future reference debris lying on the sea floor and marking its location on charts, in this case to augment existing data for the ports of Valdez, Kodiak, Seward, and Anchorage, Alaska.[8]

The five minesweepers based in Seattle and Tacoma—*Conquest, Enhance, Esteem, Implicit,* and *Pledge*—began their deployment on 7 June 1983, getting underway for Astoria, Oregon, a small town located at the mouth of the Columbia River. The group arrived the next day and was joined by *Constant* and *Gallant,* arriving from San Diego and San Francisco respectively. After embarking guests of the Navy League, with forty-two visitors aboard *Gallant* alone, the seven minesweepers made the twelve-hour scenic cruise up the winding Columbia River to Portland, Oregon for the Rose Festival. Separating the states of Washington and Oregon, the river is the chief inland tributary in the Pacific Northwest, with banks so steep in places that ships have in years past taken shelter from storms by mooring to trees.

Upon arrival in Portland, the Navy ships moored along the river wall in the heart of the city, and their crews set out to enjoy the best liberty on the West Coast. Sailors have the opportunity to enjoy a meal in the home of a congenial host or date a local girl, through a program designed to match the interests of sponsors and guests. Many crew members, believing they are more likely to win a quiet evening than a hot date, head straight for town. A daytime carnival atmosphere is replaced at night by parties. Much anticipated throughout the year leading up to the festival, these social events draw comely attendees from adjacent states as well as local areas.

On 13 June, the ships left the picturesque Rose City, framed by Mts. Hood and St. Helens, to make the return trip down river. Passing Astoria to port, they crossed the bar and turned northward along the coast of Washington. Rounding Cape Flattery the following day, they entered Puget Sound, bound via passage inland through the Straits of Juan de Fuca to Seattle.[9]

The minesweepers then, with their selected reservists embarked, left Seattle on 20 June for Alaska. The *Cayuga* accompanied the group to provide food and fuel underway. Conduct of the first of two mine exercises took place during the transit. Arriving in Alaskan waters, the MSOs proceeded in groups to different destinations to complete their portions of the second exercise, which included Q-route surveys. *Constant* and *Implicit* made for Kodiak Island and conducted mine countermeasures operations, anchoring nightly in Kodiak Bay. *Pledge* arrived in

Cook Inlet, and *Conquest* and *Esteem* operated in Prince William Sound. Following completion of the exercise, the ships entered port cities to enjoy their Fourth of July celebrations. *Implicit* visited Kodiak, *Enhance* and *Pledge*, Seward, *Conquest* and *Esteem*, Valdez, and *Constant* and *Gallant*, Anchorage (see map 7-2).[10]

Map 7-2

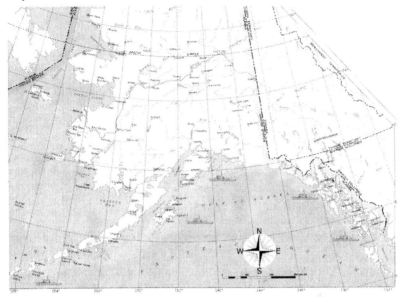

Alaska: In the mid-1980s, aged ocean minesweepers deployed to Alaskan waters to conduct Q-route surveys of major ports and demonstrate conclusively that their material condition was good enough to justify their continued existence.

The minesweepers left their respective ports for Juneau. They arrived via the beautiful Inland Passage, the crews awed by the deep blue water, sunlight glinting off icebergs, and the impressive scenery as Juneau came into view. A layer of clouds often shrouds the body of the steep mountainous island, providing a billowy backdrop for the sight of the mountaintop stabbing through the clouds and the city nestled at the water's edge at its base. The group of ships left Juneau on 9 July for Ketchikan.[11]

Reaching Ketchikan, the minesweepers moored at the Coast Guard Pier. In this rustic frontier community, armed men attired in animal furs still come into town to purchase food and supplies with nuggets and pinches of dust from gold pokes. A lot of work in Alaska is seasonal, and during the off season there is more darkness than daylight each day. Accordingly, here, as in other places, there were a lot of bars, some of them pretty tough. The commanding officer of an MSO that visited Ketchikan the following year remarked, tongue in cheek, following a night on the town, "you know you're in a good bar when you see a bloody handprint on the wall of the men's room."

The minesweepers made the return transit to Seattle via the Inland Waterway. The ships based in the Northwest arrived on 17 July at Seattle and Tacoma, while the remaining two MSOs turned southward, following a stop for fuel at Port Angeles. *Gallant* arrived in San Francisco and *Constant* moored the next day at Naval Station San Diego, marking the completion of the longest operation by a group of Pacific Fleet minesweepers in many years. The Alaskan cruise generated much public relations value, as in recent times Navy ships rarely, if ever, stopped at the port cities visited by these MSOs. The wooden ships were well received by the populace, and their presence stimulated much interest in the Navy.[12]

Alaskan Deployment—1984

Conquest, Esteem, and *Implicit* left Seattle on 14 May 1984 for San Francisco to rendezvous with other Mine Squadron 5 ships arriving from Tacoma and San Diego, and with *Excel* and *Gallant,* who were based in San Francisco. Upon arrival, the MSOs berthed at Naval Air Station Alameda, to make final preparations before sailing as a group to Hawaii for participation in RIMPAC 84, a combined naval exercise with units from the United States and other Pacific Rim nations. *Pluck,* the only remaining member of the squadron, stayed behind in San Diego, engaged as a test ship for a CNO project. Leaving the pier at the airbase on 22 May, the MSOs headed outbound in San Francisco Bay, passing north of Alcatraz Island and under the Golden Gate Bridge before setting on a southwest course. They were escorted by the amphibious cargo ship USS *Durham* (LKA 114). The ships arrived at Kahului, Maui, on 2 June, completing the transit of the Eastern Pacific and also an unofficial MSO race.[13]

Those familiar with the maximum speed of the minesweepers might believe the term "race" a bit incongruous. However, any "ordered bell" that requires propulsion engines to work hard over a long period of time is racing. The MSOs were positioned in two diamond formations of four ships each, with a faster group leading a slower group. The most economical use of fuel by the MSOs was achieved through use of two of their four main propulsion engines. Bringing a third or fourth engine online provided only a little more speed, burned more fuel, and consumed unnecessary engine use hours. The aluminum-block nonmagnetic engines fitted in minesweepers were less robust than those manufactured of steel and were supposed to be replaced after five thousand hours of use. However, because the Packard Company had gone out of business two decades earlier, there were few or no replacements, unless you counted stockpiled war reserves that were not available. Accordingly, you took care of those you had and lived with very old tired engines.

All of the above reasons notwithstanding, the propulsion plants were put to the test. Naval officers are by nature a competitive lot. The commanding officers of some of the MSOs were cagey, both about how many main engines they had online and, when queried, about their ordered feet of propeller-pitch, used instead of bell changes, revolutions, and knots to order speed changes aboard the vessels. The guide ship in one group went as fast as possible, no matter what the ordered speed, until one of the engines blew a head gasket or a "J-hose" (water hose), after which it would slow down until the necessary repairs were made and then go at top speed again. As the minesweepers neared Hawaiian waters, the commanding officer of one remarked, "Well the 'Maui-500' is over and we lost."

Tired from years of service, the Packard engines required much work by the ship's engineers to keep them running and in safe operating condition. The enginemen of one Pacific Fleet MSO elected to install drip pans beneath main propulsion engines to catch leaking oil until they could replace gaskets or rubber "O-rings" and machine mating metal surfaces to correct the hemorrhage. The ship's commanding officer, taken to task by the squadron commodore for using nonstandard lube oil while deployed to Alaska in 1985, reportedly replied, "It doesn't matter sir, the oil doesn't remain in the engines long enough to do any damage."

The minesweepers participated in RIMPAC in early June, anchoring at night off Lahaina, a popular tourist destination and historic town located on the western coast of Maui that had once been a center of the Pacific whaling industry. The mine countermeasures portion of the exercise consisted of Single-O and improved deep-moored sweeping as well as mine hunting. The MSOs berthed at the submarine base at Pearl Harbor on 14 June as a prelude to their participation in a "port breakout," a term describing the practice of minesweepers leading combatant ships out of port through a Q-route to avoid, in this case, a simulated mined channel.[14]

The time in port also provided the crews of three of the eight MSOs, preparing to continue on to Alaska, the opportunity to obtain the supplies, and particularly repair parts, necessary for the trip. A storekeeper from one MSO, hand-delivering the requisitions for these items to the base supply center, found, much to his delight, that the person filling the order did not recognize the name of his ship and, told that it was moored at the pier, assumed it was a submarine. Knowing that requirements of submarines command a higher priority than those of surface ships, the trusty sweep sailor failed to set the record straight. When word of this infraction reached the "mustang" commanding officer of one of the minesweepers, he quickly removed his current rank insignia and warfare pin, affixed his former chief's anchors and enlisted dolphins to his uniform, and set off to wheel and deal in earnest.

Conquest, Constant, Gallant, Implicit, and *Pledge* left Pearl Harbor in late June for home. As the ships neared the West Coast, they separated to make the run to their individual homeports.[15]

Excel, Esteem, and *Enhance* sailed on 9 July for Adak, Alaska with Chief Sandoval, the squadron diesel inspector, aboard *Excel* to ensure the reliability of her aged Packard engines and of the Waukesha engines of the other ships. Possessing extensive knowledge gained over many years aboard sweeps, "Sandy" would routinely arrive aboard squadron ships with his box of special tools and assist the crew in coaxing ancient engines back to life. En route, the three MSOs were joined by a USCG *Hamilton*-class high endurance cutter to provide fuel and lubricating oil during the transit. The group arrived at Adak on 20 June, mooring at the pier in sequential hull numbers to enjoy a brief stay in port before conducting a mine countermeasures exercise in nearby waters. While mine hunting in the harbor during the exercise, *Excel* located a downed aircraft whose image on the sonar display suggested an airplane of World War II vintage. The MSOs proceeded next to Dutch Harbor, Unalaska, an island located northeast of Adak in the Aleutian Islands chain.[16]

Photo 7-1

Excel, Esteem, and *Enhance* in port Adak, Alaska. During operations, *Excel* located with sonar a downed aircraft on the bottom of the bay, perhaps lost during World War II (author's collection)

Waiting on the pier to board *Excel* upon her arrival were a group of selected reservists, some of whom, having arrived the previous day, had spent their evening at the infamous "Elbow Room," ranked by *Playboy* magazine as one of the ten toughest bars in the United States. Warned by the reservists to stay away, based on the brawls they had witnessed, *Excel's* junior officers and crew immediately headed for the rustic building, constructed of logs and galvanized sheet metal roofing. Dogs lounged outside its door and stringers of fish hung from the walls. En route, a crewman from a fishing boat asked for a ride to the bar. Getting out of the vehicle, flush with money from several months of fishing in the Bering Sea, he threw a hundred-dollar bill through an open window to settle up for his ride. (The sailors promptly returned it.) The evening itself was fairly tame, with amity among Navy men, boisterous fishermen, and members of a local band beating on home-made steel drums.[17]

The minesweepers left Dutch Harbor on 1 July for Kodiak, arriving the next day for a port visit that included participation in Coast

Guard Day festivities with staff from the base and crews of ships stationed there. Bound next for Ketchikan, the ships encountered severe weather in the Gulf of Alaska before reaching port. On the 10th, the ships got underway to continue the transit of the Gulf of Alaska to Seattle. The arrival of the group on 13 August marked the completion of the deployment for *Enhance* and *Esteem*.[18]

Excel, now designating herself "The Bering Sweeper" because she had swept north of the Aleutian chain, remained in Seattle until her departure on 16 August for Astoria, Oregon. During the ensuing visit, her crew participated in parties and activities associated with the Astoria Regatta. Criteria for membership in the associated yacht club appeared to be the ownership of something that floated, as evidenced by the numbers of small boats proceeding downriver. *Excel* left port for San Francisco and moored at Naval Supply Center, Oakland on 23 August. *Enhance*, *Esteem*, and *Excel* became the first Pacific Fleet minesweepers to earn Sea Service Deployment ribbons since the last MSO deployments to the Western Pacific in 1973.[19]

Alaskan Cruise—1985

From 3 June to 25 July 1985, eight minesweepers made a cruise to Alaska with midshipmen and reservists on board for their annual training. The MSOs did not group sail during the open-ocean transit from Seattle to Alaskan waters, but instead made their way in smaller units without a larger ship accompanying them to provide replenishment underway. Following their arrival, they participated in mine countermeasures exercises that included Q-route surveys of the ports of Anchorage, Seward, Kodiak, and Adak.

Excel and *Gallant* began their deployment on 1 June, leaving their berths at Navy Supply Center, Oakland, bound for Astoria. Joined off the mouth of the Columbia River by *Enhance*, the MSOs participated in a mine exercise with HM 4 minesweeping helicopters from the amphibious assault ship USS *Tripoli* (LPH 10). That night, *Gallant* rescued a crewmember from a sunken fishing boat in heavy weather off the coast near Astoria, Oregon. She and sister ship *Excel* were standing off the entrance to the Columbia River waiting for first light to embark a pilot and cross the bar when they received warning via marine radio of a sinking boat. In pitch darkness, *Gallant* found one crewmember, and a Japanese merchant ship rescued a second. *Excel* found the body of the deceased skipper the following day. There had been only two immersion suits on board, and the captain had insisted that his crew use them. (An immersion suit insulates the wearer's body from the frigid sea and ensuing hyperthermia.) Remarking the event to the author during a subsequent interview, *Excel*'s skipper, retired Navy commander Lee Foley, noted that "the captain of the fishing boat, in the time-honored tradition of the sea, ensured the survival of his crew in the frigid seas, knowing full well that his decision would in all likelihood cost him his own life. In my view this was the epitome of gallantry and intrepidity." The minesweepers' destination, the town of Astoria, was the home of the family of the deceased. Immediately after mooring, *Excel* sailors took up a collection for the family, and her commanding officer made the man's sons honorary crewmembers. The MSOs remained in port overnight before embarking guests the next morning for the transit up the Columbia River to Portland for the famed Rose Festival.[20]

The two minesweepers left their riverside berths for Esquimalt, British Columbia, heading north upon reaching the Pacific several hours later, and arrived the following day at the Canadian Forces Base. *Excel* took advantage of the facility at Plumper Bay to check-range her degaussing system before mooring and "putting down liberty call" for the crew. That evening at the officers' club the base port engineer, a large red-haired and bushy-bearded Scotsman, commented to *Excel*'s captain and several junior officers that he had seen his ship enter port and that its stack was "smoky, smoky," informing him that he would accordingly like to meet the Chief Engineer. The stack of a ship "smoking black" means the fuel and air mixture for the engines is too rich, discharging particulates into the atmosphere, which can result in a fine for pollution. When informed that the Chief Engineer had the duty as Command Duty Officer aboard *Excel*, he roared, "Wot kind of ship are you running, Captain, that you give the Engineer the duty the first night in port?" A gregarious individual, he ended this colorful discourse with a kind offer to exchange the officers' U.S. dollars for Canadian currency at a better rate than offered in town. Following liberty in the beautiful city, *Excel* and *Gallant* left port on 14 June for Seattle.[21]

Conquest and *Esteem* sailed from Seattle on 4 June for Juneau, Alaska, arriving via the Inland Passage. On the 10th, the MSOs set a heading across the Gulf of Alaska for Kodiak Island, home of massive brown bears. A large stuffed specimen, standing erect, is displayed in a glass case at the Coast Guard base located on the island, and residents advise visitors not to venture into the woods without a rifle for protection. Kodiak is also known for its sport fishing, and one often sees, while salmon fishing on its rivers, huge Kodiak bears along the banks.[22]

Conquest and *Esteem* arrived at Kodiak on the 13th, mooring at the Coast Guard pier, and departed two days later bound for Adak, an island in the Aleutian chain that splits the Northern Pacific Ocean and Bering Sea, strategically located some thirteen hundred miles southwest of Anchorage and fourteen hundred miles from Magadan in eastern Russia.[23]

Following their visit to Esquimalt and upkeep in Seattle, *Excel*, *Gallant*, and *Implicit* departed on 18 June for Ketchikan, across the Gulf of Alaska, *Excel* with midshipmen and a few Navy League guests aboard. En route, the three ships encountered a severe storm. *Excel* lost hull sheathing, the portable firefighting pump mounted on the fo'c'sle of another sweep was ripped loose from its mount and washed overboard, and the chain locker of the third MSO flooded. Following local minesweep operations on 24 June, the ships set a course the following day for Kodiak.[24]

There *Excel*, *Gallant*, and *Implicit* enjoyed rest in port before participating in a mine exercise. They left for Cook Inlet, near Anchorage, for another mine exercise, which included extensive Q-route surveys. The crews enjoyed liberty in Anchorage over the 4th of July weekend, followed by more underway time and additional upkeep in port. The three MSOs departed on the 16th en route Juneau for a port visit before the return trip to Seattle. Arriving in the Pacific Northwest on the 26th, *Implicit* returned to Tacoma. *Excel* and *Gallant* passed through the Ballard Locks to Lake Union and moored at the NOAA (National Oceanic & Atmospheric Administration) base amidst white-hulled research ships, to enjoy, in succeeding days, the Seattle Seafair. With the arrival of *Pluck* from San Diego to participate in the festival, all nine MSOs were for the first time in recent memory located in the same port area. *Excel* and *Gallant* began their final leg home to Oakland on 31 July and arrived on 3 August.[25]

Arriving with a separate group of sweeps at Adak, *Esteem* participated in a mine exercise from 21 to 27 June, before sailing for Seward, Alaska. *Esteem* entered port in Seward for Independence Day and remained through the 8th, when she left for Kodiak Island. Upon her arrival, she moored at the Coast Guard pier for two days of liberty before sailing for Ketchikan to enjoy her final visit to an Alaskan community.[26]

Conquest, with Commander, Mine Group 1 embarked, remained in Adak until 26 June, participating in a mine exercise. She sailed the next day for Kodiak Island to celebrate Independence Day, leaving on 11 July for Seward, Alaska. Following a short three-day visit, she left for Ketchikan to join *Esteem* for the final leg to Seattle.[27]

Operation EARNEST WILL—1987 to 1990
Between 22 August 1987 and 26 April 1990, the Pacific Fleet Ocean minesweepers were directly engaged in or supporting mine clearance in the Persian Gulf as part of Operation EARNEST WILL.

Reactor Compartment Escort Operations—1991 and 1992
The symbolic tearing down of the Berlin Wall on 9 November 1989 and the ensuing and related demise of the Soviet Union prompted a post–cold war reduction in the assets of the U.S. military. Downsizing within the Navy resulted in the decommissioning of nuclear-powered surface combatants (with the exception of aircraft carriers) and scores of submarines, many at their first scheduled refueling, despite the fact that they still retained the greatest part of their service life.

The U.S. Navy does not lay-up, or lease or sell to foreign governments, nuclear-powered ships or submarines. Accordingly, they were disposed of, which required the removal of nuclear fuel and decontamination of the vessels, followed by disposal of reactor compartments and recycling of hulls. The once proud ships and submarines were towed to Naval Shipyard, Bremerton, Washington for removal of their reactor compartments prior to the cutting up of their hulls. With ships arriving at the yard faster than they could be disposed of, the bows of some were simply cut off forward of the space housing the reactor compartments. These uncontaminated sections of the vessel were re-cycled and the remaining hulks placed en masse in dry docks until the time was available for the laborious work needed to dispose of them.

The removed reactors were placed on a barge and towed down the coast of Washington and up the Columbia River for eventual transport overland to a DOE facility at Hanford, Washington. The Navy ships assigned to escort tug and tow during transit ironically included *Knox*-class frigates and MSOs, which were also in the waning years of their service lives. The almost dead escorted the deceased to their final resting places. In 1991, *Implicit* was ordered to escort the tow of a decommissioned submarine to Astoria, Oregon, and she performed these same duties again in July. The following year, *Conquest* escorted reactor tows from Sinclair Inlet at Bremerton down the Washington coast to the Columbia River and from Seattle to Astoria.[28]

ATLANTIC FLEET

During the post–Vietnam War era, Atlantic Fleet MSOs were assigned as both active-duty and reserve ships, initially to Mine Flotilla 2 on 1 April 1971. It was disestablished on 30 June 1973, whereupon all reserve MSOs were assigned to Mine Squadron 12. Reorganizations continued and on 16 July 1981, Mine Squadron 12 was redesignated Mine Group 2, and later, on 1 March 1985, Mine Squadron 2. The final change occurred in December 1991, when Mine Squadron 2 became Mine Countermeasures Group 2.

Following their transfer in the early 1970s to the Naval Reserve, the ships were initially assigned to the divisions and homeports shown below.

Ship	Division	Homeport
Affray	121	Portland, Maine
Inflict	121	Portland, Maine
Detector	121	Portsmouth, New Hampshire
Dash	121	Fall River, Massachusetts
Adroit	121	Newport, Rhode Island
Direct	123	Perth Amboy, New Jersey
Exultant	123	Perth Amboy, New Jersey
Exploit	123	Little Creek, Virginia
Fortify	123	Little Creek, Virginia
Fearless	126	Charleston, South Carolina
Dominant	126	St. Petersburg, Florida
Engage	126	St. Petersburg, Florida
Impervious	126	Mayport, Florida

There were many similarities between the employment of Atlantic Fleet and Pacific Fleet Reserve MSOs; however, due to geographic location, the East Coast–based ships provided more support to Navy laboratories for research and development and to the U.S. Naval Academy, located at Annapolis, Maryland. For the latter, the MSOs escorted yard patrol craft during treks up inland waterways and served as guest ships for the Parents' Weekend Open House.

Prior to the deployment in June 1983 of *Exultant* and *Fearless* (with active MSOs *Illusive* and *Leader*) to Europe, visits by reserve sweeps to "foreign countries" were limited to Canada; the British island of Bermuda in the North Atlantic Ocean, east of Cape Hatteras, North Carolina; islands in the Caribbean; and Central America. Following joint exercises, ocean minesweepers moored for liberty at HMC Dockyard in Halifax, Nova Scotia and visited Canso, Nova Scotia, to enjoy its annual regatta. The MSOs journeyed southward to the Caribbean Sea to participate in exercises, train at the naval base at Guantanamo Bay, Cuba, and conduct acoustic sound tests on the range at Andros Island, The Bahamas and bottom surveys of the Panama Canal.

On 1 July 1971, the status of *Dash*, *Detector*, *Direct*, and *Dominant* was changed to Naval Reserve Training (NRT) ships, a designation later changed to Naval Reserve Force (NRF) ships. As active ships, they had been based in Charleston, South Carolina, but now they were transferred to new homeports and the number of active-duty crewmen reduced, with some people transferred to other activities. Key billets were eliminated and for ten years even executive officers were absent from MSO manning. The Senior Watch officer (a collateral duty of the senior department head), whose responsibilities already prevented him from performing properly, was expected to function as the executive officer as well.[29]

Dash and *Detector* arrived at Fall River, Massachusetts and Portsmouth, New Hampshire, respectively, to join Mine Division 121. *Dominant* reported on 20 August 1971 to Mine Division 126 at St. Petersburg, Florida. The sole U.S. Navy ship located at the port's Bayboro Harbor, she was supported by a maintenance and repair unit that also supplied a pool of manpower to supplement the efforts of her nucleus crew in maintaining the ship in a ready condition at all times. *Direct* sailed into Perth Amboy, New Jersey on 27 August 1971 to comprise, with the coastal minesweeper USS *Parrot* (MSC 197), the newly formed Mine Division 123. In *September* the following year, *Exultant* joined the division.[30]

As one of her first duties in 1971, *Detector* towed the *Gato*-class diesel-electric submarine USS *Croaker* (IXSS 246) from Portsmouth, New Hampshire to Boston, Massachusetts for dismantling. Commissioned on 24 April 1944 as SS-246, *Croaker* made six patrols in the Pacific during

World War II, sinking a cruiser, four tankers, two freighters, an ammunition ship, two escort craft, and a minesweeper. *Croaker* was transferred in 1968 to the Naval Reserve for use as a trainer and participated
in various submarine operations until stricken from the Navy Register
in 1971. Saved from the "breakers," she was transferred to the Submarine Memorial Association in Groton, Connecticut and later moved
to the Buffalo Naval and Servicemen's Park in New York. She is now
part of a historical fleet that includes the guided-missile cruiser USS *Little
Rock* (CLG 4) and the destroyer USS *The Sullivans* (DD 537).[31]

In 1973 and 1974, two reserve crews were assigned to *Direct*. The
"Blue Crew" or "combined crew" was composed of "Selected Reserves" who drilled on board the first weekend of each month and
whose records were maintained aboard the ship. The "Gold Crew" received administrative support from the Naval Reserve Training Center
in Atlantic City, New Jersey and used *Direct* only as a training ship, drill-
ing usually on the third weekend of the month. The Gold Crew was
disbanded in July 1974 due to cutbacks and reorganization within the
naval reserve.[32]

As part of the post-war restructuring of the mine force, Mine
Squadron 1, located at Guam, was disestablished on 1 June 1974. One
month earlier, the remaining squadron ships—*Engage, Fortify, Impervious,* and *Inflict*—left Apra Harbor in company with the salvage ship USS
Conserver (ARS 39), bound for Long Beach via stops at Midway Island
and Pearl Harbor. Their departure from Guam marked the first time
since shortly after the Korean War that U.S. Navy wooden-hull ships
were no longer in the waters of the western Pacific. Leaving Pearl Harbor on 3 June, the MSOs left *Conserver,* her escort duties completed, behind in her homeport. After their arrival on the West Coast, the
minesweepers, reassigned to both the Atlantic Fleet and naval reserve
duty, continued on to their new homeports. *Engage* and *Impervious,*
based at St. Petersburg and Mayport, Florida, respectively, joined Mine
Division 126. *Fortify* reported to Little Creek, Virginia to join Mine Division 123 and *Inflict* to Portland, Maine to join Mine Division 121.
Fearless, based at Charleston, was transferred on 1 July 1974 to the Naval Reserve Force with no change of homeports.[33]

In early 1974, *Direct* and *Exultant* conducted a sonar search of a
proposed New York Harbor holding anchorage. A plot of the obstructions on the bottom was charted and forwarded to the harbormaster.

Ocean minesweepers were also employed by the Navy to survey the waters surrounding the sites of proposed new bases.[34]

In June 1975, *Direct* traveled to Machias, Maine to participate in the reenactment of the first naval battle of the Revolutionary War. Fought in the bay off Machias, the battle was a land and sea action that resulted in the capture by local patriots of the British schooner *Margaretta*, with the loss of only one man on the American side. The victors were equipped with sidearms, knives, and pitchforks when they attacked and seized the British naval vessel. Her captain died that night in the Burnham Tavern (which still existed at the time of *Direct*'s visit, as a well-preserved colonial inn, open to visitors). During her two-day stay, the MSO hosted over six hundred visitors before she sailed for Perth Amboy.[35]

In September of 1975, *Direct* was again engaged in duties linked to America's colonial days, having received orders to transport two Revolutionary War–era British cannon to Halifax, Nova Scotia. The two nine-pounders, weighing 3,500 pounds each, were armaments of the British vessel *Cerberus*. Cornered in 1776 by the French Fleet in Narragansett Bay, her crew scuttled her rather than surrender to the enemy. A group of historians and oceanographers from the University of Rhode Island located the wreckage of the ship and raised the cannon. As part of bicentennial goodwill gestures, it was decided the cannon would be returned to the British government for display in Greenwich, England the following year, sponsored by the Sunday *London Times*. The cannon were wrapped in cloth soaked in saltwater, sealed in Styrofoam, enclosed in long, gray, metal crates, and then loaded aboard *Direct* in Newport for transport to Halifax, Nova Scotia and delivery to the Royal Navy frigate HMS *Minerva*. *Direct* arrived in the bay in early October and, just after sunrise, a Canadian barge-crane came along her starboard side to transfer the cannon to *Minerva*. As the big guns were hoisted away, *Direct* crewmen gave them a last farewell, ending two hundred years of American possession. *Direct* then entered port to represent the U.S. Navy at the Halifax Joseph Howe Festival.[36]

In early February 1977, *Dash* and *Detector* were involved in a search for the lost bow section of the Liberian-registered oil tanker *ARGO Merchant*, which had grounded on 15 December 1976 on shoals twenty-nine miles southeast of Nantucket Island. The vessel had been eighteen miles off course. Three days later, the winds and waves picked up and on the night of 20 December, rough weather moved into the area. The following morning the tanker split in two, spilling seven million gallons of bunker oil into the sea. The wrecked ship was never salvaged, as fast moving currents buried the hull on the Nantucket Shoals. After efforts by a Coast Guard H-3 helicopter, a U.S. Navy P-3 Orion patrol plane from Patrol Squadron 44, and the *Recovery* were unsuccessful in locating the bow near Fishing Rip on Nantucket Shoals, *Recovery* requested the assistance of Mine Squadron 12. On 8 February *Dash* and *Detector* were ordered to proceed to the scene and given four areas to search. The operation attracted international interest due to the possible environmental impact of oil leaking from the bow tanks (in addition to the seven million gallons spilled upon grounding) on the nearby Georges Banks and Cape Cod resort areas. Despite ten-foot seas and twenty-five-knot winds, *Dash* located the wreckage on the first day and marked it with a buoy with less than ten-foot error. Coast Guard divers later determined that the bow tanks had been thoroughly destroyed in the grounding and posed no further threat of oil pollution.[37]

In 1977, two sets of ships, *Dominant* and *Exultant* and *Exploit* and *Inflict*, changed homeports. The purpose of the "ship swaps" was to station together minesweepers with like engines; *Exploit* would now be with *Affray*, which also had Packard engines, while *Inflict* would be collocated at Little Creek, Virginia, with other Waukesha-propelled vessels.[38]

The crews of *Dominant* and *Exultant* assembled on the pier at the naval amphibious base at Little Creek on 8 July for a cross-decking ceremony and change of command. The bulk of each crew were exchanging ships, leaving only key engineering people aboard their respective commands. The commanding officers relieved one another and their respective crews marched aboard their new ships. *Dominant*, with the former *Exultant* crew aboard, arrived at her new homeport at Perth Amboy, mooring portside to the Naval Reserve Center on the Arthur Kill. *Exultant* reached St. Petersburg, Florida and moored at the quay wall adjacent to the Naval Reserve Center at Bayboro Harbor.[39]

Exploit's homeport was changed from Little Creek, Virginia to Portland, Maine, and she arrived there on 19 September 1977. She and *Inflict* had previously swapped crewmen, and the commanding officers exchanged ships.[40]

On 16 September 1977, *Detector* got underway from her berth in Newport, Rhode Island for her annual dependent's cruise, which this year took place during the famed America's Cup finals. Everyone

Photo 7-2

Affray (MSO 511) southbound on the Ashley River, at the twin bridges in Charleston, in the fall of 1987 (courtesy of Harry Keith)

aboard the minesweeper had the opportunity to witness *Courageous*'s re-sounding victory in the second race of the competition. *Dominant* joined several other Navy vessels and civilian craft off Newport to watch the third race of the finals. The American entry won both the race and the series.[41]

On 7 March 1978, *Fearless* endeavored to clear a five-square-mile area north of Charleston Harbor Buoy "2C" of German mines possibly laid in 1942. She found no mines but did locate three ship anchors, which an archeologist later determined were of nineteenth-century vintage. The Navy presented the artifacts to the Charles Towne Landing in Charleston.[42]

Detector left Newport on 3 August 1978 for New York harbor to rendezvous with four Naval Academy yard patrol (YP) craft being used for summer training of midshipmen. She escorted them from New York to Newport, from Newport to Atlantic City, New Jersey, and from Atlantic City to Little Creek, Virginia, with port visits along the way. The training was invaluable in the development of midshipmen into naval officers and in instilling in them an appreciation for the need to stand proper watches in order to ensure the safety of vessel and crew. This was not obvious to at least one trainee. Standing watch as the officer of the deck aboard a YP operating in inland waters, and hungry, the midshipman left the bridge and went below to eat. Unfortunately, he had not been properly relieved of his watch, nor was his relief even on the bridge. A startled craft master, an officer assigned to the navigation and seamanship faculty at the Naval Academy, quickly remedied the situation and then provided some very terse guidance to the "Mid."[43]

Homeported, in some cases, in ports without adequate repair and maintenance facilities, the reserve minesweepers received necessary support when the Navy brought "elderly" naval craft out of mothballs and equipped them as floating workshops. *Exploit* underwent a repair-availability from 22 to 31 July 1979 in Newport, with the floating workshop YR 26. Launched in 1941, the unnamed vessel was manned by a contingent of reservists to provide maintenance and repair work for ships. The following year *Exploit* again traveled from Portland to Newport for a two-week "RepairEx" with the floating workshop. After being struck by the Navy, she was sunk on 28 August 1998 by the state of Texas for use as an artificial fishing reef.[44]

Northern Europe Deployment—1983

In June 1983, reserve minesweepers *Exultant* and *Fearless* deployed to Europe with active ships *Illusive* and *Leader* to join the permanent NATO squadron of mine countermeasures ships, referred to as Standing Naval Force Channel, for operations in Northern Europe and the Mediterranean Sea. This cruise, the first by Atlantic Fleet reserve MSOs, coincided with the deployment in the same year of Pacific Fleet reserve MSOs to Alaska.

U.S. Maritime Defense Zone—1986 and 1987

From 30 October to 2 November 1986, *Impervious* participated in the first major mine countermeasures exercise along the approaches to New York City, as part of the recently initiated Maritime Defense Zone (MARDEZ) Atlantic Fleet organization. The MARDEZ concept divided the East and West coasts of the United States into sectors for the command and control of mine countermeasures in support of fleet commander objectives. Surface, airborne, and explosive ordnance disposal (EOD) forces were used to facilitate the safe movement of ships in or out of port. The Atlantic Fleet gave the Coast Guard wartime responsibility for the defense of U.S. ports, which included mine countermeasures. Exercise QUICK PITCH 87 tested interoperability, command and control, and the capability of minesweepers to hunt and neutralize bottom mines laid in commercial ports. The commander of Maritime Defense Zone Sector 3, a U.S. Coast Guard admiral, conducted the exercise.[45]

Exercise FIRST SHIELD was conducted on 23 and 24 August 1986, primarily within Narragansett Bay. The objective was a breakout of a NATO reinforcement/resupply convoy from Davisville, Rhode Island. Commander, Maritime Defense Zone Sector 1 directed the exercise. Commander, Mine Division 121 coordinated the actions of *Affray* and *Exploit* as well as those of an EOD detachment embarked aboard a USCG fifty-five-foot Aids-to-Navigation boat.[46]

The following year a more elaborate MARDEZ exercise was conducted from 14 to 27 October 1987. "AGILE KNIGHT" exercised command and control during joint training with U.S. Navy, Coast Guard, and Army National Guard units. The exercise was directed by Commander, Maritime Defense Zone Sector 1, and the objective of the subordinate mine countermeasures commander, Commander, Mine Division 121, was to conduct port breakout operations from the submarine base at New London, Connecticut. Units participating in the exercise included *Affray*, one EOD diver detachment and one EOD Area Point Search Septeur, a supplemental sonar platform, two remotely operated vehicles, one USCG cutter, and several small craft.[47]

Operation EARNEST WILL—1987 to 1989

Between 6 September 1987 and 25 May 1989, *Fearless*, *Illusive*, and *Inflict* were deployed to the Persian Gulf to conduct mine countermeasures in support of Operation EARNEST WILL. Other Atlantic Fleet minesweepers served as stateside training platforms for the rotational crews that periodically replaced one another aboard the deployed ships.

Operation DESERT SHIELD/STORM—1989 to 1991

Three aged ocean minesweepers, USS *Avenger* (MCM 1), and later USS *Guardian* (MCM 5) were deployed from 1989 through 1991 to the Persian Gulf in response to the invasion by Iraq of Kuwait.

During and following DESERT STORM, remaining Atlantic Fleet MSOs were decommissioned. *Adroit, Impervious,* and *Leader* (the first two reserve ships) returned from the Persian Gulf on 9 November 1991 to Norfolk, Virginia, and were decommissioned on 12 December 1991 in a joint ceremony. The last Atlantic Fleet minesweeper to be struck was reserve ship *Exploit* on 15 December 1993.

Of twenty-seven mine warfare ships comprising the U.S. Navy surface mine force today, five of the fourteen *Avengers* and nine of twelve *Ospreys* have been redesignated naval reserve ships. The Military Sealift Command, Washington, D.C., has contracted to lease the twenty-seventh ship, the high speed vessel HSV *2 Swift,* from Bollinger/Incat in Lockport, Louisiana for use by the Navy as an interim mine warfare command and support ship (MCS) following decommissioning of USS *Inchon* (MCS 12).

The Navy accepted HSV *2 Swift* in August 2003 and there is hope that ensuing testing will validate the usefulness of the experimental vessel as a command ship, breaking a long-standing Navy practice of converting aged cast-off vessels for use as mine countermeasure support ships. USS *Epping Forest* (MCS 7), commissioned a dock landing ship (LSD 4) on 11 October 1943, was converted on 30 November 1962 to a mine countermeasure support ship, and stricken on 1 November 1968. Her replacement in Sasebo, Japan, USS *Catskill* (MCS 1), was commissioned on 30 June 1944 as a vehicle landing ship (LSV 1) and later converted to an MCS to serve as the flagship for Commander Mine Flotilla 1. The former vehicle landing ship (LSV 2) USS *Ozark* (MCS 2) was commissioned on 23 September 1944, converted to a mine countermeasure support ship on 24 June 1966, and decommissioned on 1 April 1974. USS *Orleans Parish* (MCS 6) was commissioned a tank landing ship on 31 March 1945, converted to a mine countermeasure support ship on 19 January 1959, and decommissioned on 20 May 1966.

This trend continued when the *Inchon* was converted in 1996 to serve as an MCS for Commander, Mine Warfare Command at Ingleside, Texas. Commissioned on 20 June 1970, she was decommissioned thirty-two years later on 20 June 2002. A fire in the boiler room on 19 October 2001 killed one crewmember and injured seven others, and her service ended eight months later.

8   Ships Damaged or Lost at Sea

> *Ships that sailed for sunny isles, but never came to shore.*
> Thos. Kibble Hervey, *The Devil's Progress*

Groundings and fires at sea were the most common causes of damage to, or loss of, ocean minesweepers. This is not surprising if one considers that these ships operated routinely in shallow waters, near shore, and in close proximity to a myriad of navigational hazards. Additionally, their construction of combustible wood materials, their limited outfit of damage control and firefighting equipment, and their lack of crew to operate what there was made them much more vulnerable to fire than other ship types.

Most major fires broke out in the engine rooms, generally caused by fuel or lube oil—spraying or leaking from Packard diesel main-propulsion or generator engines—striking hot surfaces and igniting. The engines installed in minesweepers are unforgiving. Manufactured of nonferrous materials to protect minesweepers from magnetic mines, they are both less durable and more maintenance intensive than other marine diesel engines. Moreover, only small numbers of relatively junior engineers are available to maintain many types of equipment crammed into a very tiny hull. The result can be disastrous. The Navy ultimately was impelled to implement rigorous engineering inspections and programs to try to control the fire hazards implicit in minesweepers, especially after *Force* caught fire and sank off Guam in 1973.

USS *PRESTIGE* (MSO 465)

The first ocean minesweeper was lost in 1958. *Prestige*, deployed with Mine Division 92 to the Western Pacific for service with the 7th Fleet, grounded at Naruto Kaikyo Strait in the Inland Sea of Japan (at 34 degrees 14 minutes north, 134 degrees 39 minutes east) at 1:35 a.m. on 23 August. At the time, *Prestige* was en route from Yokosuka to Kure in company with *Pivot* and *Pluck*. *Pivot*, valiantly attempting to free *Prestige*, also grounded on a submerged pinnacle but managed to free herself twenty minutes later.[1]

Two minutes after going hard aground on Naka Se Reef, *Prestige*'s bridge-watch team received a report of flooding in "lower sound" (the sonar equipment room). Investigation revealed a large hole, three feet by four feet, through which rocks could be seen, and several smaller holes in the hull. Personnel and all portable equipment were removed from the space, and the scuttle dogged shut to prevent the spread of flooding. The conning officer meanwhile attempted to back off the reef, using different engine orders and rudder combinations. When that failed, ship's engineers pumped sea water carried as ballast from a diesel-oil storage tank forward on the centerline to lighten the forward part of the ship. The continuing effort to back clear of the reef was unsuccessful, and the conning officer ordered "all engines stop" at 3:24 a.m.[2]

Further attempts to lighten the ship—which included launching the motor whaleboat, shifting all weight possible (including ammunition) aft, and pumping 1,600 gallons of diesel fuel over the side—failed to free the reef-gripped ship. At 4:36 a.m, *Pivot* got underway from anchorage nearby to try and pull *Prestige* free from the rocks. Her motor whaleboat took a messenger line from the stern of *Prestige* back to *Pivot*. The messenger was led through the bullnose (bow chock) by 5:00 a.m., and *Pivot* began heaving in as *Prestige* paid out her tow wire. (First light, 5:33 a.m., discovered a new three-by-one-foot hole in *Prestige*'s stem, where the bow curved to join the keel.) With the tow wire aboard and stopped off to a pelican hook on her fo'c'sle, *Pivot* backed her engines and took a strain on the wire to assist *Prestige* in freeing herself. She maneuvered, with various engine and rudder combinations, in an attempt to tow from directly astern, but the strong currents prevented her from gaining the correct position. Unsuccessful, *Pivot* cast off the tow wire. On her second attempt, she anchored five hundred yards south of *Prestige*, intending to let the flood current swing her stern into position while using her motor whaleboat to take a messenger line to *Prestige*'s stern. However, the motor whaleboat was unable to make sufficient headway against the strong current and cast off the messenger. *Pivot* abandoned the salvage effort at 11:00 a.m. and weighed anchor, heaving around with a heavy strain due to the strong current, and overheating her anchor windlass.[3]

At 4:11 p.m., while maneuvering to pass close enough to *Prestige* to send a line with a line-throwing gun, *Pivot* grounded on a submerged rock approximately 150 yards astern of the stranded minesweeper. Now *Pivot* was in difficulty, the current swinging her stern rapidly to starboard. After trying unsuccessfully with various engine and rudder combinations to back free, *Pivot* sounded General Quarters. The reports from repair parties indicated no flooding anywhere in the ship. All personnel except ship control were ordered to the fantail in an attempt to lighten the bow. *Pivot* was soon free of the rocks and backing clear. Her thirty-minute ordeal over, she proceeded northward through Naruto Kaikyo Strait to anchorage. Ship's divers went over the side to inspect the hull for damage and found the reef had shaved the keel from the stem to the sonar dome, shearing off the latter. Otherwise, no apparent damage had been done.[4]

Prestige continued to attempt to back and twist free of the reef throughout the morning. At 10:33 a.m. the bridge received a report of a new break in the forward engine room hull, caused by rock penetration. Soundings of tanks and bilges revealed six to fourteen inches of water in tanks and voids. The crew shifted weight, and the bridge backed engines and twisted the ship throughout the afternoon, trying to break free. At 6:54 p.m., frames began to give way in the forward engine room. Soon thereafter, electrical power in the machinery space was secured, and the bridge received a report of flooding at a rate of two hundred gallons per minute in the forward engine room. At 7:00 p.m. the commanding officer gave the order for all personnel to make preparations to abandon ship.[5]

Pivot's motor whaleboat came alongside *Prestige* at 7:10 p.m. to assist in disembarking crewmembers. Five minutes later, *Prestige*'s bridge received a report of a large crack in the forward engine room, in the area of the three-hundred-kilowatt minesweep generator. At 7:17 p.m., *Prestige* sent a visual SOS to two Japanese cutters that were standing by. Fourteen minutes later, *Pivot* saw all lights in *Prestige* go out. In preparation for abandoning ship, designated people had begun conducting emergency-destruction procedures. At 7:37 p.m., after radiomen had destroyed all IFF (identification of friend or foe) communications equipment, the crew began disembarking as *Pivot*'s and *Pluck*'s motor whaleboats made her side. Remaining crewmembers began destroying the minesweep gear on her fantail. At 8:03 p.m., the bridge received a report of flooding in the after engine room. *Pluck*'s motor whaleboat was away from alongside at 8:09 p.m.—a little less than nineteen hours after grounding and after a steadfast effort by the crew (and *Pivot*) to save the ship.[6]

The Japanese Coast Guard patrol craft PS-112 moored alongside *Pivot* at 10:56 p.m. to transfer additional survivors. At 11:10 p.m. the evacuation of personnel was completed. A little after midnight, *Pivot* recorded that the whole crew was safely off *Prestige*—no lives had been lost and no one was injured. Thirty enlisted men and three officers, including *Prestige*'s commanding officer, were on board *Pivot*; the remaining officers and men were aboard *Pluck. Pivot*'s motor whaleboat was away from her side at 3:30 a.m. to patrol the waters around *Prestige*.[7]

The fleet ocean tug USS *Tawakoni* (ATF 114) arrived on the scene on 24 August to assist *Prestige* but was unable to begin salvage operations the following day because all ships present were required to evade Typhoon Flossie. En route on the 24th, *Tawakoni* had encountered a strong riptide running in the Naruto Kaikyo Strait, which caused her at 1:40 p.m. to yaw forty-five degrees to either side. Passing clear of the strait at 1:45 p.m., she anchored to the northeast. Later in the day, the Service Squadron 3 staff maintenance officer came aboard in advance of the *Prestige* salvage operation, and *Tawakoni* received twelve enlisted *Prestige* personnel from *Pivot*.[8]

Early the following day, *Tawakoni*'s motor whaleboat took a salvage party to inspect *Prestige*. Following the boat's return, the fleet tug left for the typhoon anchorage in Harima Nada Inland Sea, in accordance with a CoMinDiv 92 message (250032Z August 1958). She anchored at 12:01 p.m. and got underway four hours later to ride out Typhoon Flossie in the anchorage area. The eye of the hurricane was overhead at 8:45 p.m. and moved past *Tawakoni* at 9:20 p.m., with winds shifting to the southeast. The fleet ocean tug remained underway until 6:52 a.m. on 26 August, when she anchored north of Kado Saki in seventeen fathoms of water.[9]

The commander of Mine Division 92 and the commanding officer, executive officer, and operations officer of *Prestige* came aboard *Tawakoni* in early morning to discuss the demolition of the abandoned minesweeper. During the meeting, *Pivot* anchored in Naruto Kaikyo, six hundred yards from the fleet tug. *Tawakoni*'s motor whaleboat was away at 12:38 p.m. with a salvage party for *Prestige*. The salvage party boarded the MSO at 1:20 p.m. to set a demolition charge, clearing her side at 2:02 p.m. The charge exploded at 2:12 p.m., and *Tawakoni*'s boat returned to the ship with the salvage crew four minutes later.[10]

Early the following day, 27 August, *Tawakoni*'s motor whaleboat was again away for *Prestige*, with a salvage party and demolition team from *Pivot* bearing instructions from CoMinDiv 92 regarding the placing of explosives. Two charges set the bridge and pilot house of *Prestige* on fire. At noon, motor whaleboats from *Pivot* and *Tawakoni* took salvage parties to board *Prestige*, while *Tawakoni* shifted into position for salvage work, including retrieval of the CL cable on the wreck's fantail (which provides electrical power to acoustic noise-making devices) and began heaving in after it had been made fast.[11]

Tawakoni's motor whaleboat left her side the following morning to continue the salvage efforts, and the salvage ship USS *Current* (ARS 22) arrived shortly thereafter from Pusan, Korea to assume the duties of CTG 73.4 from *Tawakoni*. *Tawakoni*'s boat returned in late morning to deliver a short section of CL cable for transfer to *Pivot*, and in late afternoon retrieved the magtail from *Prestige*.[12]

On 29 August, *Tawakoni* transferred *Prestige* crewmembers to *Current* and sailed for Yokosuka, Japan. *Current* tried unsuccessfully on 31 August and 1 September to pull the wreck of the *Prestige* off the reef. All of her subsequent salvage efforts, assisted by the auxiliary ocean tug USS *Mahopac* (ATA 196), failed, and *Prestige* was demolished, by the use of more explosives, on 5 September 1958.[13]

Upon completion of the failed salvage operation of *Prestige*, *Pivot*, after riding out a typhoon whose center passed within twenty miles of her, sailed to Sasebo for drydocking. Inspection revealed that large portions of her keel and side planking had been gouged and torn away and that her sonar dome had been smashed. However, the ship had suffered no leakage and had withstood her damage well.[14]

USS *EXULTANT* (MSO 441)

On 12 August 1960, *Exultant* caught fire off the coast of Savannah, Georgia. The ship had departed Charleston that morning in company with *Nimble*, en route Miami, Florida to join *Avenge* and *Fidelity* for a port visit in connection with the annual convention of the National Association of County Officials.[15]

That evening at 5:55, fire erupted in the after engine room and spread rapidly throughout the adjacent engineering spaces. Valiant efforts by damage control parties, with assistance from *Nimble*, extinguished the blaze, and *Exultant* was subsequently towed safely to port. *Nimble*, after first disposing of all topside ammunition, courageously moored starboard side to the burning ship, using standard mooring lines doubled with a wire aft, and had a fire and rescue party aboard three minutes later. Sadly, *Exultant*'s engineer officer and four crewmen lost their lives fighting the fire, which raged for over three hours. *Pinnacle*, en route from Jacksonville to Charleston when news of the fire reached her, and *Sagacity* also went to her aid. *Pinnacle* escorted *Exultant* while she was being towed by *Nimble* to Savannah and remained with her for three days to act as a communications ship.[16]

The following sequence of events, based upon entries from *Exultant*'s deck log, depicts the courageous actions of *Exultant*'s crew, in very grim circumstances, to put out the blazing inferno and save their ship.

- 5:55 p.m.—Class A and B fires discovered in after engine room near #1 main engine. General Quarters sounded. All main engines secured. General Quarters stations in engineering spaces overwhelmed by fire and smoke.

- 6:00 p.m.—Ship dead in the water. Class A and B fires out of control in after engine room, boiler uptakes, and all spaces amidships on the maindeck, starboard side. Firemain pressures holding up. Fire parties attempt to extinguish the fire by inserting hoses into holes chopped through the bulkheads and decks of and around the stackhouse.

- 6:15 p.m.—Class A fire spreads to messdecks. Electric wiring in fire-affected spaces is short-circuiting, causing additional hazard to fire parties.

- 6:17 p.m.—Magazine sprinkling and flooding system activated. Contents of all ammunition, demolition, and pyrotechnic lockers jettisoned.

- 6:20 p.m.—P-500 (portable emergency) pump rigged on the 01 deck, starboard side.

- 6:28 p.m.—Smoke from the boiler uptakes pouring out of vents on the stackhouse now so dense that the fantail can no longer be seen from anywhere forward of the stackhouse.

- 6:35 p.m.—USS *Nimble* (MSO 459) moors alongside to port and provides fire party and additional equipment, including fire hoses charged from her firemain.

- 6:48 p.m.—Merchant ship SS *Tropicana* standing by to render assistance.

- 6:57 p.m.—Fire confined to engineering spaces and spaces on main deck, starboard side, amidships.

- 7:00 p.m.—Ship's firemain pressure sinking, although #1 ship's service generator is still on the line.
- 7:10 p.m.—Ship listing nine degrees to starboard.
- 7:23 p.m.—Fire confined to engineering spaces. Reflash watches set in surrounding compartments. Energized electrical wiring still a hazard to firefighters.
- 7:25 p.m.—Crew mustered on station.
- 7:46 p.m.—All fires under control. #1 ship's service generator secured. P-500 pump secured. Reflash watches set in after engine room and boiler uptakes. All spaces on the maindeck level being dewatered.
- 8:00 p.m.—Class A and B reflash fire discovered in the boiler uptakes.
- 8:03 p.m.—Reflash fire extinguished using hose charged from *Nimble*.
- 8:08 p.m.—Merchant ship SS *Tropicana* departed as no assistance was needed from her.
- 8:44 p.m.—Class A and B reflash fire discovered on starboard side of after engine room.
- 8:50 p.m.—Reflash fire extinguished.
- 8:51 p.m.—List decreased by dewatering to two degrees to starboard.
- 8:55 p.m.—Remains of men previously logged as missing removed from the after engine room.
- 9:17 p.m.—One ration each of medical brandy distributed to the crew.
- 10:00 p.m.—Coast Guard ship (hull number 36445), USS *Cone* (DD 866), USS *Ellison* (DD 864), and USS *Shangri La* (CVA 38) in the vicinity to offer assistance if needed. Fire damage includes charring of forward engine room, boiler uptakes, and all spaces on the maindeck, starboard side, amidships. All electrical circuits leading through the spaces burned or charred. All machinery inoperative in these spaces, although not damaged beyond repair. Entire interior of ship blackened by smoke, and ship generally unsuitable for habitation. Engineering spaces hot, their air containing oil vapor.
- 10:05 p.m.—Commenced restowing all fire hoses in respective fire stations. P-500 pump moved to the fantail and connected to a firemain riser and an eductor in the after engine room bilge. All other usable damage control gear assembled on the fantail.
- 11:12 p.m.—Preparations commenced for tow astern of *Nimble*.
- 11:14 p.m.—Towing hawser received from *Nimble* and secured on deck.
- 11:15 p.m.—*Nimble* away to take station ahead.
- 11:33 p.m.—Ship underway in tow five hundred yards astern of *Nimble*, en route to Savannah, Georgia.

Exultant remained at Savannah only a short while before being brought to Charleston Naval Shipyard for repairs. The ship returned to duty on 28 May 1961 upon the completion of a nine-month overhaul.

As a result of this fire, MSOs were modified by the addition of an escape scuttle from the soundproof watchstander's booth in the main engine room into the magnetic cable reel well above it. The *Exultant* watch team did not have this means of escape and, trapped in the booth, perished in the flames.[17]

USS *STALWART* (MSO 493)

On 28 March 1966, *Stalwart* capsized and sank as a result of fire. At about 3:30 a.m. on 25 June, while *Stalwart* was berthed at the tender pier, Naval Station, San Juan, Puerto Rico, fire broke out in a machinery space. Shipboard personnel were immediately joined in combating the fire by the Naval Station fire department, Naval Station personnel, and numerous fire parties from other ships present. However, at 12:10 p.m., after nearly nine hours of heroic efforts, *Stalwart* capsized and sank. Luckily, no casualties or serious injuries occurred among some 250 personnel who had fought the fire.[18]

Immediately after *Stalwart* sank, the division commander established a security watch to guard the area and prevent pilferage. *Stalwart's* crew was berthed in the Naval Station barracks and was issued clothing and other personal effects since their gear had either been destroyed by the fire or gone down with the ship. The next day salvage operations began under the direction of CoMinDiv 44. First priority was removal of topside material that might be in the way of specialized salvage personnel and equipment.[19]

Commander, Service Squadron 8 assumed duties as the on-scene commander on 29 June 1966. On 5 July USS *Escape* (ARS 6) and USS *Hoist* (ARS 40) began salvage operations to right and raise the burnt and sunken hulk.[20]

Stalwart was located alongside the tender pier, resting on the bottom with an eighty-degree list to starboard. On 13 July, *Escape* shifted her berth, mooring to the Puerto Rico Dry Dock Company Pier and Tender Pier East. *Hoist* moved to an athwartship location between the tender pier and the commercial pier to position herself for recovery operations. The self-propelled seaplane wrecking derrick YSD 27 moored port side to the salvage ship. A civilian non-self-propelled eighty-ton crane barge had moored alongside *Escape*'s port side earlier and was now made up to *Hoist*'s starboard side, separating the two salvage ships.[21]

The following day, *Escape* pumped fresh water and fuel from forward to aft tanks to ballast the ship, set the maneuvering detail, and commenced, with *Hoist*, the operation to lift *Stalwart*'s bow. However, the civilian non-self-propelled crane's lift wire broke under maximum strain, placing the entire load on *Hoist* and *Escape*. The latter backed her engines full to compensate for the weight but the wire bridle connecting the tow wire to bollards on the pier parted, injuring a crewmember. Engines were stopped, the tow wire was re-rigged, and the lift operation began again. Operations had to be stopped again at dusk while bow lights were rigged aboard *Hoist*, cofferdams were fabricated and installed on *Stalwart*'s submerged fantail, and electrical submersible pumps were rigged to pump water from inside her hull. On 15 July, *Hoist*'s boatswain mates rigged two one-and-five-eighths-inch diameter parbuckling wires under the winch and through the auxiliary bow lift rollers. *Escape* placed number 2 main engine on the line for deck power and at 2:18 p.m. put number 1 and 3 main engines in the propulsion loop and began backing at fifteen revolutions per minute while taking a strain on the bow lift gear. She stopped both shafts at 3:46 p.m. *Hoist*, meanwhile, manned her lifting stations at 6:46 p.m. and resumed operations. Work was halted at 7:50 p.m. due to an excessive load on *Hoist* from the stern area of the wreck—now up by the bow. *Escape* and *Hoist* operated numerous pumps to remove water from the wreck, and by early in the morning of 16 July the bow was ten feet off the bottom with twenty-five degrees of starboard list.[22]

Hoist remanned lifting stations that afternoon and, after taking a moderate strain on main lift reels, began heaving around on all four legs of the bow lifting gear. The salvage operation continued throughout the day. The procedure was: heave around on the bow lifting gear, pause to pump water from the wreck, and heave around again. Late in the day, *Hoist* crewmembers manned heavy lift stations to ease out on the beach gear wires and parbuckling wires as a prelude to refloating the minesweeper.[23]

After raising *Stalwart* on 17 July, the two salvage ships unrigged beach gear and shifted berths to the tender pier, and *Stalwart*'s crew immediately began removing equipment, machinery, and spare parts, with preservation of material the primary objective. Two days later, *Stalwart* was dry docked for the removal and preservation of main and auxiliary machinery. By the end of August, preservation of all equipment was complete and *Stalwart* was placed "Out of Commission, Special" on 24 August 1966.[24]

By that time, all but eighteen crewmembers had been reassigned. The remaining nucleus crew was assigned the task of cleaning up and preparing *Stalwart* to be towed to Charleston. On 16 November, re sponsibility for *Stalwart* was assumed by the commanding officer of USS *Saliman* (ATF 161), an ocean tug. *Saliman* departed San Juan with *Stalwart* in tow the next day, arriving at Charleston on 22 November 1966. The U.S. Navy Sub-Board of Inspection and Survey found *Stalwart* unfit for further service and estimated the cost of repairs to be $3,500,000. The acquisition cost of *Stalwart* had been $4,920,444, and it was estimated that a new like ship would cost $7,000,000. *Stalwart* was stricken from the Navy List on 1 March 1967.[25]

The robustness, even after damage, of ocean minesweepers was documented by a 23 February 1968 message from the Atlantic Fleet commander to the Chief of Naval Operations. In response to a proposal to destroy *Stalwart* as a target, he stated:

> A review of *Stalwart* hull characteristics indicate[s] that sinking is extremely unlikely if used as a live target. Possibility of floating debris and the hulk itself constituting dangers to navigation is very high. These factors outweigh training benefits which could be derived by using *Stalwart* as target. It is therefore recommended that *Stalwart* be disposed of by means other than target to destruction.[26]

USS *AVENGE* (MSO 423)

On 6 October 1969, fire struck *Avenge* while the ship was in dry dock undergoing a $1.25 million conversion at Bethlehem Shipyard on Key Highway near Baltimore, Maryland. A large portion of the amidships section, particularly the main deck and above and the electrical wireways under the main deck, was damaged before the fire was extinguished by the U.S. Coast Guard and the Baltimore Fire Department. No casualties or injuries to personnel resulted, but except for preserving government material, no further work was performed on *Avenge*.[27]

A board of inquiry convened in October found that no action of the commanding officer, executive officer, or any other member of the crew had contributed to the fire. The shipyard had failed to put fire-resistant coverings in place prior to hot work, as required in the specifications. In the opinion of the board, the fire had originated in the bilge of the after engine room as a result of sparks or molten metal from welding or brazing, a lighted cigarette or cigar, or an electrical short. The board recommended that the shipyard be held accountable for damages.[28]

A letter dated 7 January 1970 from the Chief of Naval Operations to the Secretary of the Navy reported that restoration of *Avenge* would incur a $3.5 million deficit in Ship Construction Navy (SCN) funds and require fourteen months. In contrast, striking the ship would generate assets—$1.5 million in SCN and approximately $4.6 million in new and used material. The letter also noted that the president of the Board of Inspection and Survey had found the ship unfit for further service. *Avenge* was decommissioned three weeks later, on 31 January 1970.[29]

USS *SAGACITY* (MSO 469)

On 19 March 1970, *Sagacity* grounded in low visibility on the seaward end of the south jetty at the entrance to Charleston Harbor, causing extensive damage to her rudders, shafts, screws, keel, and hull. Aground at 4:41 p.m., the ship was refloated at about 7:00 that evening with the assistance of a Navy tug and proceeded to the MineLant piers on one shaft, accompanied by the tug. Five days later, on 24 March, *Sagacity* entered drydock in Wando Division of Deytens Shipyards for temporary repairs to ensure her watertight integrity. At completion of repairs on 29 April, she returned to Charleston.[30]

Four months later, as the Navy continued to reduce its mine force, a decision was made to inactivate *Sagacity*. The ship began pre-inactivation on 17 August 1970 in preparation for decommissioning; she was stricken from the Navy List and accepted into the Inactive Ship Facility detachment, Charleston, on 1 October. The Naval Ship Systems Command estimated that replacement of the ship, which had originally cost $5,070,854, would in current dollars cost ten million and that her scrap value was only $15,500. The Supervisor of Shipbuilding estimated that it would cost $400,000 to repair damage to the underwater hull, shafts, propellers, and sonar dome, noting that this figure did not include normal overhaul costs of approximately $200,000.[31]

USS *ENHANCE* (MSO 437)

On 17 March 1973, while participating in Operation END SWEEP and at anchor in the approaches to Hon Gai Harbor, North Vietnam, following a strenuous day of minesweeping, *Enhance* caught fire and burned at sea. During the ten preceding days she had assisted in the neutralization of the approaches to Haiphong Harbor and had been the first U.S. ship to sweep and control helicopter sweeping in the approaches to Hon Gai Harbor, north of Haiphong. At about 9:50 p.m. on the 17th, fire broke out in the forward engine room as a result of a leaking generator fuel line spraying diesel on a hot engine. The ensuing fire quickly raged out of control, forcing an evacuation of the space by the watchstanders.[32]

Enhance lost all electrical power about eight minutes after the fire was reported, but not before she transmitted a message requesting help. Even though *Enhance* was only ten miles from the support ship, it appears that other units were unsure at first of her exact location. Her crewmembers valiantly battled the flames with salt water from portable firefighting pumps and the installed aqueous-film-forming foam sprinkler system. Delivery of gasoline and foam concentrate by helicopters enabled the fire fighters to continue their effort. *Illusive* and the salvage ship USS *Safeguard* (ARS 50) soon arrived, having steamed through unswept waters. *Safeguard* moored to *Enhance*'s starboard side and provided additional firefighting water and relief firefighting personnel. By daybreak on 18 March the fire had been put out and all but fifteen crewmembers had left the ship for transfer to Subic Bay. *Enhance* was then towed to the Ship Repair Facility at Subic Bay for repair of $180,000 in damage, arriving on 23 March.[33]

The extensive fire damage to structural, mechanical, and electrical components of the forward engine room necessitated a lengthy repair period that lasted from 23 March until 8 July. Virtually every piece of equipment in that space was replaced or overhauled. In addition, the galley was remodeled because the fire had weakened the deck beneath the space and ruined the appliances. At completion of the shipyard period, *Enhance*'s crew conducted refresher training and was ready by late July to meet operational commitments.[34]

USS *FORCE* (MSO 445)

The final disastrous loss among Pacific Fleet ocean minesweepers occurred on 24 April 1973, when *Force* suffered an uncontrollable fire in her after engine room and sank in the Philippine Sea. She had left Subic Bay in the Philippines on the 21st, bound for her homeport of Guam for an overhaul and was sailing unaccompanied, as was then the custom. This was the first sinking of a U.S. Navy ship since the disappearance of USS *Scorpion* (SSN 589) with ninety-nine men on 24 May 1968.

Force had been attached to Mine Flotilla 1 and Task Force 78, which had been clearing Haiphong Harbor of mines until suspension of minesweeping operations the preceding week. The crew, forced to abandon ship when fire swept through the vessel, lowered lifeboats and left the minesweeper. No loss of life occurred, though a few personnel received burns while attempting to combat the fire prior to abandoning ship. Rescue aircraft found all sixty-five enlisted men and five officers safe in lifeboats and life rafts, 820 miles west of Guam. The castaways were picked up by the British merchant ship *Sprayness* and delivered to Okinawa.[35]

Force had sunk at 10:53 a.m., local time, on 24 April 1973, at 13 degrees 5 minutes north latitude, 131 degrees 25 minutes east longitude, in approximately 3,200 fathoms of water.[36]

In addition to the devastating conflagrations that damaged or caused loss of ships, fires of lesser scale—in one case from suspected arson—afflicted many sweeps. On 5 January 1975, while the ship was en route to San Diego, California from liberty in the Mexican resort city of Ensenada, fire broke out at 9:45 a.m. in the after engine room of *Enhance*. She had just completed a full-power trial when a lubricating oil filter vent valve failed, spraying oil onto the hot turbochargers of number 1 main engine. The engine room watchstanders were forced to evacuate the space because of heavy smoke, and *Enhance* lost electrical power in approximately ten minutes. However, she had transmitted an emergency message at 9:49 a.m. to her division mate *Pluck*, sailing in company. As the fire raged out of control, *Pluck* courageously moored alongside to assist in extinguishing the blaze. Repair parties from *Enhance* battled the fire for about two and a half hours using aqueous-film-forming foam, fire hoses, and an installed sprinkler system. Additional firefighting equipment and supplies were flown in by helicopter, and ten crewmembers were evacuated because of smoke inhalation.[37]

The fleet ocean tug USS *Cree* (ATF 84) arrived that afternoon with six personnel from the repair ship USS *Jason* (AR 8). *Cree* took the damaged minesweeper in tow after *Pluck* had cast off following ten hours

Photo 8-1

Enhance (MSO 437) on fire at sea (courtesy of MNC(SW) Mathew Prager)

of effort. *Pluck* proceeded to San Diego, where *Enhance* subsequently moored outboard of *Pluck* on 6 January 1975.[38]

Later that month, on the 27th, Atlantic Fleet minesweeper *Illusive* suffered damage as a result of arson. At 10:15 p.m., while the ship was at anchor, dense smoke began issuing from the magnetic cable reel well. For the next two hours, crewmembers fought and extinguished the fire, which had originated in the after engine room, located below the reel well. Although the ship did not suffer any structural damage or personnel injuries, the fire caused extensive damage to engine room degaussing cables, engine control wiring, and electrical lighting circuits. *Illusive* was taken under tow and arrived the next day at Naval Station Charleston. During the ensuing investigation, a watchstander admitted that he, acting alone, had set the fire that had endangered the lives of his shipmates. He was tried at general court martial, found guilty, and punished by dishonorable discharge from the naval service and confinement at hard labor for ten years.[39]

In the eleven years after *Force* was lost, additional firefighting gear was installed in all ocean minesweepers. Improvements included installation of shipwide high-temperature alarm systems to detect abnormal temperatures or fire, and, in the forward and after engine rooms, salt-water sprinklers and firefighting systems that used aqueous film-forming foam and halogenated hydrocarbon (Halon).

On 20 July 1977, *Direct* caught fire. The ship had been en route Boston when the engine room watch reported a fire, which raged quickly out of control and led to loss of electrical power. Damage control parties fought the fire with installed portable pumps and, after almost two hours, successfully extinguished it. The destroyer USS *Newman K. Perry* (DD 883) took the damaged sweep in tow, arriving at Newport on 21 July. *Direct* remained in Newport until 14 December 1977, when she was towed by a Military Sealift Command vessel to the Philadelphia Naval Shipyard.[40]

On 1 October 1979, *Direct*'s homeport was changed from Perth Amboy, New Jersey, to Charleston, the ship having been out of homeport since July 1977 as a result of the repair of the fire and the subsequent overhaul.[41]

On 27 September 1978, a second Mine Division 123 ship, *Detector*, was damaged by a fire in the after engine room while underway for crew training. At 11:59 p.m., off Long Island, New York, the crankcase of number 1 main engine exploded, setting the engine room ablaze and filling the ship with smoke. The ship immediately sounded the General Quarters alarm, and through the efforts of all hands extinguished the fire. A U.S. Navy tug towed *Detector* into port on 28 September. Fortunately, there had been no personnel casualties and only minimal material damage. *Detector* spent the remainder of 1978 at her homeport, Newport, while her crew prepared for an interim dry docking restricted availability to repair the damage. On 30 March 1979, *Detector* moved from Pier 1 at the Naval Education and Training Center to nearby Newport Shipyard.[42]

The ship returned to operational status on 3 April 1980, when she shifted back to Pier 1.[43]

Since two of four minesweepers of the same type had suffered serious fires originating in their engine rooms, on 28 September 1978 *Dominant*'s squadron commander ordered her to enter Charleston, prohibiting the ship from using her diesels until she had received a comprehensive inspection, which subsequently revealed both main engines required complete overhauls. The ship was towed back to her homeport for repairs.[44]

Fires, the nemesis of the ocean minesweepers, have also damaged modern *Avenger*-class mine countermeasures ships, giving reminder that a fire originating anywhere in a wooden vessel is a potential ship killer.

9 Operation EARNEST WILL

Trade follows the flag.
British proverb, nineteenth century

In 1980 Iraq invaded Iran, citing territorial claims to the Shatt al Arab, the embayment formed by the Tigris and Euphrates Rivers that flows southeast into the Persian Gulf and forms part of the border between Iran and Iraq (see map 9-1). A variety of antagonisms, however, had existed for a long time between the two governments, rivals for dominance in the region. The ensuing long and costly war continued until the UN arranged a cease-fire in 1988, with no clear victor having ensued. During the war, Iran suffered more than a million casualties as well as the severe disruption of its economy. The Iraqi people also suffered greatly and were to endure yet more hardship during the subsequent Persian Gulf War.[1]

FACTORS PROMPTING U.S. NAVY INVOLVEMENT IN THE IRAQ-IRAN WAR

During the Iranian War, Iraq found that although it had superior weapons its advantage was offset by Iran's numerically superior armies, and it accordingly wanted to prevent Iran from selling oil and thereby funding an improved military. Iraq established a zone off Iran's coast and notified foreign governments that it would attack ships that crossed this "line of death" to enter Iranian ports. Iraqi F-1 Mirage fighter aircraft routinely launched from bases in the north, flew southeast over the Persian Gulf, and attacked with missiles surface contacts located by radar. The guided missile frigate USS *Stark* (FFG 31) was struck by two Iraqi-launched Exocet missiles in such an attack on 17 May 1987,

Map 9-1

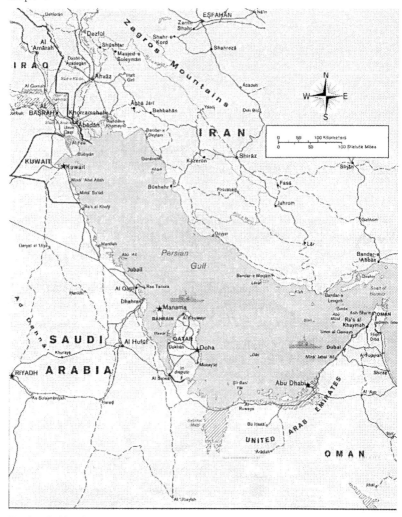

Persian Gulf: U.S. minesweepers operated from Bahrain during Operation EARNEST WILL, and from Dubai, UAE, during Operation DESERT SHIELD/STORM, to conduct mine clearance operations throughout the Persian Gulf.

causing the deaths of thirty-seven sailors, the wounding of five, and considerable damage to the ship.[2]

This was a difficult time for commanding officers of U.S. Navy ships, because the existing peacetime and wartime rules of engagement were separate and distinct and did not clearly address the gray area of operations during times when the nation was neither at peace nor at war. A commanding officer waiting for the certainty of hostile intent might allow an enemy aircraft to approach within effective missile range and find himself acting possibly too late to prevent damage to his ship. On the other hand, an Iraqi aircraft meeting parameters for engagement by shipboard weapon systems conceivably might not be flying an attack against the ship. At the time, the rules also did not allow U.S. Navy ships to protect vessels not sailing under the American flag from air or surface attack. To minimize the possibility of attack, some merchant vessels sailed with their navigation lights extinguished. Many ships did not use their radars, fearing that the Iranian Guard would be able to pinpoint their location through electronic emissions and attack them; they chose instead to navigate by satellite or visual information. Vessels also commonly operated with water from fire hoses spraying continuously onto their decks and lifeboat davit-arms down—ready, if necessary, instantly to fight fires or abandon ship.

Iran, meanwhile, was attacking ships delivering materials to Iraq and taking delivery of oil, using naval ships, aircraft, and small boats (Swedish-manufactured "Boghammers" and Boston Whaler–style craft, operated by the Iranian Revolutionary Guard). The Iranian naval order of battle included four British-built Vosper Thornycroft Mark 5 frigates that were based at Bandar e Abbas, a port city on the Strait of Hormuz; they usually operated in the waters south of the Iranian Sassan and Rostam oil fields. Purchased by the Shah of Iran, the formidable well-armed ships could obtain a top speed of 40 knots. Standard procedure for these vessels was to query the master or watch officer of a merchant vessel identified during the day by marine radio about the ship's last port of call, destination, and cargo manifest. If not satisfied with the answers, the warship would normally allow the vessel to proceed and then attack it later at night with guns or Sea-killer missiles. The frigates *Sabalan* and *Sahand*, named for two very high volcanic mountains in northwestern Iran, were particularly vicious; the commander of the former became known as "Captain Nasty" for attacking defenseless vessels and ruthlessly killing many merchant seamen.[3]

The *Pasdaran*, the Iranian Revolutionary Guard, operated forty speedboats, capable of speeds up to 50 knots, purchased from the Swedish shipbuilding firm of Boghammer Marin. Less powerful but far more maneuverable and cheaper than the frigates, the craft were armed with heavy infantry weapons, normally 12.7 and 14.5mm heavy-machine guns, Russian rocket-propelled grenade (RPG) launchers (or the Chinese version, the Type 56 Anti-Tank Grenade Launcher), and 107mm rocket launchers. Initially, these boats were under naval control, but later a naval Iranian Guard headquarters was established at Bandar e Abbas. A common tactic for the Guardsmen aboard the speedboats was to fire the shoulder-held rocket launchers at the bridges of merchant ships and rake vessels with machine gun fire to wound or kill crewmen and thereby disable or discourage the tankers. Understandably, some seamen chose not to sign on merchant ships entering the Gulf, and some insurance companies declined to insure the ships.[4]

From the beginning of the Iraq-Iran War in 1980, merchant vessels regularly suffered, in addition to aircraft and surface attacks, mine attacks by both sides in the shipping lanes of the Persian Gulf. Escalation of Iranian attacks specifically targeting Kuwaiti vessels in the latter part of 1986 prompted Kuwait to request convoy protection from other nations for its tankers. When the Soviets agreed to assist Kuwait, the Reagan administration, previously reluctant to become engaged in the conflict, decided formally to offer protection to half of Kuwait's tanker fleet by allowing it to sail under the American flag, with appropriate U.S. military protection. This decision was prompted by increased attacks on merchant shipping, especially by Iran, and the possibility that without U.S. intervention the Soviet Union would enhance its position in the region at American expense by gaining influence with countries that might otherwise prefer U.S. assistance. The West's disinclination to commit itself to protecting the smaller Arab states—Bahrain, Kuwait, Qatar, and the U.A.E.—from being drawn into the war was becoming increasingly unacceptable in terms of both Cold War and Middle East politics. On 19 May 1987, President Reagan formally announced a U.S.-Kuwaiti reflagging agreement that had been signed on 2 April:

> The use of the sea-lanes will not be dictated by the Iranians. These lanes will not be allowed to come under the control of the Soviet Union. The Persian Gulf will remain open to navigation by the nations of the World.

To comply with U.S. legal requirements, eleven of Kuwait's twenty-two tankers had their ownership transferred to the U.S. Chesapeake Shipping Company, permitting them to be protected by U.S. naval vessels.[5]

The movement of merchant convoys into and out of the Persian Gulf via the Strait of Hormuz was already dangerous due to the Iranian frigates and Boghammers operating from nearby Bandar e Abbas, and Iranian missile batteries that fired Chinese CSSC-2 "Silkworm" antiship missiles sited in the area. In an effort to stop the convoys, Iran laid mines in the Gulf shipping lanes and other areas through which the ships and their escorts might pass, having apparently taken seriously U.S. threats to destroy the missile sites if Silkworms were fired at American-led convoys. The mining of international waters by any country is considered a hostile act. However, by this action Iran made possible the deterrence, damage, or loss of vessels while allowing it to disclaim responsibility. To deploy the weapons, the Iranian Navy installed mine rails in the landing craft *Iran Ajr*, while the Iranian Guard apparently commandeered dhows (indigenous Persian Gulf sailing vessels) and outfitted them with cranes capable of laying half-ton moored mines.[6]

Originally, U.S. mine experts thought the most common mines employed were North Korean–manufactured copies of the Soviet M-08 contact mine. Later evaluation determined that the mines, of a 1908 Russian design with protruding horns, had been manufactured in Iran and had several characteristics that distinguished them as uniquely Iranian. Some of these mines broke free of their mooring cables and, with drifting MYaM contact mines laid by Iraq and Iran in the early 1980s, littered the Gulf, posing an immense threat to shipping. Iran also had a few U.S. Mark 65 ground mines inherited from the Shah, in addition to miscellaneous Soviet-designed types, among them the air-laid AMD-500 and AMG-1 as well as the ship-laid KRAB.[7]

Later in the year, the Iranians were caught in the act mining offshore shipping routes. During the night of 20 September 1987, two U.S. Army Special Forces McDonald-Douglas MH6A helicopters, operating from the guided-missile frigate USS *Jarrett* (FFG 33), discovered the *Iran Ajr* laying mines and attacked her, killing five crewmen and disabling the craft. Navy SEALs then boarded the vessel and took twenty-six prisoners (of whom one was mortally wounded), photographed her cargo of ten M-08 mines and later, following the collection of all available intelligence, took her out to deep water and scuttled her. Captured documents revealed that the vessel had been following specific orders to lay mines, three of which were found the next week twenty miles off Dubai, one of the United Arab Emirates. In addition to proving an embarrassment to Iranian President Ali Hussein Khamanei, this incident increased the country's international isolation.[8]

INITIAL U.S. NAVY INVOLVEMENT IN MINE CLEARANCE

The U.S. Navy became involved in mine clearance in the spring of 1987 when U.S. Navy explosive ordnance disposal (EOD) divers cleared ten contact mines near Kuwait's Al Ahmadi oil terminal. This operation was supported by Kuwaiti and Saudi Arabian surface forces and took place after U.S. Navy EOD divers spotted mines from a Kuwaiti Air Force helicopter. Following discovery of the mines, Commander, Mine Warfare Command deployed a quick response team and equipment from Mine Squadron 2 in the United States to Kuwait to assist in mine search and clearance. Additionally, Commander, Naval Air Force Atlantic placed helicopter minesweeping squadron HM 14 on twenty-four-hour alert status.[9]

Shortly after the Iraqi missile attack on *Stark*, the first convoy protected by U.S. Navy warships under Operation EARNEST WILL, directed by Commander Middle East Force (CMEF), began steaming toward Kuwait on 24 July 1987. Escort of the reflagged tankers and U.S. ships through the Persian Gulf to Kuwait waters and back through the Strait of Hormuz (see map 9-2) continued for three years until 16 August 1990. During this period, the U.S. Navy conducted 480 missions and escorted 640 merchant vessels.[10]

During the maiden EARNEST WILL convoy, with U.S. Navy escort ships sailing ahead and astern, the reflagged steamship *Bridgeton* struck a mine the morning of the first day, on 24 July 1987, nineteen nautical miles west of Farsi Island. Water rushing in through the resulting thirty-five- by forty-five-foot hole in her port bow flooded four compartments, reducing her speed from 16 to 5 knots, but did not stop her. Supplied with information regarding the route of the ships, Iranian Revolutionary Guards had laid three fields with some sixty mines, mostly of the M-08 type, along the convoy's path. During the following days, about a dozen mines were found in the vicinity where the tanker had been hit. The cruiser *Fox* (CG 33), destroyer *Kidd* (DDG 993), and frigate *Crommelin* (FFG 37) fell in astern of the supertanker and the steamship *Gas Princess* to take advantage of their deeper draft for protection against additional moored mines, and the convoy continued on

Map 9-2

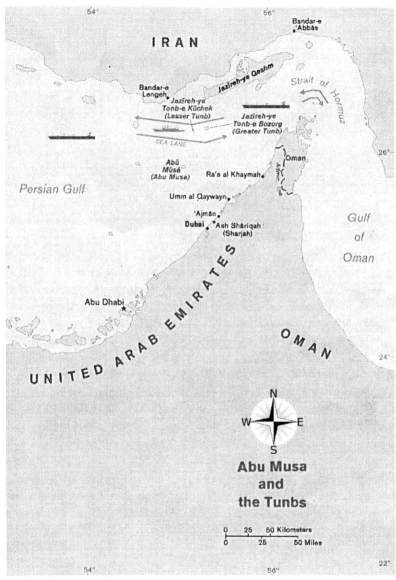

Strait of Hormuz: Navy escort ships formed up merchant convoys in the Gulf of Oman, prior to escorting them to Kuwait and back via the Strait of Hormuz.

to Kuwait. The *Bridgeton* was repaired in Dubai following her return transit and returned to service on 15 October.[11]

THE IRANIAN THREAT TO MERCHANT VESSELS

Farsi and Abu Musa Islands were the sites of two major naval bases from which Iranian Guards launched Boghammer attacks on merchant vessels. Ship convoys entering the Gulf had to skirt Abu Musa in the southern Gulf, after passing within range of Silkworm missiles located at sites around the Strait of Hormuz, and then avoid Farsi in the northern Gulf en route Kuwait. The fully loaded tankers and their escort ships ran the gauntlet the opposite way during passage out of the Gulf. However, the ship convoys were susceptible to attack anywhere along their route, as units of the Iranian Guard, which had grown to 20,000 strong by 1987, also operated from many other locations. The force of Boghammers based at Farsi and Abu Musa operated in patrols of three or four speedboats from forward bases at Kharg, Rostam field oil platforms, Larak, Sirri, the Tunbs, Qeshm, Henjam, Al Karan, and Al Farisiyah. These sites monitored maritime radio traffic between vessels and used radars installed on offshore oil platforms to locate and target merchant ships for attack.[12]

The Iranian Guard suffered its first defeat on 8 October 1987. A Boghammer and two Boston Whaler–type craft detected during a nighttime surveillance mission by MH-6 helicopters operating from the guided missile frigate USS *Thach* (FFG 43) fired upon the unseen aircraft overhead. The helicopters promptly returned fire, sinking one of the craft and damaging the others. The helicopters employed were referred to by sailors aboard ship as "sea bats" because they were stowed inside helicopter hangers by day and emerged only after dark. The pilots of the very small but lethal aircraft were Army Warrant Officers, many former Cobra pilots during the Vietnam War. Weapon systems fitted on the sides of the helicopters, a rocket launcher and 40mm gun, were not trainable, necessitating pivoting of the aircraft from side to side to engage enemy targets. The pilots maintained proficiency by targeting empty fifty-five-gallon lube oil drums provided by the ship. During these nighttime events, observers aboard *Thach* saw only gun flashes from the unseen and otherwise silent aircraft.[13]

On 16 October, while she was operating in Kuwaiti waters, the Iranian Guards attacked the U.S.-reflagged tanker *Sea Isle City* with a

Silkworm missile fired from Al Faw in northern Iran, blinding the American captain and injuring nineteen crewmen. Although the vessel was not under U.S. Navy escort at the time of the attack, President Reagan announced two days later that the United States would retaliate. The following day, on 19 October, Operation NIMBLE ARCHER was launched against Rostam Oil Field in the southern Gulf, which was being used by the Iranian Guard for command and control purposes to locate and target merchant vessels. A group of five U.S. Navy warships, the *Thach* and four destroyers, took part in the operation, which resulted in the destruction of three inactive oil platforms used by the Iranian Guard as a naval base. A Farsi-speaking linguist aboard *Thach* broadcast warnings for fifteen minutes to allow any people aboard the derricks to evacuate; an oil field boat departed before the four destroyers demolished the first derrick with naval gunfire. The second platform was damaged by explosives transported by *Thach*'s motor-whaleboat and positioned on the platform by EOD personnel. Navy SEALS set the third platform on fire after spiking antiaircraft guns and damaging a search-radar on the roof of the derrick. During all this, the commandos captured intelligence spooling from a teletype, radios, small arms, and an Iranian flag.[14]

On 22 October, the Iranian 26th Missile Brigade defiantly launched a missile at Kuwait's Sea Island Terminal, its only facility able to handle tankers of greater than 500,000 dead weight tons. In response, Washington announced six days later a ban on imports and exports from and to Iran. Moreover, Kuwait provided the United States with another floating barge base, *Winbrown 7*, and electronic reconnaissance facilities to supplement capabilities the barge *Hercules* already lent U.S. military special forces.[15]

U.S. NAVY RESPONSE TO THE MINE ATTACK ON THE SS *BRIDGETON*

Following the mine attack on *Bridgeton*, the quick-response team of Mine Squadron 2, initially deployed in June and recalled in July when diplomatic clearance was denied, departed again in late July for Bahrain to provide a mine countermeasure capability.[16]

For *Bridgeton*'s return transit from Kuwait, the team outfitted two 150-foot Kuwaiti commercial tugs, *Hunter* and *Striker*, with standard MSB (minesweeping boat) mechanical minesweeping gear, "pigs, kites, and otters" (floats, diverters, and depressors). When one-third of the tugs' civilian crews refused to undertake minesweeping, U.S. sailors deployed with Mine Division 125 and experienced men serving ashore at the administrative support unit in Bahrain manned the minesweeping tugs. *Hunter* and *Striker* were positioned ahead of the lead ship in this and ensuing convoys, with their mechanical minesweeping gear streamed astern to cut any moored mines in the convoy's path.[17]

Helicopter Squadron 14, which had been on twenty-four-hour alert in Norfolk for over a month and had been directed just days before the damage to *Bridgeton* to unpack its equipment and return to normal seventy-two-hour alert, was ordered to the Gulf; the first load of its gear was airlifted east six hours later. When the squadron's eight RH-53D Sea Stallion minesweeping helicopters arrived, they began operations and searched visually for lines of mines in advance of the convoys, supported by the amphibious assault ships *Guadalcanal* (LPH 7) and *Okinawa* (LPH 3).[18]

STANDARD MERCHANT CONVOY OPERATIONS

Convoy missions began in the Gulf of Oman with U.S. Navy escort ships searching visually and by radar for merchant vessels assigned to particular convoys. Usually the tankers were steaming or anchored near the rendezvous position; occasionally, however, ships had entered port for provisions or repairs, were late, or failed to show up. The owners of the vessels, the companies that insured them, and the seamen who sailed in them were well aware that the Persian Gulf was a dangerous place. To help form the ships into a convoy, U.S. Navy liaison officers were lowered from helicopters by a suspended line. These transfers of personnel were likely more entertaining for observers than for the participants. Ship's masts and other hazards to flight forced the helicopters to remain fairly high above the vessels; in blustery weather, the officers swung back and forth like pendulums while being lowered to the rolling and pitching decks below. Once safely aboard, they found that seasoned masters, not accustomed to answering to anyone else at sea and particularly not the U.S. Navy, did not always welcome them with open arms. Each naval liaison officer had an encrypted hand-held radio to ensure that the convoy commander (the commanding officer of one of the naval escorts) could communicate with the masters and that the latter would follow orders. Transiting through waters within range of Iranian shore-based missiles was suspenseful. Some faster ships, mindful that the merchant ship *Sea Isle City* had received considerable damage when struck by a Silkworm missile, did not want to maintain the convoy's speed, which was dictated by the capability of the slowest vessel. Since the escorts generally availed themselves of the protection afforded them by sailing astern of the more deeply drafted tankers, the masters sometimes wondered aloud about who was protecting whom.

Navy planners selected massive deep-draft, thick-hulled oil tankers to lead the convoys, believing that while a mine strike would undoubtedly damage them, it would probably not sink them, whereas a significantly smaller naval vessel would probably not survive. This logic appears well founded, based on a comparison of the damage suffered by the *Bridgeton*, with a displacement of 400,000 tons, and, later in the war, by the guided missile frigate USS *Samuel B. Roberts* (FFG 58), at 4,000 tons. The merchant tanker, at the time the largest in the world, suffered hull damage, while the Navy ship, one one-hundredth the displacement, would have sunk if not for the rapid and courageous actions of her crew.[19]

Therefore, during transits of the merchant ships in and out of the Gulf, typically one or more large tankers led the convoy, followed by a Navy warship, additional merchant ships, another naval combatant, and one or two more merchants. "Tail-end Charlie" was the slowest vessel, placed last to allow it to maintain best speed and not have to jockey its engines continuously to keep station between a ship ahead and one astern, as did the other ships. The most immediate protection from mines was provided by helicopters based aboard the Navy combatants that flew ahead of the convoy to spot moored or floating mines and destroy them with gunfire from door-mounted .50-caliber machine guns, and by the two minesweeping craft.

The final defense against mine damage aboard Navy ships was the age-old mine watch, a crewmember posted in the "eyes of the ship" to detect and report shallow moored mines and to deflect with spray from fire hoses any "floaters" close aboard.

Mark III patrol boats (PBs) of a Naval Reserve Force Small Boat Unit safeguarded the flanks of convoys from attack by small boats, shouldering away potentially hostile craft. Living conditions aboard the small PBs were stark, and the crews a colorful lot. One boat, commanded by a towering lieutenant (junior grade) with machine-gun

Photo 9-1

Crew members stand watch on the bow of the guided missile destroyer USS *Kidd* (DDG 993) to visually search for floating or shallow-moored mines as the combatant escorts the reflagged Kuwaiti tankers *Gas King, Ocean City, Sea Isle City,* and *Bridgeton* (photographer PH2 Tolliver)

cartridge belts draped across his chest, flew the skull and crossed bones of the "Jolly Roger" from its mast. Periodically the PBs would come alongside larger Navy ships for fuel, supplies, decent meals, and niceties like showers and haircuts. Associating with these craft reminded ship's company that hardship at sea was relative.

U.S. RESPONSE TO THE CONTINUED MINE THREAT

Throughout 1987, mines continued to present a threat to shipping in the Gulf. By the beginning of July, the Saudis had discovered about a dozen mines in the approaches to Mina al Ahmadi, Kuwait (see map 10-1); in early August a dhow hit a mine off Bahrain, and a mine discovered later near the Saudi Khafji off-shore oil field caused a delay in the passage of a convoy of reflagged ships.[20]

A requirement for additional capabilities to clear mines prompted the departure from Charleston on 4 August 1987 of Commander, Mine Division 125, his staff, and four MSBs (minesweeping boats) aboard the amphibious transport dock USS *Raleigh* (LPD 1) for the Persian Gulf. Six days after the group sailed, the tanker *Texaco Caribbean* was severely damaged eight nautical miles off Al Fujayrah in the Gulf of Oman by a mine probably laid six days earlier when Iranian naval forces conducted Operation "MARTYRDOM," in and around the Strait of Hormuz, to practice mock suicide attacks on simulated American ships. The next day five mines were discovered off Al Fujayrah in an area widely regarded as a sanctuary for tankers about to enter the Gulf. In recognition of the danger to shipping, the U.A.E. declared on 30 August a thirty-square-mile danger area off her eastern coast and warned merchant vessels to stay at least two nautical miles from the zone. The new mine threat spurred international action. The Royal Navy dispatched four *Hunt*-class minehunters to join a fifth vessel, and the French and Soviets deployed three minehunters and three mine-sweepers, respectively. These and the newly arrived U.S. mine counter-measures force aboard *Raleigh* combed the zone but were initially unable to discover any mines. Restrictions were briefly rescinded but then reimposed with the discovery of two more mines. Following the mining of the supply vessel *Anita*, with the loss of the vessel, four crewmen, and her owners, many ships berthed off Al Fujayrah moved to Mina al Fahal in Muscat, Oman, whose waters were regarded as safer.[21]

Their caution was apparently justified following the sinking of the research ship *Marissa I* twenty nautical miles northwest of Al Arabiyah Island. The arrival of seven Belgian, Dutch, and Italian vessels strengthened the international mine countermeasures force to about thirty vessels, which gradually eliminated the threat, although in mid-October French minehunters discovered some mines off Khawr

Fakkan, U.A.E. The mine clearance efforts continued and between 20 and 25 November, British minehunters and U.S. ocean minesweepers discovered eighteen mines off Farsi Island and northeast of Bahrain. In late September, U.S. Secretary of Defense Caspar Weinberger had visited the Gulf region and promised that the United States would guarantee freedom of navigation in the Gulf.[22]

Unfortunately, the efforts of smaller fifty-seven-foot wooden U.S. Navy minesweeping boats (MSBs) to clear mines off Bahrain Bell, an area regularly used by American vessels, were unsuccessful, and *Raleigh* returned to Charleston in late November with the staff and boats. The shallow-draft MSBs, designed for inshore mine clearance, had been used extensively and successfully during the Vietnam War for river minesweeping. Fitted with proportionally smaller mechanical minesweeping gear than the MSOs, the boats were less capable in deeper waters and covered a narrower path with each pass through a mined area.[23]

Anticipating a lengthy requirement for minesweepers to clear mines in the Persian Gulf, the U.S. Navy had earlier deployed six MSOs, three each from the Pacific and Atlantic Fleets. These ships and crews performed extremely well in very demanding conditions, clearing minefields and supporting tanker escort missions by conducting sonar surveys of hundreds of miles of navigational Q-routes. The Belgian navy participated with two MSOs, *Breydel* (M906) and *Bovesse* (M909)—former MSO hulls 504 and 506, respectively, two of thirty-six MSOs built in the United States and immediately transferred to NATO countries as part of the Mutual Defense Assistance Program. (Hereafter the designation MSO refers to the U.S. MSOs.)[24]

In order to speed the arrival of the minesweepers and save wear and tear on the ships and their crews, the MSOs were towed from the United States to the Gulf. The salvage ship USS *Grapple* (ARS 53) towed the Atlantic Fleet ships—*Fearless, Illusive,* and *Inflict*—a distance of nine thousand nautical miles. The USS *Barbour County* (LST 1195), a tank landing ship based in San Diego, towed Pacific Fleet ships *Enhance, Esteem,* and *Conquest* to the Gulf.

A year and a half later, in March 1989, the Atlantic Fleet ships returned under their own power to the United States; the Pacific Fleet MSOs remained in the Gulf until 1990. During the intervening period, the Pacific and Atlantic MSO crews rotated differently: 25 percent of the crews aboard the Pacific Fleet ships were replaced each month, whereas the Atlantic Fleet held entire crews to a four-month rotation.

Pacific Fleet Minesweepers
The three Pacific Fleet Naval Reserve Force MSOs sailed shorthanded on 20 August from Seattle, Washington, for Pearl Harbor, Hawaii, under the command of Commodore John Jackson, a reserve officer commanding Mine Division 52. The ships left members of their bridge and combat information center teams behind to take part in an advanced mine hunting training program at Oak Harbor, Washington. There the teams developed techniques to be used in the Gulf and participated aboard *Pledge* and *Implicit* in a mine exercise in Puget Sound. A few days out of Seattle, the three sweeps rendezvoused with *Barbour County* to make up the first "enhanced tow" of its kind. Upon reaching Pearl Harbor on 1 September, the MSOs broke tow before entering port and maneuvered independently to their berths.[25]

The watch teams rejoined the ships in port and crewmembers attended 3rd Fleet Persian Gulf briefings. Upon departure of the group and when clear of restricted waters, the MSOs were made up once again in tow behind *Barbour County*. Four days later, *Conquest* suffered a collision with the amphibious ship while breaking away following an alongside replenishment, receiving structural damage to her port side. Her crew made the necessary temporary shoring repairs, and, detached by Commander, 3rd Fleet, *Conquest* returned to Pearl Harbor for repairs. The rest of the group continued to Subic Bay, arriving on 25 September. During the nineteen-day transit, the ships conducted firefighting training and gunnery exercises.[26]

At the naval repair facility in Subic Bay, *Enhance* and *Esteem* were docked for voyage repairs before taking part in early October in a mine hunting and minesweeping exercise. *Barbour County* and the two minesweepers left Subic Bay on 6 October for Singapore, arriving four days later for a visit before continuing the transit to Bahrain. The group arrived at the Gulf of Oman on 24 October and awaited the guided missile frigates USS *Carr* (FFG 52) and USS *Elrod* (FFG 55) to escort it through the Strait of Hormuz. Leading the ships in formation, *Esteem* became the first U.S. MSO to arrive in the Gulf, living up to her motto—"First in the Field." (The Belgian minesweepers *Breydel* and *Bovesse* had arrived earlier as part of a five-vessel Belgian-Dutch MCM flotilla, with the Belgian command and logistics support vessel *Zinnia* and the Dutch Tripartite-class minehunters *Maassluis* [M856] and *Hellevoetsluis* [M859].) The Pacific Fleet MSOs arrived the following day at Mina Sulman, the port of Manama, Bahrain, completing their 12,300-nautical-mile journey.[27]

Barbour County's 1st Lieutenant, Lieutenant Commander Jim Taplett (previously the XO of USS *Excel*), recalls the crossing of the Pacific and Indian oceans by his vessel and her charges:

> Our short notice tasking to design and execute the first-ever enhanced tow of these minesweepers halfway around the world was a challenging experience, requiring *Barbour County* to transform herself into both a fleet tug and a replenishment ship. In addition to a wide range of on-deck towing and fueling rigs, our tank deck housed some 300 tons of logistical gear. The towing configuration was a single column formation consisting of 1,000 feet of 10-inch towing hawser connecting the towing ship to the first minesweeper, followed by some 800 feet of 8-inch hawsers between the first, second, and third minesweepers. En route Hawaii we had to re-make broken tows on several occasions and consequently refine our techniques, with particularly useful assistance from offship expertise during a brief stop in Pearl Harbor. The entire journey took only 70 days to complete and was one of the longest by minesweepers in U.S. history. Everyone aboard felt a great sense of accomplishment in delivering these mission-critical assets to the theater of operations in record time.

Conquest departed Pearl Harbor after completion of repairs to rejoin *Esteem* and *Enhance*. En route, she stopped briefly at Kwajalein Atoll, spent ten days in port or near Subic Bay participating in a mine exercise and a night at the "Man of War Anchorage" in Singapore. Leaving the City of Lions, she sailed for Colombo, Sri Lanka, the final port at which Pacific Fleet ships normally stop before entering the Persian Gulf. *Conquest* arrived on 18 November at Mina Sulman.[28]

Atlantic Fleet Minesweepers

Mine Squadron 2 ships *Fearless* and *Illusive* left Charleston on 31 August and proceeded down the Cooper River for Little Creek to rendezvous with the other two deploying ships, *Inflict* and *Grapple*. *Fearless* and *Illusive* were active-force ships, *Inflict*, like the Pacific Fleet MSOs, a Naval Reserve Force vessel. Mine Squadron 2 staff members constituted the Commander's embarked transit group staff. The commodore and members of his staff would depart on 2 October for Bahrain, the former to assume duties as the Middle East Force Mine Countermeasures Group commander.[29]

On 6 September, *Fearless*, *Inflict*, and *Illusive* began their historic voyage, in which the *Grapple* towed the three minesweepers across the Atlantic and through the Mediterranean and Red Seas to the Gulf of Oman. The Atlantic crossing was marked by rough seas and rigorous training designed to prepare the MSO crews for the hostile Middle East environment.[30]

The group entered sunny Rota, Spain on 24 September, remaining for three days of needed rest and maintenance before continuing onward toward the Persian Gulf. Leaving port, the ships passed the Rock of Gibraltar in early morning and sailed into the Mediterranean Sea. Arriving in Haifa, Israel, the sailors were able to enjoy tours of Jerusalem and the surrounding countryside. The group stood out of port on 12 October for the Suez Canal and arrived the same day in Port Said, Egypt, where it anchored, awaiting the next southbound ship convoy. Finally, in the early morning, *Illusive* led the other minesweepers through the Suez Canal.[31]

After transiting the canal, the ships continued through the Red Sea, making a brief stop for fuel at Djibouti on 21 October. The small nation, which won its independence from France in 1977, is located on the northeastern coast of Africa in the Gulf of Tadjoura. Largely a desert land, it has almost no natural resources, and many of its people are nomads. However, it is strategically located at the southern entrance to the Red Sea and offers a free port for ships using the channel.[32]

After a brief stop in Djibouti, the ships continued on their journey. On 24 October, *Illusive* suffered damage to her forecastle when another MSO's towlines became fouled in her rudderpost and turned her ninety degrees from the tow course, causing *Illusive*'s bullnose to give way under the heavy strain. Accordingly, the towline bridles were disconnected, and *Illusive* continued under her own power. After arriving in the Gulf of Oman, *Grapple* detached from the group to begin a return transit, while the three MSOs continued on to the Persian Gulf.[33]

Arriving in the Gulf of Oman, the MSOs stood by to await escort by the guided missile frigates *Carr* and USS *Gallery* (FFG 26) through the Strait of Hormuz and across the Persian Gulf. Reaching Manama on 8 November, *Illusive* received repairs to her sonar and forecastle. Manama, the largest of the islands of the independent sultanate and more liberal by Western standards than its neighbors, is a favorite

Photo 9-2

A serviceman aboard *Inflict* (MSO 454) aims an FIM-92 Stinger portable antiaircraft missile system (photographer PH1 Mussi)

vacation spot of visitors to and inhabitants of the Persian Gulf. While in port, detachments of U.S. sailors trained in the use of shoulder-mounted Stinger missiles embarked in the MSOs to provide a self-defense capability against air threats.[34]

Stateside, *Adroit* served as a training platform for the "silver" and "gold" crews (two other complete crews that would sequentially replace each other during extended operations in the Gulf) as they prepared to deploy aboard *Inflict* in the Persian Gulf.[35]

OPERATIONS IN THE PERSIAN GULF—1987

Farsi Island Mine Danger Area

Enhance got underway from Bahrain for the first time on 4 November, conducting mine hunting training near Sitrah Anchorage before sailing with *Inflict* for Jubail, Saudi Arabia. After arrival, *Enhance* became the first U.S. Navy ship to use the repair facilities there. *Inflict* performed mine countermeasures in ensuing weeks in the Farsi Island Mine Danger Area (MDA), a minefield in the vicinity of the Iranian island of Farsi, locating ten mines before arrival at Bahrain in late January. Within the first eighteen months of mine clearance operations, the MSOs would account for over fifty moored mines, clear three major minefields, and check sweep convoy tracks throughout the Persian Gulf.[36]

Photo 9-3

A crewmember paints a symbol representing a mine on the bridgewing of *Inflict*, representing the number of mines it has discovered and destroyed in Gulf shipping lanes (photographer PH1 Mussi)

Esteem conducted local operations while waiting for tasking and the arrival of the three Atlantic Fleet MSOs. Anchored nearby at Bahrain Bell was the dock landing ship USS *Mount Vernon* (LSD 39), used as both a mobile base for the minesweeping helicopters and the "MSO mother ship" for fuel, supplies, provisions, mail, and water. With the arrival of the Atlantic Fleet MSOs, *Esteem* received orders to proceed to the northern Persian Gulf. She left with *Fearless* to conduct mine hunting in the Farsi MDA. The operation began on 19 November and continued through 28 March 1988, during which time Task Unit 801.4.7 located and destroyed a total of sixteen mines. The task unit was formed, following the mining of international waterways by Iranian forces, from the six MSOs and four explosive ordnance disposal mine countermeasures detachments.[37]

Fearless, the second MSO to enter the mined area, located three mines during November; divers from EOD Mobil Unit 6, based in Charleston, South Carolina, countercharged (detonated) them. Arriving from Jubail, *Enhance* conducted MCM operations at Farsi in late November.[38]

Illusive, repairs finished to her bow and forecastle, and *Conquest*, her short respite in port completed following the long trek to the Persian Gulf, sailed from Bahrain to join the mine countermeasures effort. *Conquest* was underway in the MDA in early December, mooring briefly one day alongside the barge *Hercules*. Leased from Kuwait, *Hercules* was anchored in international waters about 40 nautical miles from Farsi. Operating from the well-equipped floating base were 200 U.S. Special Forces personnel who used communications and signal intercept equipment to collect intelligence, Army Special Forces MH-6A helicopters, and Mark III patrol boats that guarded the flanks of convoys. Navy combatant ships alternately escorted convoys and guarded the barges and minesweepers working in nearby minefields. The ships had to be vigilant, but such duty did offer some humorous moments. A ship's serviceman from a guided-missile frigate, aboard the barge to provide needed haircuts, was asked by a SEAL officer if he would like lobster for lunch. He responded: "Sir, please do not go to any trouble for me." The officer replied "No trouble at all," affixed a swim mask and flippers, dived over the side, and quickly returned with a live lobster in each hand. *Illusive* operated throughout most of December, with many hours of Q-route surveying, mine hunting, Dan buoy laying, and

Photo 9-4

Minesweeper *Illusive*, the ("MSO mothership") dock landing ship USS *Mount Vernon* (LSD-39), and a PBR Mark 2 riverine patrol boat at Sitrah anchorage (photographer PH2 Elliott)

control of minesweeping helicopters interrupted by short periods at Sitrah Anchorage for crew rest and upkeep.[39]

On 18 December, *Esteem* got underway from anchorage after receiving word of a mine drifting in the vicinity of the entrance to Bahrain's main shipping channel. Operating at night with half the crew ashore, she located and destroyed the live mine.[40]

Az Zuluf Oil Field
Enhance and *Fearless* alternately worked the Saudi Az Zuluf Oil Field in late November and early December. Moving from Farsi Island, *Enhance* began mine countermeasures operations with the Royal Saudi Navy in the oil field on 27 November. She left on the 5th of December for Sitrah Anchorage for upkeep and then entered Basrec (Bahrain Ship Repair Company) Shipyard (the first yard period for a U.S. ship at this facility). During the latter half of December, *Fearless* conducted mine countermeasures operations at Farsi, interrupted by a brief Christmas period at the Bahrain Bell and Sitrah anchorages. *Fearless* departed Farsi in late November for Bahrain. She sailed with a Saudi Arabian naval

escort on 11 December and conducted MCM operations in the oil field the following three days.[41]

The year 1987 was the most lethal of the Iraq-Iran War to ships in the Persian Gulf. Despite the presence of foreign warships during the year's latter half to provide protection for their country's merchant vessels, there were still 186 attacks against ships, with Iranian attacks outnumbering Iraqi. Although both countries specifically targeted tankers, 27.5 percent of the vessels suffering damage were other ship types. Less discriminate than missiles or gunfire, mines detonated against a variety of vessels. Through year's end, MSOs alternated working the Farsi MDA with upkeep time at Sitrah Anchorage or Bahrain Bell and time in port at Basrec Shipyard or Manama. Most ships spent a few days around Christmas at Sitrah Anchorage, and some servicemen were able to attend the Bob Hope USO show, starring Barbara Eden, Connie Stevens, Lee Greenwood, and others aboard the amphibious assault ship USS *Okinawa* (LPH 3) anchored near Bahrain.[42]

1988

During January, the MSOs were busy in the northern Persian Gulf conducting mine countermeasures and EARNEST WILL escort operations, involving exploratory mine hunting and airborne mine countermeasures control, Q-route surveys, and Dan buoy laying. Off-task time was spent undergoing maintenance at Basrec shipyard, upkeep at anchorage, or brief visits to Jubail. *Enhance* began the New Year engaged in mine hunting and providing support for ship convoys. On the 6th of January, her crew sighted a floating mine and sank it with small-arms fire.[43]

    Esteem left Sitrah in early February with *Illusive, Fearless,* and *Conquest* for the Farsi MDA, to operate near the northern mine line. *Esteem* anchored upon arrival and stayed at anchor through 11 February due to bad weather, with over twenty-knot winds and eight- to ten-foot seas. *Illusive* and *Conquest* sailed on 6 February for the King Abdul Aziz Naval Base, near the large commercial port at Jubail, Saudi Arabia. During the visit, *Illusive* hosted a reception for several distinguished guests, including Rear Admiral Less, Commander Joint Task Force Middle East Force; Rear Admiral Bernsen, Commander Middle East Force; Major General Farrington, Chief, U.S. Military Training Mission, Saudi

Photo 9-5

Bob Hope and Barbara Eden entertain crewmembers of ships deployed to the Persian Gulf aboard the amphibious assault ship USS *Okinawa* (LPH-3) anchored off Bahrain (photographer PH2 (SW) Jeff Elliott)

Arabia; and Commodore Badr, Commander King Abdul Aziz Naval Base Jubail, RSNF. Shortly afterward, Rear Admiral Less relieved Rear Admiral Bernsen and assumed a dual designation as both CJTFME and CMEF.[44]

Illusive and *Conquest* left Jubail to return to the Farsi MDA and rendezvous with the dock landing ship USS *Portland* (LSD 37) for fresh water, stores, and mail. Water for drinking, cooking, and showers was a scarce commodity in the Persian Gulf because the MSOs could not make sufficient quantities while mine hunting. Their Aquafresh evaporators used jacket water from the main engines to flash seawater to distillate; low speeds did not work the often-idling engines hard enough to reach the optimum temperature.[45]

Following her replenishment, *Conquest* moored outboard of *Illusive*, alongside *Portland*, at Jana Island, Saudi Arabia. Later in the day, *Illusive*, *Fearless*, and *Esteem* proceeded to Farsi Island, anchoring near the barge *Hercules*. *Conquest* made the two-hour transit to the northern mine danger area the following day, 19 February.[46]

While *Conquest* and *Illusive* were enjoying their port visit in Jubail, the weather abated, allowing *Esteem* to conduct MCM operations. She located one mine, and a team of EOD divers was embarked to detonate it. *Enhance* arrived in the northern Persian Gulf mid-month for mine countermeasures operations. Upon her return, *Illusive* resumed her role as an MCM control ship for minesweeping helicopters working the Farsi mine danger area.[47]

Following a short dry-docking period, *Inflict* left Bahrain to conduct MCM operations for the remainder of the month. *Fearless*, *Conquest*, *Esteem*, and *Enhance* departed the Farsi area on 19 February with *Portland* and the guided missile frigate USS *McClusky* (FFG 41) for Sitrah Anchorage. (*Fearless* remained underway in the central Gulf for most of the remainder of the month.)[48]

Conquest, *Enhance*, and *Esteem*, having completed crew turnover and required maintenance, sailed in late February for the Farsi MDA. *Conquest* anchored upon arrival near the barge *Hercules* and entered the MDA nine hours later. She remained on task through early March, anchoring each night near the barge for crew rest.[49]

March began with all MSOs, less *Fearless*, conducting mine countermeasures in either the Farsi MDA or northern Persian Gulf; *Fearless* was at Sitrah Anchorage outboard of the amphibious transport dock USS *Trenton* (LPD 14), preparing for a change of command. The blue crew turned over to an eager gold crew, which had trained aboard *Leader* and *Exultant* in Charleston. Resuming operations, *Fearless* located and assisted EOD Mobile Unit 6 divers in destroying three Iranian mines during the month.[50]

Esteem worked the Farsi MDA during the first half of March, before mooring at Mina Sulman Pier to offload mine shapes and minesweeping gear prior to making a port call at Doha, Qatar—the first such visit by a U.S. Navy warship in over twenty years. Qatar, an independent emirate occupying a peninsula projecting into the Persian Gulf, lies a short distance southeast of Bahrain. Because the channel to Doha is both narrow and shallow, *Esteem* was an ideal visitor, though larger ships, including the *McClusky*, have since entered the nation's capital city. Summers are not ideal; the daytime temperatures on the mostly flat and sandy peninsula average a very hot 108 degrees.[51]

Early April found *Illusive*, *Esteem*, and *Inflict* working the Farsi mine danger area. *Illusive* located a suspected M-08 mine, previously found by *Fearless*, confirming it with visual remotely operated vehicle (ROV) identification. EOD Mobile Unit 2 Detachment 46 divers destroyed the mine using countercharges. Despite this success, the MSOs generally had difficulty in identifying mine-line contacts using their Super Sea Rover remote mine locators and, because the units had no mine neutralization capability, they relied on EOD personnel for mine destruction. *Conquest* and *Enhance* joined the ships on 5 April, having completed repair periods at Basrec Shipyard.[52]

Az Zuluf Oil Field

Conquest, *Enhance*, *Illusive*, and *Inflict* conducted MCM operations during the second week of April in the Az Zuluf Oil Field. At completion, *Conquest* left for the Bahrain Oil Field in the central Persian Gulf. *Illusive*, *Inflict*, and *Enhance* sailed to conduct Q-route surveys near Kuwait.[53]

Southern Persian Gulf Mine Danger Areas

At the completion of MCM operations, *Fearless* arrived on 6 April at Jubail for a rest in port. Her stay was cut short due to the near sinking of the *Samuel B. Roberts* by an Iranian-laid moored mine. Returning to Bahrain following convoy escort duty, the frigate's lookouts sighted three mines ahead in waters northeast of Qatar. Unfortunately, while cautiously backing away from this threat, she detonated a fourth mine in a field of M-08 mines that the Iranian Guard had laid the previous day. The concussion from the mine lifted main propulsion engines from their foundations, broke the keel of the ship, and caused serious fire and flooding. Fortunately, no crewmembers were killed, although ten were wounded. The resulting extensive flooding required the crew to ignore the doctrine to first put out fires and then control flooding; they had to concentrate on dewatering the ship to keep it afloat. *Fearless*, *Illusive*, *Inflict*, *Conquest*, and *Enhance* immediately proceeded to the central Persian Gulf, where the incident had occurred. During the transit a floating MYaM mine was spotted and later destroyed by EOD divers. On 16 April the MSOs began mine clearance operations with EOD Mobile Unit 2 Detachment 46 divers in the Shah Allum mine danger area.[54]

The U.S. Navy launched Operation PRAYING MANTIS two days later in response to Iran's offensive mining attack against the *Samuel B. Roberts*. The targets selected were two gas/oil separation platforms, now Iranian Guard bases, with the hopes of engaging the Iranian frigate *Sabalan* under "Captain Nasty." On 18 April, three surface action groups (SAGs) of three ships each and tactical aircraft from the carrier USS *Enterprise* (CVN 65) went into battle, with two SAGs going after the Sassan and Sirri platforms and the third searching for the *Sabalan*. Following arrival at the first platform and preparatory naval gunfire support, Cobra gunships delivered covering fire while helicopters inserted first Marines via fast rope on the Sassan rig, then SEALs to collect intelligence and set demolition charges. Fifteen hundred pounds of plastic explosives turned the platform into an inferno. The plan for the destruction of the Sirri platform was similar, but one of the initial naval gunfire rounds struck a compressed gas tank, setting the platform ablaze and making the insertion of personnel unnecessary.[55]

Following launch by Iran's Combattante-II-class patrol boat *Joshan* of a Harpoon missile that passed down the port side of the cruiser USS *Wainwright* (CG 28), the frigate USS *Simpson* (FFG 56) engaged the patrol boat with a SM-1 standard missile. *Wainwright* and *Simpson* then hit the Iranian with several additional missiles and finished her off with naval gunfire. The *Sahand* was similarly sunk off Larak Island by naval aircraft and the destroyer USS *Joseph Strauss* (DDG 16). After the Iranian frigate directed naval gunfire and missiles at an A-6, the plane retaliated with a Harpoon, a laser-guided bomb, and Skipper weapons. A war-at-sea strike launched from *Enterprise* (six A-7s and one A-6 aircraft) followed up the initial attack with Walleye, Skipper, and 1,000 pound bombs and, in a successive attack, aircraft-launched Harpoons coincided with a Harpoon shot by the *Strauss*. The *Sahand* sank a few hours later. *Sabalan* was located leaving Bandar e Abbas by another group of A-6s that had earlier neutralized four Boghammers after they attacked the U.S. tug *Willy Tide* and a U.S.-run and -manned oil rig in the Mubarak field off the U.A.E., sinking one and causing the other three to run aground at Abu Musa Island. The lead A-6 dropped a

500-pound laser-guided bomb down her stack to stop the infamous frigate dead in the water. With additional aircraft overhead ready to attack and another carrier-launched war-at-sea strike inbound, higher authority decided to terminate offensive operations and the command of "Captain Nasty" was subsequently towed into Bandar e Abbas.[56]

The heavily damaged *Samuel B. Roberts* returned to her homeport at Newport, Rhode Island aboard the Dutch heavy-lift vessel *Mighty Servant 2*. She later returned to service following a first-of-its-kind modular repair at Bath Iron Works, Portland, Maine.[57]

Conquest and *Illusive* sailed from Sitrah on 19 April for the QCX 101 Oil Field. *Enhance*, *Inflict*, and *Fearless* were already near the Rostam MDA, with the guided missile frigate USS *Sides* (FFG 14) providing protection. *Esteem* departed Jubail on 20 April and joined the other MSOs the following day.[58]

Through the remainder of April and the first half of May, all six U.S. minesweepers, as well as vessels from Belgium, the Netherlands, Britain, and Italy conducted mine hunting operations, concentrating on three major mine danger areas—Farsi Island, Shah Allum, and Rostam. *Esteem* located an M-08 shallow moored contact mine on 22 April; while prosecuting this mine she drifted to within fifteen feet of another M-08 mine. As the ship backed cautiously away, her watch team detected additional mines by sonar. Meanwhile, *Inflict* conducted mine clearance in the Shah Allum and Rostam minefields, finding and exploding five mines. Her crew had red snapper for supper one night, retrieved after the force of explosions killed and floated them to the surface. In five days, the MSOs, working with thirteen allied ships, located and destroyed seven mines. This mission completed, the sweeps transited south to the Rostam mine danger area, where in the following three days they destroyed five additional mines. During the preceding five months, Task Unit 801.4.7 had destroyed a total of thirty mines and cleared three minefields.[59]

With Shah Allum minefield operations nearing completion, *Conquest*, *Enhance*, *Inflict*, and *Illusive* moored at Basrec Shipyard in early May, while *Esteem* and *Fearless* continued their labors. *Illusive* departed on 7 May for the Rostam MDA. During the next four months, she spent eighty-three days at sea, fifty-eight consecutive, searching more than 250 miles with sonar, clearing more than a hundred miles with mechanical minesweeping gear and participating in a successful salvage operation.[60]

Bahrain Oil Field

On 19 May, *Conquest, Enhance, Illusive, Esteem,* and *Fearless* transited with *Trenton* to the Bahrain Oil Field. The following day, *Conquest* began local operations until arrival at Sitrah Anchorage on 24 May, followed by more local operations through the end of the month. *Fearless* moored at Basrec Shipyard on 21 May, joining *Inflict,* which at the completion of intense operations in the central Gulf entered the yard for maintenance and turnover from the gold to the silver crew. *Inflict* left Basrec Shipyard on 23 May and led an EARNEST WILL convoy two days later.[61]

During the three-month period of June through August 1988, Iran and Iraq reached a cease-fire agreement; the cruiser USS *Vincennes* (CG 49) accidentally shot down an Iranian airliner while engaged in combat with several Iranian small surface craft; and the U.S. Navy conducted several more EARNEST WILL convoy escort missions.

The MSOs continued to conduct operations in the central and northern Persian Gulf, mine hunting and leading EARNEST WILL convoys, with maintenance at Mina Sulman, Bahrain, and the King Abdul Aziz Naval Base. Visits to Jubail allowed some crewmen to participate in a traditional Arab tent feast.[62]

Fearless sailed from Sitrah Anchorage on 24 June for the northern Persian Gulf to conduct, with *Esteem,* aircraft search and salvage operations. *Fearless* used her remotely operated vehicle to find a sunken U.S. helicopter, and *Esteem* located a sunken Iranian F-14.[63]

In late July, MSOs arrived in Mina Sulman and moored alongside the amphibious transport dock USS *Dubuque* (LPD 8) for a visit by the Secretary of the Navy.[64]

Farsi Island Area

In late August, *Conquest, Enhance, Esteem, Fearless, Illusive, Inflict,* and a Navy explosive ordnance disposal team began a coordinated mine clearance effort of a known minefield in a 150-square-nautical-mile area of the northern Persian Gulf. Through the combined efforts of the MSOs and EOD divers, the remaining mines of the field, first discovered in the area in early 1988, were located and neutralized; in late September, the Farsi Island commercial ship transit route was declared safe.[65]

Fearless briefly left the operating area in early September for a visit to Dubai, a sheikhdom in the United Arab Emirates, for two days of rest. While the ship's officers and chief petty officers hosted a reception for local British and American expatriates, the crew partook of the local culture.[66]

Support of Operation EARNEST WILL

The ocean minesweepers continued to mine hunt and conduct mechanical minesweeping along various commercial transit routes in the northern and central Persian Gulf to ensure continued safe navigation by merchant convoys. *Illusive* mine hunted more than 500 nautical miles of the Gulf, swept more than 360 miles, and provided mine countermeasures support for ten convoy missions. Operations were interspersed with time in port at Mina Sulman, Basrec shipyard, or at Sitrah Anchorage.[67]

In early October, *Enhance* moored alongside USS *LaSalle* (AGF 31) in Mina Sulman. *LaSalle*, the Middle East Force flagship for more than a decade, was commonly referred to by U.S. sailors as "the galloping ghost of the Arabian Coast" because of her white exterior, so painted to reflect heat from the searing sun.[68]

Fearless left Basrec Shipyard on 26 November for operations in the central Persian Gulf Kingfisher test bed area, a test mine danger area. While the ship was at Sitrah Anchorage in late December, Secretary of Defense Frank Carlucci presented the commanding officer and crew with a Navy Unit Commendation for their efforts in the detection and destruction of mines located in the Farsi mine danger area. (The other MSOs received similar awards.) The minesweepers proceeded to Abu Dhabi the day before Christmas Eve for a quiet holiday, returning to Sitrah for a short availability with the destroyer tender USS *Acadia* (AD 42).[69]

1989

In early 1989, the ocean minesweepers continued to conduct mine countermeasures operations in the northern and central Persian Gulf under operational control of Commander, Joint Task Force Middle East. The year witnessed a lasting cease-fire between Iraq and Iran, the countries that had planted the minefields discovered the previous year. The easing tensions resulted in the dissolution of Middle East Force Mine Countermeasures Group Command, and the three Atlantic Fleet MSOs returned to their homeports in March. The Pacific Fleet minesweepers would spend most of the year keeping proficient at their mine-countermeasures skills while continuing to hunt known mine danger areas for further signs of mining. No moored or bottom sea mines were located by any vessel engaged in MCM operations, although floating varieties were occasionally discovered in the Gulf.[70]

Esteem departed Sitrah Anchorage in early January in company with the *Raleigh*, minesweepers *Conquest*, *Illusive*, and *Inflict*, and the motor vessel MV *Falcon Services* for operations in the northern and central Persian Gulf to continue the Q-route surveys necessary to certify EARNEST WILL convoy lanes safe for passage. The *Raleigh*, with Commander, Middle East Force Mine Countermeasures Group embarked, was the MSO mother ship during these operations. This operation was to be the last mass search of regions where mines had been discovered the preceding year.[71]

This tasking continued in February; the MSOs anchored each night at the completion of the day's work. Daily minesweeping operations normally required crews to be up each morning two hours before daylight, underway at daylight, and minesweeping until dusk. This routine was broken only by fuel and mail brought by charter tugs. In all, the MSOs swept 494 miles of routes during this period, certifying as safe the last Q-routes to be cleared in the Persian Gulf after twenty months of continuous effort.[72]

The Atlantic Fleet MSOs returned in March to Bahrain to prepare for the return transit to the United States. *Illusive* first entered Basrec Shipyard and then moved to Mina Sulman before returning to the yard. *Inflict* went alongside *Acadia* for a maintenance period and then moved to Basrec. At completion she moved to Sitrah Anchorage for yet more maintenance, this time alongside the destroyer tender USS *Puget Sound* (AD 43). *Fearless* spent time alongside the tank landing ship USS *Peoria* (LST 1183) in Mina Sulman and at Basrec and Sitrah Anchorage. On 26 and 27 March, she hosted a congressional delegation that included Senators Garn, Hollings, and Inouye, who toured *Fearless*, talked with crewmembers, and congratulated them on a job well done.[73]

ATLANTIC FLEET MSOS' JOURNEY HOME

On 30 March 1989, *Inflict*, *Illusive*, and *Fearless*, in company with *Peoria*, began their long journey home. The advanced age and small size of the ships made living conditions difficult. Aboard the short-handed *Inflict*, a port-and-starboard underway watch rotation was necessary. The group of ships experienced seas of nearly six feet directly on the beam the first day, followed by a brief period of calm as they transited the North Arabian Sea. Seas became rough again as the ships passed through the Strait of Bab el Mandeb and into the Red Sea. From this point on rough weather was normal, with conditions becoming particularly challenging in the western Mediterranean and in the Atlantic, where the ships frequently encountered twelve- to eighteen-foot waves, sometimes on the beam.[74]

During the first week of April, *Fearless* conducted a channel survey of Hodeidah Harbor, Yemen Arab Republic, to allow the guided missile frigate USS *Underwood* (FFG 36) to deliver critical security assistance items.[75]

Port and starboard watches for *Inflict* crewmembers continued. Reveille was at 5:00 a.m. to ensure that personnel standing the midwatch had a short break. Despite an attempt to optimize work and rest, every member of the ship was standing watch and working between 15 and 20 hours a day. Water permeated the ship in heavy seas, and constant effort was required to maintain sanitation and even minimal levels of comfort. Nevertheless, the engineering plant and all auxiliary equipment operated at peak performance, and machinery used remarkably little lube oil despite the age of the ship. Electronic gear functioned as designed and, through the efforts of her crew, *Inflict* arrived in her homeport with all equipment operational.[76]

But many miles would pass under their hulls before the ships returned home. The MSOs transited the Suez Canal and accomplished an unexpected Mediterranean-style moor in Port Suez. Following departure on the morning of 17 April, the task group formally "chopped" to the U.S. 6th Fleet and set a course for Catania, Sicily for fuel, food, and much-needed rest. At completion of the visit, the ships departed for Palma de Mallorca, Spain. This visit provided ample time for everyone to enjoy liberty. Palma was perhaps the crew's favorite liberty port; experiences there were much recounted aboard *Inflict* long after her departure. The group then transited the Strait of Gibraltar and arrived at Rota, Spain to provision prior to crossing the Atlantic Ocean. The salvage ship USS *Opportune* (ARS 41) joined the ships at this time. She would accompany the group past Bermuda and then, as the ships split up, continue with *Inflict* on to Little Creek.[77]

On 6 May, the group began the long transit across the Atlantic. Conditions were rough, but the crews kept busy making preparations for their arrival and dealt with conditions as best they could. The MSOs refueled from the *Peoria* every third day. Watch-standing burdens lessened as the ships transitioned from 6th Fleet's area of responsibility to a lower threat area. On 23 May 1989, *Inflict* conducted her final astern refueling from *Peoria* and received permission to detach to proceed on duties assigned, which were to continue on to her homeport. *Illusive* left the group the same day for Mayport, Florida, arriving there after almost a two year-absence.[78]

As *Inflict* approached the Little Creek channel on 25 May to proceed into port, her sister ship *Fortify* was on hand to greet her with a spray of multicolored water and blasts from the ship's whistle. The 9,284-mile transit was over. However, the lengthy deployment had exacted a toll; on 30 March 1990, *Inflict* was decommissioned and made ready for tow to the Portsmouth Naval Inactive Ship's Maintenance Facility. The crew debarked and her commissioning pennant was hauled down from the mast for the last time. *Illusive* was also decommissioned that day and *Fearless* on the following.[79]

REMAINING OPERATIONS IN THE PERSIAN GULF

Enhance joined the other MSOs in late January 1989 in mine countermeasures operations in the central Persian Gulf, where from February through April she primarily operated, making a port call to Dubai and visiting Jubail for ten days, during which she made runs on the range to check her degaussing system. *Conquest* also utilized the range and, after leaving Jubail in early February, alternated training at sea with time alongside the tenders *Acadia* and *Puget Sound* through the end of March, with a visit to Abu Dhabi. In April and May, she conducted MCM operations in the central Persian Gulf and called in late May at Ras al Khaymah, United Arab Emirates.[80]

Conquest conducted mine countermeasures operations in June and July in the central and northern Gulf, making a visit with *Enhance* to Dubai in late July. Dubai was, and is, a popular liberty port among American and British sailors. Being the trade hub of the Persian Gulf, it offers a variety of goods at reasonable costs; for leisure, a Western-style seaman's club is available, complete with a swimming pool, rock and roll music, and plenty of beverages. To provide a modicum of decorum, and in respect to Arab culture, the club is located inside a walled compound, away from the main downtown area.[81]

Enhance operated in July and August, while *Conquest* was at the Bahrain Ship Repair Company shipyard for a maintenance period, in the northern and central Gulf, conducting Q-route surveys and training.[82]

Throughout the first week in September, *Enhance* and *Esteem* conducted survey operations in the Rostam Oil Field. During the operation, *Enhance* located five Iranian M-08 mine cradles. In October, *Enhance* conducted MCM operations and training in the central Persian Gulf, visited Jubail mid-month before entering Basrec shipyard for maintenance, and, in late October, took part in the salvage and recovery of a downed U.S. Army helicopter. In November, she returned to Rostam Oil Field, located an M-08 mine cradle, and assisted EOD divers with its recovery.[83]

In December a decision was made to bring the remaining minesweepers home from the Persian Gulf. Because the cease-fire had continued to hold in the Persian Gulf, and as no new mines had been found, the need for a U.S. mine countermeasures presence had declined. The arrival of *Enhance* and *Esteem* at Basrec for maintenance and crew turnover was the first step in the preparation for their departure. Crew rotation had become a routine event, as many crewmen returned for second or third tours in the Gulf. Changes of command had also become both routine and informal affairs, with most taking place on the fantails of the ships and in working uniform.[84]

PACIFIC FLEET MSOS' JOURNEY HOME

Conquest, Enhance, and *Esteem* spent February 1990 at the Bahrain Ship Repair Company shipyard, their crews engaged in laying up equipment and drawing down supplies and personnel in preparation for heavy-lift of the three MSOs to Seattle. The ships moved to Sitrah Anchorage for docking aboard the motor vessel *Super Servant 3*. *Esteem* served as the home for a twenty-man caretaker crew aboard the heavy-lift vessel to perform required maintenance on the minesweepers during the transit. The remaining crewmembers from the three ships flew home.[85]

Super Servant 3 left Bahrain on 7 March and moored on 26 April at Pier 27, Seattle, Washington. The following day was devoted to crew turnover and returning to service laid-up machinery necessary for undocking. The heavy-lift ship moved in late afternoon to the Seattle anchorage to prepare for undocking the three MSOs, whose return followed twenty-eight months in the Persian Gulf.[86]

A FORESHADOWING OF BITTER DESERT STORM LESSONS

Neither the Joint Chiefs of Staff nor the U.S. Central Command had seriously considered mines in planning Persian Gulf operations, and following the mine strike to SS *Bridgeton*, Commander Middle East Force later admitted there had been no attempt to check the route for mines despite intelligence warning of their presence. However, to be fair, at the time, without even a nominal mine countermeasures force in the Gulf, such action would have been limited to surveillance by helicopters along the planned convoy route in the hope of sighting any mines that might be close to the surface. The Navy's entire stateside mine force consisted of an almost entirely reserve force of thirty-year-old ocean minesweepers, a few minesweeping boats, and two dozen RH-53D Sea Stallion helicopters.[87]

Despite these limitations, the mine force had performed its mission in the Persian Gulf, although its success was admittedly against low-technology Iranian mines based on a pre–World War I Russian design. However, there was room for optimism. Around the time that the six used-up MSOs returning home from the Gulf were struck from service, the first vessel in a new class of ships to replace the ocean minesweepers, the mine countermeasures vessel USS *Avenger* (MCM 1), was commissioned. Fifty feet longer and 500 tons greater in displacement, it was designed to be more seaworthy than the MSOs and to house newer and more sophisticated equipment. With a planned class of only fourteen vessels, the *Avengers* would have to be very good, as history had repeatedly shown that it takes a considerable amount of time to counter sizeable numbers of easily obtained sea mines employed by a knowledgeable and determined adversary. Unfortunately, design limitations and complications occurring during construction were to have serious consequences for the new class.

10 Operation DESERT SHIELD/STORM

The mine issues no official communiqués.
Admiral William V. Pratt, USN
5 October 1942

A CALL TO ARMS

Following the protracted Iraq-Iran War of 1980–1988, dictator Saddam Hussein continued to pour his nation's resources into his war machine instead of rebuilding Iraq's economy. In a country numbering only eighteen million people, he maintained a million men under arms, accelerated nuclear and biological weapons research programs, and produced chemical weapons on a large scale. Because of vast expenditures in conjunction with a large national debt incurred during the war with Iran, Iraq faced bankruptcy by early 1990. Having made no effort to pay off the debt, estimated to be as high as $80 billion, Saddam was unable to borrow additional funds because foreign bankers viewed Iraq as an extreme credit risk. He also refused to pay neighboring Arab countries the collective $37 million debt owed them, claiming that Iraq had incurred the financial obligation defending its Arab brethren against the common Persian enemy. At a summit gathering of Arab Cooperation Council members in February 1990, Saddam asked Jordan's King Hussein and Egypt's President Hosni Mubarak to inform the Gulf states that not only was his country adamant about not paying back the debt owed them, it urgently needed a loan of an additional $30 billion. He added, "Let the Gulf regimes know that if they do not give the money to me, I will know how to get it." Unsuccessful in obtaining the funds he needed to fuel his militaristic agenda, Saddam accused Kuwait and the United Arab Emirates (U.A.E.) at an Arab Cooperation Council meeting held on 30 May of waging economic warfare against

Iraq by overproducing oil and thereby driving down market prices. He then demanded that Kuwait pay billions of dollars to Iraq to compensate for its economic sacrifices during the war with Iran and grant Iraq economic concessions. Kuwait's Emir, Sheik Jabir Ahmed Sabah, flatly rejected these demands. On 2 August 1990, Iraq invaded and seized in a single day the diminutive emirate, which is slightly smaller than the state of New Jersey, located on the western Persian Gulf between Iraq to the north and Saudi Arabia to the south.[1]

America's response to this act of aggression and potential threat to other countries in the region was swift. On 6 August, following agreement by King Faud to allow U.S. military forces to deploy to Saudi Arabia, President George Herbert Walker Bush ordered the immediate execution of Operational Plan 1002-90. The military objectives of the plan were to establish a force in the region capable of deterring further Iraqi aggression, to build and integrate forces sent by other nations, to enforce UN sanctions against Iraq, and to defend Saudi Arabia from an Iraqi attack. General H. Norman Schwarzkopf, Commander in Chief of the U.S. Central Command (USCincCent) headquartered in Tampa, Florida, began deploying combat forces to the operational theater on 7 August. Less than six months after the last ocean minesweepers to participate in the Iraq-Iran War returned to Seattle, four Atlantic Fleet mine warfare ships received orders back to the Gulf on 10 August 1990. Minesweepers *Adroit* (MSO 509), *Impervious* (MSO 449), *Leader* (MSO 490), and *Avenger* (MCM 1) were dispatched on short notice to establish a U.S. mine countermeasures presence in support of Operation DESERT SHIELD. (USS *Guardian* [MCM 5] later relieved *Avenger*.)[2]

During their tour in the Gulf, the U.S. ships made important contributions to Operation DESERT STORM as part of a multinational mine countermeasures (MCM) force. The ships initially assisted minesweeping helicopters performing precursor sweeping and conducted their own mine clearance operations in the northern Persian Gulf. Following mine strikes to the amphibious assault ship USS *Tripoli* (LPH 10) and cruiser USS *Princeton* (CG 59), in a supposedly benign area seaward of enemy shore-based Silkworm missile battery range, the three MSOs led the crippled vessels to safe waters. In preparation for the start of ground warfare following the air campaign, MCM forces swept naval gunfire support lanes to enable the battleships USS *Missouri* (BB 63) and USS *Wisconsin* (BB 64) to fire their sixteen-inch guns at shore targets. At the end of the short war and disclosure by

Iraqi authorities of the locations of their minefields and minelines, responsibility for clearing them was allocated among the eight countries contributing major MCM forces. Great Britain joined the MCM effort during DESERT STORM and, following the war, Belgium, France, Germany, Italy, Japan, and the Netherlands as well. As its top priority, the allied force cleared the navigational routes leading into Kuwaiti anchorages and ports in order to facilitate the resupply and reconstruction of the Emirate. The secondary task was to clear remaining Iraqi minefields.

In spite of the best efforts of the crews of the four wooden ships, helicopters, and EOD divers, the U.S. Navy MCM flotilla was not adequate to the task at hand in the Gulf War, due to its small size. Although overall as capable as any force, due to its complementary components, there were insufficient U.S. assets to perform the quantity of mine clearance desired in the time available. This untenable condition was made worse by the demurral of all but one of America's allies to commit forces to mine clearance efforts until after the end of the war, which in large part precluded a planned amphibious assault on a Kuwaiti beachhead. One might argue this is a moot point in view of the coalition's victory; however, it highlights the fact that nations often act in their own self-interest, which makes problematic any U.S. dependence on others for a particular warfare capability. Senior Marine Corps leaders wanted the 17,000 U.S. Marines aboard amphibious ships off Kuwait to make a landing, designated "DESERT SABER," and pressed hard until a week before the ground war began to be a part of the offensive operations. However, enemy mining of beaches and adjacent surf zone and other fortifications along the shore, as well as other considerations, prevented this action. General Schwarzkopf and local Navy and Marine Corps commanders believed that the required mine clearance would be too time consuming and pose danger to allied forces operating inside the artillery range of enemy forces ashore. (Although unknown at the time, there were also large numbers of Iraqi mines lying in deeper waters between the ships and the shoreline.) Moreover, shore bombardment to prepare for a landing could have harmed Kuwaiti civilians and damaged property. The risks did not seem worth the potential military gain. Yet, in a ruse, conspicuous preparations for a landing continued so that the Marine presence aboard the ships would force Iraqi Army troops positioned to oppose any movement ashore to remain in place, in essence removing them from the enemy order of battle.[3]

U.S. MINE FORCE PRE-DEPLOYMENT PREPARATION

Stateside in the summer of 1990, war with Iraq was not certain and no one could predict that the deploying ships would encounter large numbers of Iraqi-laid mines in a crescent-shaped area (see map 10-1) along the Kuwaiti coastline. When the vessels departed for the Gulf, the majority of each ship's company remained in their respective homeports for pre-deployment training. The remainder, including the commanding officers of *Avenger, Leader,* and *Impervious*, accompanied the ships as they were carried to the Gulf by a heavy-lift vessel. Skeleton crews remained aboard the minesweepers for communications, to perform required maintenance, and generally to ensure safety and material readiness. Stateside, *Defender* (MCM 2), *Exploit* (MSO 440), and *Exultant* (MSO 441) trained the nucleus crews. The training emphasis was mine countermeasures, engineering, damage control, and fire fighting, as well as chemical, biological, and radiological defense.[4]

By 1 October 1990, sailors left behind had rejoined their ships in the Persian Gulf.[5] The ships themselves had been transported to the Gulf on board the Dutch Wijsmuller Line motor vessel *Super Servant 3*. Moving them had been an enormous challenge because of the technical difficulties associated with the heavy-lift operation, which involved putting ships of two different types onto what is essentially a big floating truck. Complicating matters was *Avenger*'s length and fiberglass-sheathed wooden hull, the bow of which after loading protruded out over the stern of the mammoth transport. Preparation for loading the ships took several days and the evolution itself entailed sixteen hours of very exacting work. The motor vessel departed Norfolk, Virginia on 28 August and arrived at Mina Sulman, the port of Manama, Bahrain on 30 September 1990. The minesweepers were floated off three days later and entered Basrec (Bahrain Ship Repair Company) Shipyard in Bahrain for a short maintenance period. Leaving the yard to join the U.S. Mine Countermeasures Group, the ships arrived at the Sheik Zayed MCM base, a five-acre site at Port Zayed in Abu Dhabi, U.A.E., which had only opened on 12 October, and continued to prepare for wartime operations. Captain David J. Grieve, U.S. Navy, the commodore of Mine

Map 10-1

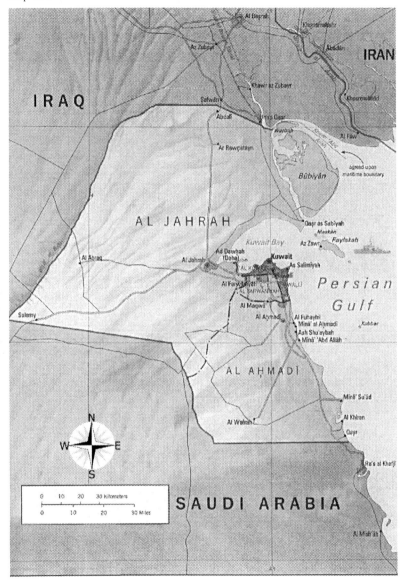

Kuwait: Beneath the waters of a crescent-shaped area along the Kuwaiti coastline lurked large numbers of Iraqi-laid mines.

Group 1 who would deploy to command the U.S. Mine Countermeasures Group (ComUSMCMGru), had not wanted to be based in Saudi Arabia because it was both too restrictive and too close to the combat area to conduct the training and certification necessary to prepare the force for operations.[6]

Photo 10-1

Avenger (MCM 1), *Adroit* (MSO 509), *Leader* (MSO 490), and *Impervious* (MSO 449) aboard the partially submerged *Super Servant* 3 prior to offloading at Bahrain (photographer Cdr. John Charles Roach)

The deployment of *Avenger* marked the first operational employment of an MCM 1-class ship. She was outfitted with the newest mine-detection sonar and remotely operated mine-neutralization vehicles (MNVs), as well as traditional minesweeping gear salvaged from ocean minesweepers struck from service. Mine-neutralization vehicles can confirm the presence of mines and lay explosive neutralization charges—greatly reducing hazards to Explosive Ordnance Disposal (EOD) divers as well as providing an alternative to their use. The ocean minesweepers also carried remotely operated vehicles to identify mines. Grieve remarked after the war that putting *Avenger* into the fray was a bad idea because as the lead ship for a new class of ships she was not yet ready for wartime operations. She was the first new mine warfare ship built for the U.S. Navy in twenty-six years and equipped with a sonar system that was not a production model, and other equipment and machinery of unproven reliability (it was necessary to replace all four of her propulsion engines during her time in the Gulf). Moreover, *Avenger* had been designed for deep ocean work and was actually more vulnerable to influence mines than were the ocean minesweepers. The new technology she incorporated presented challenges, and the two yards (Peterson Builders and Marinette Marine) constructing the fourteen vessels in the class had been faced not only with the same difficulties as those who built wooden ships in the 1950s, but also with those caused by the erosion of the naval expertise necessary to help guide them. Additionally, as both shipyards were vying for award of Navy contracts for the remaining ships in the class, there was little incentive for them to share lessons learned with one another.[7]

Grieve arrived in the Gulf from Mine Group 1 headquarters at Naval Air Station, Sand Point, Washington on 3 October to exercise operational and tactical command of the U.S. mine countermeasures forces supporting the multinational force assembled to liberate Kuwait. Later, active duty and reserve personnel from the Seattle, Washington area served in theater as personnel were rotated. Active duty and reserve personnel from the Mine Warfare Command, Mine Squadron 2, and Craft of Opportunity Mine Squadron 22 comprised the remaining members of the ad hoc ComUSMCMGru staff. The following day, huge Military Airlift Command C-5 Galaxy and C-141 Starlifter transport planes began delivering Helicopter Mine Countermeasures (HM) Squadron 14 and its six helicopters. Operational units of the U.S. MCM Group included the three MSOs, one MCM 1-class ship, six MH 53E Sea Dragon minesweeping helicopters, and more than twenty Navy EOD teams and their support craft, two commercial tugs outfitted for diving operations.[8]

The MH 53E helicopters were initially based ashore in Abu Dhabi, U.A.E., in lieu of aboard a "large-deck" amphibious ship from which they operate best. Commander, U.S. Naval Forces, Central Command (ComUSNavCent) and the amphibious task force commander were initially loath to dedicate a major vessel, essential for the conduct of amphibious aerial assault, to the mine clearance mission. The guidance provided to Grieve was to operate from Abu Dhabi and to prepare the mine force for operations, with the issue of a flagship to be addressed if mine clearance in the northern Gulf was needed to support offensive operations. He was also asked to explore options for operating the helicopters from shore or resurrecting the barge *Hercules*, utilized as a mobile base during the Iraq-Iran War. These possibilities, as well as the potential use of an amphibious transport dock (LPD), were eventually discarded and the helicopter carrier USS *Tripoli* (LPH 10) was assigned to provide dedicated support to the mine force. Vice Admiral Henry Mauz, Commander Seventh Fleet, was the first Commander U.S. Naval Forces, Central Command. He was relieved of his duties by Vice Admiral Stanley Arthur on 1 December 1990.[9]

PREPARATIONS FOR WAR

An immediate mine force need was training in local waters near Abu Dhabi to gain certification of readiness to clear mines. The MSOs' training prior to their deployment order had focused largely on engineering readiness, very important due to the advanced ages of the ships, but not the full range of what they would be required to do in the Gulf, and *Avenger* was not yet ready for combat operations. Accordingly, the four U.S. mine countermeasures ships spent much time training to conduct mine clearance in support of amphibious landings; practiced joint helicopter, ship, and explosive ordnance disposal operations; trained against mine simulators; and conducted combined exercises with the Royal Navy and Royal Saudi Naval Forces. In early November, the three MSOs and *Avenger* participated in a combined U.S. and United Kingdom mine countermeasures exercise that included six mine warfare ships maneuvering in formation with their Double-O mechanical sweep gear deployed astern. (The Double-O maneuver streams two explosive cutter-laden wires astern, one to port and one to starboard.) *Leader* operated with EOD Mobile Unit 5 to develop tactics to counter the expanding Iraqi mine threat. The U.S. ships used the Royal Navy's portable degaussing range at Dubai to measure their magnetic signatures and verify the effectiveness of measures taken to minimize risk from mines, including the removal of magnetic material and the calibration of equipment.[10]

The relatively high magnetic and acoustic signatures of the U.S. MCM ships would limit their use during DESERT STORM primarily to support U.S. minesweeping helicopters performing precursor sweeps, while a British MCM flotilla performed the bulk of the mine clearance. The magnetic signature of *Avenger* was significantly higher than the British *Hunt*-class minehunters, and the signatures of two of the three MSOs, while lower than *Avenger*'s, were higher than that of a *Hunt*. Since NATO's inception in 1949, the United States had increasingly relied on its allies to perform the bulk of any mine clearance required during wars and conflicts, while it dedicated its resources to offensive capabilities, and had became particularly dependent upon them following the massive post–Vietnam War downsizing of the mine force. Consequently, the U.S. Navy could now field only a few old MSOs (a majority of its ocean and all of the coastal and inshore minesweepers were long gone from service) and the unproven first new mine countermeasures vessel to be constructed since 1961. The vulnerability of its dependence on allies to conduct the preponderance of any mine clearance requirements was highlighted when only the British MCM vessels joined the United States during DESERT STORM. The Royal Australian Navy contributed a clearance diving team for mine countermeasures in shallow waters. During the postwar period, however, six additional countries would contribute ships to the Coalition mine clearance operations.[11]

Eight British *Hunt*-class minehunters would conduct mine clearance during DESERT STORM and postwar operations, supported by survey ships assigned as "motherships" for the mine countermeasures vessels, as well as a logistics supply ship. HMS *Cattistock* (M 31), HMS *Atherstone* (M 38), and HMS *Hurworth* (M 39), in company with survey ship HMS *Herald* (H 138), left Britain on 13 August 1990 for the Persian Gulf. This group was joined later by HMS *Ledbury* (M 30) and HMS *Dulverton* (M 35), and in April 1991 three newly arrived *Hunts* replaced the first three on station in the Gulf.[12]

The small but sophisticated British ships utilized Lynx and Sea King helicopters as mine spotters and carried some of the most advanced mine countermeasures equipment then available, as well as embarked EOD divers, reflecting the longstanding emphasis placed on mine warfare within the British Navy and its expertise in conducting it. Each ship was constructed of glass-reinforced plastic and nonmagnetic metals to minimize its magnetic field or "signature" and its propulsion system was designed for minimum noise, thereby reducing its "acoustic signature" as well. Interestingly, the magnetic signatures of the *Hunts* were lower than those of the U.S. ships despite the use of Deltic diesel marine engines fitted in the Royal Navy vessels. The use of the readily available proven engines, manufactured of durable magnetic materials, resulted in a cost effective and reliable propulsion plant. The disturbances these engines would otherwise make to the Earth's magnetic field (and thereby trigger magnetic sea mines) were compensated for by an advanced degaussing system fitted in the ships.[13]

The Saudi Arabian Navy offered in early February 1991 to assist with mine clearance, but Commander Middle East Force directed it instead to clear the area off the coast of northern Saudi Arabia, where the guided-missile frigate USS *Nicholas* (FFG 47) had identified minelike objects with her Kingfisher sonar while escorting *Missouri* in fire support areas RK1 and RK2. This put Saudi Arabia's MCM ships,

Addriyah (MSC 412), *Al Quysumah* (MSC 414), *Al Wadi'ah* (MSC 416), and *Safwa* (MSC 418) out of the principal effort.[14]

After spending the Thanksgiving holiday in Abu Dhabi, the U.S. mine countermeasures ships continued to conduct local operations, after which *Leader* and *Avenger* transited to Bahrain for a maintenance period at Basrec Shipyard. A message from ComUSNavCent set mid-January 1991 as the target for launching Operation DESERT STORM. The coalition plan envisioned a phased air, naval, and ground offensive operation against Iraq executed over a period of approximately one month. Far from home and on the eve of hostilities, the sailors spent the Christmas holiday in Bahrain or Abu Dhabi. A Bob Hope special show, starring entertainers Brooke Shields, Marie Osmond, and the Pointer Sisters, provided a measure of diversion for some.[15]

CREW ROTATIONS

In order to maintain three MSOs on station during Operations DESERT SHIELD and DESERT STORM and yet keep crew deployments to a maximum of six months, Commander, Mine Squadron 2 developed and implemented a plan for rotating crews, not hulls, from stateside. This arrangement helped ensure the continuous alertness required for mine clearance during long periods of high-intensity operations. *Avenger*'s crewmembers remained aboard through an extended stay in the Gulf, as there were no replacements available to operate and maintain her unique equipment. This followed heavy tasking before deployment with lead ship activities and separation from family and friends due to shipyard periods out of homeport. The minesweepers found the Persian Gulf a harsh environment. During the summer, when air temperatures can reach 120 degrees or higher and seawater used to cool machinery is near a hundred degrees, there is little relief from the sun. The problem is exacerbated by the rapid growth of mussels in equipment heat-exchangers, restricting the flow of cooling seawater. These conditions, combined with periodic sandstorms blowing across the Gulf, made living conditions almost unbearable at times. Although sailors—and particularly minesweep sailors—are tough, the inability of air conditioning systems to cool adequately communications and other vital combat systems jeopardized the ships' ability to complete their missions. The limitations of equipment, not human endurance, normally determined mission success or failure. In all, eleven crews were embarked in five U.S. mine warfare ships.[16]

Schedule of Deployments

USS *Adroit*	(30 September 1990–12 October 1991)
—*Adroit*	30 Sep 1990–23 Jan 1991
—*Exploit*	23 Jan 1991–8 Jun 1991
—*Constant*	8 Jun 1991–12 Oct 1991
USS *Impervious*	(30 September 1990–12 October 1991)
—*Impervious*	30 Sep 1990–13 Apr 1991
—*Engage*	13 Apr 1991–12 Oct 1991
USS *Leader*	(30 September 1990–12 October 1991)
—*Leader*	30 Sep 1990–7 Mar 1991
—*Exultant*	7 Mar 1991–26 Jul 1991
—*Affray*	26 Jul 1991–12 Oct 1991
USS *Avenger*	(30 September 1990–25 July 1991)
—*Avenger*	30 Sep 1990–25 Jul 1991
USS *Guardian*	(12 June 1991–13 January 1992)
—*Guardian*	12 Jun 1991–15 Oct 1991
—*Devastator*	15 Oct 1991–13 Jan 1992

PRE-DESERT STORM PLANNING AND PREPARATION

As the New Year dawned, the U.S. mine countermeasures ships and helicopters were training in the southern Persian Gulf off their base at Abu Dhabi. In mid-October, shortly after the arrival of the American MCM forces in the Gulf, ComUSNavCent guidance directed the commander of the U.S. amphibious task force to formulate plans for an amphibious assault at Ras al Qulaya, Kuwait, located about twenty miles north of the Saudi Arabian border. The operational objectives of "DESERT SABER" were to interdict enemy lines of communications south of Kuwait City, fix enemy forces along the coast, and establish a beachhead or port area to sustain American forces in Kuwait. In early December, the specified landing site shifted to Ash Shuaybah, approximately ten miles further north into Kuwait. The advantage of Ash

Shuaybah over Ras al Qulaya was that it lay further behind Iraqi lines and had more favorable hydrography.[17]

On 30–31 December, ComUSNavCent held an amphibious planning conference aboard the amphibious command ship USS *Blue Ridge* (LCC 19) in the port of Dubai. NavCent's objective for the assault was to tie down Iraqi forces in eastern Kuwait prior to commencement of the ground war; support U.S. Marine forces; establish a beach or port for supplying ground forces; and link up with Marine forces ashore. However, one of the problems of the proposed assault was the projected amount of time it would take to conduct mine-clearance operations, which could not start until after the existing Iraqi threat to mine countermeasures forces had been reduced. Clearance of the very large areas the amphibious force required to support the beach assault, and the associated timelines, could not be met with the relatively modest mine countermeasures force. Following much discussion about the objectives of the operation and associated requirements and potential pitfalls, agreement to reduce the size of some areas was reached. However, the overall scope of proposed work was still too great. Captain Grieve emphasized that U.S. mine countermeasures ships were not designed to search mixed moored contact and influence minefields without minesweeping helicopters first performing precursor sweeps. He planned to use the helicopters to sweep shallow moored and sensitive influence mines, and, accordingly, wanted a helicopter carrier assigned from which to operate the MH 53s. He also highlighted the vital importance of British participation in the mine clearance operations, which would shorten considerably the time necessary to complete the work, especially because the *Hunt*s with their very low magnetic signatures would not require precursor sweeps as the American ships did. However, while the Royal Navy minehunters were not as vulnerable as the U.S. ships to being sunk or damaged by influence mines buried in silt on the seafloor, they also could not locate them by minehunting and therefore could not eliminate the threat. The existing environmental information predicted a high mine burial rate, which turned out to be incorrect, but reminded everyone that minehunters, which possess no capability to sweep mines, cannot counter what their sonars cannot find. So, while the *Hunt*s were great ships, they did not provide the complete answer. The overarching U.S. plan for mine clearance was to mine hunt if possible. For mines that were buried in silt, and thus unhuntable, to minesweep—and, if minesweeping was necessary, employ helicopters first as they were less suspectible to damage than the mine countermeasures ships. In spite of these and other anticipated problems and the reservations of some people about the viability and value of an amphibious assault, the planning continued.[18]

ComUSNavCent was concerned at this time about minefields off Kuwait and drifting mines in the other areas of the Persian Gulf in which NavCent ships were operating. On 21 November, NavCent intelligence reported evidence of mining activity off Ras al Qulaya in southern Kuwait, perhaps since 7 November, to which area a potential Iraqi minelayer had made at least four or five short trips. By year's end, intelligence personnel estimated that there were 180 to 250 moored contact and bottom influence mines in the Persian Gulf. They believed, however, that they knew the general location of these mines and of the two semicircles of mines Iraq was thought to be planning to lay off the coast of Kuwait. By the time DESERT STORM began, planners concluded that Iraq had completed the inner circle in December and was nearing completion of the outer; subsequent events would prove this inference invalid in respect to both location and numbers of mines. However, the NavCent staff was "hamstrung" by incomplete intelligence upon which to base its analysis. The USCincCent rules of engagement prohibited U.S. forces from engaging and destroying Iraqi minelayers unless caught in the act, and during this period USCincCent would not allow NavCent surveillance in areas where the Iraqis might be laying mines, to minimize the possiblity that poking around the northern Gulf might provoke an Iraqi attack before the buildup of adequate coalition forces in Saudi Arabia. Mine warfare typically faces such a quandary. During the period immediately preceeding a possible war, when military commanders may desire to destroy the potential enemy's capability to lay mines should conflict result, diplomatic efforts are normally taking place to try to avoid hostilities. Accordingly, destroying potential shipkillers while they are still in storage at mine depots or in transit aboard minelayers before the enemy can sow them in waters used by friendly forces would be viewed by one's adversary as an act of war and likely undo all efforts in progress to maintain the peace.[19]

The critical importance of mine countermeasures forces to safe navigation and military operations in the Gulf had been given additional emphasis shortly before this meeting. On 21 December 1990, Saudi Arabian naval forces discovered the first drifting mine in the Az Zuluf Oil Field, located off the Saudi Arabian coast southeast of the border with

Kuwait. Five days later, a second mine was discovered and numbers three and four on 30 December. By 1 January, a total of six floating mines had been found. The Saudis soon found number seven in the eastern half of the Persian Gulf. On 8 January a drifting mine was reported about thirty nautical miles northeast of Bahrain, and by 13 January, the drifting mine count would reach twenty, although the NavCent staff did not believe that all reports of sightings were valid, as it is easy during conditions of restricted visibility or in choppy seas to misidentify small floating objects, such as trash bags discarded by ships, as mines. Initially, the staff did not know whether the real mines were moored types that had broken loose or the Iraqis had deliberately set them adrift—nor did it make much difference. Drifting mines could damage combatants throughout the Gulf, although the risk was the greatest in the northern part. Ships operating at night that did not require fast speeds for transit or, in the case of those operating aircraft, to create the necessary relative winds across the flight deck, steamed at bare steerageway in the belief that less water passing under their hulls meant less likelihood of encountering a mine.[20]

In the preferred procedure for destruction of drifting mines, a helicopter carried two men, either an EOD team or two SEALs, to the scene. The divers jumped into the water, swam to the mine, and attached a time-delayed charge to it. They then swam away, were winched up by the helicopter, and from a safe distance detonated the explosive. In a few cases when coalition forces discovered a drifting mine, they towed it ashore for intelligence exploitation, the analysis of its capabilities, by experts. By war's end, coalition forces had destroyed 109 floating mines.[21]

Since mid-December, prior to receipt of a formal initiating directive, NavCent forces had been planning an amphibious assault into Ash Shuaybah, about thirty miles north of the Saudi-Kuwaiti border. The Iraqis had started preparing coastal defenses against the possibility of such an operation in August and they now had three infantry brigades deployed in nine battalion-size strongpoints defending Ash Shuaybah. To assault these defenses, the NavCent amphibious force had seventeen thousand Marines. Major Marine units embarked aboard thirty-one amphibious ships were the 4th MEB (Marine Expeditionary Brigade), 5th MEB (Special Operations Capable), and 13th MEU (Marine Expeditionary Unit [Special Operations Capable]). Including logistics and commercial vessels, the Amphibious Task Force contained

Photo 10-2

An explosive ordnance disposal (EOD) diver attaches plastic explosives to a mine found floating in the Gulf during Operation DESERT STORM (photographer PH1(DV) Noel Guest)

forty-three ships. The Persian Gulf Battle Force was prepared to support the landing with three carriers, two battleships, and dozens of escorts.[22]

For an amphibious landing, mine countermeasures forces would have to clear four areas: the sea echelon area, where amphibious ships would operate; fire support areas (FSAs), where battleships would conduct naval gunfire operations; lanes to the sea echelon area and FSAs; and lanes from the sea echelon area to the beach for landing craft delivering Marines ashore. Before the mine countermeasures force could begin their painstakingly slow work, the coalition forces would have to eliminate or reduce to an acceptable level the threat posed to the unarmed vessels by Iraqi aircraft, patrol boats, Silkworm missiles, shoulder-fired missiles from shore or small boats, and artillery. A separate issue was the threat from the beach, largely guns sited on the tops of buildings as well as in miscellaneous fortifications. The planned mine countermeasures would require the ships and helicopters to work inside the ranges of these weapons and the aircraft would have to fly lower than the buildings. Additionally, mine clearance, which by its nature is always dangerous, was expected to be even more so due to the presence of multiple types of mines. Several options for clearance levels and time to complete the effort were considered. One was a two-week period to achieve for most of the areas a confidence level of eighty percent clearance, based on availability of a large deck ship from which to operate the helicopters and several key assumptions about the specific types of mines the mine force might encounter during the operation. When asked by a flag officer about clearance of the potentially remaining 20 percent mines, Grieve replied, "Your ships going through the area sweep them." This was not meant to be a humorous answer, but rather to drive home the point that there is never any certainty of 100 percent mine clearance, and that to have any chance of achieving it with the existing small mine force would require a prohibitive amount of time that would not support the planned date for an amphibious assault.[23]

DESERT STORM operations plans promulgated in January made it clear that the primary role of the amphibious forces would be to deceive the Iraqis. The amphibious force would conduct feints, demonstrations, and other activities to create the impression of a forthcoming major amphibious assault along the Kuwaiti and Iraqi coasts. The objective was to fix the Iraqi Republican Guards while the main ground attack took place in the western desert. But the operation plans also directed ComUSNavCent to be prepared to conduct amphibious operations to seize specific objectives in conjunction with Marine forces operating inside Kuwait.[24]

MINE COUNTERMEASURES BEGIN

After months of training, the U.S. MCM group rendezvoused north of the training area off Dubai, United Arab Emirates, on 13 February 1991 to begin its transit to the northern Gulf. It comprised the amphibious assault ship USS *Tripoli* (LPH 10), with Captain Grieve and his staff and MH 53 minesweeping helicopters embarked, ocean minesweepers *Adroit, Leader*, and *Impervious*, and mine countermeasures ship *Avenger*. Also aboard the flagship to support the operation were Commander Destroyer Squadron 22, the commander of the U.S. naval surface combatants assigned to provide the group force protection and his staff, as well as four Marine Cobra gunships to fly cover for the minesweeping helicopters. Five Royal Navy minehunters, *Ledbury, Dulverton, Atherstone, Cattistock*, and *Hurworth* and support ship *Herald*, sailing from Bahrain, joined their U.S. Navy counterparts the following day. The British MCM force would operate as a separate but coordinated group, with Grieve the overall commander and responsible for the airborne mine countermeasures, while Commander Jon Scoles, Royal Navy, managed the mine clearance conducted by the ships. Both U.S. and RN naval surface combatants were assigned to provide protection for the MCM forces during these operations.[25]

The MCM Group and its accompanying support ships remained near Farsi Island before continuing the remaining 150 miles to Point Echo, a position that intelligence had earlier indicated lay along a line of existing mines, and later discounted—but which proved a reality, as it was the Manta line that *Princeton* hit. The intelligence at the time estimated that several minefields existed south of Point Echo. The group arrived on the morning of 16 February and commenced mine clearance operations in an area shoreward of the main mine belts discovered later, except for the Manta line. The ships subsequently moved seaward and into the minefield because of a Silkworm cruise missile threat. *Princeton* served as the local antiair warfare commander and provided protection for MCM and Naval Gunfire Support Groups. The latter group included the battleships *Missouri* and *Wisconsin*, and several other warships to provide the battleships and mine countermeasures ships protection against surface and air threats.[26]

Navy priorities for the MCM operations off Kuwait were first to clear a "Faylaka fire support area," designated FSA F1, from which a battleship could shell enemy positions ashore, and then a sea echelon area needed to position amphibious ships for a planned amphibious raid on Faylaka Island, held by the 440th Iraqi Marine Infantry Brigade. Proponents believed that a raid, prior to a subsequent amphibious assault on Ash Shuaybah in southern Kuwait scheduled to take place two days after the beginning of the ground war, would destroy Iraqi capabilities on the island, create uncertainty, serve as a diversion prior to "G-day," and help prevent any last-minute shifts of enemy troops to the west. There was not unanimous support for this plan, as some NavCent planners believed the raid, codenamed "DESERT SLASH," scheduled to occur one or two days before the ground war, would delay the amphibious assault on Ash Shuaybah due to a requirement to consolidate and reload the amphibious ships following the operation. Ultimately, USCincCent cancelled both the raid and the subsequent Ash Shuaybah assault, codenamed "DESERT SABER," because of the inability of MCM forces to clear mines in time, risk of collateral damage inside Kuwait, risk of Marine Corps casualties and potential morale boost to Iraqi troops should this occur, and because the operations were deemed unnecessary. Tasking for U.S and Royal Navy MCM forces in mid-February was, upon completion of FSA F1, to clear another fire support area (FSA F2) to allow a second battleship to shell targets inside Kuwait.[27]

The planned MCM operation had a dual purpose: to clear fire support and a sea echelon area for the Faylaka raid and to support the deception required for the proposed Ash Shuaybah assault. Unbeknownst to the MCM Group, six minefields and four minelines lay orientated in a crescent shape beneath the shallow waters in the immediate and adjacent areas off the coast of Kuwait in which they were to operate. To reach Point Echo, the MCM ships and their escorts would have to steam through minefields containing both moored and influence mines. Iraqi minefield plans surrendered following the war showed the approach channel crossed mineline 7; however, the planned FSAs and sea echelon area contained no mines. Of course, the NavCent forces were not privy to this information at the time.[28]

On the morning of 16 February, *Tripoli*, *Avenger*, *Adroit*, and the British *Hunts* crossed minefields 4 and 5 on their way to start mine clearance operations at Point Echo, located about sixty nautical miles east of the Kuwaiti coastline. The guided-missile frigates USS *Jarrett* (FFG 33) and USS *Curts* (FFG 38) took station to provide air defense in minefield 4. *Princeton* crossed minefields 4, 5, and 7, and the destroyer USS *Foster* (DD 964) and other ships operated in and around these minefields for the next forty-eight hours, unaware of the danger that lurked beneath them.[29]

The MH 53E helicopters operating from the *Tripoli* began influence and mechanical sweeping supported by the U.S. MCM ships. The Royal Navy vessels began minehunting the designated channel leading from Point Echo to Point Foxtrot at the rear of the sea echelon area. To the west of it lay the fire support areas from which, once cleared, battleships could shell Faylaka Island and positions inside Kuwait itself. On 17 February, the MH 53s began mechanical sweeping of the channel from Point Foxtrot to Point Golf, the forward boundary of the sea echelon area, while the U.S. mine countermeasures ships remained near Point Echo. After the British MCM ships found no mines in the channel leading to Point Foxtrot, they began searching the sea echelon area.[30]

That night, having received intelligence that Iraq planned a Silkworm missile attack against *Tripoli*, Rear Admiral William Fogarty, Commander, Middle East Force (ComMidEastFor), ordered the temporary suspension of MCM operations and the withdrawal of U.S. MCM forces to the east beyond the range of the land-based missiles. *Princeton* moved to the west to position herself between the threat and the mine countermeasures ships. After midnight on 18 February, the danger of a missile attack apparently having passed, the MCM force was ordered back to resume operations. To counter the threat of drifting mines, the mine countermeasures ships fell in astern of *Tripoli* in a column formation during the return transit because the LPH could station large numbers of lookouts with night vision devices high above the water.[31]

In the early hours of 18 February, *Tripoli* struck a moored contact mine, probably a LUGM-145, and received severe hull damage, a sixteen-by-twenty foot hole, ten feet below the waterline and just forward of the starboard beam. *Impervious*, *Leader*, and *Avenger*, coming to the amphibious ship's aid, detected sonar images of minelike objects near her, and Grieve decided to anchor the LPH while the minesweepers sorted out the threat. *Avenger* located a line of nine probable mines and *Leader* ten minelike objects nearby. *Leader* and *Impervious* began searching for a safe route to lead *Tripoli* out of the dense minefield into which she had stumbled. The plan was to proceed north to intercept the track used coming into the area, believing it a safe route. Following receipt of orders to move farther out to sea, due to another Silkworm threat, the two ocean minesweepers led the stricken amphibious ship to safety in the darkness, helped by mal-deployed and inert mines. Later that morning *Princeton*, operating about ten miles northwest of *Tripoli*, was rocked by two exploding bottom influence mines, which caused significant structural damage and put one propeller shaft and one rudder out of action. *Adroit* proceeded to the area and swept a channel through which the salvage vessel USS *Beaufort* (ATS 2), led by the minesweeper, towed the damaged cruiser from the minefield to safety. Later that day, *Avenger* located and "danned" a line of nine moored mines in the immediate vicinity of the *Tripoli* mine strike. Dan buoys are normally used to mark safe channels for vessel traffic, but can also be used to identify hazards to shipping. When required, the bright orange buoys are rigged with anchors and lead or cement "clumps" (weights) to prevent drifting and are pushed off the fantail at predetermined positions to signal danger to all vessels trafficking through an area.[32]

The crews of *Tripoli* and *Princeton* fought hard to successfully control mine-inflicted flooding and damage that, although severe and requiring shipyard repairs to correct permanently, was not debilitating. *Tripoli* was able to continue her mission for several days, until completion of MCM operations immediately prior to commencement of the ground war. *Princeton* quickly restored her missile strike and antiair defense capabilities, reassumed duties as the local antiair warfare coordinator, and provided defense for the MCM Group until relieved.[33]

After completing the immediate task of assisting naval units to get out of the "*Tripoli* minefield," a junior officer on board *Avenger* performed an underwater inspection to check for damage to the sonar from a fish-trap buoy and recovery line the ship had snared. Encounters with fish-trap recovery lines in shallow waters were a hazard for the MCM ships' underwater equipment and hull appendages during operations at night. Searching for mines is painstakingly slow because high-frequency sonar works best at low ship speeds. Accordingly, to clear even a small area in a reasonable time, ships must work continuously until either crew fatigue or a need for provisions or fuel forces them to leave the field. By day, a minesweeper can alter course to avoid fish-trap buoys but, of course, it cannot see these hazards at night. Conversely, a ship might choose not to alter course if doing so might leave a portion of the minefield unsearched. The possible consequences include damage to the sonar or to other equipment protruding from the hull.[34]

For the remainder of 18 February, U.S. MCM forces concentrated on escorting all ships east of the minefield located by *Tripoli*. Thereafter, the British and U.S. MCM forces would continue the work they had already begun by clearing a thousand-yard-wide approach channel about eighteen nautical miles long from Point Charlie to Echo, then another fifteen nautical miles to Point Foxtrot. Previous MCM efforts had already partially cleared the section of the channel from Point Echo to Foxtrot. The MCM forces would now create a newly designated Battleship FSA (BBFSA) by expanding the width of the channel previously worked by the helicopters from Point Foxtrot to Point Golf to two thousand yards. In order to complete the mine clearance necessary for the amphibious raid and assault scheduled to take place within days, it was necessary to find ways to save time. Accordingly, the helicopters conducted no precursor mechanical sweeps prior to the *Hunt*-class ships' minehunting the Point Charlie-to-Echo channel and only a single magnetic sweep in parts of the channel. This action allowed them to concentrate on mechanical sweeping to increase the width of the channel from Point Foxtrot to Golf to serve as the BBFSA and on influence sweeping in both the Point Echo-to-Foxtrot and Foxtrot-to-Golf segments of the channel. The reduced number of helicopter sweeps somewhat increased the danger to the British ships that were minehunting in the Charlie-to-Echo channel, but would have greatly increased the danger to the more vulnerable U.S. MCM ships to an unacceptable level. Accordingly, the U.S. MCM ships' only mine clearance effort during the war occurred on 21 February, when they worked the Charlie-to-Echo channel just completed by the British. In late afternoon on 24 February, the U.S. helicopters and British MCM ships completed mine clearance in the BBFSA area to an eighty percent confidence level, and *Tripoli* sailed for Jubail, Saudi Arabia for much-needed structural repairs. The hole in her hull had grown larger, to thirty-by-twenty feet, and her keel was now separated from the shell plating by about eight feet. If bulkheads 26 and 31, providing watertight integrity, gave way in heavy seas, additional flooding would result and cause her to founder or capsize. Her remaining on station to support the helicopter MCM operations enabled use of the BBFSA by *Missouri*, which began firing her sixteen-inch guns against Faylaka Island about 9:00 p.m. on 23 February and at targets inside Kuwait about 5:00 a.m. the following morning to support the deception of an amphibious assault. This followed a decision by CincUSCent on the eve of the commencement of the ground war to cancel the planned amphibious raid and amphibious assault.[35]

On 23 February, in a scheduled change of command, Rear Admiral Raynor A. K. Taylor relieved Rear Admiral Fogarty as Commander Middle East Force, and the following day, in another routine turnover, Captain David Vail relieved Captain Grieve as Commander, U.S. Mine Countermeasures Forces. Admiral Taylor soon thereafter sailed his flagship USS *LaSalle* (AGF 3) north to embark the U.S. MCM Group staff that, following the departure of *Tripoli*, had moved temporarily aboard *Missouri*. From Jubail, *Tripoli* would continue to support helicopter operations until a sister ship, USS *New Orleans* (LPH 11), was designated her replacement.[36]

February 24th was the official date of the commencement of a U.S.-led UN Coalition ground offensive that would liberate Kuwait in four days. On that date, *Avenger* was steaming in formation with other units under the tactical control of *Tripoli*, prior to the departure of the amphibious ship for Jubail. For the next two days, *Avenger* conducted minehunting operations and led the *LaSalle* to the BBFSA. The latter task is no longer necessary due to the accuracy of GPS navigation. A traditional duty of mine countermeasures ships has been to lead other Navy vessels through cleared channels (Q-Routes) to open waters, as errors in navigation might result in an otherwise avoidable encounter with mines remaining outside the safe area. However, since minesweepers can now assign exact GPS coordinates to cleared areas or remaining mines, and other Navy vessels use their GPS navigation to avoid them, a "lead through" is generally now a misuse of MCM assets—which

Photo 10-3

The commanding officer of the amphibious assault ship USS *Tripoli* (LPH 10) inspects mine damage to the vessel as it sits in dry dock awaiting repairs (photographer JO1 Gawlowicz)

Photo 10-4

The battleship *Wisconsin* (BB-64) fires a round from one of her 16-inch guns at an Iraqi target in Kuwait (photographer unknown)

could normally be better employed clearing mines, particularly since few large ("high value") escorted vessels are willing to proceed at bare steerageway, the optimum speed for mine countermeasures ships using sonar to survey the waters through which they pass.[37]

On the evening of 25 February, the battleship *Missouri* and her escorts steamed in the fire support area off Ash Shuaybah, while the MCM forces continued mine clearance operations. The British frigate *London* provided protection for HMS *Herald* (A 138), the MCM control ship anchored in the center of the BBFSA, a ten-mile-long by one-mile-wide swept channel, supporting an all-British MCM force composed of *Atherstone, Cattistock, Dulverton, Hurworth,* and *Ledbury.* The minehunters continued to extend the swept channel toward the Kuwaiti coast to create a safe path to FSA F1. These operations continued both as part of the deception and so *Missouri* could get closer to the coast and reach more targets inland. The ships faced danger both below and above the water as they operated west of the Naval Gunfire Support Group and accordingly outside effective air defense cover.[38]

On 27 February, *Avenger* located a glass-reinforced plastic-encased Manta mine similar to those that had damaged *Princeton* nine days earlier. Long thought by experts to be "undetectable" by sonar, it was the first bottom influence mine found intact during combat. It was subsequently marked using the ship's MNV and detonated by divers from EOD Mobile Unit 6 through use of neutralizing charges. A few days later, *Avenger* sailed to Bahrain for a maintenance period. She returned in mid-March to the Kuwaiti operational area and resumed minehunting.[39]

POSTWAR MINE CLEARANCE

Coalition forces declared a cessation of offensive operations on 28 February 1991, and three days later on 3 March a formal cessation ceremony between Iraqi and Coalition troops took place at the Safwan airfield, located in southeastern Iraq just north of the Kuwait-Iraq border. At Safwan, Iraqi officials handed over plans showing the location of six separate minefields (MF 1 through 6) and four mine lines (ML 7 through 10). The Iraqis identified the locations and numbers of moored contact and bottom influence mines, but provided no additional details. During the postwar period, an allied MCM force, composed of units from nine nations, had three important tasks: clearing harbors, opening Q-routes (safe passages) through minefields and into Kuwaiti ports, and clearing the Iraqi minefields.[40]

By 23 April, British, French, and Australian EOD divers had cleared the Kuwaiti harbor areas. Though they found no mines in the harbor areas, they removed sunken boats, removed or exploded live ordnance, and destroyed eighty-two sea mines that had washed ashore, either broken free of their moors or purposely set adrift by the Iraqis.[41]

During DESERT STORM, only Britain and the United States had participated in the mainstream mine countermeasures effort. Following the cessation of hostilities, Australia, Belgium, France, Germany, Italy, Japan, and the Netherlands participated in the postwar mine clearance operations. Japan joined the effort only after considerable internal debate about the constitutionality of its armed forces' involvement in the multinational operation, and its forces, following their arrival on 1 June in the Gulf, operated independently of those of the other countries. Because of the sensitivity of some other countries about operating under U.S. command, the participants agreed to divide responsibilities for mine clearance geographically. The minesweepers from Belgium, France, Germany, Italy, and the Netherlands operated as an independent Western European Union (WEU) force.[42]

A Belgian MCM flotilla—the logistics support ship *Zinnia* (A 961) and two *Tripartite*-class minehunters, *Iris* (M 920) and *Myosotis* (M 922)— had actually begun defensive-only mine countermeasures operations under Western European Union operational control in the Gulf of Oman on 23 September 1990. On 17 January 1991, as Operation DESERT STORM began, the flotilla proceeded toward the Persian Gulf. Belgium made the decision on 27 February to deploy the older *Aster*-class minesweeper *Dianthus* (M 918) to augment its ships and, following the cease-fire, began mine-clearing operations off Kuwait. The Belgian flotilla was reinforced by three Dutch *Tripartite*-class minehunters—*Haarlem* (M 853), *Harlingen* (M854), and *Zierikzee* (862)—and five French *Tripartite*-class minehunters—*Aigle* (M 647), *Cassiopee* (M 642), *Orion* (M 645), *Pegase* (M 644), and *Sagittaire* (M 650)—accompanied by the French mine disposal tender *Pluton* (M 612) and the minesweeper support tender *Loire* (A 615). The *Tripartite*-class vessels, constructed as part of a joint Belgium, France, and Netherlands shipbuilding venture, were delivered to their respective countries between 1983 and 1989. The last Belgian ships departed the Gulf on 14 July 1991.[43]

Britain continued combined operations with the United States until 15 April, when its MCM ships joined the WEU force. At month's end, minehunters HMS *Brecon* (M 29), HMS *Brocklesby* (M 33), and HMS *Bicester* (M 36) replaced *Cattistock*, *Atherstone*, and *Hurworth*, and survey ship HMS *Hecla* (A 133) relieved *Herald* of her mine countermeasures support ship duties. *Bicester*, a veteran of the 1982 Falklands Campaign, would during the aftermath of the war earn the distinction of clearing more mines than any British mine countermeasures ship since World War II. [44]

The *Exultant* crew took over *Leader* on 7 March; the original departing crew arrived in the United States and assumed responsibility for *Exultant*. During the next five months, *Leader* located a total of twenty-seven mines, most of which were bottom influence types, notoriously more difficult to find than moored mines. Unfortunately, *Leader* detonated an influence mine while streaming her magnetic and acoustic gear and was laid up for a month while repairs were made to her number 2 main propulsion engine. The extensive damage to the MSO gave reminder that influence minesweeping is dangerous and even more so at night, when it is more difficult to rescue the crewmembers of damaged or sunk ships. Accordingly, given the choice, minehunting is a more effective and economical method of clearing mines than minesweeping. "Minehunt if you can, minesweep if you must" says the current wisdom. However, minesweeping is necessary when sea munitions are buried or otherwise un-huntable, or conditions require both hunting and sweeping to ensure adequate clearance. Thus, while minehunters appeal to budget conscious policy makers, because they are smaller and less expensive to acquire and operate than minesweepers, they also have less utility. Equipped with sonar only, they cannot counter acoustic or magnetic mines that must be swept because they are buried in silt or hidden by ridges or water conditions that impede the pathway of acoustic waves trying the pierce the seemingly tranquil sea.[45]

In early March, a set of Q-routes was defined, forming a set of interconnecting channels extending from mine-free areas into several Kuwaiti ports. The British and U.S. MCM forces set the clearing of the initial Q-routes as their top priority. The first Q-route leading into Kuwait was an extension of the channel the British minehunters had swept during DESERT STORM as a fire support area. Extending this channel was the quickest way to open a clear route. On 12 March, the ComUSNavCent flagship *LaSalle* and British minehunter *Cattistock* led a three-ship convoy, consisting of a Soviet merchant vessel and two U.S. Military Sealift Command ships through the Q-route into Kuwait to deliver badly needed water and supplies. The first ships to visit Kuwait after the war, theirs was a brave act, as most mariners would prefer not to enter, at least initially, swept but not yet tested previously mined waters.[46]

British and U.S. MCM forces then started clearing a deep-water channel through which larger vessels could transit into Kuwait, which they completed on 24 May. After opening these navigational routes, British and American forces shifted their efforts to clearing their assigned minefields. (French and Belgian MCM forces, in turn, completed most of the Iraqi minefields assigned to them before clearing the Q-route to Mina Saud, Kuwait.) *Avenger* cleared Q-routes and mine hunted in Mine Danger Area 9 and Mine Line 7 in late March and April, initially hunting mines in the deep-water ship channel. While working in the much shorter and narrower approach to nearby Ras al Qulayah Naval Base, *Avenger* received small-caliber gunfire from shore;

however, no damage was done and the attackers were not identified. After spending 28 March in Mina Ash Shuaybah, Kuwait, she resumed minehunting in the Kuwaiti area through late April.[47]

Avenger in late April conducted sonar condition checks at particular locations to predict equipment performance against certain types of mines, and located using her minehunting sonar six bottom-influence manta mines, neutralizing them with explosive charges deployed by her remotely-controlled mine neutralization vehicle. During the same period, *Leader* conducted clearance operations in Minefield 5 and Mine Line 7 (*Adroit* also worked Minefield 5.) [48]

Avenger arrived at Bahrain on 27 April for a maintenance period before departing for Abu Dhabi, from whence she began her long voyage home on 1 June. While *Avenger* was in port, *Adroit* conducted mine clearance operations in Minefield 5 (also worked by *Impervious*).[49]

Avenger's relief in the Persian Gulf, *Guardian*, continued her predecessor's success, locating and destroying multiple mines. *Guardian* had left the United States on 1 May 1991 carrying a 2,500-gallon fuel bladder secured with cargo nets on her fantail to extend her range. Escorted first by a U.S. Navy and then a U.S.N.S. tug, she conducted a brief turnover with *Avenger* in the Red Sea en route to the Persian Gulf. After her arrival in Abu Dhabi on 12 June, she conducted degaussing ranging, mine hunting, and gunnery exercises for five days. *Guardian* anchored to receive orders from ComUSMCMGru, fuel, and provisions and then departed for Mine Danger Area (MDA) 7, Minefield 5. She located her first mine on 21 June and several more in ensuing days. The destruction of the first mine noticeably jolted the ship and resulted in numerous dead floating fish; subsequently, *Guardian* moved farther away from the mines before detonating explosive charges. The following day she moored with *Leader* and *Adroit* outboard of the nuclear-powered cruiser USS *Texas* (CGN 39), returning the following day to Mine Danger Area 7. *Texas* and later the destroyer USS *Merrill* (DD 976) assumed both flagship and support duties for the mine warfare commander and his MSO/MCM ships. In total, *Guardian* located and neutralized with her MNV twenty-nine mines, one MOB, fifteen LUGM-145s, and thirteen UDM acoustic influence bottom mines.[50]

After a short period in Bahrain, *Guardian* left with *Adroit* and *Leader* for the northern Gulf for minehunting operations in Mine Danger Area 10. *Guardian* mine hunted and as necessary moored alongside

Photo 10-5

Adroit and *Leader* conducting mine-clearing operations with an MH-53E Sea Dragon minesweeping helicopter (photographer PH2 Rudy D. Pahoyo)

Texas to refuel. On 17 July, she steamed back to MDA 7, Minefield 5, for three days of operations before departing for Abu Dhabi with *Adroit* and the *Merrill*.[51]

Leaving Abu Dhabi in late July, *Guardian* sailed in company with *Leader* (with ComUSMCMGru embarked) for Mine Danger Area 10. *Guardian* hunted in MDA 10 and Mine Line 9 (near Iraq and Iran) until 10 August. At completion of mine-hunting, *Guardian* moved to Point Delta, outside the Mine Danger Area. Mine Line 9 was actually located about two miles north of where U.S. forces believed it to be, in shallow, brackish, almost chocolate milk–colored water, eight to ten miles off the coastline. Because the currents were too strong to permit the use of *Guardian*'s Mine Neutralization Vehicle, EOD divers using handheld sonars and Global Positioning System navigation sets defused the mines. Due to limited visibility, the divers entered the water about twenty feet from the estimated positions of the mines and then walked forward with one hand held in front of them until they located the mines by touch. This was a very dangerous operation, made more so by a requirement to exploit (recover for intelligence) vice destroy the mines with explosive charges. Following orders to recover at least one of each type of mine, EOD divers had to render safe mines they could not see and with which they might not be familiar. During one such evolution, divers found on the sea bottom a small rubber raft containing a dead Iraqi pilot. The body was turned over to Japanese officials who returned the deceased to the Iraqi government.[52]

Mine clearance operations in Mine Danger Area 10 were complicated by navigational and political dangers. In addition to the hazards imposed by the mines, the waters were too shallow in some areas for U.S. Mine Warfare ships and no international agreement specified where Iraqi and Iranian territorial waters ended and international waters began. The United States considered the line of demarcation to be three miles from shore; Iraq and Iran claimed their territorial waters extended twelve miles out. Further complicating matters was a disagreement over where the shoreline began. The United States measures the shoreline of a country at mean low water. Iran considered mudflats exposed at low tide as its shoreline, extending claimed territorial waters by about two miles. To preclude a fishing boat or some other small craft from later being blown up, the U.S. Navy wanted to clear all the mines located in MDA 10, some in Iranian waters. Iran would not allow U.S. mine forces to operate in her waters but did subsequently permit the Japanese to conduct mine clearance operations.[53]

On 12 August, *Guardian* left the operational area for a brief period in Kuwait City before proceeding to Bahrain, mooring in Mina Sulman. She departed on 24 August for the northern Gulf to search for a downed Saudi Arabian helicopter. After an unsuccessful search, Saudi Arabian authorities cancelled the operation.[54]

Guardian thereafter worked the waters off the Kuwaiti coast. She initially minehunted by day in Box Bravo Two, anchoring outside suspect waters at night, then Box Sierra Two and finally off Ash Shuwaikh, Kuwait. On 13 September she got underway for Jubail, Saudi Arabia. After only one day in port, she searched successfully for a lost H-53 helicopter from USS *Peleliu* (LHA 5). On 17 September, *Guardian* sailed with *Adroit, Leader,* and *Merrill* for Bahrain. *Guardian* spent the next four weeks in port or conducting local operations nearby, preparing to turn over *Guardian* to the crew of *Devastator* (MCM 6). She left the Bahrain area once during this period to make a short trip to Abu Dhabi.[55]

During the postwar clearance period, which lasted through 10 September 1991, at least one of the four U.S. MCM ships was engaged continuously in mine hunting and mine clearance. The WEU countries completed mine clearance in their assigned areas on 20 July, and the U.S. and Japanese Self-Defense Maritime Force on 10 September. However, authorities did not consider some of the "mine danger areas" completely safe for the passage of merchant vessels until many years after the war, and warned mariners about transiting these areas with annotations on charts. Considering that mines sown during World War II were still being found washed ashore or located by divers and MCM ships decades later, it is obviously prudent, given the choice, to avoid formerly mined waters.[56]

Responsibilities for postwar mine clearance by country for individual and/or shared areas and the resulting efforts are summarized in the following table. These totals do not include mines located in other areas in the Persian Gulf. Moreover, it is important to highlight that totals of mines found and areas cleared by MCM forces of individual nations are useful in describing the scope and success of the operation, but the effectiveness of individual ships or classes of ships cannot be accurately determined based solely on the numbers of mines they cleared. Minehunting is painstakingly slow, and this task is made more challenging by poor water or seafloor conditions that degrade the effectiveness of sonar or by debris littering the bottom that must be evaluated as either "mine like" or "non-mine like" before the search for real mines can continue. Also, since an area must be meticulously searched before the possibility that mines may lie beneath its serene waters can be discounted, searching waters that ultimately contain few or no mines might consume as much or more time than clearing those that conceal many potential ship killers. Conversely, the goal may not be to find mines, but instead to identify areas in which it is relatively safe for ships to operate. The risk in counting mines is that results can lead to the wrong conclusions. Some people erroneously discounted the importance of the U.S. minesweeping helicopters because they did not sweep (detonate) any mines in the Gulf. However, since most of the Iraqi influence mines were not properly armed, and were thus essentially decoys, it would not have been possible for either helicopters or ships to detonate them by sweeping. Additionally, because their type and condition were unknown at the time, their presence actually slowed operations—since they could not be swept, much slower minehunting operations were necessary to locate and deal with each one. The existing challenges reaffirmed the value of mines as sea denial weapons, as no matter what form is required mine clearance is very time consuming and inherently dangerous. Today, the most effective method remains the use in concert of mine countermeasures vessels (able to both hunt and sweep), minesweeping helicopters, and explosive ordnance disposal divers. The inability of the U.S. and British MCM Forces to clear the large areas necessary to support an amphibious landing was not due to a lack of skilled capabilities, but instead to a paucity of ships, helicopters, and divers.[58]

Mid-October also marked the end of the deployments of the three ocean minesweepers, who had participated throughout the northern

Country	Assigned Areas (minefield, mineline)	Number of MCM Ships	Number of Bottom Mines	Number of Moored Mines	Square nautical miles of Minefield Areas cleared	Square nautical miles of Q-Route Areas Cleared
Belgium	MF 1,2 ML 8	3	64	211	140	0
France	MF 1,2 ML 8	2	68	134	130	27
Germany	MF 3,6 ML 7	2	28	64	65	0
Italy	MF 6 ML 7	4	11	60	65	0
Japan	MF 5 ML 10	4	21	10	55	0
Netherlands	MF 3	3	3	35	20	0
United Kingdom	MF 4	5	59	125	95	0
United States	MF 5 ML 7,9,10	5	48	106	163	218
Total		**28**	**302**	**745**	**733**	**245**

Note: The total mines found by the U.S. Navy include the two bottom influence mines and the moored contact mine that damaged *Princeton* and *Tripoli*, respectively.[57]

Persian Gulf in the largest mine clearance operation since the Korean conflict. Although debris, LUGM-145 mine-anchors, bombs, and other non-mine objects littering the sea floor adversely affected MCM operations, coalition forces destroyed or neutralized more than thirteen hundred enemy mines by campaign's end. The five U.S. MCM- and MSO-class ships had located 120 mines, searching approximately 163 square miles of mined waters. Conditions in the operating areas had been favorable for minehunting; water depth, average-to-good bottom conditions, and limited burial of mines contributed to good sonar performance. However, tidal currents, which often limited the employment of divers, MNVs, and ROVs to slack water, made neutralization of the mines generally more difficult than detection. Below is a summary of areas cleared by the U.S. ships:[59]

Area	Square Miles
Minefield 5	90
Mine Line 7	22
Mine Line 9	26
Mine Line 10	9
Al Ahmadi	4
Al Faud	1
Al Shuaybah	11
Total	163

RETURN HOME

On 12 October, the heavy-lift motor vessel *Super Servant 4* left Abu Dhabi with the minesweepers *Adroit*, *Impervious*, and *Leader* secured on deck. The merchant vessel arrived at Norfolk on 9 November. Earlier, on 25 July, *Avenger* had entered Charleston after a seven-week transit, bringing to a close her eleven-and-a-half-month deployment. After departing Dubai on 1 June, *Avenger* transited the Strait of Hormuz to begin her journey home. Highlights of the voyage included passage through the Suez Canal, a port visit in Naples, four days of liberty in Port Vendres, France and a brief stop in Rota, Spain.[60]

DECOMMISSIONING

Within a month of their return home, *Adroit*, *Impervious*, and *Leader* were decommissioned in a joint ceremony on 12 December 1991. Although they were not the last ocean minesweepers to leave service (*Implicit* was decommissioned at Tacoma, Washington on 30 September 1994), Operation DESERT SHIELD/STORM was essentially the MSOs' final hurrah. Eight days after the three MSOs were decommissioned, on 20 December 1991, the U.S. Mine Countermeasures Group that had been "stood up" for DESERT SHIELD was disestablished. USS *Guardian*, the last MCM ship remaining in Gulf waters, departed on 15 January 1992.[61]

THE WAY FORWARD

Avenger was the first ship of its class to deploy, the first to locate a Manta fiberglass-cased-influence mine in combat, and the first U.S. Navy unit to deploy EOD divers to deal with an influence mine. General Schwarzkopf saluted the officers and men of *Avenger* for a job well

done, telling them: "Your contribution to the multinational mine clearance operations in the northern Persian Gulf was exemplary." However, overall, the performance of the U.S. mine countermeasures ships
had been inadequate. General Schwarzkopf later indicated that the
Navy's very, very antiquated minesweeping fleet frankly just could not
get the job done. To be fair, the words "small and" could be inserted
between the second "very" and "antiquated," as the ocean minesweepers did a fine job; they just could not clear the multitude of mines deployed by Iraq in the unrealistic timelines some people imagined were
possible. Initially the MSOs' sonars performed better than *Avenger*'s
and, because the minesweep generators installed in the older ships produced higher current to pulse through magnetic cables ("magtails")
streamed astern, they also had a much more powerful sweep capability.
Despite being under-funded, -manned, and -maintained for many years,
the ocean minesweepers performed the mission as well as the newest, albeit it not fully proved, U.S. Navy mine countermeasures ships.[62]

Today, the U.S. Navy's fourteen *Avenger*-class mine countermeasures
ships and twelve *Osprey*-class coastal minehunters provide unique capabilities that do not exist through any other means or measures, although
research is being conducted to try to find other ways by which to detect
and destroy mines. The MCM ships provide onscene, around-the-clock
mine clearance capabilities, limited generally only by crew fatigue and
particularly bad sea conditions. The use of minesweeping helicopters
and divers are equally important, because they provide different and
complementary capabilties. When minehunting is not possible, it is necessary to sweep, and when minesweeping is required, helicopters are the
first choice. However, although minesweeping helicopters cover mined
waters more rapidly than ships while posing less risk to crewmen, they
cannot operate at night or during reduced visibility. Similarly, although
EOD divers can locate and deal with mines (as well as exploit them for
intelligence collection), they are limited by fatigue and depth of water
and are at extreme risk when working in murky waters in which they cannot see hazardous ordnance. At the present time, minehunting and
sweeping vessels still provide the best all around solution to problems
that arise when hostile forces mine waters in which Navy or merchant
ships must operate. Capabilities of individual ships notwithstanding,
history has repeatedly reminded military commanders that sea mines are
deadly and that large numbers of ships, helicopters, and divers are required to clear them in a reasonable period of time.

Photo 11-1

Mine Countermeasures Vessel USS *Gladiator* (MCM 11), one of the fourteen *Avenger*-class ships currently in service that were replacements for the sixty-five U.S. Navy Ocean Minesweepers (painting by Richard DeRosset)

11 Conclusion

A historic review of the service of ocean minesweepers provides many valuable lessons learned, and perhaps some that have been forgotten as well. It shows that the four decades of experience with this ship type provide a good deal of information about how and how not to employ mine warfare vessels. It reveals the enduring good practices that must continue as well as some new ones that might be enacted. Above all, it suggests that the employment of current mine force ships cannot duplicate that of the MSOs for the simple reason that the priority and nature of Navy missions have evolved and changed to address new challenges facing the United States and its allies.

CURRENT REALITY

To begin with, there exists no requirement today for mine warfare vessels to support the U.S. space program or to deploy routinely to the Western Pacific, Caribbean, North Atlantic, or Mediterranean for duty as ready mine force ships. However, while two *Avengers* at Sasebo and two *Avengers* and two *Osprey*-class coastal minehunters (USS *Cardinal* [MHC 60] and USS *Raven* [MHC 61]) at Manama, Bahrain represent forces that are presently supportable by the Navy, they will not satisfy the Combatant Commanders' requirements for mine warfare vessels in Southeast and Southwest Asia. Hostilities would require deployment of additional mine-clearing ships, which the Navy should transport to the operational theater aboard chartered heavy-lift ships, sparing heavy wear and tear on the minesweepers before they even begin their main tasking. Ideally, the mine force should include a dedicated support ship that could carry four MCMs or MHCs like a heavy lift ship, perform repairs, and provide logistics support for the ships, as well as support the embarked mine countermeasures staff while keeping up with the battle group. The Navy must not forget that the use of a large number of modern, sophisticated mines by a knowledgeable adversary would require a very large mine countermeasures force if military operations necessitated removal of the threat in a reasonable amount of time. Such a force of U.S. mine warfare ships does not exist today. One hesitates even to speculate about how long it might take to come up with a force commensurate with past requirements, but it would be substantial.

The Navy today must be considered woefully short of mine countermeasures ships, a condition resulting from post–Vietnam War decommissioning of large numbers of ocean and coastal minesweepers, constructed as a result of the bitter lessons of the Korean War. Most of those remaining in service were transferred to the Naval Reserve Force, where for the duration of their service they were undermanned, -funded, and -maintained. Inherent shortcomings in both the size and condition of the mine force were exposed but did not unduly inhibit operational requirements during the Iraq-Iran War because the aged ships encountered simplistic Iranian-manufactured mines based on pre–World War I technology, and highly competent assistance was available from allied forces. The bulk of the mines encountered during the Persian Gulf War were also simplistic, and some were not even deployed correctly. Moreover, the strategy eventually employed to win the war helped disguise deficiencies in mine warfare capability. Had the 17,000 Marines aboard the ships off Kuwait, who were unable to land because of Iraqi mines, been necessary for victory or if their absence had resulted in large numbers of casualties, the inadequacy of mine forces in DESERT STORM may have been as significant as at Wonsan.

In the early 1970s, minesweeping helicopters operating from amphibious ships seemed for a time capable of performing the bulk of any mine clearance in lieu of minesweepers. This development may have led some to believe that a relatively small force of mine countermeasures ships would be sufficient to deal with any future requirements (clearance was accomplished at Haiphong Harbor by only ten ocean minesweepers and a modest number of minesweeping helicopters) and that the Navy no longer required a large force of ocean minesweepers. The idea was to use helicopters to perform mine clearance in shallow waters and the planned *Avenger*-class mine countermeasures ships for any deep-water work.

Using minesweeping helicopters for precursor minesweeping seemed ideal because, towing sleds at twenty-five mph, they cover water more rapidly than minesweepers, and they are less vulnerable to mines than ships. However, helicopters have weaknesses and limitations. They cannot operate during low visibility or at night, are not as effective as ships against deep mines, and cannot remain on station to operate around the clock. Also in the 1970s EOD divers seemed to provide an alternative to traditional minesweeping. They can locate and deal with mines with considerable precision. However, they are severely limited by fatigue and water depth and are at risk working in murky water where they cannot see the ordnance. The use of marine mammals is another option. However, sea lions, which must visually sight mines, are thwarted by opaque waters, and dolphins, which rely on built-in sonar, work only for expensive restaurant-quality fish and require a large ship with a well-deck to gain access to portable pools of water that house them when they are not employed. The simple truth is the mine force should encompass all of these capabilities because they complement one another. Experience has shown that helicopters, divers, and marine mammals cannot replace mine countermeasures ships, but can do some things better and are able to work in waters not accessible to the surface vessels.

Planners concerned about the shortcomings of the U.S. mine force often attempt to promote a more robust and capable force by citing numbers of mines laid in past conflicts, the lengthy time it would take to open critical ports or channels to merchant shipping and naval vessels should mining occur, historic mine-to-ship kill ratios, and related data. Most of their arguments fall on deaf ears, or at best result in issuance of policy papers but no additional funding. The reasons are the culture of the Navy and its biases, as well as practical concerns. The most powerful Navy "unions" are the aviation, submarine, and surface ship communities, within each of which are further stratifications based on perceived military importance or career desirability.

Why is the mine warfare career path held in such low esteem? There are many reasons—some cultural, some pragmatic. First, the U.S. Navy does not generally like mines, sea denial weapons that once in the water limit its access, and "Mahanian navies" (those whose ideology derives at least in part from U.S. naval historian Captain Alfred Thayer Mahan's *The Influence of Sea Power Upon History, 1660–1783*) do not like sea denial. Moreover, the Navy suppressed the story of the greatest U.S. success through use of mines, Operation STARVATION (the mining of Japan's sea lanes in WWII), because of its concern about how the role of the new Air Force would affect the Navy, since

Army Air Corps bombers had planted most of the mines, and fear of a possible consolidation of the armed forces. The 12,135 mines dropped in Empire waters by the B-29 Super Fortresses of the 21st Bomber Command sequentially impaired the movement of Japanese naval units, destroyed seaborne communications among her great industrial zones, blockaded major commercial ports, and finally placed all of Japan under a total mine blockade. The operation ultimately resulted in the loss of or damage to 670 ships vital to the delivery of food and supplies necessary for survival. So effective was the mining effort that shortly before the United States dropped the atomic bomb on Hiroshima, Japanese industrialists warned military leaders that if the war went on another year, seven million Japanese would die of starvation.

Second, if the submarine force is the "silent service," mine warfare is the "unknown service" within the Navy, receiving few resources and little publicity. The mine force has been for decades a "backwater entity," relying in large part on reservists to augment active duty personnel manning and supporting its ships, with few senior officers with sufficient influence or remaining service to champion it.

Another reason is the warrior persona, which leads officers to aspire to command a destroyer-type ship and seek a progression of career assignments leading to this goal. Moreover, mine warfare has not traditionally been viewed by officers as particularly exciting or noble work, a perspective that is not unique to the U.S. Navy. A First Lord of the British Admiralty once characterized it as "unpleasant work for a naval man, an occupation like that of rat-catching."

Finally, unlike every other type of Navy ship, mine warfare vessels (constructed for a specific purpose) are rarely needed for their primary mission and thus are in a sense a garrison force. Since in both war and peace the Navy never has enough combatant ships to meet its existing commitments for ships on station around the world, there is an organizational reluctance to allocate many fiscal, personnel, and material resources to mine warfare. During post–Cold War downsizing, some within the Navy questioned why, in a fleet with a battle force of less than 300 ships, 27 of the fleet units were mine warfare vessels. As of this writing, although Navy leaders have proclaimed mine warfare a high priority, the service plans to decommission within the next two years all of the *Osprey*-class mine hunters, reducing the surface mine force to a mere fifteen ships, one of which is the leased experimental mine warfare command ship HSV *2 Swift*.[1]

Yet, despite research in progress to find technology that will provide better ways to locate and destroy mines more quickly, the United States currently still needs mine countermeasures ships, and numbers of these vessels count. Whereas advances in other warfare technology, such as the modern stealth bomber, have proven more effective than a tenfold or even hundredfold increase of 1950s era bombers, such is not the case with improvements in mine warfare. While the *Avenger*-class mine countermeasures ships currently in service have improved navigation and an integrated combat systems suite that includes a remotely operated vehicle for use in mine destruction, they are essentially "stretched" ocean minesweepers fitted with gear salvaged from their predecessors. The smaller *Osprey*-class minehunters, which unlike the *Avengers* have no capability to perform minesweeping, would be valuable only as dive platforms for EOD divers in the event their sonar should fail during mine clearance operations.

Since the Navy currently has such a small countermeasures force, only fourteen *Avengers* and twelve *Ospreys*, the durability and reliability of the unique machinery and equipment fitted in them is also an issue. Considerable resources were expended after the Korean War both to improve the capability of ocean minesweepers to locate and dispose of mines and to increase the reliability of their engines. Experience has shown that when constructing other small vessels such as buoy tenders, salvage ships, and ocean tugs, it is possible to procure off-the-shelf reliable steel-block diesel engines. However, the same cannot be said of ocean minesweepers fitted with Packard or Waukesha engines, or *Avenger-* and *Osprey*-class ships employing Isotta Fraschini engines. Longstanding reliability problems with the Packards necessitated much time and money to maintain and repair them, and this problem continued with the Italian engines.

Like their predecessors, the *Avengers* have suffered reliability issues with propulsion engines, generators, and other equipment. While this book focuses primarily on the collective history of post–Korean War ocean minesweepers, any cursory study of their successors would conclude that the same problems plague the Navy's present-day mine warfare community. Minesweeping helicopters, explosive ordnance disposal divers, marine mammals, and supporting organizations and research laboratories have been in the past, and are today, similarly under-resourced, -funded, and -championed.

It follows, therefore, that much can be learned by studying MSO history. Although many of the ship-type weaknesses were corrected in the subsequent design of the *Avenger-* and *Osprey*-class ships, some persistent challenges remain—chiefly the reliability and robustness of equipment and machinery and the utilization of the active duty and reserve personnel that crew the ships. This conclusion describes improvements made in the current mine warfare ships, highlights the shortcomings that still exist, and discusses post–Cold War force structure changes that affect today's mine force. It ends with recommendations regarding the future utilization of *Avenger-* and *Osprey*-class ships, including their active involvement in homeland security, and with proposals for the acquisition of their eventual successors.

OVERVIEW OF THE SERVICE OF THE MSOS

The possibility that a country hostile to the United States might mine its coastal ports or waterways or those of its overseas allies to prevent free movement of Navy and merchant shipping (as happened most recently during both the Iraq-Iran and Persian Gulf Wars) mandates maintaining a capable surface mine force, although historically only a very small portion of the service of ocean minesweepers has been devoted to mine clearance. (In theory, of course, the existence of a ready mine force would serve to inhibit the use of sea-emplaced munitions by adversaries in the first place.)

For these reasons, fleet commanders faced with more requirements than assets are challenged to consider how to employ the small, relatively slow, and lightly armed vessels when they are not engaged upon their principal mission. The result is that minesweepers have traditionally served as "maids of all duties." Admiral Rickover commanded, as a lieutenant commander, the minesweeper USS *Finch* (AM 9), a 188-foot vessel built in 1918 to sweep mines in the North Sea. After reporting aboard on 17 July 1937 at Tsingtao, China, he found that most of her time was spent performing mundane duties for Commander, U.S. Asiatic Fleet in the Far East—carrying supplies, transporting Marines, performing towing and salvage work, and participating in the Yangtze River Patrol. The tradition of assigning mine warfare ships a myriad of tasks continued during the service of the ocean minesweepers—some, had they been available, better performed by steel-hulled ships.[2]

For many reasons, MSOs were not ideally suited as patrol ships during the Vietnam War, suffering limitations in speed, sea-keeping, crew size, and storage for fuel and food. However, the ships could and did carry out their tasking by boarding and searching vessels themselves, by working with patrol aircraft to extend their search capabilities, and by acting as "mother ships" in support of faster and more heavily armed patrol craft. The Navy addressed some of these design inadequacies when, in 1971, it converted *Assurance* (MSO 520) and *Alacrity* (MSO 521) to towed-array-surveillance-system (TASS) vessels. In addition to being fitted with unique equipment needed for their new mission, the ships also received the greater fresh water production and fuel storage capacity required for extended patrols.

The relative differences in speed between the hunter and its prey, however, are important. Since most vessels today are faster than Vietnamese junks and sampans, modern mine countermeasures ships are useful only to interdict merchant vessels or craft required to proceed slowly while navigating restricted or shallow waters, such as when in inland waterways or while entering or leaving port.

During the Vietnam War, the shallow draft and excellent maneuverability of the MSOs helped to offset their slow speed, and they were ideal for roles that required the least expenditure of resources to get the job done. In the absence of small ships, even cruisers had to be used for jobs well beneath their dignity and destroyers for things never dreamed of when designers laid out their blueprints. The versatility of the MSOs (and modern mine warfare ships) was one of their strengths, and they proved their worth in a variety of ways. When large-scale interdiction of Vietnamese vessels was needed, a picket of destroyers could only cover so much of the ocean, and there were areas where they could not go due to shallow water or restricted maneuvering. The MSOs filled in for more powerful ships very well as long as their radar and radio could identify danger and they could call for help in time. As a result, a U.S. Navy ship could be in a required location at a required time. The use of ocean minesweepers completed the circle of interdiction better than a destroyer-and-cruiser-only picket could have, even had there been enough of the larger hulls.

The MSOs could also operate close to shore or inshore, and were used during the war to transfer both men and materials ashore. They also visited ports that "deeper hulls" just could not get to because of shallow water depth. President Eisenhower's People to People program, for instance, was greatly enhanced by small ships visiting small cities. The friendship and mutual respect resulting from sailors painting schools and churches, providing medical aid, donating clothing and schoolbooks, and participating with their hosts in sports events and local festivals benefited all involved. It also helped the United States develop and strengthen alliances.

During the Vietnam War, ocean minesweepers used their gun mounts to engage in combat with enemy forces, including armed trawlers, ashore and at sea, and the combat action ribbons they received were awarded for gun actions, not mine clearing. Fitted with a 40mm gun, the minesweepers were relatively well armed for small ships and could defend themselves against armed merchants being used for smuggling. As the ships were modernized, however, the mount was removed to make room for the winch for a variable-depth-sonar and replaced with a smaller 20mm gun. The 20mm gun mounts, with admittedly lesser capabilities, still gave the MSOs a very real bite and continued to be used throughout the war. Following the war, however, they too were removed, leaving only .50-caliber machine guns for the detonation of floating mines, and seemingly during the ensuing decades the concept of self-defense for MCM ships was lost within the U.S. Navy. This is not true of the mine countermeasures ships of most foreign navies, as a review of their capabilities will attest.

The Royal Navy *Hunt*s, for instance, are fitted with a 30mm mount, 2 x 20mm guns, and two smaller general-purpose machine guns, which provide the mine countermeasures vessels a credible self defense while deployed outside the United Kingdom, and enable them to function in a secondary role as patrol craft while performing fishery protection duties in home waters. Belgian/Dutch/French *Tripartite*-class minehunters are equipped with a 20mm gun and two smaller 12.7mm machine guns, and Japanese mine warfare ships similarly employ a 20mm gun as their major armament. Many small countries without large formidable navies have long utilized mine warfare ships for coastal protection duties. In contrast, there has traditionally been little interaction between non-deployed U.S. Navy 2nd and 3rd fleet units and U.S. Coast Guard missions, except for utilization of aged Navy ships for counter-drug operations. However, with the Coast Guard now stretched thin with myriad historic and new homeland security duties, during a period in which a majority of the Navy's few mine warfare ships have been relegated to the reserves, it is time to adopt the proven model of countries not long afforded the relative, and constantly diminishing, security of large ocean expanses.

Possessing high-frequency, high resolution sonar, ocean minesweepers were employed routinely during peacetime to locate a variety of items on the ocean floor, a requirement that still exists today.

OCEAN MINESWEEPER SHORTCOMINGS

Design Flaws and their Operational Impact

Mine warfare ships constructed of non-ferrous metal and wood to minimize the threat presented by magnetic mines have inherent weaknesses that do not exist in steel-hulled ships. This does not imply that the mine warfare vessels are too fragile for regular employment, but suggests that they should be used sparingly by commanders to carry out extended non–mine warfare related duties so as to preserve the service life of equipment and machinery that due to limited demand can be difficult to obtain and expensive to replace.

The ocean minesweepers suffered much wear and tear during their repetitive long transits back and forth between the United States, the Mediterranean, and the western Pacific for operations with the 6th and 7th Fleets. In 1987, to support Operation EARNEST WILL and in order to preserve the service life of the vessels, a salvage ship and tank landing ship each towed three MSOs to the Persian Gulf. In transit, one of the Pacific Fleet minesweepers was damaged while refueling underway and an Atlantic Fleet ship while made-up in tow. Two years later, the Atlantic Fleet vessels returned to the United States under their own power and were then decommissioned. In early 1990, the Navy transported the Pacific Fleet minesweepers home aboard the heavy-lift ship *Super Servant 3*, vice under their own power or by tow. That fall, the Navy deployed three MSOs and USS *Avenger* (MCM 1), the lead ship in a new class of mine countermeasures ships, to the Persian Gulf aboard a heavy-lift ship in support of Operation DESERT SHIELD/STORM. The MSOs returned to the United States in 1991 aboard *Super Servant 4*. *Avenger* sailed home earlier.

Habitability Issues and Their Operational Impact

Deck seams in the ocean minesweepers generally opened in heavy seas, soaking berthing spaces and areas throughout the ships. It was not unusual in bad weather conditions for crewmembers, eager to lay below after enduring hours of cold salt spray and often seasickness, to find their bunks permeated with water that had rained down or sloshed from adjacent decks. When the MSOs operated in hot and humid tropical climates, sailors often had difficulty sleeping, as air-conditioning did not initially exist and there was limited air circulation inside the ships. Eventually, air-conditioning plants were installed in conjunction with upgraded electronics and communications equipment that required cooling. The berthing spaces of ships fully modernized now had air-conditioning serving them as well, although crewmen in the other ships still suffered.

Such hardships are minimized or absent in *Avenger*-class ships. The hull, weather decks, and deck housing are sheathed in fiberglass and other synthetic materials that keep out the sea. With hulls fifty feet greater in length than the MSOs, the *Avengers* ride better in rough seas and have the space needed for improved habitability. Minesweep sailors are now afforded air-conditioning in all living and electronic equipment spaces and relatively spacious berthing with associated lounges in which they may relax, read, and view movies from collections on board.

One MSO shortcoming that still plagues mine warfare vessels is inadequate production of distilled water, due to the operations in which they routinely engage and sometimes the areas in which those operations are conducted. The *Avengers* possess two means by which to make water: a distiller that uses main propulsion engine jacket-water to flash sea water to distillate and an electrically-powered reverse-osmosis unit. The latter equipment is able to produce potable water for crew use, but not the distilled, mineral-free water required for engine cooling. When ships are mine hunting at slow speeds to optimize sonar ranges, their propulsion engines do not work hard enough to produce hot engine jacket-water needed for optimum distiller operation. Moreover, when the ships are operating in areas with high seawater injection temperatures (ninety degrees or greater), the distillers also make little or no water. In the 1960s, the engineers of MSOs assigned to Windward Passage patrols near Cuba were forced to fill empty lube oil drums (lined with plastic bags) with distilled water to supplement what they could make underway.

Much knowledge hard-won by generations of MSO sailors was gradually lost over time as a result of the downsizing of the mine force. As the Navy began in the early 1970s to decommission large numbers of ocean minesweepers (and all of the smaller coastal minesweepers) not surprisingly the pool of people possessing extensive mine warfare experience shrank. This phenomenon continued as additional MSOs were struck and those remaining in service deployed less often. Finally, at about the time the last MSOs were leaving service, the Navy decided to consolidate the replacement mine force, fourteen *Avengers* and twelve *Ospreys*, at Ingleside, Texas. An unfortunate consequence of this policy was that many of the few "old salts" still on active duty retired or sought duty aboard other types of ships, vice leaving the areas in which they had homesteaded for many years. Additionally, because portions of MSOs' ship histories, particularly those recording combat duty during the Vietnam War, remained classified until the recent past, many lessons learned were not available for consideration by subsequent generations of minesweep sailors.

The *Avengers* based in Bahrain did adopt one practice employed by MSOs conducting MARKET TIME patrols off the coast of Vietnam: the use of awnings to shield topside watchstanders from the sun. Local craftsmen fabricated the coverings, supporting poles, and cross members from materials at hand. Because ordinary (magnetic) steel was used for the strength members, however, the ships had to leave the rigs ashore during mine hunting operations. A similar rig, properly designed and fabricated of non-magnetic materials, would greatly benefit ships operating in areas of extreme temperatures. Not only did the awning provide crewmen relief from the searing sun, its configuration also caused a Venturi effect, creating a relative breeze blowing across the decks below the covering.

Other challenges the MSOs faced still exist today in different forms. Ocean minesweepers engaged in Operation MARKET TIME patrols off Vietnam had to worry about running over fish stakes, large wooden poles driven into the sea floor to provide an offshore moorage for fishing boats. A nighttime encounter with these obstructions could foul or damage propellers or other running gear. *Avengers* working mine danger areas in the Persian Gulf encountered fish trap tending lines that could also damage sonar elements protruding below the ships. Although easy to see and avoid during the daytime, they, like the fish stakes, presented risk to the ships during nighttime operations. This weakness should be corrected during design of a next-generation vessel, perhaps through use of a "rope guard" or similar device that wouldn't impede sonar transmission and reception, but which operators could deploy beneath the ship's hull, along with the sonar transducer while minehunting, to deflect lines, cables, and such away from exposed mission-critical components.

Ship Armament and Self-Defense Capabilities

Modern U.S. mine warfare ships have no credible gun mount, and thereby minimal self-defense capability, which was not always the case. The MSOs employed their 40mm gun mounts frequently during the Vietnam War in support of land forces ashore, in counter fire on enemy shore batteries, and in sea battles, in one of which USS *Endurance* (MSO 435) helped send an armed steel-hulled trawler to the bottom. The 40mm guns were replaced by smaller 20mm mounts during modernization to make space on the fo'c'sle for a hoist for the improved sonar, and eventually the less capable 20mm guns were removed as well, leaving the ships largely defenseless.

In the decades since, the tradition of fitting gun mounts in mine warfare ships has been neglected, perhaps because of a belief that minesweepers would only be at risk while performing mine clearance off enemy shores, during which time combatant ships would be available to provide force protection, or concern that installation of a gun mount would unduly increase the ships' magnetic signatures. Yet, the MSOs often operated alone or in pairs during hostile conditions and this practice still prevailed in the late 1990s in the Persian Gulf. Modern mine warfare ships might be most at risk while operating alone, as were intelligence-gathering vessels USS *Liberty* and USS *Pueblo* in the 1960s when attacked by Israeli and North Korean forces. Moreover, modern pirates demonstrate regularly how small high-speed craft can readily prey upon much larger vessels.

If back-fitting gun mounts in existing ships is not possible, the ships should be heavily armed with machine guns and shoulder-mounted weapons. This capability would help deter possible aggressors (the ships are slow and may operate in coastal waters where piracy is not unknown) and provide them a greater self-defense capability against enemy military forces or, in the world today, terrorists conducting asymmetrical warfare. Moreover, since the Navy now has far fewer ships, it makes sense to better arm those remaining. As a Navy Captain serving in the Pentagon during the force reductions in the 1990s once remarked to me, "When you have fewer gunfighters, each one better have two guns."

Manning Issues—Mix of Active Duty and Reserve Personnel

Prior to the post-Vietnam reduction in the mine force, the MSOs were manned with full crews composed of active duty personnel. As the Navy transferred many of the remaining ships to the Reserve Force, however, crews were drawn down to half their original strength, with reservists comprising the balance of the crew. Although this was a successful cost-saving strategy, because the reservists were normally only on board one weekend a month, it left the active-duty crew severely undermanned the remainder of the time. Not surprisingly, material condition and operational readiness declined, and in the absence of the reservists, the small active-duty crews were forced to operate ships shorthanded.

One might argue that the Navy mine countermeasures mission (and the Navy's role in additional homeland security tasking) best belong to local reservists because they have complete and persistent knowledge of the harbors and coastal areas in which the ships operate. This point is valid; however, as the post-Vietnam MSO experience demonstrated, too much reliance on part-time sailors places an unfair burden on full-time undermanned crews and impairs readiness.

Additionally, reservists who drill for many years aboard the same ship provide a continuity of knowledge and collective experience of great value to a crew comprised of full-time sailors transferred between duty stations more frequently. Moreover, as most reserves are longtime inhabitants of the areas in which their ships are based, they do have persistent knowledge of local waters. Nonetheless, to ensure adequate material readiness and the ability of Naval Reserve ships to operate at sea when Reservists are not aboard (which is much of the time), a sufficient number of active duty personnel must be assigned. Recognizing that use of reserves is linked to affordability, it's time to reduce in size or eliminate the now unnecessary layer of management created to train and administer the Naval Reserve and use the savings to pay for more full-time sailors. The mission of the TAR (Training and Administration of Reserve) Program, comprised of full-time former active duty personnel, is to provide the support necessary to prepare Naval Reservists to conduct prompt and sustained operations in support of U.S. national interests. However, because Naval Reserve direct support to active duty Navy units shrank more during post–Cold War downsizing than the bureaucracy created to oversee a much larger

Naval Reserve, some leaders rightly question the relative merit and necessity of the TAR program. A rear admiral serving in the Pentagon during the late 1990s observed about a similar situation, "If we keep receiving less program funding and don't reduce overhead, pretty soon all we'll have left is a headquarters staff, with no money for the mission it exists to support." The Naval Reserve exists to augment active duty forces and, in today's much smaller Navy, unit readiness is particularly important. The post–Vietnam War model of reducing the numbers of active duty sailors assigned to ocean minesweepers by fifty percent, with citizen-sailors (usually only aboard ship one weekend a month) comprising the balance of the crew, was a dismal failure. Naval reservists should augment Naval Reserve Force ship crews comprised of a majority of active-duty sailors, not function as a cost-saving and unsatisfactory alternative. Moreover, reservists working directly for the fleet units they support would enable the Navy to develop the skilled personnel it needs during mobilization. It should not shortchange its mine warfare ships on a day-to-day basis by funding unnecessary management with resources that could be used for mission. Monies for greater "tooth-to-tail" ratio can be found by reducing, or eliminating altogether, existing "shore" Naval Reserve bureaucracy.[3]

Given that today the Navy has fewer ships than at any time since before World War I, it is important that it optimize those that it does have. Some reasonable suggestions related to the employment of mine warfare ships might include:

- Fully man them with active duty personnel;
- If deployed overseas, transport them aboard heavy-lift vessels to conserve machinery life;
- Provide them greater self-defense capabilities; and,
- Employ them, when not engaged in their primary mine warfare mission, for historic fleet as well as new roles.

A discussion of these points and a proposed new role for modern mine warfare ships follows the below section.

POST-COLD WAR FORCE STRUCTURE CHANGES

Significantly Fewer Combatant and Small Naval Vessels
The chapter on the Iraq-Iran War describes convoy escort duty (Operation EARNEST WILL), a mission the Navy had not performed much since World War II and one that it now has much less capability to

perform. During post–Cold War downsizing in the 1990s, the Navy decommissioned large numbers of escort vessels in order to retain its capital ships and to fund additional construction of types able to project power ashore (aircraft carriers, cruisers, and destroyers). Many whole ship classes were struck, including *Pegasus*-class patrol combatant missile ships; *Bronstein*, *Brook*, *Garcia*, and *Knox*-class frigates; *Charles F. Adams*, *Farragut*, and *Kidd*-class destroyers; and *Leahy* and *Belknap*-class cruisers, as well as some older nuclear-powered cruisers and steam-propelled aircraft carriers. The Navy also transferred service ships and tugs to the Military Sealift Command and decommissioned many tenders and repair ships. The small vessels remaining in service today include mine warfare ships, salvage ships, submarine rescue ships, and *Cyclone*-class patrol craft. The latter were constructed for use by Navy SEALs, but ultimately proved too large and too slow for many special operations missions. With increased Navy emphasis on the use of capital ships to project power ashore in support of land forces and for ballistic missile defense, two questions arise:

- Are some fleet commander requirements not being met or not being performed as well as possible?
- Can the Navy utilize its remaining small ships to conduct their primary missions and also perform other traditional fleet—and possibly some new homeland security—duties?

POTENTIAL NEW SECONDARY ROLE FOR SMALL NAVAL VESSELS

For the *Avenger*- and *Osprey*-class ships (the successors of the former ocean and coastal minesweepers), there remain traditional mine countermeasures, search and salvage, support for research and development (albeit more limited), and showing-the-flag missions, as well as possible use in support of homeland security scenarios. The world has changed and, based on the threat that terrorists pose to U.S. harbors and facilities, current utilization of mine force vessels (and other small ships such as the *Cyclone* patrol craft) should be carefully examined and modified as appropriate to best employ them.

Given fewer ships and the same or increased commitments worldwide, the Navy might well consider using mine warfare vessels to help safeguard port facilities and harbors, vulnerable as these sites are to acts of sabotage. The mine warfare community has extensive experience working in and around harbors, bays, and sea approaches. MSOs spent much of their service life conducting patrols, surveillance of ships, and harbor security duties at bases around the world. The ocean minesweepers also conducted Q-routes (sonar surveys) of major ports and their approaches to chart bottom debris in order to be able to discount it in the event of hostile mining, and could employ the same technology to detecting underwater explosive devices. Employment of a mine countermeasures vessel in response to a terrorist-threat scenario is not without precedence. USS *Gallant* (MSO 489) received short-notice operational tasking on 9 January 1980 after the Sacramento Port Authority received a phone call claiming that a group calling themselves "The Patriotic Scuba Divers of America" had mined the Sacramento Deep Water Ship Channel to prevent the departure of a Soviet merchant ship from the Port of Sacramento with a load of grain. Underway within a matter of hours, *Gallant* commenced mine hunting and minesweeping operations in the ship channel. After she had searched the waters for several days without finding any indications of emplaced munitions, the Port Captain reopened the channel and the Port of Sacramento resumed normal operations. During the interim period, however, ship movement came to a standstill while the minesweeper painstakingly located, identified, and eliminated as potential threats many automobiles, refrigerators, and other debris littering the bottom. Considered merely odd as the time, in the wake of 9/11, the threat of placement of mines in America's ocean approaches, bays, harbors, or inland waters today would obviously cause great trepidation and, if real, potentially grave consequences.

The presence of *Avenger-* and *Osprey*-class ships in major ports along the East and West Coasts would in itself help deter terrorist actions. The ships would provide an onsite capability to locate explosives through use of their shipboard sonars or by working with and supporting explosive ordnance disposal divers. Additionally, if the ships were utilized to assist the Coast Guard in inspecting vessels and craft entering or leaving port, they could host law enforcement detachments that could operate from them with zodiac boats to offset the ships' slow speeds. Now is the time for U.S. Navy mine warfare ships to bolster the U.S. Coast Guard. Moved into the Department of Homeland Security in 2003 and given the added responsibilities of patrolling the nation's 361 ports and 95,000 miles of coastline, the Coast Guard is woefully short of vessels and many of the aged ones that it does have are deteriorating at record rates due to the additional demands made upon them

"Coast Guard plagued by breakdowns: Aging fleet could threaten service's anti-terror mission," proclaims the title of a 6 July 2005 issue of *USA Today*. The article notes:

> Key members of Congress, maritime security experts and a former top Homeland Security Department official say that the fleet is failing and that plans to replace the Coast Guard's 88 aging cutters and 186 aircraft over the next 20 years should be accelerated.

The commandant of the Coast Guard told Congress that his equipment is failing at unacceptable rates and provided several examples of equipment breakdown or degradation. For instance, since 2001 there have been twenty-three hull breaches—holes that let in water—requiring emergency drydock repairs in the forty-nine 110- and 123-foot patrol boats. The chairwoman of a Senate Coast Guard subcommittee, Senator Olympia Snowe (R-Maine), concluded: "This nation must understand the dire situation in which the Coast Guard now finds itself." She favors replacing the "deepwater" fleet over the next ten to fifteen years. Snowe further calls a White House plan to increase the length of time scheduled to replace the "deepwater" ships from the current twenty-year plan to twenty-five years (to save costs in the short term) a "violation of common sense" amidst mounting concern that terrorists will try to sneak weapons of mass destruction into the United States through its wide-open ports.

Basing *Cyclones*, small high-powered patrol boats, with groups of mine warfare ships would provide local commanders a faster and more heavily-gunned vessel to complement the sonar-equipped ships and enable the diesel-powered vessels to mutually support one another. Navy minesweepers, salvage ships, and patrol craft, along with Coast Guard vessels, have traditionally worked close to shore, albeit for their own Service or (within the Navy) for their own communities. It is past time for the Navy and Coast Guard to align more closely these small vessels to increase operational synergy and mutual support, particularly desirable goals in a smaller force of ships. The Navy has already transferred tactical control of three of its thirteen *Cyclone*-class patrol craft to the Coast Guard for use as homeland security assets. The *Avenger*- and *Osprey*-class ships could similarly be dispersed among major East and West Coast ports for joint employment by both the USN 2nd and 3rd fleet commanders for Navy missions and the Coast Guard for homeland security tasking.

The Navy's mine warfare ships are currently all based at Ingleside, Texas. This consolidation occurred for a variety of reasons including deficiencies in the mine force and Congressional action that closed unnecessary bases to free monies to fund the operating forces. The Navy made a policy decision to close Naval Station, Charleston and other aged bases and relocate displaced ships to the newer "strategic" homeports that had been intended for a planned 600-ship Navy. Ingleside originally was supposed to house both an aircraft carrier and a battleship surface action group. When fleet downsizing eliminated this possibility, the Navy relocated to the Gulf Coast facility all its mine warfare ships, the former Charleston-based mine warfare command and school, a squadron of minesweeping helicopters, and some EOD detachments. The movement of the ships also reflected Navy belief that, because the Soviets no longer posed a threat to U.S. ports, it no longer required ships to be based in a number of locations to clear mines rapidly if required.

This logic may not be as valid today. Following the decommissioning of *Inchon* in 2002, the Navy no longer has a dedicated command ship at Ingleside from which minesweeping helicopters and EOD detachments can operate in concert with mine warfare ships. If the elements of the mine force can no longer operate together in one location, do they need to be based together? A related question is: Were a majority of the weaknesses noted during Operation DESERT STORM due to deficiencies in command and control and synergy between the elements of the mine force, or because the mine warfare ships and helicopters had been under-funded, -resourced, and -maintained for years? Hopefully there will be no return to the ineffective post-Vietnam Reserve MSO model, which the transfer of a majority of today's mine warfare ships to the Naval Reserve may nevertheless signify. (As of this writing, a provision of the Congressional Base Closure and Realignment legislation awaiting final approval would result in the closure of the mine warfare base at Ingleside, decommissioning of all twelve *Osprey*-class minehunters, and transfer of the ten *Avenger*-class ships based at Ingleside to San Diego.)

An alternative use of the *Avenger*- and *Osprey*-class ships would be to fully man and fund them for employment in myriad fleet tasks and homeland security roles, when not occupied by mine warfare training requirements and infrequent mine clearance operations. Small groups of similar-type ships could be homeported along the East and West

Coasts for joint employment by the Navy and Coast Guard, the Navy exercising operational control for the mine warfare mission and other fleet commander requirements and the Coast Guard taking tactical control of the ships for homeland security tasks.

Reservists should be assigned to support full active-duty crews, instead of as a cost-saving and unsatisfactory alternative. This method would allow the Navy to develop the additional mine warfare personnel it needs during mobilization and not shortchange the ships on a day-to-day basis.

Another important benefit would be that fully-manned and -funded ships could and should be used as full-time fleet units, not moored pier-side as floating training platforms. As the MSOs demonstrated, small ships can perform a variety of tasks for which destroyers or cruisers are either not available or not ideal, for (due to small crew size and minimal fuel consumption) a fraction of the cost of the surface combatants. Mine warfare ships have long been the poor cousins of the surface combatant navy, and it is time to bring them into the fold. Longstanding reliability problems should be corrected and the ships returned to full fleet partnership, small groups of the same type of ships based at major port areas to help ensure their commonality and maintainability. In addition, the small ships of the Navy can team with Coast Guard patrol craft to safeguard U.S. ports and facilities when not engaged in other missions.

NEXT GENERATION SHIPS

If significant breakthroughs in research and development are achieved, the backbone of the next generation mine force may be completely unlike the *Avenger* and *Osprey* mine countermeasures ships that comprise the surface mine warfare component today. However, the challenges that the physics of the ocean present minesweepers have not changed and, since the advent of these types of vessels in World War I, there have been relatively modest improvements in technology, suggesting that these ships will continue to be relevant for the foreseeable future.

The capabilities of the U.S. Navy surface mine force have been in decline for over thirty years, ever since massive downsizing of the ocean and coastal minesweeper force began near the end of the Vietnam War. Advocates for a larger Navy, or one that should at least not be reduced further in size, often compare the relatively modest numbers of ships today with the formidable fleets of the past. This argument has merit when quantity is more important than quality, such as during Operation MARKET TIME when a greater number of ships with less capabilities was more desirable than fewer ones with more capabilities. A counter to this argument is that a larger Navy is both unaffordable and unwarranted because modern ships have substantially more ability to deliver ordnance on target than their predecessors did. However, because there have not been quantum technological improvements in the capabilities of mine countermeasures ships, numbers of these vessels still do matter. Mine clearance is painstakingly slow and, when necessary, must be accomplished to preclude denial of the use of the waters in which embedded weapons lie. The use of mines by enemy forces overseas has periodically during the past fifty years delayed or precluded planned U.S. military operations and, if employed in American ports, harbors, or approaches, could result in the losses of ships and their crews, bringing trade and shipping to a standstill.

Despite these realties, Navy majority leadership has never embraced mine warfare, and since the post–Korean War shipbuilding program that produced the MSOs and other mine craft has not devoted sufficient resources to produce state-of-the-art mine countermeasures vessels. The same cannot be said of other mission areas, as witnessed by nuclear-powered ships and submarines, conventional sophisticated surface combatants, and high technology aircraft. Perhaps it is time to acknowledge formally the longstanding deficiencies in mine warfare, as documented by a host of naval officers and researchers, including Lott in *Most Deadly Sea*, Hartmann in *Weapons That Wait*, Marolda in *Operation Endsweep*, and Melia in *Damn the Torpedoes*, and consider a different approach to the problem.

In contrast to the United States, Great Britain has placed great emphasis and effort on its ability to perform mine countermeasures ever since Germany repeatedly mined its waters in World War I (and again during World War II) in an effort to prevent it from receiving by sea both the war materials and food it needed, and thereby make it capitulate. Moreover, the British invented most of the mine countermeasures equipment and techniques still in use today. The United States has generally, since World War I, copied, adopted, or modified for use in its own ships equipment installed in or employed by British minesweepers. Since Great Britain may well be our most stalwart ally, and we both speak and write a common language (negating potential inter-operability problems), it is time to engage in a joint shipbuilding effort advantageous to both countries.

The most recent example of British prowess occurred during Op-eration DESERT STORM, when HMS *Hunt*-class minehunters per-formed the bulk of mine clearance because it was considered too dangerous to send the U.S. ships against particular Iraqi-laid mines due to their higher magnetic ship signatures. The *Hunt*s were less susceptible to damage from mines because of their overall lower ship signatures, de-spite the magnetic Deltic diesel engines fitted in them. The Royal Navy selected proven, reliable, and less costly magnetic engines constructed of durable materials for its mine warfare vessels, and compensated for the greater disturbances they made to the Earth's magnetic field through use of installed state-of-the-art degaussing systems. This phi-losophy has proved superior to that adopted by the U.S. Navy over the past fifty years for construction of ocean, coastal, and inshore mine-sweepers, and their successors, *Avenger* and *Osprey* class mine counter-measures ships and coastal minehunters. (After German introduction of magnetic mines during World War II rendered its antiquated steel-hulled minesweepers obsolete, the U.S. Navy first converted wooden-hulled fishing boats to coastal minesweepers and eventually employed 481 wooden "Yard-class" auxiliary motor minesweepers to counter the new menace. Powered by durable steel-block engines, the scrappy 136-foot ships routinely crossed great ocean expanses to dis-tant theaters of operations. However, although their wooden hulls made them less susceptible to the mines, the durable [magnetic] equip-ment and machinery fitted in them still put them at risk. Accordingly, when the U.S. Navy later undertook construction of a large number of modern post–Korean War minesweepers, it sought to reduce the ships' signatures through use of non-magnetic engines and other machinery and equipment, and the best degaussing then available.) The propul-sion plants of these ships were beset throughout their service with reli-ability problems, and, in retrospect, the use of less expensive and more reliable engines and proven modern degaussing systems in the *Avenger*s and *Osprey*s would have been much better than the exotic engines chosen, which have also proved to be maintenance intensive and un-reliable. Following the war, the commander of the U.S. Naval Forces, Admiral Arthur, said of U.S. capabilities, "everyone in the world had better minesweepers out there than I did." Entry into a joint ship construction project with the U.K. would save the United States scarce funds it would otherwise spend on its own research and development efforts and lower the unit costs of the mine countermeasures vessels for both it and Great Britain, since the associated overhead would be spread among more ships leaving the yard.

In this manner, a very capable next generation mine counter-measures ship could result, economical enough to be purchased in sufficient quantities to expeditiously clear mines when called upon to do so. Because MCM ships advanced enough to counter modern sophisticated mines cannot be constructed overnight, a sufficient number of mine countermeasures vessels must be available when needed. This in essence demands a credible "garrison force" of ships, the expense of which, admittedly, would be hard to justify if infrequent mine clearance were its only mission. The continued threat of terrorism and associated requirements to safeguard ports and harbors mandates today, as during the Vietnam War, a greater number of vessels to carry out the mission, none of which need be the expensive multi-mission cruisers and destroyers designed to engage enemy forces or to project power ashore via the employment of Tomahawk missiles. Most current coastal requirements are being met by a stretched U.S. Coast Guard that could be augmented with Navy mine countermeasures ships.

Prolonged operations during the Vietnam War stole the life from both ocean and coastal minesweepers, but mine countermeasures ships assisting the Coast Guard in ensuring the safety of the ports in which they were based would have no requirements to make long transits to reach areas of operations. Moreover, these ships would be operating routinely in the same waters to maintain proficiency in their primary mine warfare mission and would know them intimately.

What form might a next generation mine countermeasures ship take? First, it would have reliable engines (compensated for by an adequate degaussing system), an advanced combat systems suite integrating advanced sonar, navigation system, and minehunting vehicle, and means to defend itself from mines and enemy forces. Second, it would be designed for and fitted with the gear (utilizing both the most advanced and most reliable technology) necessary to deal with all types of mines. Third, it would employ the latest fire suppression and firefighting equipment. Fourth, it would be seaworthy and provide as much comfort as possible for its crew during extended operations. Finally, after Navy planners had considered how best to utilize it when it was not performing mine countermeasures, additional capabilities would be added in modular form so that they could be quickly removed to return the vessel to its baseline minesweeper or minehunter configuration. It would be desirable for a mine countermeasures ship performing homeland security duties to have a credible gun mount installed on its fo'c'sle as well as other automatic weapons elsewhere. Because such armament and associated ammunition would likely increase the ship's susceptibility to damage from magnetic mines, it could be designed for removal, along with other metal items, during the traditional "magnetic materials off-load" that precedes entering a minefield. A multi-role modular ship concept was used for Danish *Thetis*-class fishery protection frigates, which could be quickly reconfigured for a number of individual peacetime roles, including surveillance, mine warfare, fast patrol boat, antisubmarine, and environmental operations.[4]

The concept of adding modular features to a baseline mine countermeasures vessel with requisite low magnetic and acoustic signature could be expanded to allow for more significant differences (based on individual customer desires) between ships from the same builder's yard. One example of a very economical and versatile vessel is the German-designed Type-209 diesel submarine built by the West German company HDW (*Howaldtswerke Deutsche Werft*) at Kiel. Between 1967 and 1995, twelve countries contracted for construction of fifty-four of the 1000-ton displacement vessels. The most frequently constructed conventional submarine class in the West due to superior features, good submerged range, speed, and handling aspects, as well as economical cost, its original displacement increased in some cases by as much as fifty percent based on customer requirements. The additional size and space were needed to accommodate increases in range, crew quarters, added electronic equipment, and increased diving depth. The net result was the emergence of the "Type 209 family" comprising very varied submarines as members.[5]

Since U.S. involvement in the post–World War I clearance of sea mines in the North Sea, there have been considerable improvements in the design, construction, and employment of mine countermeasures ships, as well as repeated painful reminders of the importance of mine-sweepers. Nonetheless, the Navy has generally provided the mine warfare community scant resources and for the most part ignored it between infrequent occurrences of enemy mine employment. Following incidents in which the Navy has had too few minesweepers to clear offensive mines in some reasonable amount of time, or has suffered ship losses, its leaders have investigated how the service found itself in a disadvantageous position and pledged increased funding and other support necessary to correct the problem. However, as memories of existing shortcomings fade and other pressing requirements for resources take precedence, the mine force, without the large numbers of senior officers to champion it that mark the surface combatant, aviation, and submarine communities, continues to receive only meager handouts. I hope this history of MSO service will help change a long-existing Navy culture and "mainstream" perceptions of the mine force so that the sailors who go down to the sea in wooden ships will receive the same level of support and consideration for their service as those who sail in steel-hulls, upon or under the sea.

Appendix A MSOs of the Atlantic and Pacific Fleets

Atlantic Fleet		Pacific Fleet	
USS *Ability*	(MSO 519)	USS *Acme*	(MSO 508)
USS *Adroit*	(MSO 509)	USS *Advance*	(MSO 510)
USS *Affray*	(MSO 511)	USS *Conflict*	(MSO 426)
USS *Aggressive*	(MSO 422)	USS *Conquest*	(MSO 488)
USS *Agile*	(MSO 421)	USS *Constant*	(MSO 427)
USS *Alacrity*	(MSO 520)	USS *Dynamic*	(MSO 432)
USS *Assurance*	(MSO 521)	USS *Embattle*	(MSO 434)
USS *Avenge*	(MSO 423)	USS *Endurance*	(MSO 435)
USS *Bold*	(MSO 424)	USS *Energy*	(MSO 436)
USS *Bulwark*	(MSO 425)	USS *Engage*	(MSO 433)*
USS *Dash*	(MSO 428)	USS *Enhance*	(MSO 437)
USS *Detector*	(MSO 429)	USS *Esteem*	(MSO 438)
USS *Direct*	(MSO 430)	USS *Excel*	(MSO 439)
USS *Dominant*	(MSO 431)	USS *Firm*	(MSO 444)
USS *Engage*	(MSO 433)*	USS *Force*	(MSO 445)
USS *Exploit*	(MSO 440)	USS *Fortify*	(MSO 446)*
USS *Exultant*	(MSO 441)	USS *Gallant*	(MSO 489)
USS *Fearless*	(MSO 442)	USS *Guide*	(MSO 447)
USS *Fidelity*	(MSO 443)	USS *Illusive*	(MSO 448)*
USS *Fortify*	(MSO 446)*	USS *Impervious*	(MSO 449)*
USS *Illusive*	(MSO 448)*	USS *Implicit*	(MSO 455)
USS *Impervious*	(MSO 449)*	USS *Inflict*	(MSO 456)*

Atlantic Fleet		**Pacific Fleet**	
USS *Inflict*	(MSO 456)*	USS *Leader*	(MSO 490)*
USS *Leader*	(MSO 490)*	USS *Loyalty*	(MSO 457)
USS *Nimble*	(MSO 459)	USS *Lucid*	(MSO 458)
USS *Notable*	(MSO 460)	USS *Persistent*	(MSO 491)
USS *Observer*	(MSO 461)	USS *Pivot*	(MSO 463)
USS *Pinnacle*	(MSO 462)	USS *Pledge*	(MSO 492)
USS *Rival*	(MSO 468)	USS *Pluck*	(MSO 464)
USS *Sagacity*	(MSO 469)	USS *Prestige*	(MSO 465)
USS *Salute*	(MSO 470)	USS *Prime*	(MSO 466)
USS *Skill*	(MSO 471)	USS *Reaper*	(MSO 467)
USS *Stalwart*	(MSO 493)		
USS *Sturdy*	(MSO 494)		
USS *Swerve*	(MSO 495)		
USS *Valor*	(MSO 472)		
USS *Venture*	(MSO 496)		
USS *Vigor*	(MSO 473)		
USS *Vital*	(MSO 474)		

Sixty-five total ships
* Six ships served in both the Atlantic and Pacific Fleets.

Appendix B Unit Award Citations

Unit Awards (in chronological order)

USS *Endurance* (MSO 435)	November 1965–June 1966
Task Force Sixty-Five	20 January–15 April 1966
Mine Division Seventy-Two	11 November 1966–6 May 1967
Manned Spacecraft Recovery Force Atlantic (TF 140)	1 July 1967–26 July 1969
Mine Division Ninety-One	1 October 1965–30 June 1966 and 1 September 1967–31 May 1968
USS *Firm* (MSO 444), USS *Embattle* (MSO 434), and USS *Loyalty* (MSO 457)	5 May–7 September 1968
Commander Task Group 194.0	18 October–5 December 1968
Minesweeper Special (MSS 1)	20 June–15 October 1969
USS *Endurance* (MSO 435)	November 1970
Commander Task Force 115	2 March–15 December 1972
USS *Alacrity* (AG 520) and USS *Assurance* (AG 521)	8 August–30 November 1974
USS *Illusive* (MSO 448)	28 September 1978–25 June 1979
USS *Leader* (MSO 490)	28 September 1978–25 June 1979
Mine Countermeasures Task Group 1-81	27 April–8 October 1981
Task Unit 801.4.7	19 November 1987–23 April 1988
Arabian Gulf Battle Force	17 January–7 February 1991
USS *Adroit* (MSO 509)	13 May–1 June 1991

THE SECRETARY OF THE NAVY
WASHINGTON

The Secretary of the Navy takes pleasure in commending

USS ENDURANCE (MSO-435)

for service as set forth in the following

CITATION:

For exceptionally meritorious service from November 1965 to June 1966 while serving as a unit of Task Force 115, engaged in anti-infiltration patrols off the coast of Vietnam. During this period, USS ENDURANCE (MSO-435) on repeated occasions closed the coast to counter the attacks of hostile forces ashore in support of threatened and beleaguered allied units under attack. While in pursuit of her primary mission, ENDURANCE displayed initiative, imagination and professional competence to a unique degree, pioneering in the development of tactics for the deployment of multiple small units while maintaining at all times the highest standards of morale, aggressiveness and efficiency. By the extraordinary and collective heroism of her crew, and by her exceptionally meritorious conduct in refining the techniques appropriate to her task, ENDURANCE upheld the highest traditions of the United States Naval Service.

All personnel attached to and serving on board USS ENDURANCE during the period designated above, or any part thereof, are hereby authorized to wear the Navy Unit Commendation Ribbon.

Paul H. Nitze

Secretary of the Navy

THE SECRETARY OF THE NAVY
WASHINGTON

The Secretary of the Navy takes pleasure in commending

TASK FORCE SIXTY-FIVE

for service as set forth in the following

CITATION:

For exceptionally meritorious service from 20 January to 15 April 1966 in support of salvage and recovery operations of great importance to the United States Government. Following the mid-air collision between two U. S. Air Force aircraft over the Mediterranean Area on 17 January 1966, a large amount of wreckage and debris, including a nuclear weapon, was scattered over the countryside and adjacent sea areas in the vicinity of Palomares, Spain. The United States Government undertook a commitment to the Government of Spain to restore the area to its original condition by removing all wreckage and debris, and locating and recovering the missing nuclear weapon. At the direction of the Chief of Naval Operations, Commander SIXTH Fleet established Task Force SIXTY-FIVE in support of that effort. In undertaking, and successfully accomplishing all assigned tasks in what was probably the largest and most difficult deep-sea search ever conducted by any country in the world, personnel of Task Force SIXTY-FIVE consistently demonstrated an exceptionally high order of professionalism, ingenuity, enthusiasm, and determination. Innovations were developed and put into operation which permitted the location and recovery of the missing nuclear weapon from a depth of 2,850 feet. This remarkable achievement, along with the development of other capabilities in the field of undersea salvage, attests to the skill, knowledge and training of Task Force SIXTY-FIVE personnel, and reflects great credit upon themselves and the United States Naval Service.

All personnel attached to and serving with Task Force SIXTY-FIVE during the period designated above, or any part thereof, are hereby authorized to wear the Navy Unit Commendation Ribbon.

Paul R. Ignatius

Secretary of the Navy

CHIEF OF NAVAL OPERATIONS

The Secretary of the Navy takes pleasure in presenting the
MERITORIOUS UNIT COMMENDATION to

MINE DIVISION SEVENTY-TWO

for service as set forth in the following

CITATION:

For meritorious service from 11 November 1966 to 6 May 1967
while serving with friendly foreign forces engaged in armed conflict
against communist insurgent (Viet Cong) forces in the Republic of Vietnam. Mine Division SEVENTY-TWO units, consisting of USS FIRM
(MSO-444), USS EMBATTLE (MSO-434), USS FORCE (MSO-445), USS
PRIME (MSO-466), and USS REAPER (MSO-467), spent a total of 576
ship days on coastal surveillance (MARKET TIME) operations in support of United States Navy and Vietnamese Navy efforts to prevent Viet
Cong attempts to infiltrate men and material into the Republic of Vietnam. In addition to conducting vigorous, daily, anti-infiltration patrols,
Mine Division SEVENTY-TWO units actively supported Operations
SURFLINE, FARRAGUT, and DECKHOUSE VI. Their action during these
operations was instrumental in the success of friendly forces, and contributed significantly to the heavy losses sustained by the enemy. Mine
Division SEVENTY-TWO units were also instrumental in recovering the
sunken dredge DONG NAI in Vung Tau Harbor, assisted in extinguishing
a shipboard fire on the merchant ship RUTGERS VICTORY, and aided
many drowning, ill, or distressed Vietnamese fishermen. The outstanding
professionalism, courage, and devotion to duty displayed by the officers
and men of Mine Division SEVENTY-TWO throughout their deployment,
contributed greatly to the success of the counterinsurgency effort in the
Republic of Vietnam and were in keeping with the highest traditions of
the United States Naval Service.

All personnel attached to and serving with Mine Division SEVENTY-TWO during
the above-designated period, or any part thereof, are hereby authorized to wear the
Meritorious Unit Commendation Ribbon.

For the Secretary,

T. H. Moorer

T. H. Moorer
Admiral, United States Navy
Chief of Naval Operations

THE SECRETARY OF THE NAVY

WASHINGTON

        The Secretary of the Navy takes pleasure in presenting the MERITORIOUS UNIT COMMENDATION to

MANNED SPACECRAFT RECOVERY FORCE ATLANTIC (TF-140)

for service as set forth in the following

CITATION:

        For meritorious service while supporting the National Aeronautics and Space Administration's APOLLO manned space-flight operations in the Atlantic from 1 July 1967 to 26 July 1969. The Manned Spacecraft Recovery Force Atlantic conducted recovery operations vital to the success of Project APOLLO in coordinated operational employment of numerous disparate Navy, Air Force, Marine and Army units and civil agencies. The painstaking planning and attention which this Task Force devoted to each of the eight APOLLO missions resulted in flawlessly-executed Atlantic recoveries. Consistently meeting and sustaining the highest standards of excellence throughout its recovery mission, and in the development and perfection of astronaut and spacecraft recovery techniques and procedures, the Manned Spacecraft Recovery Force Atlantic, by its expertise, alertness, and dedication, reflected great credit upon itself and the National Aeronautics and Space Administration, and upheld the highest traditions of the United States Naval Service.

Secretary of the Navy

CHIEF OF NAVAL OPERATIONS

The Secretary of the Navy takes pleasure in presenting the MERITORIOUS UNIT COMMENDATION to

MINE DIVISION NINETY-ONE

for service as set forth in the following

CITATION:

For meritorious service from 1 October 1965 through 30 June 1966 and from 1 September 1967 through 31 May 1968 while serving as a unit of Task Force 115 and Task Group 70.5 during combat operations off the coast of the Republic of Vietnam. Displaying outstanding initiative and skill, the units of Mine Division NINETY-ONE carried out vital roles in support of free-world forces by providing naval gunfire support and illumination, support of Coastal Group actions, and in the coordinated destruction of enemy forces that attempted to infiltrate the coast of the Republic of Vietnam on the night of 29 February/1 March 1968. Further, division personnel demonstrated outstanding courage, perseverance, and aggressive prowess in the clearance of minefields which seriously hampered operations of major SEVENTH Fleet units. Throughout their deployment with the SEVENTH Fleet, the officers and men of Mine Division NINETY-ONE were instrumental in the successful conduct of numerous and varied missions in support of combat forces. Their exemplary skill, versatility, and dedication in the performance of mine countermeasures operations, aircraft salvage operations, anti-infiltration patrols, and support of Free World Military Assistance Forces were in keeping with the highest traditions of the United States Naval Service.

All personnel attached to and serving with Mine Division NINETY-ONE during the above-designated periods, or any part thereof, are hereby authorized to wear the Meritorious Unit Commendation Ribbon.

For the Secretary,

T. H. Moorer

T. H. Moorer
Admiral, United States Navy
Chief of Naval Operations

CHIEF OF NAVAL OPERATIONS

The Secretary of the Navy takes pleasure in presenting the MERITORIOUS UNIT COMMENDATION to

USS FIRM (MSO-444)
USS EMBATTLE (MSO-434)
USS LOYALTY (MSO-457)

for service as set forth in the following

CITATION:

For meritorious service from 5 May to 7 September 1968 while serving with friendly foreign forces engaged in armed conflict against enemy forces in the Republic of Vietnam. USS FIRM, USS EMBATTLE, and USS LOYALTY spent a total of 252 ship-days under the operational control of Commander Task Force 115 conducting coastal surveillance (MARKET TIME) operations in support of United States Navy and Vietnamese Navy efforts to prevent Communist attempts to infiltrate men and material into the Republic of Vietnam. In addition to conducting vigorous, daily, anti-infiltration patrols, the ships participated in numerous sonar searches for downed friendly aircraft, dispensed medical assistance to distressed or injured Vietnamese seafarers, and provided naval gunfire support to friendly forces in-country. The outstanding professionalism, courage, and devotion to duty displayed by the officers and men of USS FIRM, USS EMBATTLE, and USS LOYALTY throughout this period contributed greatly to the success of the counterinsurgency effort in the Republic of Vietnam, and were in keeping with the highest traditions of the United States Naval Service.

For the Secretary,

E. R. Zumwalt, Jr.
Admiral, United States Navy
Chief of Naval Operations

By virtue of the authority vested in me as President of the United States and as Commander-in-Chief of the Armed Forces of the United States, I have today awarded

THE PRESIDENTIAL UNIT CITATION (NAVY)

FOR EXTRAORDINARY HEROISM TO

COMMANDER TASK GROUP 194.0
(Units Participating in Operation SEA LORDS)

 For extraordinary heroism and outstanding performance of duty from 18 October to 5 December 1968 while engaged in armed conflict against enemy forces in the Republic of Vietnam. Commander Task Group 194.0 initiated and prosecuted the first of several interdiction campaigns to sever enemy lines of communication and resupply and to establish the legal government in areas previously held by the enemy. The naval units engaged in Operation SEA LORDS consistently displayed the striking power and professionalism which were to mark this and following campaigns. Tasked with routing a myriad of enemy forces from their previous sanctuaries, personnel of Commander Task Group 194.0 ventured courageously into little-known canals and back-water areas, fighting valiantly through countless intense enemy rocket and automatic weapons attacks. The naval units, through their persistent and aggressive strikes against enemy strongholds, were eminently successful in their campaign to interdict enemy resupply routes and base areas throughout the lower Mekong Delta region. The courage, professionalism, and dedication displayed by the officers and men of Commander Task Group 194.0 reflected credit upon themselves and were in keeping with the highest traditions of the United States Naval Service.

Richard Nixon

CHIEF OF NAVAL OPERATIONS

        The Secretary of the Navy takes pleasure in presenting the MERITORIOUS UNIT COMMENDATION to the

MINESWEEPER SPECIAL (MSS-1)

for service as set forth in the following

CITATION:

        For meritorious service from 20 June to 15 October 1969, during which time the new Minesweeper Special was delivered to the Navy, fitted out, given a preliminary evaluation of effectiveness, and tested to determine its ability to withstand underwater shock. Without benefit of formal training or previous experience with the type of command and control facilities installed in the Minesweeper Special, the officer-in-charge and crew members assigned undertook the task of developing the unit from an unknown and untried entity to an operationally tested and capable mine countermeasures platform. Faced with predictions that the converted liberty ship would be severely restricted in its maneuverability and would have to be towed wherever it went, the crew displayed exceptional seamanship in demonstrating the maneuverability of the Minesweeper Special at Charleston, South Carolina. The next task was to measure its survivability during shock tests accomplished in an area near Key West, Florida. Exhibiting the utmost in courage and perseverance, the Minesweeper Special crew remained aboard during the detonation of ten explosive charges, personally overseeing each detail before, during, and after each shot. Upon completion of the highly successful shock tests, the crew once again displayed expert seamanship by safely moving the unit from Key West to Charleston, under its own power. Their overall commendable performance resulted in bringing the Minesweeper Special concept in mine countermeasures significantly closer to becoming a reality. By their skill, teamwork, diligence, and loyal devotion to duty, the individual crew members of the Minesweeper Special reflected credit upon themselves and the United States Naval Service.

        For the Secretary,

E. R. Zumwalt, Jr.
Admiral, United States Navy
Chief of Naval Operations

THE SECRETARY OF THE NAVY

WASHINGTON

The Secretary of the Navy takes pleasure in presenting the
NAVY UNIT COMMENDATION to

USS ENDURANCE (MSO-435)

for service as set forth in the following

CITATION:

For exceptionally meritorious achievement in action against a
heavily armed, enemy infiltration trawler in November 1970. When the
enemy trawler began its approach to the coast of the Republic of Vietnam,
USS ENDURANCE, a lightly armed ship, maneuvered into a favorable
position to intercept the trawler. With consummate skill, she assumed a
course to avoid alerting the enemy vessel and gained a most advantageous
position. Immediately after the trawler entered the waters of the Republic
of Vietnam, ENDURANCE closed and challenged. In the ensuing engagement at a range of 1,000 yards, she utilized both her armament and
searchlight for maximum advantage. The spirited gun action delayed the
movement of the trawler until more heavily armed ships could close and
assist. After being hit repeatedly by the gunfire of ENDURANCE and the
assisting units, the trawler stopped, exploded, and sank. The courage,
resourcefulness, and fighting spirit of the officers and men of USS
ENDURANCE were in keeping with the highest traditions of the United
States Naval Service.

Secretary of the Navy

John W. Warner

CHIEF OF NAVAL OPERATIONS

        The Secretary of the Navy takes pleasure in presenting the
MERITORIOUS UNIT COMMENDATION to

COMMANDER TASK FORCE 115

for service as set forth in the following

    CITATION:

        For meritorious service during the period 2 March 1972 to 15 Decem-
    ber 1972 in connection with the interdiction of enemy supply lines into
    the Republic of Vietnam. Maintaining a close vigil over 1,200 miles of
    coastline, Task Force 115 (United States Naval Coastal Surveillance
    Force) created one of the most effective coastal barriers in naval his-
    tory. Large quantities of insurgent war materials were destroyed or
    captured. In addition, Task Force 115 units conducted almost daily naval
    gunfire support missions, completed numerous search and rescue oper-
    ations, carried out hundreds of psychological warfare missions and
    medical civic action programs, and conducted training programs for Viet-
    namese naval personnel which culminated in the turnover of the total
    Coastal Surveillance System and the operational control of the entire
    inner and outer coastal barriers to the Vietnamese Navy. The profes-
    sionalism, courage, and dedication displayed by the officers and men of
    Task Force 115 were in keeping with the highest traditions of the United
    States Naval Service.

                        For the Secretary,

                        E. R. Zumwalt, Jr.
                        Admiral, United States Navy
                        Chief of Naval Operations

THE SECRETARY OF THE NAVY
WASHINGTON, D. C. 20350

The Secretary of the Navy takes pleasure in presenting the
MERITORIOUS UNIT COMMENDATION to

USS ALACRITY (AG-520)
and
USS ASSURANCE (AG-521)

for service as set forth in the following

CITATION:

For meritorious service while operating in the Mediterranean Sea from 8 August 1974 to 30 November 1974. By their
superb performance and dedication to duty, the officers, men,
and civilian personnel of USS ALACRITY and USS ASSURANCE
accomplished an operational mission of great significance for
the United States Navy. Through their display of professionalism, ingenuity, and resourcefulness, another link in the United
States chain of defensive warfare system was forged and tem-
pered. The outstanding performance of the personnel of USS
ALACRITY and USS ASSURANCE, under arduous and trying
conditions and operational constraints, reflected credit upon
themselves and was in keeping with the highest traditions of
the United States Naval Service.

William Middendorf

Secretary of the Navy

THE SECRETARY OF THE NAVY
WASHINGTON, D.C. 20350

        The Secretary of the Navy takes pleasure in presenting the
MERITORIOUS UNIT COMMENDATION to

USS ILLUSIVE (MSO 448)

for service as set forth in the following

CITATION:

        For meritorious service while serving as a member of
the Standing Naval Force Channel (STANAVFORCHAN), North
Atlantic Treaty Organization (NATO) Mine Countermeasures
(MCM) Squadron from 28 September 1978 to 25 June 1979. USS
ILLUSIVE was required to observe and to evaluate NATO MCM
capabilities and to emphasize and reaffirm the United
States' ability and determination to support NATO with a
viable MCM force. ILLUSIVE's crewmembers responded enthusiastically and aggressively to this extremely challenging
mission, and exhibited innovative and highly effective
operational planning and execution throughout the entire
period of deployment. The skillful utilization of all available MCM assets up to those limits imposed by the severe
operational environment enabled ILLUSIVE to achieve an
exceptional record of operational performance which was unexceeded throughout STANAVFORCHAN. The crew's achievements
enhanced greatly the overall performance and facilitated the
successful accomplishment of the NATO Squadron's endeavors.
By their indefatigable efforts, uncompromising commitment to
excellence, and steadfast devotion to duty, the officers and
enlisted personnel of USS ILLUSIVE (MSO 448) reflected
credit upon themselves and upheld the highest traditions of
the United States Naval Service.

                                        E. Hidley

                              Secretary of the Navy

THE SECRETARY OF THE NAVY

WASHINGTON. D.C. 20350

The Secretary of the Navy takes pleasure in presenting the MERITORIOUS UNIT COMMENDATION to

USS LEADER (MSO 490)

for service as set forth in the following

CITATION:

For meritorious service while serving as a member of the Standing Naval Force Channel (STANAVFORCHAN), North Atlantic Treaty Organization (NATO) Mine Countermeasures (MCM) Squadron from 28 September 1978 to 25 June 1979. USS LEADER was required to observe and to evaluate NATO MCM capabilities and to emphasize and reaffirm the United States' ability and determination to support NATO with a viable MCM force. LEADER's crewmembers responded enthusiastically and aggressively to this extremely challenging mission, and exhibited innovative and highly effective operational planning and execution throughout the entire period of deployment. The skillful utilization of all available MCM assets up to those limits imposed by the severe operational environment enabled LEADER to achieve an exceptional record of operational performance which was unexceeded throughout STANAVFORCHAN. The crew's achievements enhanced greatly the overall performance and facilitated the successful accomplishment of the NATO Squadron's endeavors. By their indefatigable efforts, uncompromising commitment to excellence, and steadfast devotion to duty, the officers and enlisted personnel of USS LEADER (MSO 490) reflected credit upon themselves and upheld the highest traditions of the United States Naval Service.

E. Hidalgo.

Secretary of the Navy

THE SECRETARY OF THE NAVY

WASHINGTON, D.C. 20350

      The Secretary of the Navy takes pleasure in presenting the
MERITORIOUS UNIT COMMENDATION to

MINE COUNTERMEASURES TASK GROUP 1-81

for service as set forth in the following

CITATION:

      For meritorious service from 27 April 1981 to 8 October 1981
while conducting bilateral/multilateral mine countermeasures
operations in the Northern Atlantic and Mediterranean theaters.
Participating in five major exercises, Mine Countermeasures (MCM)
Task Group 1-81 achieved the first complete integration of the
United States Navy's surface, sub-surface, and airborne mine coun-
termeasures assets. This integrated employment of AMCM/SMCM/EOD
Units created a total force concept and demonstrated to Allied
Nations a profound capability for surface and airborne mine-
sweeping, as well as mine hunting and mine disposal techniques.
This unique deployment of MCM forces displayed the U.S. Navy's
effectiveness in responding to hostile mining threats worldwide.
Exhibiting considerable flexibility in organization, MCM Task
Group 1-81 displayed the ability of the United States to deploy a
naval mine countermeasures force to integrate or augment existing
NATO/Allied minesweeping forces. By their extraordinary accomplishments, superb performance, and unrelenting dedication to
duty, the officers and enlisted personnel of Mine Countermeasures
Task Group 1-81 reflected credit upon themselves and upheld the
highest traditions of the United States Naval Service.

Secretary of the Navy

THE SECRETARY OF THE NAVY

WASHINGTON

    The Secretary of the Navy takes pleasure in presenting the NAVY UNIT COMMENDATION to

TASK UNIT 801.4.7

for service as set forth in the following

CITATION:

    For exceptionally meritorious service in conducting Mine Countermeasure (MCM) Operations in and against three Iranian minefields in the Persian Gulf between 19 November 1987 to 23 April 1988. Following the mining of international waterways by hostile Iranian Forces, Task Unit 801.4.7 and participating units was formed from Ocean Minesweepers (MSO's) and Explosive Ordnance Disposal MCM Detachments. Mine Countermeasures Operations commenced for the Task Unit on 19 November 1987 in a minefield in the vicinity of the Iranian Island of Farsi. From then until 28 March 1988 the assigned units located and destroyed a total of 16 mines in the "Farsi Mine Danger Area." Shortly after this tasking was completed, USS SAMUEL B. ROBERTS (FFG 58) struck a mine at Shah Allum in the central Persian Gulf. All six minesweepers and their embarked explosive ordnance disposal personnel conducted a high speed night transit through heavy seas, and were in place the next day to conduct five days of mine countermeasures operations with 13 allied MCM ships, resulting in the destruction of seven mines. Their mission at Shah Allum completed, the Task Unit then transitted south to the "Rostam Mine Danger Area" where they destroyed five additional mines in the next three days. During this five-month period, the Iron Men in the Wooden Ships of Task Unit 801.4.7 faced great dangers in the successful destruction of a total of 30 mines and the clearance of three minefields. By their determination, professionalism, and complete dedication to duty, the officers and enlisted personnel of Task Unit 801.4.7 and participating units reflected great credit upon themselves and upheld the highest traditions of the United States Naval Service.

Secretary of the Navy

THE SECRETARY OF THE NAVY
WASHINGTON

The Secretary of the Navy takes pleasure in presenting the NAVY UNIT COMMENDATION to

ARABIAN GULF BATTLE FORCE

for service as set forth in the following

CITATION:

For exceptionally meritorious service in action during Operation DESERT STORM from 17 January 1991 to 7 February 1991. The units of Arabian Gulf Battle Force performed superbly in combat and provided extraordinary logistics support for coalition ships, significant air strike capability, close air support, and Naval gunfire support for ground and sea forces. Often operating in mine filled waters and under continued threat of shore and air launched cruise missiles, their endurance and perseverance provided the necessary sustainment, ensuring a swift and successful campaign. The units of the Arabian Gulf Battle Force combined air and surface warfare to eliminate the Iraqi Navy as a potential threat. Their personal bravery, bold initiative, and resolute determination helped set the stage and execute the stunning coalition victory.

By their superior resourcefulness, indomitable fighting spirit, and courageous dedication to duty, the officers and enlisted personnel of the Arabian Gulf Battle Force reflected great credit upon themselves and upheld the highest traditions of the United States Naval Service.

Secretary of the Navy

THE SECRETARY OF THE NAVY
WASHINGTON

      The Secretary of the Navy takes pleasure in presenting the NAVY UNIT COMMENDATION to

USS ADROIT (MSO 509)

for service as set forth in the following

CITATION:

      For exceptionally meritorious service while conducting mine countermeasures operations in support of United States mine clearance efforts in the Northern Persian Gulf from 13 May to 1 June 1991. USS ADROIT (MSO 509) vigorously conducted continuous offensive mine countermeasures which resulted in the successful prosecution and eradication of two multi-segmented Iraqi mine lines. During this time, as the only United States Minesweeper in the Northern Persian Gulf, ADROIT operated alone with her embarked explosive ordnance disposal detachment in the live Iraqi minefields for 18 days under the constant danger of a mine strike. Moving rapidly up the Iraqi minelines, ADROIT aggressively sought out and marked for destruction 55 Iraqi moored mines. Displaying exceptional professionalism and team work, ADROIT's mine hunting team detected, classified, and marked each mine-like contact for disposal. ADROIT's zealous and safe prosecution of these moored and bottom mines was a driving force in the success of the United States Mine Countermeasures efforts in the Northern Persian Gulf and directly contributed to the opening of the Kuwaiti sea lanes. By their inspiring courage, superior resourcefulness, steadfast devotion to duty, the officers and enlisted personnel of USS ADROIT (MSO 509) reflected great credit upon themselves and upheld the highest traditions of the United States Naval Service.

Secretary of the Navy

Notes

Overview Notes:

1. G. K. Hartmann, *Weapons That Wait* (Annapolis, Md.: Naval Institute Press, 1979), p. 15; Arnold Lott, *Most Dangerous Sea* (New York: Ballantine Books, 1966), pp. 220–228; originally Lott, *Most Dangerous Sea: A History of Mine Warfare, and an Account of U.S. Navy Mine Warfare Operations in World War II and Korea* (Annapolis, Md.: Naval Institute Press, 1959), pp. 288–295.

2. Lott, *Most Dangerous Sea*, pp. 269, 275–277.

3. Ibid., pp. 269, 275–277; Hartmann, *Weapons That Wait*, pp. 78–81.

4. Lott, *Most Dangerous Sea*, pp. 14–15, 64.

5. Ibid., pp. 33–38, 129.

Chapter 1 Notes:

The above account is probably unfamiliar to many readers. Few people are aware that there were still wooden ships in the U.S. Navy during the Vietnam War (or for that matter today), and fewer still that they engaged there in combat operations. In *Most Dangerous Sea*, Arnold Lott recounts the compelling and thorough history of U.S. Navy Mine Warfare through the end of the Korean War. Readers interested in those details are referred to his excellent book. The information contained herein traces the service of sixty-five ocean minesweepers from their commissioning following the Korean War to the end of the service of the last ships remaining in the class following the Persian Gulf War. It is only a portion of the rich post–Korean War history of U.S. Navy mine warfare.

1. E-mail message from Capt. Charles R. Schlegelmilch, USN (ret.), of 23 March 2004; CO USS *Endurance* (MSO 435) letter MSO435:SRW:tnb ser 026-70 of 28 November 1970; account of engagement by Capt. Paul A. Lutz, USCG, commanding officer of *Sherman*, www.uscg.mil/hq/g-cp/history/VTN_Lutz_Sherman.html (accessed 8 March 2004); www.uscg.mil/Pancarea/rush/history/combat1.htm (accessed 8 March 2004).

For their key roles in the destruction of the trawler, *Sherman*'s commanding officer and executive officer received the Bronze Star, and other crewmembers received awards of lower precedence. John Wisinski, a well-known Coast Guard artist, depicted the destruction of the trawler by *Sherman* in a 1972 painting that her commanding officer donated to the Coast Guard Academy.

I describe the steel-hulled enemy ship as a trawler because it is referred to as such in references, and because the generic term "infiltration trawler" was commonly used for such vessels during the Vietnam War, but a more accurate classification would be "coaster" (small general cargo ship). After viewing an aerial photograph of the vessel found in USCGC *Rush*'s 1970 cruise book, maritime artist Richard DeRosset believes that it was either a small coastal freighter or a tanker converted to a freighter, noting that it shared the characteristics and features of small cargo ships built in European countries. These included tapered and domed stacks, sharp raked bow, cruiser stern, tripod masts, and slanted weather deck openings in the superstructure.

2. E-mail message from Capt. Charles R. Schlegelmilch, USN (ret.), of 23 March 2004.

3. Ibid.

4. Ibid.

5. Conversation and e-mail messages from Capt. Charles R. Schlegelmilch, USN (ret.), on 11 and 23 March 2004; CO USS *Endurance* (MSO 435) letter MSO435:SRW:tnb ser 026-70 of 28 November 1970.

6. BM2 Michael Wark, "Memories of Vietnam," www.ussendurance.org/Wark.htm (accessed 2 November 2002), and additional information obtained from him via e-mail messages and phone conversations.

7. Conversation and e-mail messages from Capt. Charles R. Schlegelmilch, USN (ret.), on 11 and 23 March 2004.

8. BM2 Michael Wark, "Memories of Vietnam," www.ussendurance.org/Wark.htm (accessed 2 November 2002), and additional information obtained from him via e-mail messages and phone conversations.

9. Conversation and e-mail messages from Capt. Charles R. Schlegelmilch, USN (ret.), on 11 and 23 March 2004; CO USS *Endurance* (MSO 435) letter MSO435:SRW:tnb ser 026-70 of 28 November 1970; e-mail message from Capt. Charles R. Schlegelmilch, USN (ret.), on 1 February 2005.

10. Conversation with Michael Wark of 13 March 2004.

11. Account of engagement by Capt. Paul A. Lutz, USCG, commanding officer of *Sherman*; Conversation with Michael Wark of 13 March 2004.

12. Wark, "Memories of Vietnam," and additional information obtained from him via e-mail messages and phone conversations.

13. Conversation with Capt. Charles R. Schlegelmilch, USN (ret.), on 11 March 2004; CO USS *Endurance* (MSO 435) letter MSO435:SRW:tnb ser 026-70 of 28 November 1970; Ship's Cruise Book entry.

14. Commander U.S. Naval Forces Vietnam letter FF5-16/N33:sn 3480 serial 01092 of 1 December 1970; Harbor Clearance Unit 1 Command History for 1970, http://members .aol.com/jackrogue/70hist.html (accessed 4 March 2006).

15. *Endurance* ship's history for 1970; CTU 73.4.2 P naval message of 301110Z November 1970; CTU 73.4.2 OP naval message of 021001Z December 1970; Admin ComNavForv P naval message of 041337Z December 1970; Harbor Clearance Unit 1 Command History for 1970, http://members.aol.com/jackrogue/70hist.html (accessed 4 March 2006).

16. *Dynamic* ship's history for 1970; e-mail message from Capt. Charles R. Schlegelmilch, USN (ret.), on 23 March 2004.

Chapter 2 Notes:

1. Tamara Moser Melia, *"Damn the Torpedoes": A Short History of U.S. Naval Mine Counter-measures, 1777–1991* (Washington, D.C.: Naval Historical Center, 1991), p. 95.

2. *Force* ship's history for 1955.

3. Arnold Lott, *Most Dangerous Sea: A History of Mine Warfare, and an Account of U.S. Navy Mine Warfare Operations in World War II and Korea* (Annapolis, Md.: Naval Institute Press, 1959), pp. 160, 231.

4. www.geocities.com/Pentagon/Bunker/2170/philiprhodes.html.

5. *Engage* ship's history for 1955; *Implicit* ship's history for 1965.

6. *Observer* ship's history; n.d.

7. *Embattle* and *Reaper* ship's history for 1960; *Implicit* ship's history for 1965.

8. *Energy* and *Pivot* ship's history for 1967–68; *Implicit, Nimble,* and *Skill* ship's history for 1967; Lott, *Most Dangerous Sea*, p. 63.

9. *Engage* and *Fortify* ship's history for 1968–70; Lott, *Most Dangerous Sea*, p. 73.

10. *Engage* and *Fortify* ship's history for 1968–70; *Avenge* ship's history for 1968.

11. Bob Adelwerth, USN (ret.), quoted in Dick Lewis, "102 MSOs," www.geocities.com/Pentagon/Bunker/2170/102msos.html (accessed 24 March 2002); *Assurance* ship's history for 1958.

12. *Assurance* ship's history for 1958; Lewis, "102 MSOs"; *Ability* ship's history.

13. *Avenge* and *Pivot* ship's history for 1955; *Firm* ship's history for 1960.

14. Benjamin W. Lankford Jr. and John E. Pinto, "Developments in Wooden Mine-sweeper Hull Design since World War II," *NavShips Tech News*, August 1967.

15. *Valor* ship's history for 1955; *Illusive* ship's history for 1955–57.

16. *Loyalty* ship's history for 1961–65; *Agile* ship's history for 1968.

17. Adelwerth, quoted in Lewis, "102 MSOs."

18. Lankford and Pinto, "Developments in Wooden Minesweeper Hull Design since World War II."

19. *Pledge* ship's history for 1966; *Endurance* and *Venture* ship's history for 1967; Dale Henry, former ST1 and *Fearless* crewmember from 1963 to 1965, e-mail of 8 May 2001.

20. *Energy* and *Pivot* ship's history for 1967–68; *Implicit, Nimble,* and *Skill* ship's history for 1967.

21. *Endurance* ship's history for 1967.

22. Ibid.

23. CoMinWarFor command history for 1972–73; OpNavNote 5030 OP-904K serial 2239P90 of 18 January 1973; CNO message date-time-group 172140Z May 1972.

24. *Assurance* ship's history for 1973–74; *Fearless* ship's history for 1973.

25. *Alacrity* ship's history for 1973–74; *Fidelity* ship's history for 1974.

26. *Alacrity* ship's history for 1973–74; Mike Cosgrove, CDR, CEC, USNR (ret.), Minecraft Sailors Biographies, http://nmsoa.org/msbio.html (accessed 14 December 2005).

Chapter 3 Notes:

1. Tamara Moser Melia, *"Damn the Torpedoes": A Short History of U.S. Naval Mine Counter-measures, 1777–1991* (Washington, D.C.: Naval Historical Center, 1991), pp. 78–79.

2. Ibid., p. 83.

3. Ibid.

4. Arnold Lott, *Most Dangerous Sea: A History of Mine Warfare, and an Account of U.S. Navy Mine Warfare Operations in World War II and Korea* (Annapolis, Md.: Naval Institute Press, 1959), pp. 20, 285; G. K. Hartmann, *Weapons That Wait* (Annapolis, Md.: Naval Institute Press, 1979), p. 80.

5. *Venture* ship's history for 1959; Melia, *"Damn the Torpedoes,"* p. 95.

6. *Pledge* ship's history for 1975; *Leader* ship's history for 1974.

7. CoMinDiv 82 command history for 1968.

8. *Guide* ship's history for 1968.

Chapter 4 Notes:

1. *Direct* ship's history for 1956.

2. *Dash, Detector,* and *Dominant* ship's history for 1956.

3. *Dash* ship's history for 1956; *The New Book of Knowledge* (New York: Grolier, 1996), vol. 12, pp. 406–7.

4. *Dash* and *Detector* ship's history for 1956; *The New Book of Knowledge,* vol. 12, p. 461; vol 1, p. 68.

5. *Detector* and *Dominant* ship's history for 1956.

6. Flanders and Flanders, *Dictionary of American Foreign Affairs* (1993), pp. 351–52.

7. *Nimble, Pinnacle, Sagacity,* and *Skill* ship's history for 1958.

8. Flanders and Flanders, *Dictionary of American Foreign Affairs,* p. 352.

9. Ibid.; *The Lebanon Operation (15 July–25 October 1958)* and *Airborne Operations* (2.3.7 AC.F)—TAB D—U.S. Army Center for Military History.

10. *Pinnacle* and *Sagacity* ship's history for 1958; CoMinRon 7 command history for 1958.

11. *Adroit, Aggressive, Fidelity,* and *Stalwart* ship's history for 1958.

12. *Nimble* and *Pinnacle* ship's history for 1958.

13. *Detector* and *Dominant* ship's history for 1958.

14. *The New Book of Knowledge* vol. 1, p. 68; vol. 20, p. 370; www.mil.be/navycomp/ops/index.asp?LAN=E&PLACE=1 (accessed 25 November 2004).

15. *Fearless* and *Valor* ship's history for 1959; *The New Book of Knowledge,* vol. 20, p. 367.

16. *Valor* ship's history for 1959; John Riker, former *Valor* crewmember, e-mail of 8 May 2001.

17. Riker, e-mail of 8 May 2001.

18. Ibid.

19. Ibid; www.cherbourg.com/right.htm.

20. Riker, e-mail of 8 May 2001.

21. *Valor* ship's history for 1959–60.

22. Joe Gross, former officer aboard *Pinnacle,* e-mail of 9 May 2001.

23. *Avenge, Exultant, Fearless, Fidelity,* and *Valor* ship's history for 1961–62.

24. *Exultant, Fearless, Fidelity,* and *Valor* ship's history for 1961–62; Encyclopedia Britannica (1970), vol. 7, p. 570.

25. *Dash, Detector, Direct,* and *Dominant* ship's history for 1961–62.

26. Ibid.

27. *Agile, Aggressive, Bold,* and *Bulwark* ship's history for 1962; *Swerve* ship's history for 1966.

28. Encyclopedia Britannica (1970), vol. 6, p. 878; *Dictionary of American Foreign Affairs* (1993), p. 145.

29. *Dictionary of American Foreign Affairs,* pp. 145–46.

30. Ibid., p. 146.

31. *Encyclopedia Americana International Edition* (1990), p. 306; *Dictionary of American Foreign Affairs,* p. 146.

32. Bob Adelwerth, www.geocities.com/Pentagon/Bunker/2170/naval_quarantine_of_cuba.html (accessed 19 April 2001).

33. Mike Goss, e-mail message to author, 5 June 2002.

34. *Encyclopedia Americana International Edition,* p. 306.

35. *Ability, Notable, Rival,* and *Salute* ship's history for 1962.

36. CoMinDiv 82, Command History for 1962.

37. *Dictionary of American Foreign Affairs,* p. 147.

38. *Adroit, Venture,* and *Direct* ship's history for 1963; CoMinDiv 44 command history for 1963; Colin Wilson, *Mysteries of the Universe* (New York: DK Publishing, Inc., 1997), p. 24; William P. Quinn, *Shipwrecks along the Atlantic Coast* (Orleans, Mass.: Parnassus Imprints, 1988), p. 174.

39. *Affray, Alacrity,* and *Observer* ship's history for 1965. There is no record for 1965 in *Exploit's* ship's history file, but she was a member of the division during this period.

40. Al Hines, "Memories of Shipboard Life," www.geocities.com/Pentagon/Base/8361/mso509history.html (accessed 13 April 2001); Frank, "Memories of Shipboard Life," www.geocities.com/Pentagon/Base/8361/mso461history.html (accessed 13 April 2001).

41. *Alacrity* and *Observer* ship's history for 1965; Richard K Kolb, "Cold War along the Cactus Curtain," pp. 5–6, www.vfw.org/magazine/jan99/36.shtml (accessed 31 December 2001).

42. *Encyclopedia Americana International Edition,* p. 274; *Dictionary of American Foreign Affairs,* p. 164.

43. *Encyclopedia Americana International Edition,* p. 274; *Dictionary of American Foreign Affairs,* pp. 164–65; www.vfw.org/magazine/jan99/36.shtml (accessed 31 December 2001).

44. *Alacrity* and *Observer* ship's history for 1965; Kolb, "Cold War along the Cactus Curtain," pp. 5–6.

45. *Dash, Detector, Direct,* and *Dominant* ship's history for 1965; *Dictionary of American Foreign Affairs,* p. 165; Kolb, "Cold War along the Cactus Curtain," pp. 5–6.

46. *Dash, Detector, Direct,* and *Dominant* ship's history for 1965; Capt. Ronald Moser, USN (ret.), 5 November 1999.

47. *Nahant* ship's history for 1961; *Directory of American Naval Fighting Ships* (1969); Arnold Lott, *Most Dangerous Sea: A History of Mine Warfare, and an Account of U.S. Navy Mine Warfare Operations in World War II and Korea* (Annapolis, Md.: U.S. Naval Institute Press, 1959), pp. 54–56.

48. *Dictionary of American Foreign Affairs,* p. 165.

49. Randall C. Maydew, *America's Lost H-Bomb! Palomares, Spain, 1966* (Manhattan, Kansas: Sunflower University Press, 1997), p. 3.7; www.cdi.org/issueB/nukeaccidents/accidentB (accessed 18 August 2000); www.propl.org/2000/accident/cdilist (accessed 18 August 2000); Joint Committee on Atomic Energy Interoffice Memorandum, 15 February 1968; Center for Defense Information; www.brook.edu/fp/projects/nucwcost/palomares.

50. Flora Lewis, *One of Our H-Bombs is Missing* (New York: McGraw-Hill, 1967), p. 148, 159–160, 182; Maydew, *America's Lost H-Bomb! Palomares, Spain, 1966,* pp. 44, 83–84, 95, 102–104; *Nimble* and *Sagacity* ship's history for 1966; CoMinDiv 84 command

history for 1966; www.cdi.org/issues/nukeaccidents/accidents.htm (accessed 18 August 2000).

51. Lewis, *One of Our H-Bombs is Missing*, pp. 162–163; Maydew, *America's Lost H-Bomb! Palomares, Spain, 1966*, pp. 89, 93–94; *Skill* ship's history for 1966; CoMinDiv 84 command history for 1966.

52. Maydew, *America's Lost H-Bomb! Palomares, Spain, 1966*, p. 84; *Ability* and *Notable* ship's history for 1966; CoMinDiv 85 command history for 1966; Steve Walter, "Memories of Shipboard Life," www.geocities.com/Pentagon/Base/8361/mso468hiBtory.html, (accessed 13 April 2001).

53. Lewis, *One of Our H-Bombs is Missing*, p. 162; Maydew, *America's Lost H-Bomb! Palomares, Spain, 1966*, p. 102; *Notable* and *Salute* ship's history for 1966; Walter, "Memories of Shipboard Life."

54. *Rival* ship's history for 1966; Walter, "Memories of Shipboard Life."

55. Walter, "Memories of Shipboard Life."

56. Ibid.

57. Lewis, *One of Our H-Bombs is Missing*, p. 184; *Notable*, *Rival*, and *Salute* ship's history for 1966; Walter, "Memories of Shipboard Life."

58. Lewis, *One of Our H-Bombs is Missing*, p. 225, 234; Maydew, *America's Lost H-Bomb! Palomares, Spain, 1966*, p. 88; *Notable* and *Salute* ship's history for 1966; Walter, "Memories of Shipboard Life."

59. *Ability*, *Notable*, *Rival*, and *Salute* ship's history for 1966; CoMinDiv 85 command history for 1966; www.brook.edu/fp/projects/nucwcost/palomares.

60. *Adroit*, *Swerve*, and *Sturdy* ship's history for 1966; CoMinDiv 44 command history for 1966.

61. Dennis L. Moore, NCC, USN (ret.), e-mail of 27 April 2001.

62. *Bold* ship's history for 1967.

63. CoMinDiv 45 command history for 1967.

64. CTG 44.9 message-date-time group 2312322 August 1967.

65. Ibid.; CTU 44.9.5 message-date-time group 2214502 August 1967.

66. CoMinDiv 45 command history for 1967; *Alacrity* ship's history for 1967; CTG 44.9 message-date-time group 2312322 August 1967; CTU 44.9.5 message date-time-group 2214502 August 1967; CTU 44.9.5 message date-time-group 2218502 August 1967.

67. *Fidelity* ship's history for 1967.

68. *Sagacity* and *Skill* ship's history for 1968.

69. *Affray* and *Bold* ship's history for 1968; Dennis L. Moore, NCC, USN (ret.), e-mail of 30 April 2001.

70. *Agile* and *Bold* ship's history for 1969.

71. *Force* and *Prestige* ship's history for 1957; *Thrush* and *Falcon* ship's history for 1959.

72. *Agile* and *Bold* ship's history for 1969; Dennis L. Moore, NCC, USN (ret.), and former *Bold* crewmember, e-mail of 9 May 2001.

73. *Agile* and *Bold* ship's history for 1969.

74. *Dash* and *Direct* ship's history for 1970.

75. Ibid.

76. Ibid.

77. Ibid.

78. Ibid.

79. Ibid.

80. Ibid.

81. Ibid.

82. Ibid.

83. *Dash* and *Direct* ship's history for 1970; CTG 60.1 message date-time-group 291535Z September 1970; Naval Vessel Register, 28 January 2000.

84. *Dash* and *Direct* ship's history for 1970.

85. Ibid.

86. Ibid.

87. Ibid.

88. *Vital* ship's history for 1971; Mike Cosgrove CDR, CEC, USNR (ret.), Minecraft Sailors Biographies, http://nmsoa.org/msbio.html (accessed 14 December 2005).

89. *Alacrity* ship's history for 1971.

90. *Vigor* ship's history for 1971 and 1972; *Fidelity* and *Fearless* ship's history for 1972.

91. SecNav, 15 October 1998.

92. *Affray* ship's history for 1973; *Chico Enterprise-Record*, Sunday, December 29, 2002, Section 3C.

93. *Exploit* ship's history for 1974.

94. *Illusive* and *Leader* ship's history for 1978.

95. Ibid.; www.mso-belgium.org/en/stanavforchan/stanavforchan_en.htm.

96. *Illusive* and *Leader* ship's history for 1978.

97. Ibid.

98. Ibid.

99. Ibid; http://encarta.msn.com/index/conciseindex/67/067B9000.htm.

100. *Illusive* and *Leader* ship's history for 1978.

101. *Illusive* and *Leader* ship's history for 1979.

102. Ibid.

103. Ibid.

104. Ibid.

105. Ibid.

106. Ibid.

107. Ibid. *Leader* ship's history identifies the port the two ships visited as Portland, England; *Illusive* ship's history, Portsmouth.

108. Ibid.

109. Ibid; www.fwkc.com/encyclopedia/low/articles/1/1015000282f.htm.

110. Ibid.

111. Ibid.

112. *Exultant* ship's history for 1980.

113. Ibid.

114. *Leader*, *Fidelity*, and *Illusive* ship's history for 1980.

115. *Illusive* ship's history for 1980.

116. *Dominant* and *Engage* ship's history for 1980.

117. CoMinGru 2 command history for 1980.

118. *Dash* ship's history for 1980.

119. *Leader*, *Fearless*, and *Illusive* ship's history for 1980.

120. *Direct*, *Exultant*, and *Impervious* ship's history for 1980.

Chapter 5 Notes:

1. *The New Book of Knowledge* (New York: Grolier, 1996), vol. 17, p. 347.

2. www.ksc.nasa.gov/history/mercury/mercury-goals.txt (accessed 14 December 1998).

3. Ibid.; www.space.com/news/spacehistory/spacechimp_010717html (accessed 31 December 2001).

4. www.ksc.nasa.gov/history/mercury/mercury-spacecraft.txt (accessed 14 December 1998).

5. *Ability* and *Notable* ship's history for 1961; CoMinDiv 85 command history, CMD85/DLK:dlk 5750 serial 6 of 8 January 1962; www.ksc.nasa.gov/history/mercury/flight-summary.txt (accessed 14 December 1998).

6. *Ability* ship's history for 1961.

7. *Ability* and *Notable* ship's history for 1961; www.history.navy.mil/branches/avchr9.htm (accessed 17 August 2000). Note: this reference indicates the space capsule landed in the sea 302 miles down range from Cape Canaveral; www.ksc.nasa.gov/history/mercury/flight-summary.txt.

8. www.history.navy.mil/branches/avchr9.htm; www.ksc.nasa.gov/history/mercury/flight-summary.txt; *Exploit* ship's history for 1961.

9. www.history.navy.mil/branches/avchr9.htm.

10. *Exploit, Observer, Pinnacle,* and *Sagacity* ship's history for 1962; CoMinDiv 82 command history, CMD82/RNG:ad 5750 serial 175 of 30 November 1961; www.history.navy.mil/branches/avchr9.htm; www.ksc.nasa.gov/history/mercury/flight-summary.txt.

11. *Sturdy* and *Swerve* ship's history for 1962; CoMinDiv 44 command history, CND44/CLP:rj 5750 serial 127 of 31 December 1963; www.history.navy.mil/branches/avchr9.htm; www.ksc.nasa.gov/history/mercury/flight-summary.txt; www.intrepidmuseum.org/about_b-info.html (accessed 31 December 2001).

12. *Alacrity* and *Affray* ship's history for 1962; www.history.navy.mil/branches/avchr9.htm; www.ksc.nasa.gov/history/mercury/flight-summary.txt.

13. *Adroit* and *Stalwart* ship's history for 1963; CoMinDiv 44 command history, CND44/CLP:rj 5750 serial 127 of 31 December 1963; CoMinDiv 43 command history, CMD43/01:rs 5750 serial 11 of 28 January 1967; www.history.navy.mil/branches/avchr9.htm; www.ksc.nasa.gov/history/mercury/flight-summary.txt.

14. www.history.navy.mil/branches/avchr9.htm.

15. www.ksc.nasa.gov/history/gemini/flight-summary.txt (accessed 14 December 1998).

16. Ibid.

17. *Bold* and *Bulwark* ship's history for 1964.

18. *Observer* ship's history for 1964; *Agile* ship's history for 1965; www.history.navy.mil/branches/avchr9.htm.

19. *Swerve* ship's history for 1965; CoMinDiv 44 command history, CMD44/DJP:cd 5750 serial 238 of 21 December 1965; www.history.navy.mil/branches/avchr9.htm; www.ksc.nasa.gov/history/gemini/flight-summary.txt.

20. *Nimble* and *Skill* ship's history for 1965; www.history.navy.mil/branches/avchr9.htm; www.ksc.nasa.gov/history/gemini/flight-summary.txt.

21. *Avenge* and *Exultant* ship's history for 1965; CoMinRon 8 letter 5750 serial 77 of 28 January 1966; www.history.navy.mil/branches/avchr9.htm; www.ksc.nasa.gov/history/gemini/flight-summary.txt.

22. *Fearless* and *Fidelity* ship's history for 1965; CoMinRon 8 letter 5750 serial 77 of 28 January 1966.

23. *Ability* ship's history for 1965; CoMinRon 8 letter 5750 serial 77 of 28 January 1966; www.history.navy.mil/branches/avchr9.htm; www.ksc.nasa.gov/history/gemini/flight-summary.txt.

24. www.history.navy.mil/branches/avchr9.htm; www.ksc.nasa.gov/history/gemini/flight-summary.txt.

25. *Fidelity* ship's history of 1966; CoMinDiv 82 command history, CMD82:SWO:cs 5700 serial 13 of 31 January 1967; www.history.navy.mil/branches/avchr9.htm; www.ksc.nasa.gov/history/gemini/flight-summary.txt.

26. www.history.navy.mil/branches/avchr9.htm.

27. *Nimble* ship's history for 1966; www.history.navy.mil/branches/avchr9.htm; www.ksc
    .nasa.gov/history/ gemini/flight-summary.txt.

28. www.history.navy.mil/branches/avchr9.htm; www.ksc.nasa.gov/history/gemini/
    flight-summary.txt.

29. Ibid.

30. Ibid.

31. www.ksc.nasa.gov/history/apollo/apollo-goals.txt (accessed 15 December 1998).

32. Ibid.

33. SecNavInst 1650.1D, change 4 of 21 August 1971.

34. *Avenge* ship's history for 1966.

35. www.history.navy.mil/branches/avchr9.htm; SecNavInst 1650.1D, change 4 of 21 Au-
    gust 1971; www.ksc.nasa.gov/history/apollo/apollo-goals.txt.

36. Ibid.

37. Ibid.

38. Ibid.

39. www.history.navy.mil/branches/avchr9.htm; www.ksc.nasa.gov/history/apollo/
    apollo-goals.txt.

40. www.ksc.nasa.gov/history/apollo/apollo-goals.txt.

41. *Alacrity* and *Exploit* ship's history for 1972; www.ksc.nasa.gov/history/apollo/
    apollo-goals.txt.

42. www.ksc.nasa.gov/history/apollo/apollo-goals.txt.

43. *Adroit, Alacrity, Assurance,* and *Fidelity* ship's history for 1972; Capt. Ronald Moser,
    USN (ret.), 12 November 1999; www.ksc.nasa.gov/history/apollo/apollo-goals.txt.

44. Capt. Ronald Moser, USN (ret.), 12 November 1999; Cdr. Michael Cosgrove, CEC,
    USNR (ret.), 30 April 2001.

45. *The New Book of Knowledge*, vol. 17, p. 348; www.nasm.edu/apollo/apollolaunches.

Chapter 6 Notes:

1. *Engage, Fortify, Impervious, Inflict,* and *Loyalty* ship's history for 1955–56.

2. Ibid.

3. *Engage, Fortify, Inflict, Impervious,* and *Loyalty* ship's history for 1958.

4. Flanders and Flanders, *Dictionary of American Foreign Affairs*, 1993, p. 500.

5. *Constant, Energy, Pivot, Pluck,* and *Prestige* ship's history for 1958; CoMinDiv 92 command history for 1958.

6. Flanders and Flanders, *Dictionary of American Foreign Affairs*, p. 500.

7. *Constant, Energy, Pivot*, and *Pluck* ship's history for 1958–59; CoMinDiv 92 command history for 1971.

8. Mike Goss, e-mail message to author, 20 September 2003.

9. *Loyalty* ship's history for 1962; CoMinRon 7 command history for 1962; www.agriterra .org/-wise/536/5214.html (accessed 31 December 2001).

10. 1962: Operation Dominic/JTF 8 Part #1, www.militarybenefits.com/HomePage/ UnitPage-History/1,13506,201337/707237,00.html (accessed 12 July 2003); *Loyalty* ship's history for 1962; CoMinRon 7 command history for 1962.

11. www.enviroweb.org/issues/nuketesting/hew/usa/tests/dominic (accessed 17 August 2000); *Radiation at Johnston Atoll; cleaning up the Cold War*, pp. 3–4, www.agriterra.org/ -wise/536/5214.html (accessed 31 December 2001); Summary of the USS *Inflict*, MSO-456, Activities and Participation during the Dominic I Operation (1962) (Not in Area of Event during detonation; 1 background reading for Recovery Operations), www.osti.gov/cgi-bin/opennetnewgate?headline (accessed 12 July 2003); Dominic I Operation (1962) Shot Unit Locator Worksheet for the USS *Inflict*, MSO 456, Commanded by L. E. Denny commencing 1/1 to 11/3, 1962 (Observed one event from a distance, but not in the area), www.osti.gov/cgi-bin/opennetnewgate?headline.

12. Logbook of USS *Engage*, MSO 433, Commanded by W. H. Atkin, assigned to Pacific Fleet during Dominic I Operation, commencing November 1 to 7, 1962 (witnessed Kingfish and Tightrope Events), www.osti.gov/cgi-bin/opennetnewgate?headline; diagrams of locations of naval vessels at Johnston Atoll, www.aracnet.com (accessed 12 July 2003); William Arkin and Joshu Handler, "Naval Nuclear Accidents: The Secret History," *Greenpeace* 14, no. 4 (1989) 16; Joshua Handler, Amy Wickenheiser, and William Arkin, "Naval Safety 1989: *The Year of the* Accident," *Greenpeace*, Neptune Papers no. 4 (1990): 25; J. Daniel Mathis, e-mail to pdxavets@aracnet.com of 23 January 2002, subject: Dominic I; *Loyalty* and *Inflict* ship's history for 1962.

13. *Engage, Fortify*, and *Impervious* ship's history for 1962; USS *Fortify* Operation Dominic Operational Profile 1962, www.military.com/HomePage/UnitPageHistory (accessed 7 July 2003).

14. Www.enviroweb.org/issues/nuketesting/hew/usa/tests/dominic; *Fortify* ship's history for 1962.

15. *Inflict* ship's history for 1960.

16. CoMinDiv 93 message date-time-group 290956Z August 1961; DoD Office of Public Affairs News Release number 856–61; Tamara Moser Melia, *"Damn the Torpedoes": A Short History of U.S. Naval Mine Countermeasures, 1777–1991*, (Washington, D.C.: Naval Historical Center, 1991), p. 91; *Encyclopedia Americana International Edition* (1990), p. 279.

17. *Leader* ship's history for 1961.

18. *Encyclopedia Americana International Edition*, p. 279.

19. *Esteem, Gallant*, and *Pledge* ship's history for 1961.

20. Ibid.

21. *Conquest, Esteem, Gallant, Illusive,* and *Pledge* ship's history for 1961.

22. *Gallant* and *Illusive* ship's history for 1961–62.

23. *Esteem, Gallant, Illusive, Conquest,* and *Pledge* ship's history for 1962.

24. Ibid.

25. *Conquest* and *Illusive* ship's history for 1968–69.

26. *Fortify, Inflict,* and *Loyalty* ship's history for 1966.

27. *Endurance* ship's history for 1968.

28. Ibid.

29. Ibid.

30. *Conflict* and *Endurance* ship's history for 1968; CoMinRon 9 letter FC4-7/9-01:rn 1650 Ser: 194-68 of 31 May 1968.

31. *Fortify, Constant,* and *Pluck* ship's history for 1966.

32. *Pluck* ship's history for 1966.

33. *Pluck, Endurance, Fortify,* and *Persistent* ship's history for 1966.

34. *Conflict* and *Endurance* ship's history for 1968; CoMinRon 9 letter FC4-7/9-01:rn 1650 Ser: 194-68 of 31 May 1968; *Enhance* and *Illusive* ship's history for 1969; *Advance, Guide,* and *Pivot* ship's history for 1970.

35. Mark Bradley's memories of Vietnam, www.ussleader.org/Leader%20in%20VM.htm (accessed 20 November 2003).

36. Ibid.

37. *Conflict, Dynamic, Endurance, Implicit,* and *Persistent* ship's history for 1965.

38. *Conflict* ship's history for 1965.

39. *Implicit* ship's history for 1966.

40. *Endurance* ship's history for 1966.

41. *Conflict* and *Persistent* ship's history for 1966.

42. *Loyalty* ship's history for 1966.

43. Ibid.

44. Ibid.

45. Ibid.

46. *Conflict, Endurance,* and *Persistent* ship's history for 1968; CoMinRon 9 letter FC4-7/9-01:rn 1650 Ser: 194-68 of 31 May 1968.

47. *Conflict* and *Endurance* ship's history for 1968; CoMinRon 9 letter FC4-7/9-01:rn 1650 Ser: 194-68 of 31 May 1968.

48. CoMinRon 9 letter FC4-7/9-01:rn 1650 Ser: 194-68 of 31 May 1968; *Conflict* ship's history for 1968.

49. *Persistent* ship's history for 1968.

50. *Endurance* ship's history for 1968; CoMinRon 9 letter FC4-7/9-01:rn 1650 Ser: 194-68 of 31 May 1968.

51. *Persistent* ship's history for 1968.

52. *Endurance* ship's history for 1968.

53. *Conflict, Endurance,* and *Persistent* ship's history for 1968.

54. Citation for the Presidential Unit Citation identifying units eligible to receive the award.

55. D. J. Robinson, e-mail of 13 July 2003.

56. USS *Washoe County* (LST 1165) ship's history for 1968.

57. Commander U.S. Naval Forces Vietnam Navy News Release of 18 October 1969, "Sea Lords Completes First Year of Operations."

58. Ibid.

59. Ibid.

60. *Illusive* ship's history for 1968.

61. *Advance* and *Guide* ship's history for 1970.

62. *Conflict, Endurance,* and *Persistent* ship's history for 1968; CoMinRon 9 letter FC4-7/9-01:rn 1650 Ser: 194-68 of 31 May 1968; Melia, *"Damn the Torpedoes,"* p. 92; Edward J. Marolda, ed., *Operation End Sweep: A History of Minesweeping Operations in North Vietnam,* (Washington, D.C.: Naval Historical Center, 1993), pp. 7–8.

63. *Endurance* ship's history for 1968; CoMinRon 9 letter FC4-7/9-01:rn 1650 Ser: 194-68 of 31 May 1968; G. K. Hartmann, *Weapons That Wait,* (Annapolis, Md.: Naval Institute Press, 1979), pp. 187–88.

64. Melia, *"Damn the Torpedoes,"* pp. 95–97.

65. *Guide* ship's history for 1970; Marolda, *Operation End Sweep,* pp. 7–8.

66. Melia, *"Damn the Torpedoes,"* pp. 93–95; Peter Bayliss with Ralph Grambo, "Small Ships Heavy Boats and the Perils of the Long Tau Shipping Channel," http://academic.uofs.edu/faculty/gramborw/atav/bayliss.htm (accessed 19 February 2005).

67. Melia, *"Damn the Torpedoes,"* pp. 93–95; Bayliss and Grambo, "Small Ships, Heavy Boats."

68. Malcolm Muir, Jr., *Black Shoes and Blue Water: Surface Warfare in the United States Navy, 1945–1975* (Washington, D.C.: Naval Historical Center, 1996), p. 159.

69. Marolda, *Operation End Sweep,* pp. xi, 4.

70. *Loyalty* ship's history for 1972; Marolda, *Operation End Sweep,* pp. xi, xiii, 11, 17, 25, 45, 47; Melia, *"Damn the Torpedoes,"* p. 77.

71. Marolda, *Operation End Sweep,* pp. 11, 18.

72. Ibid., pp. 13, 16–17.

73. *Loyalty* ship's history for 1972; Marolda, *Operation End Sweep*, pp. xi, xiii, 11, 17, 25, 45, 47; Melia, *"Damn the Torpedoes,"* p. 77.

74. *Force* and *Inflict* ship's history for 1972.

75. *Inflict* ship's history for 1972; Marolda, *Operation End Sweep*, pp. 39, 119–120; *Engage* ship's history for 1973.

76. *Leader* ship's history for 1972.

77. *Enhance*, *Illusive*, and *Leader* ship's history for 1972.

78. *Engage* and *Fortify* ship's history for 1973; http://guadalupeao32.tripod.com/sweep.htm (accessed 12 April 2001); Hartmann, *Weapons That Wait*, pp. 152–53; Arnold Lott, *Most Dangerous Sea: A History of Mine Warfare, and an Account of U.S. Navy Mine Warfare Operations in World War II and Korea* (Annapolis, Md.: U.S. Naval Institute, 1959), p. 253; Marolda, *Operation End Sweep*, pp. 50, 77, 79, 115.

79. *Conquest* ship's history for 1973; Marolda, *Operation End Sweep*, p. 34.

80. *Engage*, *Fortify*, and *Impervious* ship's history for 1973; CoMinRon 5 command history for 1973, FC/3/5:10.2 5750 serial N1/18 of 7 March 1974; Marolda, *Operation End Sweep*, pp. 57, 59.

81. Hartmann, *Weapons That Wait*, pp. 152–53; Marolda, *Operation End Sweep*, pp. 59, 64.

82. *Engage*, *Fortify*, and *Impervious* ship's history for 1973.

83. *Engage*, *Enhance*, and *Fortify* ship's history for 1973; Marolda, *Operation End Sweep*, pp. 34, 66.

84. *Engage*, *Enhance*, and *Fortify* ship's history for 1973; Marolda, *Operation End Sweep*, pp. 70, 72.

85. *Engage* and *Fortify* ship's history for 1973; Marolda, *Operation End Sweep*, p. 77.

86. *Conquest*, *Engage*, *Fortify*, and *Impervious* ship's history for 1973; Marolda, *Operation End Sweep*, pp. 75, 78.

87. Hartmann, *Weapons That Wait*, pp. 152–53; Lott, *Most Dangerous Sea*, p. 253; Marolda, *Operation End Sweep*, pp. 50, 77, 79, 115; *Directory of American Naval Fighting Ships* (1969), vol. 4, pp. 228–229, 487.

88. *Conquest*, *Engage*, *Fortify*, *Impervious*, and *Inflict* ship's history for 1973; Marolda, *Operation End Sweep*, pp. 81–82.

89. *Conquest*, *Engage*, *Esteem*, *Illusive*, and *Impervious* ship's history for 1973; http://guadalupeao32.tripod.com/sweep.htm; Hartmann, *Weapons That Wait*, 152–53; Lott, *Most Dangerous Sea*, p. 253; Marolda, *Operation End Sweep*, pp. 50, 77, 79, 115.

90. Hartmann, *Weapons That Wait*, p. 153; Marolda, *Operation End Sweep*, pp. 59, 122.

91. *Engage*, *Esteem*, *Illusive*, and *Impervious* ship's history for 1973; Marolda, *Operation End Sweep*, pp. 86–88, 122.

92. *Esteem* ship's history for 1973; "Memories of Shipboard Life," www.geocities.com/Pentagon/Base/8361/mso438history.html (accessed 13 April 2001); Sam McCrow,

(PN3/2 1971–1974) retired LDO, e-mail of 29 April 2005; Thomas Braden, RM3 aboard *Esteem*, e-mail of 1 May 2005.

93. *Engage, Enhance, Esteem*, and *Inflict* ship's history for 1973.

94. Ibid; Marolda, *Operation End Sweep*, p. 122; *Fortify* ship's history for 1973.

95. Marolda, *Operation End Sweep*, pp. xiv, 109–110.

96. Ibid., pp. 109–110.

Chapter 7 Notes:

1. Dennis L. Moore, NCC, USN (ret.), e-mail message to author, 9 May 2001.

2. *Conquest* and *Implicit* ship's history for 1982; CoMinRon 5 command history for 1982.

3. *Conquest, Implicit*, and *Pledge* ship's history for 1982.

4. *Gallant, Esteem*, and *Excel* ship's history for 1982.

5. *Implicit* and *Pluck* ship's history for 1982.

6. *Implicit* ship's history for 1982.

7. *Implicit* ship's history for 1982; CoMinGru 1 command history for 1983.

8. CoMinGru 1 command history for 1983.

9. *Constant, Gallant*, and *Pledge* ship's history for 1983.

10. *Conquest, Constant, Esteem, Gallant, Implicit*, and *Pledge* ship's history for 1983.

11. *Conquest, Enhance, Esteem*, and *Pledge* ship's history for 1983.

12. *Constant, Conquest, Esteem, Gallant, Implicit*, and *Pledge* ship's history for 1983.

13. *Constant, Conquest, Esteem, Excel, Gallant*, and *Implicit* ship's history for 1984.

14. *Excel* and *Gallant* ship's history for 1984.

15. *Conquest, Esteem, Excel, Gallant*, and *Implicit* ship's history for 1984.

16. *Esteem* and *Excel* ship's history for 1984.

17. Ibid.

18. Ibid.

19. Ibid.

20. *Excel, Gallant*, and *Implicit* ship's history for 1985; CoMinGru 1 command history for 1985; Cdr. Lee Foley, USN (ret.), e-mail of 13 March 2006.

21. *Excel* and *Gallant* ship's history for 1985.

22. *Conquest* ship's history for 1985.

23. Ibid.

24. *Excel, Gallant*, and *Implicit* ship's history for 1985.

25. Ibid.; CoMinGru 1 command history for 1985.

26. *Esteem* ship's history for 1985.

27. *Conquest* and *Esteem* ship's history for 1985.

28. *Implicit* ship's history for 1991; *Conquest* ship's history for 1992.

29. *Dominant* ship's history for 1971–81.

30. *Dash, Detector, Direct*, and *Dominant* ship's history for 1971; *Exultant* ship's history for 1972.

31. *Detector* ship's history for 1971; www.maritime.org/hnsa-croaker.htm (accessed 17 September 2002); www.geocities.com/CapeCanaveral/1056/croaker.htm (accessed 17 September 2003).

32. *Direct* ship's history for 1973–74.

33. *Engage, Fearless*, and *Impervious* ship's history for 1974.

34. *Direct* ship's history for 1974.

35. *Direct* ship's history for 1975.

36. Ibid.

37. *Dash* and *Detector* ship's history for 1977; CoMinRon 12 command history for 1977; William P. Quinn, *Shipwrecks along the Atlantic Coast* (Orleans, Mass.: Parnassus Imprints, 1988), p.191.

38. *Exploit* and *Inflict* ship's history for 1977.

39. *Dominant* and *Exultant* ship's history for 1977.

40. *Exploit* and *Inflict* ship's history for 1977.

41. *Detector* and *Dominant* ship's history for 1977.

42. CoMinRon 12 command history for 1978.

43. *Detector* ship's history for 1978.

44. *Exploit* ship's history for 1979–80.

45. *Impervious* ship's history for 1987.

46. CoMinDiv 121 command history for 1986.

47. CoMinDiv 121 command history for 1987.

Chapter 8 Notes:

1. *Prestige* ship's history file for 1958; CoMinDiv 92 command history for 1958; *Pluck* decklog for 24 August 1958.

2. *Prestige* quartermaster's log for 23 August 1958; *Tawakoni* decklog for 25 August 1958.

3. *Prestige* quartermaster's log for 23 August 1958; *Pivot* decklog for 23 August 1958.

4. *Pivot* decklog for 23 August 1958.

5. *Prestige* quartermaster's log for 23 August 1958.

6. *Pivot* decklog for 23 August 1958; *Prestige* quartermaster's log for 23 August 1958.

7. *Pivot* decklog for 23 August 1958.

8. *Tawakoni* decklog for 24 August 1958.

9. *Tawakoni* decklogs for 24 and 25 August 1958.

10. *Tawakoni* decklog for 26 August 1958.

11. *Tawakoni* decklog for 27 August 1958.

12. *Tawakoni* decklog for 28 August 1958.

13. *Tawakoni* decklog for 29 August 1958; *Current* decklogs for 28 and 31 August 1958; *Current* decklog for 1 September 1958; CoMinDiv 92 command history for 1958.

14. *Pivot* ship's history for 1958.

15. *Exultant* ship's history for 1960; CoMinDiv 82 command history for 1960.

16. *Exultant, Nimble,* and *Pinnacle* ship's history for 1960; CoMinDiv 82 command history for 1960; CoMinLant message date-time-group 130230Z August 1960; *Nimble* decklog for 12 August 1960.

17. *Exultant* ship's history for 1960; CoMinDiv 82 command history for 1960; Bob Adelwerth, "Memories of Shipboard Life," www.geocities.com/Pentagon/Base/8361/mso441history.html (accessed 13 April 2001).

18. *Stalwart* ship's history for 1966; CoMinDiv 44 command history for 1966; Jerry Coppage, "Memories of Shipboard Life," www.geocities.com/Pentagon/Base/8361/mso509history.html (accessed 13 April 2001).

19. *Stalwart* ship's history for 1966.

20. *Escape* decklog for 5 July 1966; ComServRon 8 letter, N-2 4740 serial 100R of 24 September 1965; *Hoist* decklogs for 3, 4, and 14 July 1966.

21. *Hoist* decklogs for 12, 13, and 14 July 1966; *Escape* decklog for 13 July 1966.

22. *Escape* decklog for 14 July 1966; *Hoist* decklogs for 14 and 15 July 1966.

23. *Hoist* decklogs for 15 and 16 July 1966.

24. *Stalwart* ship's history for 1966; ComServRon 8 letter, N-2 4740 serial 100R of 24 September 1965; *Escape* decklog for 17 July 1966.

25. *Stalwart* ship's history for 1966–67; Senior Member, U.S. Navy Sub-Board of Inspection and Survey Norfolk letter MSO493/9030/rem serial 26 of 1 August 1966.

26. CincLantFlt message date-time-group 231842Z February 1968.

27. *Avenge* ship's history for 1969; *Baltimore Sun,* October 7, 1969.

28. CoMinRon 5 naval message date-time-group 301452Z October 1969.

29. CNO letter OP-434P/dlh serial 01P43 of 7 January 1970.

30. *Sagacity* ship's history for 1970; CoMineLant naval message date-time-group 200630Z March 1970; CNO letter OP-434P/dlh serial 1040P43 of 21 August 1970.

31. *Sagacity* ship's history for 1970; NavShipSysComHQ naval messages of date-time-groups 312210Z July 1970, 102026Z August 1970, and 012019Z October 1970.

32. *Enhance* ship's history for 1973.

33. Commander Mine Warfare Force command history for 1973; *Enhance* ship's history for 1973.

34. *Enhance* ship's history for 1973.

35. *Force* ship's history for 1973; CoMinRon 1 command history for 1973.

36. ComSeventhFlt naval message date-time-group 240346Z April 1973; *Evening Star and Daily News*, Washington, D.C., April 24, 1973; CNO letter serial 434P/652 of 4 May 1973. While assigned as the engineering officer to a guided missile frigate in 1987, the author met a former crewmember of the *Force*. By that time a chief petty officer and the officer in charge of a self-propelled fuel oil barge, he told me that it had seemed as though only about fifteen minutes passed after the fire started before *Force* was gone and he was in the water, swimming. Debris from the ship washed ashore at Grande Island in Subic Bay. Maritime artist Richard DeRosset, then a young sailor stationed aboard the amphibious transport USS *Paul Revere* (LPA 248), recalls finding some of the flotsam. He salvaged the teak chart table for use in his private boat; regrettably, the wardroom table, its legs missing, was too large for him to carry off. He also recalls seeing on the beach a plywood fire-station cover, approximately four feet by four feet in size.

37. *Enhance* and *Pluck* ship's history for 1975.

38. Ibid.

39. *Illusive* ship's history for 1975.

40. *Direct* and *Dash* ship's history for 1977.

41. *Direct* ship's history for 1977.

42. *Detector* and *Dash* ship's history for 1978.

43. *Detector* ship's history for 1978–79.

44. *Dominant* ship's history for 1978.

Chapter 9 Notes:

1. *The New Book of Knowledge* (New York: Grolier, 1996), vol. 9, pp. 310, 316.

2. Jay E. Hines, "Confronting Continuing Challenges : A Brief History of the. United States Central Command," www.centcom.mil (19 March 1997), p. 6; www.history.navy.mil/faqs/faq56-1.htm (accessed 31 December 2001).

3. Martin S. Navias and E. R. Hooton, *Tanker Wars: The Assault on Merchant Shipping during the Iran-Iraq Conflict, 1980–1988*, (London: I.B. Tauris, 1996), p. 122.

4. Ibid., pp. 122–123.

5. Tamara Moser Melia, *"Damn the Torpedoes": A Short History of U.S. Naval Mine Counter-measures, 1777–1991* (Washington, D.C.: Naval Historical Center, 1991), p. 120; Capt.

Ronald Moser, USN (ret.), 14 August 2000; Navias and Hooton, *Tanker Wars*, p. 130–132, 140.

6. Melia, *"Damn the Torpedoes,"* p. 120; Hines, "Confronting Continuing Challenges," p. 6; Navias and Hooton, *Tanker Wars*, pp. 140–143.

7. Ibid.

8. Navias and Hooton, *Tanker Wars*, p. 146.

9. CoMinRon 2 command history for 1987; Melia, *"Damn the Torpedoes,"* p. 120.

10. Hines, "Confronting Continuing Challenges," p. 6.

11. Navias and Hooton, *Tanker Wars*, pp. 143–144.

12. Ibid., pp. 151–152.

13. Ibid., p. 153.

14. Ibid., pp. 153–154.

15. Ibid., pp. 154–155.

16. CoMinRon 2 command history for 1987.

17. Hines, "Confronting Continuing Challenges," pp. 6–7; Melia, *"Damn the Torpedoes,"* pp. 120–21.

18. CoMinRon 2 command history for 1987; Melia, *"Damn the Torpedoes,"* pp. 121–22.

19. www.history.navy.mil/faqs/faq56-1.htm (accessed 31 December 2001).

20. Navias and Hooton, *Tanker Wars*, p. 144.

21. Ibid., pp. 144–145.

22. Ibid., p. 145.

23. CoMinRon 2 command history for 1987, 5750 serial N1A/146 of 22 March 1988; Melia, *"Damn the Torpedoes,"* p. 122.

24. www.geocities/com/Pentagon/Bunker/2170/102msos.html (accessed 26 October 2000).

25. *Conquest, Enhance*, and *Esteem* ship's history for 1987; *Barbour County* cruise book for 1987–88.

26. *Conquest, Enhance*, and *Esteem* ship's history for 1987.

27. Ibid.; *Barbour County* cruise book 1987–88; www.mso-belgium.org/en/gulf_war/gulf_war_en.htm (accessed 26 October 2000); Cdr. James Taplett, USN (ret.), e-mail of 1? March 2006.

28. *Conquest* ship's history for 1987.

29. CoMinRon 2 command history for 1987, 5750 serial N1A/146 of 2 March 1988; *Fearless* and *Illusive* ship's history for 1987; CoMinRon 2 command history for 1987, 5750 serial N1A/146 of 22 March 1988.

30. *Fearless* and *Illusive* ship's history for 1987.

31. Ibid.

32. *Fearless* ship's history for 1987; *The New Book of Knowledge*, vol. 4, 232–233.

33. *Fearless* and *Illusive* ship's history for 1987.

34. Ibid.; CoMinRon 2 command history for 1987, 5750 serial N1A/146 of 22 March 1988.

35. *Adroit* ship's history for 1987.

36. *Enhance, Esteem, Fearless,* and *Inflict* ship's history for 1987; Melia, *"Damn the Torpedoes,"* p.123.

37. *Esteem* and *Fearless* ship's history for 1987; Citation for SecNav Navy Unit Commendation awarded to Task Unit 801.4.7.

38. *Enhance, Esteem,* and *Fearless* ship's history for 1987.

39. *Conquest* and *Illusive* ship's history for 1987; Navias and Hooton, *Tanker Wars*, p. 146.

40. *Esteem* ship's history for 1987.

41. *Enhance* and *Fearless* ship's history for 1987.

42. Navias and Hooton, *Tanker Wars*, p. 157.

43. *Conquest, Enhance, Esteem, Fearless, Illusive,* and *Inflict* ship's history for 1988.

44. *Conquest, Esteem, Fearless,* and *Illusive* ship's history for 1988.

45. *Conquest* and *Illusive* ship's history for 1988.

46. *Conquest, Esteem,* and *Illusive* ship's history for 1988.

47. *Enhance, Esteem,* and *Illusive* ship's history for 1988.

48. *Esteem, Fearless, Illusive,* and *Inflict* ship's history for 1988.

49. *Conquest, Enhance,* and *Esteem* ship's history for 1988.

50. *Fearless* ship's history for 1988; CoMinRon 2 command history for 1988, 5750 serial N1A/027 of 24 January 1989.

51. *Esteem* ship's history for 1988; *The New Book of Knowledge*, vol. 16, pp. 2–3.

52. *Conquest, Enhance, Esteem, Fearless, Illusive,* and *Inflict* ship's history for 1988; Melia, *"Damn the Torpedoes,"* p.123.

53. *Conquest, Enhance, Fearless, Illusive,* and *Inflict* ship's history for 1988.

54. *Enhance, Esteem, Fearless, Illusive,* and *Inflict* ship's history for 1988; Commander Naval Surface Group Four command history for 1988, 1989, and 1990: 5750 006:006A serial 152 of 19 April 1989, 5750 006:006A serial L0021 of 1 March 1990, and 5750 005 serial L1017 of 26 February 1990, respectively; Navias and Hooton, *Tanker Wars*, pp. 170–171; David F. Winkler, "Operation Praying Mantis Blows a Hole in Iranian Navy," Navy League, September 2003, www.navyleague.org/sea_power/sep_03_45 .php; www.history.navy.mil/faqs/faq56-1.htm (accessed 31 December 2001).

55. Navias and Hooton, *Tanker Wars*, p. 171; Capt. Bud Lanston and Lt. Cdr. Don Bringle, "The Air View: Operation Praying Mantis," U.S. Naval Institute *Proceedings*

(May 1989); Capt. J. B. Perkins, "The Surface View: Operation Praying Mantis," U.S. Naval Institute *Proceedings* (May 1989).

56. Ibid.

57. Commander Naval Surface Group Four command history for 1988, 1989, and 1990: 5750 006:006A serial 152 of 19 April 1989, 5750 006:006A serial L0021 of 1 March 1990, and 5750 005 serial L1017 of 26 February 1990, respectively.

58. *Conquest* and *Esteem* ship's history for 1988.

59. *Esteem, Fearless, Illusive,* and *Inflict* ship's history for 1988; Citation for SecNav Navy Unit Commendation awarded to Task Unit 801.4.7; *Illusive* ship's history indicates the U.S. task unit located and destroyed five M-08 mines in the Shah Allum minefield by 8 May, and then proceeded to the Rostam MDA and cleared six more M-08 mines; "Sailors remain proud of role in Persian Gulf," *Providence Journal,* 30 November 1988.

60. *Conquest, Enhance, Illusive,* and *Inflict* ship's history for 1988.

61. *Conquest, Enhance, Esteem, Fearless, Illusive,* and *Inflict* ship's history for 1988.

62. *Fearless* ship's history for 1988.

63. Ibid. Note: *Esteem* ship's history for 1988 indicates that she was moored at Basrec Shipyard from 23 June to 6 July, the period *Fearless* ship's history indicates she conducted aircraft salvage operations; www.history.navy.mil/faqs/faq56-1.htm (accessed 31 December 2001).

64. *Enhance* and *Inflict* ship's history for 1988.

65. *Conquest, Enhance, Esteem, Fearless, Illusive,* and *Inflict* ship's history for 1988; ComDesRon 8 command history for 1988, 5750 Ser 01/25 of 20 January 1989.

66. *Enhance* and *Fearless* ship's history for 1988.

67. *Fearless, Illusive* and *Inflict* ship's history for 1988.

68. *Enhance* ship's history for 1988.

69. *Fearless* ship's history for 1988.

70. CoMinGru One command history for 1989, 5750 serial N3/094 of 6 April 1992; *Esteem* ship's history for 1989.

71. *Conquest, Esteem, Illusive,* and *Inflict* ship's history for 1989.

72. *Fearless, Inflict,* and *Illusive* ship's history for 1989.

73. Ibid.

74. *Inflict* ship's history for 1989.

75. *Fearless* and *Illusive* ship's history for 1989.

76. *Inflict* ship's history for 1989.

77. Ibid.

78. *Inflict* and *Illusive* ship's history for 1989.

79. *Inflict* ship's history for 1989.

80. *Conquest* and *Enhance* ship's history for 1989.

81. Ibid.

82. *Conquest* and *Enhance* ship's history for 1989.

83. *Enhance* and *Esteem* ship's history for 1989.

84. Ibid.

85. *Esteem* ship's history for 1990.

86. *Conquest* and *Esteem* ship's history for 1990; CoMCMGru 1 command history for 1989, 5750 serial N3/093 of 6 April 1992.

87. Navias and Hooton, *Tanker Wars*, p. 144.

Chapter 10 Notes:

1. Edward J. Marolda and Robert J. Schneller, Jr., *Shield and Sword: The United States Navy and the Persian Gulf War* (Washington, D.C.: Ross & Perry, 2001), pp. 45–48.

2. Ibid., p. 57; Commander Mine Warfare Command (hereafter ComMineWarCom), command history for 1990; CoMinRon 2 command history for 1990; Cdr. Steven Lehr, USN, 3 November 1999.

3. Lawrence Freedman and Efraim Karsh, *The Gulf Conflict 1990–1991* (Princeton, N.J.: Princeton University Press, 1993), 391–93; Capt. David Grieve, USN (ret.), 11 August 2005.

4. *Avenger* and *Leader* ship's history for 1990; Cdr. Steven Lehr, USN, 3 November 1999.

5. CoMinRon 2 command history for 1990.

6. ComMineWarCom command history for 1990; *Leader* ship's history for 1990; Capt. George Smith, USN, 19 October 1999; Marolda and Schneller, *Shield and Sword*, p. 77; Capt. David Grieve, USN (ret.), 11 August 2005.

7. Commander Mine Countermeasures Group Two (hereafter CoMCMGru 2), command history for 1991; Marolda and Schneller, *Shield and Sword*, p. 141; Capt. David Grieve, USN (ret.), 11 August 2005.

8. Marolda and Schneller, *Shield and Sword*, p. 75; www.history.navy.mil/wars/dstorm/ds5.htm (accessed 12 November 2004).

9. Marolda and Schneller, *Shield and Sword*, pp. 75, 137; Capt. David Grieve, USN (ret.), 11 August 2005.

10. Marolda and Schneller, *Shield and Sword*, p. 141; Capt. David Grieve, USN (ret.), 11 August 2005.

11. Marvin Pokrant, *Desert Storm at Sea: What the Navy Really Did* (Westport, Conn.: Greenwood Press, 1999), p. 239; Marolda and Schneller, *Shield and Sword*, p. 263; www.navsource.org/archives/11/05idx.htm (accessed 25 November 2004); Capt. David Grieve, USN (ret.), 11 August 2005.

12. Pokrant, *Desert Storm at Sea*, p. 98; Marolda and Schneller, *Shield and Sword*, pp. 77, 262–263; Jeremy Olver, www.btinternet.com/~warship/Feature/gulf.htm (accessed 13 November 2004); Capt. David Grieve, USN (ret.), 11 August 2005.

13. Pokrant, *Desert Storm at Sea*, p. 98; Marolda and Schneller, *Shield and Sword*, pp. 77, 262–263; Olver, www.btinternet.com/~warship/Feature/gulf.htm; ComMineWarCom command history for 1990; CoMCMGru 2 command history for 1991; Cdr. Steven Lehr, USN, 3 November 1999; Capt. David Grieve, USN (ret.), 11 August 2005.

14. Pokrant, *Desert Storm at Sea*, pp. 193, 195–196, 198.

15. *Leader* ship's history for 1990; Cdr. Steven Lehr, USN, 3 November 1999.

16. CoMCMGru 2 command history for 1991; Capt. David Grieve, USN (ret.), 11 August 2005.

17. Pokrant, *Desert Storm at Sea*, pp. 201–206.

18. Ibid.; Marolda and Schneller, *Shield and Sword*, p. 251; Capt. David Grieve, USN (ret.), 11 August 2005.

19. Pokrant, *Desert Storm at Sea*, pp. 208–209; Capt. David Grieve, USN (ret.), 11 August 2005.

20. Pokrant, *Desert Storm at Sea*, pp. 69–70, 91, 210, 234.

21. Ibid.

22. Ibid., p. 98.

23. Ibid., p. 108; Capt. David Grieve, USN (ret.), 11 August 2005.

24. Pokrant, *Desert Storm at Sea*, p. 95.

25. Ibid. pp. 154, 157; www.history.navy.mil/wars/dstorm/ds5.htm (accessed 12 November 2004); Capt. David Grieve, USN (ret.), 11 August 2005.

26. Pokrant, *Desert Storm at Sea*, pp. 154, 157; Capt. David Grieve, USN (ret.), 11 August 2005.

27. Pokrant, *Desert Storm at Sea*, pp. 126–127, 154, 157, 220.

28. Ibid. p. 157.

29. Ibid.; www.history.navy.mil/wars/dstorm/ds5.htm.

30. Pokrant, *Desert Storm at Sea*, p. 157.

31. Ibid. p. 159.

32. CoMCMGru 2 command history for 1991; *Avenger* ship's history for 1991; Pokrant, *Desert Storm at Sea*, pp. 160–162; Marolda and Schneller, *Shield and Sword*, pp. 264–267.

33. www.history.navy.mil/wars/dstorm/ds5.htm.

34. *Avenger* ship's history for 1991.

35. Pokrant, *Desert Storm at Sea*, pp. 162–167, 170.

36. Marolda and Schneller, *Shield and Sword*, pp. 267–268; Pokrant, *Desert Storm at Sea*, pp. 166, 173; Capt. David Grieve, USN (ret.), 11 August 2005.

37. *Avenger* ship's history for 1991; CoMCMGru 2, command history for 1991; www.chinfo
.navy.mil/navpalib/ships/battleships/wisconsin/bb64-wi.html, (accessed 25 November 2003); www.chinfo.navy.mil/navpalib/ships/battleships/missouri/bb63-mo.html
(accessed 25 November 2003); Capt. David Grieve, USN (ret.), 11 August 2005.

38. Pokrant, *Desert Storm at Sea*, pp. 174–175.

39. *Avenger* ship's history for 1991; www.history.navy.mil/wars/dstorm/ds5.htm.

40. Edlow and Carroll, "Performance of U.S. and UK Surface Mine Countermeasures Systems During Post–Desert Storm Mine Clearance"; Capt. Richard Farrell, USN (ret.),
12 November 1999; Pokrant, *Desert Storm at Sea*, pp. 192–193.

41. Pokrant, *Desert Storm at Sea*, p. 193.

42. Ibid., pp. 193, 195–196, 198; http://es.rice.edu/projects/Poli378/Gulf/gwtxt_ch7
.html#Countermine%20Warfare (accessed 25 November 2004).

43. www.mil.be/navycomp/ops/index.asp?LAN=E&PLACE=3 (accessed 25 November 2004).

44. Pokrant, *Desert Storm at Sea*, p. 98; Marolda and Schneller, *Shield and Sword*, pp. 77, 262–263; Jeremy Olver, www.btinternet.com/~warship/Feature/gulf.htm;
ComMineWarCom command history for 1990; CoMCMGru 2 command history for
1991; Cdr. Steven Lehr, USN, 3 November 1999.

45. PAO *Exultant* ship's history for 1991; CoMCMGru 2, command history for 1991;
Capt. David Grieve, USN (ret.), 11 August 2005.

46. Pokrant, *Desert Storm at Sea*, p. 194; Marolda and Schneller, *Shield and Sword*, p. 318.

47. *Avenger* ship's history for 1991; Pokrant, *Desert Storm at Sea*, pp. 194, 196.

48. *Avenger* ship's history for 1991; Edlow and Carroll, "Performance of U.S. and UK Surface Mine Countermeasures Systems During Post–Desert Storm Mine Clearance";
CoMinRon 2, command history for 1991; www.history.navy.mil/wars/dstorm/
ds5.htm.

49. *Avenger* ship's history for 1991; Edlow and Carroll, "Performance of U.S. and UK Surface Mine Countermeasures Systems During Post–Desert Storm Mine Clearance";
CoMinRon 2 command history for 1991.

50. *Guardian* ship's history for 1991; Capt. George Smith, USN, 19 October 1999.

51. *Guardian* ship's history for 1991; CoMinRon 2 command history for 1991.

52. *Guardian* ship's history for 1991; Capt. George Smith, USN, 19 October 1999; Capt.
Richard Farrell, USN (ret.), 12 November 1999.

53. Ibid.

54. *Guardian* ship's history for 1991.

55. Ibid.; Capt. George Smith, USN, 19 October 1999.

56. Edlow and Carroll, "Performance of U.S. and UK Surface Mine Countermeasures Systems During Post–Desert Storm Mine Clearance;" Capt. Richard Farrell, USN (ret.),
12 November 1999.

57. Edlow and Carroll, "Performance of U.S. and UK Surface Mine Countermeasures Systems During Post–Desert Storm Mine Clearance"; Pokrant, *Desert Storm at Sea*, pp. 193, 195–196, 198.

58. Marolda and Schneller, *Shield and Sword*, p. 263; Capt. David Grieve, USN (ret.), 11 August 2005.

59. Edlow and Carroll, "Performance of U.S. and UK Surface Mine Countermeasures Systems During Post–Desert Storm Mine Clearance."

60. CoMinRon 2 command history for 1991; *Avenger* ship's history for 1991.

61. CoMinRon 2 command history for 1991.

62. Iler, *Observer*, 2; *Avenger* ship's history for 1991; Marolda and Schneller, *Shield and Sword*, p. 263; Capt. David Grieve, USN (ret.), 11 August 2005.

Chapter 11 Notes:

1. Arnold Lott, *Most Dangerous Sea: A History of Mine Warfare, and an Account of U.S. Navy Mine Warfare Operations in World War II and Korea* (Annapolis, Md.: U.S. Naval Institute Press, 1959), pp. 17, 224–228; Capt. David Grieve, USN (ret.), 11 August 2005.

2. Norman Polmar and Thomas B. Allen, *Rickover: Controversy and Genius* (New York: Simon and Schuster, 1982), pp. 86–89.

3. Captain Stuart J. Cvrk, U.S. Naval Reserve, and Captain Richard E. Robey, U.S. Naval Reserve, "It Is Time to Transform the Naval Reserve," U.S. Naval Institute *Proceedings* (August 2003), http://www.usni.org/proceedings/Articles03/PROcvrk08.htm (accessed 22 March 2006).

4. Barry Clarke, Jurgen Fielitz, and Malcolm Touchin, *Coastal Forces* (London: Brassey's, 1994), p. 155.

5. *Asian Defense Journal* (December 1997): 53–54.

Index